A

BOOK

The Philip E. Lilienthal imprint
honors special books
in commemoration of a man whose work
at University of California Press from 1954 to 1979
was marked by dedication to young authors
and to high standards in the field of Asian Studies.
Friends, family, authors, and foundations have together
endowed the Lilienthal Fund, which enables UC Press
to publish under this imprint selected books
in a way that reflects the taste and judgment
of a great and beloved editor.

D1052864

The costs of publishing this book have been defrayed in part by the Hiromi Arisawa Memorial Awards from the Books on Japan Fund. The awards are financed by The Japan Foundation from generous donations contributed by Japanese individuals and companies.

MILLENNIAL MONSTERS

ASIA: LOCAL STUDIES/GLOBAL THEMES

Jeffrey N. Wasserstrom, Kären Wigen, and Hue-Tam Ho Tai, Editors

Millennial Monsters

Japanese Toys and the Global Imagination

ANNE ALLISON

Foreword by GARY CROSS

UNIVERSITY OF CALIFORNIA PRESS

Berkeley   Los Angeles   London

University of California Press, one of the most distinguished university presses in the United States, enriches lives around the world by advancing scholarship in the humanities, social sciences, and natural sciences. Its activities are supported by the UC Press Foundation and by philanthropic contributions from individuals and institutions. For more information, visit www.ucpress.edu.

University of California Press
Berkeley and Los Angeles, California

University of California Press, Ltd.
London, England

Library of Congress Cataloging-in-Publication Data
Allison, Anne, 1950–
  Millennial monsters : Japanese toys and the global imagination / Anne Allison ; foreword by Gary Cross.
    p.   cm.—(Asia—local studies/global themes ; 13)
  Includes bibliographical references and index.
  ISBN 978-0-520-24565-5 (pbk. : alk. paper)

  1. Toys—Japan.   2. Games—Japan.   3. Animated films—Japan.
4. Video games—Japan.   5. Consumer goods—Japan.   6. Toy industry—Japan.   7. Toys—Japan—Marketing.   8. Philosophy, Japanese.   9. Japan—Social life and customs.   I. Title.   II. Series.
GN635.J2A55   2006
688.7′20952—dc22   2005025770

Manufactured in the United States of America
15   14   13   12
10   9   8   7   6   5
The paper used in this publication meets the minimum requirements of ANSI/NISO Z39.48-1992 (R 1997) (Permanence of Paper). ∞

To Charlie

Contents

Illustrations

Foreword

GARY CROSS

Those of us who work in the often uncharted jungles of American and European popular and commercial culture are continually encountering the "monsters" of Japan—those often cute and cool critters that, especially of late, seem to have crashed onto the scene. They make us wonder: Where did they come from? Why have they so captured the imagination of children and adults on a global scale? I have often thought a really informed book about why and how Japanese popular culture has succeeded in becoming (with American pop culture) the leading exporter of fantasy, especially to the young, would go far in explaining both cultural globalization and contemporary children's commercial culture. In these covers, we have that book.

Of course, much of Japanese fantasy in *anime,* comic books, video games, and toys has been influenced by the West. For the first sixty years of the twentieth century, the Japanese playthings industry was indebted to German and especially American innovation. Linkages between Japanese and American children's consumption were well established by the 1930s, when Louis Marx, the famous American manufacturer of windup Popeyes and racist "Alabama Coon Jiggers," outsourced production to Japan. After World War II, Japan became an exporter of robots and space toys made of tin cans to an American market eager for science-fiction and space themes: Japanese spaceships looked like hastily recycled tanks and other war toys, and the toy figures looked alien to Westerners because Japanese toy makers could not afford to license images of movie and TV icons like Flash Gordon and Space Cadet.

By the late 1960s, however, Japan was producing quality Datsuns and other cars for export, and it exploited the development of transistor and digital technology to drive American and European manufacturers of TVs, radios, and stereos out of business. Still, few in the West seemed to take Japanese popular culture seriously. Until recently, the memory of cheesy Godzilla movies shown for laughs on late-night television seemed to epitomize Japanese popular culture. The revolutionary Walkman was widely embraced, but not Japanese music. Japan got its own Disneyland in 1983, a decade before Europe, but, while it had its own character, Tokyo Disneyland was still derivative. Yet all this began to change noticeably in the 1990s with the coming of *Mighty Morphin Power Rangers, Sailor Moon, tamagotchi,* and *Pokémon,* along with *anime* movies, video games, and much else.

One factor behind this transformation was the fact that the business models of Japanese manufacturers of playthings were consistent with American models of merchandising and manufacturing fantasy; they did not stick with the more parent-friendly approach of European toymakers. As early as the 1920s, toy and children's-book producers had learned the art of sliding characters and stories across "platforms" of fantasy. While British and German doll and toy makers stuck to miniaturizing adult life (e.g., through dolls' houses and vehicles) and usually maintained a didactic tone, Japanese manufacturers were influenced by American innovation in children's fantasy by cross-marketing characters from comic books and illustrated stories in the form of dolls, toys, and games. Tying toys and dolls to children's fantasy narratives was key to Disney's success in the 1930s, when Mickey Mouse became a global "friend" via sand pails, toothbrushes, and comic books as well as through Saturday-morning gatherings of "Mickey Mouse Clubs," which met to watch his cartoons in neighborhood cinemas. The merchandising of *Pokémon* sixty years later followed the same path. The proliferation of Hasbro's GI Joe "dolls" and military gear in the 1960s and the endless action-figure montages of the 1980s—perhaps best seen in the dizzying array of character goods spun off from the three *Star Wars* movies of 1978 to 1983—were adopted by the Japanese. Despite the pressures of education, work, and family, Japanese commercial culture, like the American one, invited children into a fantasy world of playful stories and toys divorced from adults' memories and expectations that children should "train" for adulthood in play. Even the Japanese cultivation of images of the "cute" in Hello Kitty and Pikachu has been influenced by German and American dolls and comic-strip characters from a century ago. Japanese "millennial monsters" are part of a wider and older world of children's fantasy.

But none of this takes away from the striking impact of Japanese imagination on today's children's culture. Nor should it obscure the fact that Japan's millennial monsters represent something new. As Anne Allison shows us, what is new and important for understanding our own times is the way that Japanese stories are told and how their characters behave and interact. From a superficial perspective, in fact, the Power Rangers are just another group of superhero fighters, appearing at the end of an era of action-figure warriors that began in the late 1970s. But this would miss the point. Japanese children's fantasy is different and seems to be defining children's culture in the twenty-first century just as American dream makers did in the twentieth.

This book tells why and how this happened by relating postwar Japanese society to children's fantasy culture. Even more interesting is Allison's linking of Japanese social experience to the globalization of contemporary consumer culture, of which children's longings are in the vanguard. Japanese dream makers capture the hopes and frustrations of life in the global economy more effectively than America's Disney. This is a big and provocative claim often wrapped in postmodernist packaging, but it is rich, thoughtful, and compelling.

Allison skillfully situates the well-known 1950s images of Godzilla within the despair of recently defeated and oppressed Japan, and relates the technological obsession of Astro Boy to the peculiarly Japanese longing for renewal in a high-tech world. With much sensitivity, *Millennial Monsters* contextualizes the seemingly contradictory world of Japanese fantasy within both the economic boom that began in the 1960s and the subsequent bust of the 1990s. With a deep knowledge of a culture foreign to most Westerners, Allison shows why disciplined and overworked Japanese longed for materialist fantasies. Technologically advanced capitalism produced a loss of place and community, and feelings of alienation from parents and the past. All this created longings for identity via the "friendly" characters of comic books, toys, and cartoons, as well as merchandise emblazoned with images of these characters. Allison shows very concretely how consumption has become a replacement for social contact, and how portable entertainment—in the form of *Pokémon* video games and handheld electronic pets—offers an alternative to place and to older kinds of relationships.

Japanese children's fantasy is riddled with technological imagery, not in a simple celebratory fashion, as with American and European electric trains, construction toys, and science sets of the early twentieth century, but through machines that are infused with techno-animism, or personality and animistic traits. Unlike the fixed world of Western children's fantasy, Japanese stories and character play are about continual transformation, or polymorphous perversity. Japanese cartoons, video games, and action-figure sets are even more foreign to American adults than were the *Star Wars* toys of the early 1980s (which were at least modeled after older Western traditions of heroism). Japanese stories experiment with more unexpected disruptions of old stereotypes (as in the case of *Sailor Moon*, with its fashionable female fighters and its edgy interpretation of the cute). *Pokémon*, or pocket monsters, are simultaneously pets and fighters, exchanged but also battled with.

Yet this is more than a story of Japanese culture and childhood. The Japanese experience is increasingly a global one, and its success in adapting to the demands of the American market and convincing American children to adapt to its aesthetics is part of the story. Western children may embrace Japanese imagination because it is "foreign" and thus "cool," but they also do so because it fits the stresses and aspirations of the postmodern age and helps them cope.

Americans, long used to hegemony in popular culture, as well as in the political, economic, and military realms, may find this recentering of global imagination hard to accept. Disney's nostalgia and cultivation of the cute and of fantasy places may continue to have global appeal, as is evidenced by the ongoing success of Walt Disney World and its spawn in France, Japan, and, soon, Hong Kong. But Japanese have captured the frustrations and longings of a world now beyond nostalgia and dreams of magical places through an ever-changing fantasy of polymorphous perversity and techno-animism: a world of millennial monsters.

Acknowledgments

This book on the fantasies of toys and the global heat of Japanese "cool" today has been a foray into unusual (dare I say alien?) territory for an anthropologist. Yet my travels have hardly been solitary, and many people have supported this project and generously assisted me along the way.

I am fortunate to have had the research for *Millennial Monsters* amply funded. For financing one year of fieldwork in Japan (1999–2000), I thank the Fulbright Program at the Japan–U.S. Educational Commission (which also provided assistance in a myriad of other ways) as well as the Social Science Research Council. My home institution, Duke University, was generous in not only funding shorter trips to Japan and all the United States–based research, but also in granting me a one-semester leave to write the book; I am grateful to the Asian Pacific Studies Institute, the College of Arts and Sciences, and the Arts & Sciences Council at Duke University.

In Japan, people graciously took time out of busy schedules to answer my questions about toys, character merchandise, Japanese youth, and monster traditions. From scholars in research institutions to executives in toy and publishing companies, and from children and their parents to toy designers and cultural critics, many people greatly assisted my research. For their generosity in interviews, I thank Fujita Akira at Shōgakukan Production; Stephen Alpert at Studio Ghibli; Ron Foster, Hori Takahiro, and Bill Ireton at Warner Brothers; Iwata Keisuke at TV Tokyo; Kamio Shunji and Sano Shinji at Tomy Company; Kondō Sumio and Takayama Eiji at Kodomo Chōsa Kenkyūjo; Tim Larimer at Time; Stuart Levy at Mixx Entertainment (now TokyoPop); Steven Murawski at Grey Daiko Advertising; Sengoku Tamotsu at Nihon Seishōnen Kenkyūjo; Shimamoto Tatsuhi at Hakuhōdō (Seikatsu Sōgō Kenkyūjo); Takashi Shintarō at Media Factory, Takei Reiko at Dentsū Inc.; Bruce Weber at Mattel Japan; and Takeda Masanobu. In addition, I am grateful to the countless children who assembled for group sessions or individual interviews. Kubo Masakazu at Shōgakukan Inc., Professor Nakazawa Shin'ichi, and Okamoto Keiichi at Dentsū were particularly helpful in the interviews they gave me; I learned immeasurably from them all. I am also indebted to Yoshimi Shunya for the good chats we had about global youth trends, nomadic technology, and *Pokémon* and for the affiliation he facilitated for me the year I was in Japan at the Shakai Jōhō Kenkyūjo, Tokyo University. I greatly appreciate the help of fellow Fulbrighters and other scholars during my time in Japan, including Frank Baldwin, Jason Cremerius, Michael Foster, Jonathan Hall, Peter Kirby, Iwabuchi Koichi, John McCreery, Tessa Morris-Suzuki, Mark Abe Noynes, Numazaki Ichirō, Neil Rae, Kerry Ross, Shiraishi Saya, Hosokawa Shūhei, David Slater, Ueno Chizuko, and Fujimoto Yukari. I also thank Itō Rena, who was endlessly resourceful as my Japan-based research assistant even when I returned to the States. To Nick Bestor I owe my introduction to the intricate world of *Pokémon*. And I appreciate the friendship of Kuse Keiko.

In the United States, I was fortunate in both the time and access that people in the (children's) entertainment industry accorded me. This was particularly true in my research on *Pokémon*, where virtually all the main players responsible for the marketing of the property in the United States generously granted me interviews: Rick Arons at Wizards of the Coast; Nancy Carson, Nancy Kirkpatrick, and Massey Rafoni at Warner Brothers; Paul Drosos at Hasbro; Norman Grossfeld at 4Kids Entertainment; Jessica Pinto at Kids WB; and Gail Tilden at Nintendo of America. I am particularly thankful to Al Kahn at 4Kids Entertainment, who met with me three times and was endlessly helpful in laying out the marketing history of *Pokémon* and other Japanese imported properties in the United States. I am also grateful for other interviews on *Power Rangers* and *Sailor Moon* with Barry Stag at Bandai America, Paul Kurnit at Griffin/Bacal, and Mark McClellan and Jean Morra at Saban Entertainment. Prior to my yearlong fieldwork in Japan, I was given a wonderful introduction to the world of toy marketing and advertising when I participated in the visiting professor program sponsored by the Advertising Educational Foundation. For my assignment to the Hasbro crew working on *Pokémon* at Grey Advertising, I thank Sharon Hudson at AEF, Mack O'Barr for arranging this, and particularly David Biebelberg and all those at Grey who so generously gave their time to me.

As in Japan, I learned much about the toys/cartoons/games in my study from children. I am thankful to all those who enlightened me through interviews or by allowing me to play with them. In particular, I thank the kids in my Greeley, Colorado, study, and especially Amy and Paul Rotunno for setting it up; I also thank their two children, Mitch and Allison Rotunno. I also thank my next-door neighbors Jake and Emma Bogerd for our multiple *Pokémon* playdates and for all they taught me.

Throughout the long years of researching and writing *Millennial Monsters,* I have been grateful for the support of many colleagues: Hideko Abe, Jonathan Allum, Harumi Befu, Ted Bestor, Elizabeth Chin, Leo Ching, Ian Condry, Dwayne Dixon, Mark Driscoll, Katherine Frank, Alessandro Gomarasca, Andy Gordon, Larry Grossberg, Mizuko Itoh, Sharon Kinsella, Ken Little, Ralph Litzinger, Gabriella Lukacs, William Matsui, Susan Napier, Diane Nelson, Jennifer Prough, Kathy Rudy, Miriam Silverberg, Steve Snyder, Laurie Spielvogel, Linda White, Kären Wigen, Ken Wissoker, Jane Woodman, Christine Yano, and Tomiko Yoda. Since its inception, I have been given many opportunities to speak about my research at various stages and in various iterations. I thank all those who extended these invitations and all the audiences who gave me such useful feedback at the Abe Fellowship Program, the Annenberg School of Communication at the University of Southern California, the College of the Atlantic, Dartmouth College, the Humanities Center at Wesleyan College, the Japan Society, Randolph Macon College, the Reischauer Institute at Harvard, Stanford University, the University of British Columbia, the University of Kansas, the University of Oklahoma, the University of Virginia, Western Michigan University, and Yale University. I am particularly grateful for the opportunity to participate in a conference (held at the East West Center in 2001) devoted entirely to the global diffusion and glocalization of *Pokémon.* For a wonderful collaboration, I thank my fellow participants and particularly Joe Tobin for overseeing both the conference and the edited volume that emerged from it *(Pikachu's Global Adventures).* In 2004 I participated in another, differently stimulating seminar (at the School of American Research) on youth and globalization. For all I learned—about my own paper on *Pokémon* and that of others—I am thankful to the co-organizers, Debbie Durham and Jennifer Cole, and my coparticipants: Brad Weiss, Ann Annagnost, Barrie Thorne, Tobia Hecht, Paula Fass, and Connie Flanagan. And to the members of my writing group at Duke—Priscilla Wald, Maureen Quilligan, Laura Edwards, and Adrienne Davis—I am deeply indebted for their endlessly sharp advice and the gentleness with which they dispensed it.

For a few more, I have very special thanks. The University of California Press has been wonderful in the production process, and I thank everyone who has worked on *Millennial Monsters.* In particular, I am grateful to my editor, Sheila Levine, for her long support and patience, and to Randy Heyman for his help and expertise in managing permissions. I was fortunate in the reviewers the press solicited; all were remarkably savvy and astute, and the book benefited enormously from them. I thank all three reviewers for their thoughtfulness: Takayuki Fujitani, Purnima Mankekar, and Bill Kelly. To Bill I owe even deeper thanks: for his multiple reads of my manuscript, for his unwavering support and advice, and for the invitation to Yale and into his graduate seminar. Over the years and mainly through email, Hyung Gu Lynn has fueled my imagination and knowledge of the Japanese pop cultural scene. Victoria Nelson came to my assistance when the writing was slogging to a standstill; her savviness in seeing me through was invaluable. I am fortunate to have the friendship of Kuga Yoshiko, who, in all my trips to Japan, offers me bountiful resources, a generous spirit, and good drinks. Orin Starn has been the best friend and colleague I could hope to have. Always sharp, infinitely available, and steadfastly wise, he has my deepest thanks. My sons, David and Adam Platzer, have been in the skin of this project from the beginning. It was Adam's passion for Japanese cyber-warriors that got me going on this and David's willingness to help me with Game Boy technology that gave me an edge with *Pokémon*. For all we've been through, and for all their faith and encouragement along the way, I thank them both. I am fortunate in having a mother whose enthusiasm for this project kept me smiling on days I was blue. Last, it is my partner, Charlie Piot, who has been my strongest supporter throughout. During all those times of doubt, struggles for clarity, and attempts to write the grant (in a "grantese" I owe, frankly, to him), he was there for me. It is Charlie who has shown me and taught me about the "gift"—from going to Japan and endlessly theorizing the capitalism of monsters to forging through difficulties together. To him, I give not thanks but the promise of a return gift.

Enchanted Commodities

Peter and His *Yu-Gi-Oh!*

The boy is sixteen years old: a good student, a star athlete, and college-bound. A colleague's son, Peter is polite but bored as we chat on a warm North Carolinian fall day in 2003. When the subject turns to hobbies, however, and I ask about Japanese fads, the sober-looking youth immediately transforms. Practically jumping out of his seat, he announces, "I'm obsessed with *Yu-Gi-Oh!*"—an obsession his father confirms while confessing total ignorance about the phenomenon himself. A media-mix complex of trading cards, cartoon show, comic books, video games, movie, and tie-in merchandise that became the follow-up global youth hit on the heels of *Pokémon*, *Yu-Gi-Oh!* entered the U.S. marketplace in 2001, promoted by the New York–based company 4Kids Entertainment. Here, as my teenage interviewee makes clear, lies a fantasy world where monsters, mysteries of ancient Egypt, and tough opponents all entwine in card play—his preferred venue of *Yu-Gi-Oh!* play, as well as that of his (mostly male) high school buddies.

As I learned from fieldwork over the last decade, there is a veritable boom these days in Japanese fantasy goods among American youth. This is not the first time, of course, that U.S. mass culture has been influenced by Japan; Japanese cartoons like *Speed Racer* have played for years, for example, and *Godzilla* was such a hit in the 1950s, it spawned Japanese monster sequels for decades. But as one twenty-something young man told me recently, J-pop (Japanese pop) is far more ubiquitous today. According to him, properties like *manga* (comic books) and *anime* (animation) are "kicking our ass" because they are better, more imaginative, and way beyond what Hollywood can muster in terms of edginess, storytelling, and complex characterizations. The comparison with American pop culture is instructive. For what is new here is not simply the presence of Japanese properties in the

United States or the emergence of American fans (I routinely meet diehards who, raised on *Godzilla* or *Speed Racer* as youths, have carried the flame into middle age). Rather, it is the far greater level of influence of Japanese goods in the U.S. marketplace these days and upon the American national imaginary/imagination.

As with Peter, part of the appeal of the game play is its novelty. Whether because of the Japanese script, foreign references, or visual design, *Yu-Gi-Oh!* has a feel that is distinctly non-American. Retaining, even purposely playing up, signs of cultural difference is more the trend today than simple Americanization of such foreign imports.

In 2003, for example, when the popular Japanese youth (comic) magazine *Shōnen Jump* was released in the United States, it was formatted to be read Japanese style, from right to left. Yet, why such an aesthetic is enticing seems to do "less with a specific desire for things Japanese than for things that simply represent some notion of global culture"—as a reporter writing in the *New York Times* has said about the current *manga* craze in the United States. For the "Google generation," worldliness is both an asset and a marker of coolness (Walker 2004:24). But whether the attraction is coded as global culture or as culturally Japanese, it involves not only a perceived difference from American pop but also a constructed world premised on the very notion of difference itself—of endless bodies, vistas, and powers that perpetually break down into constituent components that reattach and recombine in various ways. And, as with Peter and his *Yu-Gi-Oh!* cards, the pleasure of play here is studying, mastering, and manipulating these differences: an interactive activity by which something foreign soon becomes familiar.

Pokémon at LAX

It is a fall day in 1999, and a crowd of children gathers excitedly by a window at LAX airport. Gazing at the runway in front of them, they are captivated by a 747 just landing from Japan that has been magically transformed into a huge flying monster toy (figure 1). Cartoonishly drawn down the side of the aircraft is a figure recognizable even by adults: yellow-bodied and red-cheeked Pikachu, the signature fantasy creature from the biggest kids' craze of the decade, *Pokémon*. Known for its cuteness and electric powers, Pikachu is one of the original 151 *pokémon* (short for "pocket monsters"; there are now more than 300) that inhabit an imaginary world crafted onto a media-mix entertainment complex of electronic games, cartoons, cards,

Figure 1. Mobile culture/character carriers: the ANA *Pokémon* jet. (Courtesy of Shōgakukan Production.)

movies, comic books, and tie-in merchandise.[1] By 1999, what had started modestly as a Game Boy game in Japan three years earlier had become a megacorporation and the hottest kid property in the global marketplace. Given the currency and spread of the *Pokémon* phenomenon, it is hardly surprising that children would thrill at the sight of its popular icon Pikachu plastered on the side of what otherwise would be a mere vehicle of transport. More remarkable is that an airline, a business usually prone to promoting the "seriousness" of its service to adults, would willingly turn itself into an advertisement and carrier for a children's pop character. Remarkable as well is the fact that this fantasy fare causing such a splash in the United States came not from Disney or Hollywood but from Japan.

For the children hugging the window at LAX airport, excitement comes from seeing a familiar pop figure extended onto what is a new and unexpected playing field: a passenger plane. Yet for those traveling inside the carrier, the encounter goes much further than an external facade; it defines, in fact, the entire flight experience. Attendants dress in *pokémon*-adorned aprons, and passengers are surrounded by images of the pocket monsters on everything from headrests to napkins to food containers and cups. For in-flight entertainment, there are *Pokémon* movies and videos. And, disembarking from the plane, passengers receive a goody bag (like those at a birthday party) filled with *Poké*-treats—a notebook, badge, tissue container, comb. To fly on an All Nippon Airways (ANA) *Pokémon* jet is akin to visiting a theme park; it means total submergence in *Poké*-mania, from the body of the plane to one's own bodily consumption of food and fun. According to an ANA ad aimed at Japanese children, such an atmosphere promises not only recreation but also intimacy and warmth: "It's all *Pokémon* inside the plane. Your happy *Pokémon* friends are waiting for you all!!!" *(Kinai wa zenbu Pokémon da yo. Tanoshii Pokémon no nakamatachi ga minna o mat-teru yo)*. Commodities of play and travel become personal friends on an ANA jet thematized as pop culture.

Another ad, directed as much to adults as to kids, evokes similar sentiments (figure 2). The image, drawn to resemble the material of a snuggly sweater, shows a huge smiling figure of Pikachu set against a background of a blue sky dotted with fluffy white clouds. Flying into Pikachu's tummy and scaled at about one-tenth the figure's size is an ANA plane that looks as if it is trying to cuddle up against the monster. The cartoon plane has a disproportionately large head and a small tail that flips up cutely as if it were a baby bird practicing its flying technique. Against what is both a playful image and an image of playfulness, the message reads across the top, "Enjoy Japan!" or "Make Japan fun!" *("Nippon o tanoshiku shimasu!")*. Here the referent for fun has shifted; *Pokémon* jets are not only imaginary friends but also vehicles for viewing, experiencing, and selling Japan. By appropriating Pikachu, this ad sells domestic travel around Japan for ANA airlines but also carries another message about the prominence of Japanese play industries in a national economy that has suffered a debilitating recession since the bursting of the Bubble in 1991. Exports in fantasy and entertainment goods (comic books, animated cartoons, video games, consumer electronics, digital toys) have skyrocketed in the last decade, providing much needed revenues at home and making Japan not so much a fun site (as the ad promotes) as a leading producer of fun in the global marketplace today. Douglas McGray (2002), an American reporter, has referred to this as Japan's GNC (gross national cool), noting how the stock in Japanese cultural goods has recently soared (the *Pokémon* empire alone has sold $15 billion in

Figure 2. Plane as jumbo toy: advertisement for the ANA *Pokémon* jet. (Courtesy of Shōgakukan Production.)

merchandise worldwide). Here the commodification of play becomes a national resource and cultural capital for Japan.

Crossover Vehicles/Global Culture

In such crossover character goods as *Yu-Gi-Oh!* and the ANA *Pokémon* jets, Japanese "cool" is traveling popularly and profitably around the world and insinuating itself into the everyday lives and fantasy desires of postindustrial kids from Taiwan and Australia to Hong Kong and France. This global success in transactions of images, imaginary characters, and imaginative technology marks Japan's new status in the realm of what is sometimes called soft power (by Joseph Nye and others) and cultural power (by the mass media and government officials in Japan). This is a recent development, because even when Japan was most economically strong (through the Bubble years and at the height of its economic superpowers in the 1980s), its influence in the sphere of culture (images, ideas, films, publications, lifestyle pursuits, novels) penetrated little further than its own national borders. Curiously, though, along with the bursting of the Bubble, Japan has started to soar in one domain of its economy: creative goods whose value outside (as well as inside) the country is taking off like never before. And, at the same time that Japan's place in cultural production rises in the worldwide marketplace, so does the hegemony once held in this sphere by the so-called West and particularly the United States begin to erode.[2]

What interests me in these new global flows of Japanese children's properties are the ways in which fantasy, capitalism, and globalism are conjoined and (re)configured in toys like *Yu-Gi-Oh!* trading cards and an ANA *Poké*-jet. The lines between these categories blur here, for whereas *Yu-Gi-Oh!* is more clearly a play product marketed to youth, a *Poké*-jet extends the meaning of "playtoy" in a new direction by (also) being a clever marketing strategy to extend profits for a capitalist corporation not usually associated with children's entertainment. Further, according to some people at least, both these products are also vehicles of/for Japan's "cultural power"—high-tech fun goods that, in traveling popularly around the world these days, are spreading Japan's reputation as a first-class producer of imaginative fare. As a group of American kids (aged eight to eighteen) told me in 2000, the associations they hold of Japan are neither of kimonos, tea ceremonies, or kamikaze pilots nor of Honda, Toyota, or Mitsubishi but of Nintendo video games, Sony's Walkman, and *Pokémon*. It is as consumers and players of Japanese *manga, anime,* video games, trading cards, and entertainment technology (Walkman, Game Boy, Sony PlayStation) that postindustrial youth today—an ever-increasing demographic in consumerism more generally—relate to Japan.[3] And, given their abiding fandom of such properties, many of these kids also said they hoped to learn about Japan, study the language, and travel there one day. This is a fascinating shift from the early postwar period, when few American kids were interested in studying Japan at all, to the 1980s (the era of the Bubble economy), when Japanese-language classes were filled by eager American students hoping to do business someday in Japan, to the present, when Japanese fantasy creations are inspiring a wave of Japanophilia among American and global youth.

What exactly is it about Japanese *anime* or video games that is driving such a worldwide appetite to consume these virtual landscapes and imaginary fairy tales at this particular moment? Further, how are we to understand the interest(s) paid this "soft business" by the Japanese themselves, by a press that reports on the success of *Pokémon* overseas as front-page news, by writers who have proclaimed Japan the new "empire" of character goods, and by a government that is treating *manga* and *anime* like national treasures? From both sides, that is, made-in-Japan fantasy goods are becoming invested these days with particular kinds of (affective, aesthetic, financial, trans/national) value in the global marketplace where they are bought and sold with much vigor.

How to excavate, decipher, and situate these sets of values is the aim of *Millennial Monsters*. To be sure, the orbit of the Japanese play market today is global, and this is how I refer to it throughout the book. I have chosen, however, to focus on two specific sites in this traffic: Japan as the generator and the United States as one of many consumer marketplaces for Japanese cultural goods today. This is in part because these are the two sites in which I have lived and conducted research, but also because of the long-standing and particular attributes the United States brings to this nexus of trade/politics/play/power with Japan. Because of its size and wealth, the United States is a coveted market. It is also loaded with symbolic cachet for the dominance U.S. cultural industries have held in setting the trends and standards of mass entertainment around the world. In Japan, too, and particularly during the decades following its defeat and occupation by the United States, American influence on popular culture and, more generally, on shaping desires for a lifestyle marked by modernity, materialism, and McDonald's has been strong.

But in this era of late-stage capitalism and post–cold war geopolitics, global power has become more decentered, and American cultural hegemony has begun to disperse. In what Iwabuchi Kōichi (2002) refers to as the "recentering" of globalization, there is a rise today in new sources of cultural influence in global trendsetting (such as Japan) and also an expansion of new consumer marketplaces (such as China). As he and other scholars have pointed out, it is important to study such recentered globalization outside the scope of a Western anchor: looking, as he does, for example, at how Japan operates as a cultural broker and power in the "inter-Asia" region (of China, Taiwan, Hong Kong, Singapore, Malaysia, South Korea, Thailand).[4] Equally important, however, is to test what is happening in the old center of global culture itself, the United States, examining what kind of influence Japanese goods are actually exerting in the market and on the imaginations of American kids in this moment of changing globalization.

Throughout *Millennial Monsters*, I tack between Japan and the United States and move dialectically between the level of fantasy and play and that of context and the politico-economic marketplace. The book is organized around three main issues: (1) fantasy—the composition and grammar given to the imaginary characters and fanciful world(view)s at work in specific entertainment products from Japan that have been globally successful in recent years; (2) capitalism—the ways in which these products are marketed for both domestic and global sales, and are inflected and shaped by the conditions in which children actually live in specific places (namely, the United States and Japan); and (3) globalization—how the flow of Japanese character goods into the globalized market of the United States actually takes place and is invested with certain (and competing) meanings, interests, and identities (such as Japanese, American, and transcultural).

A case in point is Miyazaki Hayao's evocative *anime* movie *Sen to Chihiro no Kamikakushi (Spirited Away)*. Released in 2001 by Studio Ghibli, *Spirited Away* was the highest-earning movie to date in Japan and won an Academy Award in the United States for best animated film (in 2002). In Japan, sentiments congealed around what the movie expressed about lost (cultural) values. A tale about displacement and loss (a young girl, moving to a new town, is temporarily stuck in an abandoned theme park and is separated from her parents, who are turned into pigs for their slothful eating habits), the movie is also redemptive (the girl learns how to work in a bathhouse for spirits and, trusting in herself and her new loyalties to spirited allies, earns the return of her family to the "real" world). The movie is arguably an allegory about millennial capitalism, as all the characters save Sen (the young girl, whose name is changed to Chihiro) are grossly self-interested and materialistic (her parents pig out on food, and her fellow workers in the bathhouse gorge on everything from leftover food to the gold dispensed by "No-face," the mysterious spirit who also consumes a few workers in return). Notably, the heroine becomes a paragon not only of hard work and loyalty to friends but also of sobriety; she refuses to consume anything (figure 3) except two old-fashioned rice balls *(onigiri)*, which, given to her by Haku, her new friend, she forces down along with tears.[5] These rice balls—a sign of traditional food, traditional values—were reproduced as a plastic toy and accompanied the release of *Sen to Chihiro no Kamikakushi* in Japan; embodying the pathos evoked by the film, they circulated as a mini-fad for months.[6]

In the United States, *Spirited Away*—released by Disney—earned rave reviews from both critics and audiences, making it one of the most popular Japanese movies to circulate in the United States (*Pokémon: The First Movie*, beat it in sales, however, though *Shall We Dance?*, released in 1997 and considered a success at the time, earned far less).[7] By contrast, Miyazaki's earlier *anime Princess Mononoke*, released in November 1998 (the same week as *Pokémon: The First Movie*), did far less well and was treated as obscure Japanese fare. Why *Spirited Away* was so much better received is undoubtedly due to a number of factors, including the fact that adults flocked to the theater (much as in Japan, where *anime* is considered a

Figure 3. Refusing gold: the anticonsumption stance of Sen in Miyazaki Hayao's *Sen to Chihiro no Kamikakushi (Spirited Away)*. (From the book *Spirited Away*, vol. 4 [San Francisco: VIZ Media]; courtesy of Studio Ghibli.)

serious medium not limited to kids).[8] And what they, as well as children, picked up about the film was a story with an intriguing and different cultural coding: one whose appeal came largely, it seems, from the intermixture of a spirit world (otherworldly, haunting, intriguing) with that of a contemporary, modern, and familiar setting. The fantasy here triggered not nostalgia for lost traditions but fascination with something different: the recognizable signs of modernity (dislocation, separation, and materialism) reenchanted with spirits, witches, and a tough girl—what Arif Dirlik has called the "articulation of native culture into a capitalist narrative" (1997:71). What precisely was appreciated and understood in the fantasy of *Spirited Away* differed, that is, between these two audience bases. Yet both brought to it shared experiences as well: of living in a world conditioned by postindustrialism, global capitalism, and—as their contingent effects—dislocation, anxiety, and flux.

Where's the Fix?
Animistic Technology and Polymorphously Perverse Play

Similar to the way in which *Pokémon* moves from mere images on the exterior of an aircraft to the total immersive experience of a flying theme park, there is a polymorphous perversity in Japanese play products in how they spread—and incite desires—across various surfaces, portals, and avenues for making and marketing fun. As Freud ([1910] 1963) has used the term, pleasure that is polymorphously perverse extends over multiple territories, can be triggered by any number of stimuli, is ongoing rather than linear, and invites a mapping of gendered identity that is more queer than clear.[9] Such a construction of pleasure, I will argue, is key to the appeal of Japanese play products—the reason they have earned world renown and have sold so successfully in the global marketplace of popular (kids') culture today.[10] Indeed, the spread of kid-oriented fantasy creations across ever-new borders, media, and technologies defines this business more than anything, making Japanese children's goods a ubiquitous presence in a world itself marked by shifting identities, territories, and commodity trends.

These properties, recognized worldwide as the cutting edge of postindustrial youth and blended, as in the case of ANA, with capital(ism)s of various kinds, include Game Boy (Nintendo's handheld game system); Walkman (Sony's portable tape player that revolutionized music listening); the *Mighty Morphin Power Rangers* (the live-action television show, originally produced by Tōei Studios, that ignited a worldwide "morphin" craze in the mid-1990s); Hello Kitty (the cute white cat by Sanrio currently boasting thirty-five hundred specialty shops around the world); *Mario Brothers* (video software by Nintendo, whose Mario is more popular with American kids today than Mickey Mouse); *Sailor Moon* (a cartoon and comic about female superheroes with toy merchandise marketed by Bandai); *tamagotchi* (Bandai's handheld electronic game that hatches a virtual, digital pet); and, of course, *Pokémon*. In all these goods, polymorphous perversity is produced, at one level, through marketing and product development. A property that begins in one iteration is continually refashioned and regrafted onto new forms (from a Game Boy game to an ANA *Poké*-jet, for example).

But what is considered a principle of perpetual innovation (or perpetual obsolescence) in product design, in fact, drives capitalist production all over the world today and is not in itself unique to Japan (except perhaps in degree). Far more distinctive is how the very construction of fantasy across the spectrum of Japan's "soft power" is itself one of polymorphous perversity—of mixing, morphing, and moving between and across territories of various sorts. In the television series *Power Rangers,* for example, teenagers transform into warriors empowered by both spirits and cybernetic technology to battle evil foes. In the technology of Walkman, the act of listening to music is transformed from a more stationary soundscape into the body itself, becoming a prosthetic attachment/experience. Such a logic of creative reconstruction is particularly well suited to today's world of rapid change, speeded-up economy, and flows (of people, goods, ideas, and capital) across geographic borders marking global capitalism. It accounts, in part, for the zeal with which Japanese cool has been taken up by (kid) consumers around the world today; its techno-spun fantasies of mutable identities and disjunctive imaginaries are in sync with lived experiences of fragmentation, mobility, and flux.

But why has Japan assumed the cutting edge in a popular play aesthetics that could be called postmodern, in what theorists of late capitalism call the cultural logic of late capitalism, or virtuality, in what Manuel Castells calls the cultural logic of today's informational global capitalism (Castells 1996; Harvey 1989; Jameson 1984)? Is there something distinctive about Japan as a particular place/culture/history or about Japanese cultural industries that accounts for the production of a fantasy style that is gaining so much currency in global circuits today? I want to suggest that Japanese "cool" is certainly rooted in the industry itself—in the design, marketing, and creative strategies that have been adopted and promoted through consumptive practices over the years—but also, and more important in my mind, is the influence of two other factors: one historical and the other involving consumer aesthetics. The first factor is the specific conditions and policies in postwar Japan that shaped both the nation's mass fantasies and the vehicles through which they are communicated in particular ways. This starts with the wholesale disrupture, defeat, and despair Japan found itself in following the war that fed a popular imaginary in the 1950s of mixed-up worlds, reconstituted bodies, and transformed identities—monstrosities of various types. This was exemplified by the movie spectacle *Gojira (Godzilla)*, which, released in 1954 and spawning a host of monster sequels, featured a country terrorized by a prehistoric beast that, thanks to nuclear testing by Americans in nearby waters, mutates into an atomic weapon. Though Japan's historical fate at Hiroshima and Nagasaki was rendered dystopically in *Gojira*, the country's exposure to New Age technology was configured far more utopically in what was arguably the other most popular mass fantasy of the early postwar period, *Tetsuwan Atomu* (Mighty Atom).

Designed as a *manga* and, later, a television cartoon by Japan's leading animator, Tezuka Osamu, Tetsuwan Atomu was a high-tech robot, crafted by the head of the Ministry of Science as a replacement for the son he lost in an accident. With a boyish body, admirable character traits (sweet, industrious, altruistic), and mechanical superpowers (including a nuclear reactor as a heart), Atomu embodied the future of Japan: a technological powerhouse rebuilt from the dead. Both these pop icons from the 1950s were hybrid entities that, birthed from horrendous events, cross over and remix different eras. Following the concept of polymorphous perversity, they also were figures at odds with what Freud called the paternal signifier: a father figure dictating the familial drama by which normal/normative desires are structured.[11] Atomu is a boy (whose "father" abandons him for not growing bigger like a real boy and later becomes deranged), and Gojira is a monstrous antifather (trying to destroy rather than defend the human world). Reflected historically here, amid all the other upheavals experienced by Japan/ese following the war, is the collapse of paternal authority (from the desacralizing of the emperor to the national condemnation of the military leaders who had misled the country into a disastrous war—a discrediting of fathers that trickled down to the male soldiers who returned to the family and household, where adult men no longer commanded ultimate respect). Thus, the dismembering of the nation—physically, psychologically, socially—in wartime and the postwar years helped propel a particular fantasy construction I am referring to here as one of polymorphous perversity: of unstable and shifting worlds where characters, monstrously wounded by violence and the collapse of authority, reemerge with reconstituted selves. By contrast, the 1950s in the United States was an era of (comparative) domestic stability and postwar pride yielding a different tropic orientation in pop culture: the presumption of family intactness and paternal authority underwriting such shows as *Father Knows Best*, *Ozzie and Harriet*, and *Leave It to Beaver*.

But another factor is at work in the development of a consumer and entertainment style internationally recognized today as "Japanese." This is more an aesthetic proclivity, a tendency to see the world as animated by a variety of beings, both worldly and otherworldly, that are complex, (inter)changeable, and not graspable by so-called rational (or visible) means alone. Drawn, in part, from religious tendencies in Japan, these include Shintoism (an animist religion imparting spirits to everything from rivers and rocks to snakes and the wind) and Buddhism (a religion routed from India through China adhering to notions of reincarnation and transubstantiation). To be clear, I have no interest here in facile generalizations that pose animism as an essential, timeless component of Japanese culture as if the latter itself is stable, coherent, and homogenously shared by all Japanese (which it is not). Diverse orientations and behaviors certainly exist in Japan today (as in the past), and social trends have also changed, sometimes radically, over time. Yet it is also accurate to say that, fed in part by folkloric and religious traditions, an animist sensibility percolates the postmodern landscape of Japan today in ways that do not occur in the United States. Investing material objects and now consumer items with the sensation of (human/organic/spiritual) life, such New Age animism perpetually (re)enchants the lived world. This runs against the grain of Weber's thesis of the disenchantment accompanying capitalism. In this sense (and others), Japan offers an alternative capitalism to what modernization theory claimed in the 1950s would be the standardized (Western) form capitalism would take in any and all countries across the world.

This animist unconscious (a term I borrow from Garuba 2003) is particularly vibrant and noticeable in certain practices in twentieth- and twenty-first-century Japan. Included here is its industry of fantasy production where, in postwar properties like *Tetsuwan Atomu*, for example, one sees a universe where the borders between thing and life continually cross and intermesh.[12] The entire world here is built from a bricolage of assorted and interchangeable (machine/organic/human) parts where familiar forms have been broken down and reassembled into new hybridities: police cars are flying dog heads, and robots come in a diversity of forms from dolphins and ants to crabs and trees. Not only is boundary-crossing promiscuity rampant here, in the sense that there seems no limit to what can be conjoined and cross-pollinated with something else, but also technology *(mecha)* is a key component to the way life of all kinds is constituted—a priority the Japanese state placed on technology as well in its reconstruction efforts following the war. Taking account of the centrality of *mecha* in Japanese play goods throughout the postwar period to the present, I call this aesthetic *techno-animism.*

As we will see, techno-animism is a style that is deeply embedded in material practices of commodity consumerism. In reenchanting the everyday world (ANA jets that convert to a flying Pikachu), this linkage also reproduces a consumer capitalism tied to commodities that stand (in) for fun, release from everyday stress, and the warmth of intimacy and friendship (one is surrounded by "friends" when traveling on a *Poké*-jet). This is where polymorphous perversity (detached from fathers) and techno-animism (reconfiguring intimate attachments) join together.[13] Plugging consumers into cutely fun techno-toys, properties like *Pokémon* provide access to imaginary worlds but also map the desire to find meaning, connection, and intimacy in everyday life onto commodified apparatuses (goods/machines). Brand-name goods and trendy or chic fashions are so fetishized in the popular consciousness in Japan as to make this a consumer culture of excessive proportions even in post-Bubble times. Affective ties are formed with such objects, particularly when they are endowed with techno-animism: a cell phone accessorized by a Pikachu strap, a Sony PlayStation equipped with a karaoke system for the home.

Social critics often lament the materialism of contemporary Japanese society, referring to it as a culture of transparency where people value personal acquisitions far more than they do the interpersonal relations once so key, it is often believed, in social traditions. But this trend, too, has historical roots in the postwar period: the replacement of subjection to emperor and group by the primacy of the individual in the democratization following the war (and according to the strictures of the "democratic" constitution imposed by the occupying forces in 1947), and of the turn by the national polity from militaristic takeover of Asia to industrial production, with its goal of material abundance for Japanese citizens. Today, after decades of a corporatist drive to perform and a consumerist orientation to seek individual pleasure(s), there is a profound unease *(fuan)* in Japan, piqued by the current recession that has led to a rise in unemployment, layoffs, homelessness, and suicide. In this moment of economic downturn, there is nostalgia for a past that is remembered and (re)invented as utopically communitarian: a time when people were plugged into each other rather than into headsets or computers. In what is said to be today's era of heightened "solitarism," people seek out companionship, but ironically (or not), the form this often takes is commodification itself: a machine or toy purchased with money that is wired into the (individual) self. "Healing" and "soothing" *(iyasu, iyashikei)* are perpetual tropes in the marketplace of play goods these days, and increasingly adults as well as kids engage the animate inanimateness of fantasy fare as "friends," or even "family." Said to be a relief from the stresses caused by consumer capitalism (and its downswing in Japan since the bursting of the Bubble), such devices are also capitalistic: commodities and things that stand (in) for spirits and kin. Such encodings of intimacy, consumerism, and techno-social interactions are part of Japanese play equipment as it travels so popularly around the world today, becoming familiar and familial to global kids.

A Postmodern Currency: Character Merchandise

Since the 1970s the cyberpunk author William Gibson has written Japan into his novels as the frontier of the new cyber world order. His sci-fi descriptions of Japan bleed into those of the world at large: a landscape in which borders dissolve, bodies continually transform, virtuality is more real than reality, and space simultaneously collapses and opens up into multiple dimensions. This is a world not unlike that described by Michael Hardt and Antonio Negri in *Empire* (2000), their study of global conditions at this moment of the millennial crossover. Today's empire, they say, is a place where the ideology of the world market dovetails with that of postmodernism, differences proliferate, and mobility, diversity, and mixture are the very conditions of possibility (for communities, corporations, existence). Space is always open, modernist distinctions (private/public, inside/outside, self/other) disappear, and power is exercised not through nations or disciplinary institutions (family, state, school) but through international bodies and corporations (the United Nations, the World Bank, Microsoft, CNN). In this era of globalization, *flexibility* and *portability* are keywords for the ways in which bodies, capital, and material objects continuously move through and inhabit (shifting) space.

Flexibility and portability are also signature features for the new wave of Japanese children's properties circulating so widely in the global marketplace. In the imaginative universe of this play empire, bodies of multiple kinds are broken down, recombined, newly invented, and fluidly transported (teenagers morph into cyborgs, virtual pets are raised on digital screens, ANA planes transform into *Pokémon* theme parks). This construction and characterization of play have been fostered by specific conditions and trends in postwar Japan. They are also resonant with the millennial era/world of empire in which postindustrial kids across the world are navigating the dispersals, fluctuations, and deterritorializations of everything from bodies and identities to relationships and basic sustenance. This book will examine how Japanese play properties articulate (in Stuart Hall's usage of the word) these different planes—postwar Japan/millennial empire, play/capitalism, culture/commodity, globalism/localism.

While my subject is the business of Japanese play, I am not interested in simply tracing the history and operation of the kids' entertainment industry in Japan. Rather, I aim to track the ways in which specific children's properties have emerged in Japan, have circulated in export markets outside Japan (specifically, the United States), and have been imprinted with meanings and pleasures of various kinds (including the new imprint of Japan as a producer of cuteness and "fun," as encoded in the ANA travel campaign). The book is organized around four waves of entertainment properties, selected for the timing and differential treatment and success with which they entered the U.S. and global marketplace, and also for the diversity of play product/fantasy they represent (superheroes, girl morphers, virtual pets, collectible monsters across the media of cartoon, comic book, electronic games, and media-mix empires). In all cases, I concentrate on the production and circulation of these entertainment waves within Japan, as well as their marketing and reception in the United States. My time frame runs from the year 1993, when the Japan-based *Mighty Morphin Power Rangers* (a live-action television show about teenagers who morph into superheroes to save the world, and humanity, from destruction) was successfully launched (but heavily Americanized) in the United States and elsewhere, to 2000, a pinnacle year following Japan's sensational successes with the *Pokémon* craze (a media-mix empire of Game Boy game, comic, cartoon, movies, cards, and toy merchandise structured as a virtual world with hordes of pocket monsters that players try to discover, catch, and collect). In between *Power Rangers* and *Pokémon*, I also examine *Sailor Moon* (*Bishōjo Sērā Mūn*, the comic and cartoon about a female team of transforming superheroes)—a property that initially bombed in the States but was later picked up as a cult favorite—and the virtual pet, encased in an electronic handheld egg, called *tamagotchi*, a toy that had a huge but short-lived fandom in the United States.

This fantasy fare, I believe, is best regarded as a type of currency: goods that are bought and sold. At the same time, it consists of imaginary creations that both extend and collapse the materiality of play products into other dimensions. To borrow from Walter Benjamin (1999), this is a business of enchanted commodities. Play creatures like *pokémon* are packaged to feed a consumer fetishism that, in this age of millennial and global capitalism, penetrates the texture of ordinary life in ever more polymorphous ways. Circulating in Japan by means of fads, these have been—starting in the 1970s and peaking again in the late 1990s—a "cute" *(kawaii)* craze (also called a "character" craze) grafted around lines of merchandise such as those of the company Sanrio, known for their bright colors, miniaturization, and hordes of small articles as well as other pop cultural forms generally associated with girliness, fun, and childhood, such as writing in a childish script known as *burikko*. Today some white-collar workers *(sararīman)* even adopt a *burikko* style of endearing cuteness in an effort to retain jobs in this recessionary climate. Characters, often designed to be cute, come in toys, backpacks, lunch boxes, clothes, theme parks, telephones, wristwatches, bread, snacks, key rings, and icons promoting everything from neighborhood meetings and government campaigns to banks and English schools. These commercialized creations—including Doraemon (a blue robotic cat), Kittychan (Sanrio's femmy white cat, also called Hello Kitty), Tarepanda (a droopy, cuddly panda), and Pikachu—sell, and are sold by, a number of commercial interests by projecting an aura of fancy and make-believe.

These play characters are brands used, in turn, to brand other commodities—ANA airlines, for example, with its *Pokémon* campaign—yet they also function as transmitters of enchantment and fun as well as intimacy and identity. As presented in a book on character merchandising published by Dentsū (1999), the largest advertising firm in Japan, play characters have become a popular strategy used by groups, products, and companies of various sorts to stake their own identity and differentiate it from that of others. Adopting a language commonplace for the discussion of cute character goods in Japan, the book's authors also state that the aim of those in the business of marketing these properties is to make them "close" to consumers. "Closeness" means, in this context, both extending a product's range of play to make it as intimate for fans in as much of everyday life as possible (from toys to food, clothes, phones, and airplanes, for example) and capitalizing on the popularity of an already established character to foster an intimacy in others for the goods in question, whether this be a product, a company, or a country (Dentsū 1999).

Japanese play goods become a currency for multiple things (identity, closeness, coolness, comfort), and they also travel in multiple circuits—friendship, pop culture, corporations, the global marketplace. Carrying Doraemon phones or Pikachu key chains is customary among Japanese *sararīman,* and the *tamagotchi* virtual pets, a fad in 1996–97 (with a new edition in 2004), were as popular with young working women (OLs, which stands literally for office ladies) as with kids. Like the ANA planes, however, the play goes much further for certain consumers and attaches to a body of technologized machines—Game Boys, video systems, Palm Pilots, cell phones, iPods, and electronic devices of all kinds—that are used increasingly to navigate ever more of life and the world. Information, communication, and friendship are sought along with entertainment. So, for example, one might use a cell phone *(keitaidenwa)* as a fashion accessory or for e-mail, Web surfing, game playing, downloading programs that feature play characters (a new service started in 2000), and communicating with friends, many of whom may never materialize beyond the phone (remaining mere phone acquaintances and, thus, almost as virtual as the favorite choices for phone straps—pop characters like Doraemon, Hello Kitty, or Pikachu).

A keyword in marketing cell phones to Japanese is *wearability,* given that *keitaidenwa* are adopted mainly for personal use in Japan, and the average Japanese urbanite spends far more time walking, biking, or commuting on trains than riding in cars (figure 4). Detached from any specific space for use (home, car, office), the cell phone becomes affixed instead to the body. Portability, in other words, makes it prosthetically personal—not just a machine that is owned and used but an intimate part of the self (as reflected by the vast attention paid by Japanese to cell phone brands, fashions,

Figure 4. Techno-animism: the spirit(s) of capitalistic Japan. (*New Yorker* cover, March 18, 2002; illustration by Christoph Niemann.)

and accessorization). Here physical intimacy overlaps and converges with the psychological intimacy promoted by the new fads and marketers of cute character goods in Japan. A big appeal of a Miffy or Pikachu is that people become attached to them, taking their virtuality as a source of personal amusement, companionship, even identity. No wonder, then, that these characters become such a medium for bodily wear and personal expression, accessorizing objects that ride closest to bodies and "selves"—T-shirts, underwear, even dildos (as in the case of the Kitty-chan dildo).

Commodities with Market and Affective Value

No wonder, too, that the success such character goods as *Pokémon* are having overseas is seen as a symbol not only of Japan's rising cultural power *(bunka pawā)* in global circles but also of its ability to cultivate international "friendships." As a reporter for one of Japan's leading newspapers, the *Asahi Shinbun*, wrote in his account of the splash the first *Pokémon* movie made in the United States (it was the top-ranking movie of the week, yielding revenues in excess of even Disney's *Lion King*) in 1999: "This is amazing. And it's possible that, if we can maintain these spectacular results, we'll outrun Disney in a country where Disney is a pronoun for the United States itself. . . . Why have we been so successful? Well, first, we cultivated the foreign market and then we pushed friendship towards Japanese products" (Hamano 1999:4).

What is called "friendship" here is made both to and through products, and the acclaim a Japanese movie has in the States is read as a sign of both economic and cultural merit. Similarly, in another article in *Asahi Shinbun*, the reporter describes how he was filled with tremendous pride when he saw *Pokémon* trading cards being sold even in U.S. grocery stores. Noting how the Japanese entertainment market still imports many goods from the United States and how, after the war, Japan could only "hold out its stomach in pride" again when Japanese companies like Sony and Toyota became common names in the States, he adds that "Japanese culture has at last produced products that circulate well in the US marketplace." In summing up his viewpoint, he writes: "Products *[shōhin]* are the currency by which Japanese culture enters the United States" (Kondō 1999:4).

What matters here is not just the purchase of Japanese goods in the United States but the type of cultural product the game *Pokémon* or the movie *Spirited Away* represents. To penetrate the U.S./global marketplace with this type of popular property is seen as a crossover triumph for Japan: a move that makes Japan recognizable not merely as an industrial power (whose "hard" technology of automobiles, VCRs, and televisions has been exporting well since the 1970s) but also as a producer of play fantasies that, transmitted through "soft" technology (comic books, cartoons, the software for video games), grab the hearts and imaginations of kids around the world. Indeed, Japanese pop (cool) is booming across Asia from Hong Kong and Taiwan to China, South Korea, and Singapore (Koh 1999). One of the attractions of J-pop in these countries is said to be its "Asian" aesthetic that resonates as more familiar than Western-produced fare.[14] In non-Asian countries, by contrast, the same style is popular for its "coolness" and the very difference this poses to homegrown fantasies. (Many U.S. fans of the various properties discussed in this book have said they like Japanese mass culture precisely because it is so "unlike" anything American.) But no matter the reasons for their popularity in different places, the very fact that Japanese play products are spreading globally is a sign back home that something identifiably "Japanese" is becoming recognized, appreciated, and picked up around the world.

At one level, this marker of Japaneseness is literal: explicitly tagging these goods as "made in Japan," a practice that breaks from the commonplace policy of many Japanese companies in the postwar era when exporting overseas. Because Japan's national identity was considered a deficit both in Asia (because of Japan's legacy as brutal colonizer) and in the West (where the Japanese brand was considered too parochial, foreign, and—with popular fare like the 1950s hit movie *Godzilla*—kitschy), it tended to be effaced or deleted when goods (particularly cultural goods) left the country.[15] This practice of "denationalizing" (*mukokuseki*) Japanese products is starting to lift. The new mood is apparent in the case of *Pokémon*, which, despite undergoing adjustments in different marketplaces (called *localization* or *glocalization*, as in global brands that are altered in local markets), has been recognized worldwide as Japanese.[16] But the marker of Japaneseness operates on another level as well: of capturing an aesthetic, expressive, or spiritual sensibility deeply linked, it is often thought, to what is culturally unique about Japan and its people. For the cultural critic Miyadai Shinji, properties like *tamagotchi* derive from a sense of "enjoying life now" that stems not from traditional culture but from a lifestyle orientation that developed in Japan over the postwar era (Miura and Miyadai 1999). Okada Toshio, a game designer and lecturer at Tokyo University, believes the quality captured by play goods like *Pokémon* is "cuteness," which, because Japanese are particularly skilled in crafting it and because it is "one thing that registers for all people," may well be the nation's resource for "working foreign capital in the twenty-first century" (Yamato 1998:244). And, as described in the economic journal *Nihon Keizai Shinbun*, it is the "expressive strength" (*hyōgenryoku*) of Japanese traditional arts that is fueling what is becoming the "international common language" of *manga*, *anime*, and video games today. The market for these three industries has surpassed that of the car industry within the past fifteen years in Japan, forming an *anime*, *komikku* (comic), and game industrial zone (for Japan, what the Silicon Valley is for the United States) that may well be the root of the new twenty-first century's center for culture and recreation (*Nihon Keizai Shinbun* 1999:3).

For still others, what is both distinct and compelling about a fantasy product like *Pokémon* is the "Japanese sensibility" *(yasashisa)* it captures that, characteristic of Japan's spiritual culture, is transmitted to present-day kids and helps them to face the next century (Nagao 1998:142). This intermixture of the old (spirituality) with the new (digital/virtual media) in Japan exemplifies what I have earlier dubbed techno-animism: animating contemporary technology and commodities with spirits and recuperating cultural traditions with New Age practices. Nagao Takeshi, the author of a book on *Pokémon*, explicitly uses the Japanese word—*yōkai*—for spirits and otherworldly beings of various kinds to identify the hordes of pocket monsters that, inhabiting the virtual terrain of *Poké*-world, are what players strive to capture in operating the game (137). The latter are artificially constructed, but their "fakeness" or "non-aliveness" is not so different from that of the traditional *yōkai*, whose meaning and value in the cultural cosmology are those of a (polymorphously perverse) being that hovers between two worlds—one, phenomenal, the other, more noumenal (189). In both cases—the game space of *Pokémon* and a cultural milieu that accommodates *yōkai*—an animist logic prevails in which the borders between human and nonhuman, this-worldly and otherworldly, are far more permeable than fixed.

Different, in this sense, from the common Euro-American worldview— where humans center existence and the distinction between life and death is more definitively conceived—this also constitutes a more general aptitude in daily Japan for animating, spiritualizing, or altering the material world that is at once playful and deadly serious. Such a worldview borrows from folkloric and religious traditions, where (theoretically) everything, even robots, is credited a spirit—as argued by the author of *The Buddha in the Robot*, a robotics professor at the University of Tokyo and also a Zen Buddhist priest (Mori 1981). The aesthetic or technological manipulation of nature has a spiritual dimension; intervention by human hands can be seen to enable the ideal or potential of life to be more fully realized. Examples include the traditional art of bonsai, in which trees, extracted from nature, are carefully pruned to grow into a longer-living and more perfected version of the original, and virtual beaches today that, enclosed within a dome, artificially reproduce (and outperform) the natural outdoors. Such practices enchant everyday life, where such enchantment is neither discredited nor devalued for being at odds with the "real" or "authentic."

Combining disjuncture elements (future with the past, organic with mechanic) is a signature of Japanese play products as well. In *Mighty Morphin Power Rangers* and *Sailor Moon*, the central trope is transformation: ordinary teenagers morph into superheroes battling witches, demons, and beasts who, like the Rangers, have powers rooted in ancient spirits or animals as much as in cybertechnology. And the designer of the *tamagotchi* virtual pets has said his aim was to create a "strange species of life" (Yokoi 1997): organisms culled from both the (naturally) familiar and the (artificially) fantastic—a masked head perched on stick legs, a big-lipped octopus sporting a beret wired with a periscope.

It is this crossover quality (of polymorphous perversity and techno-animism) that more than anything is seen to capture, and serves to identify, such play fare as distinctly Japanese. And this compulsion to remix or blur borders is also at work in the way made-in-Japan cultural products can appropriate elements from other cultures and still be regarded (in Japan, at least) as "Japanese." In *manga* and *anime*, for example, scenes are frequently set in other countries, and characters often appear Caucasian. Few Japanese, however, regard any of this as "foreign" (and though Americans, I have found, are constantly perturbed by the tendency, the same remixing of cultural codes is appearing ever more in United States–made fare as well these days).[17] Similarly, Hello Kitty, one of the biggest and most global icons of Japanese cool today, was given an English name when first designed in the 1970s because—as its creator has explained—anything American was fad-dishly popular in those days, but few Japanese had the means to actually travel to the United States themselves. Making Kitty-chan part American gave this character greater appeal to Japanese (and perhaps global) consumers. And "playing" with identity has only continued. In 2001, Sanrio officially announced that Kitty now had a last name (White), making this most profitable and popular of Japanese playtoys a mouthless cat with the name Kitty White (McGray 2002).

In such a property, the line between authenticity and inauthenticity collapses. For it is not Japan in some literal or material sense that is captured and transmitted in the new global craze of Japanese cool, but rather a particular style. And it is as trademark and producer of this distinctive style that Japan has acquired new notoriety in the global marketplace of popular culture today.

Technology Begets Mythology:
Healing and Nomadicism, Enchantment and Illumination

In a book on *Pokémon*, the anthropologist Nakazawa Shin'ichi (1998) has written that Japan is a world leader in products that not only capture children's imaginations but also yield enormous profits—a combination that

Figure 5. Cute profits: fantasy toys and global sales. (*New Yorker* cover, November 1, 1999; illustration © 1999 Harry Bliss.)

may seem paradoxical (figure 5). Yet it is precisely this paradox, he concludes, that "encapsulates the direction in which capitalism is headed today" (personal interview, May 2000). Indeed, we live in an era in which the imagination plays an increasingly important role in the (global) economy and is ever more embedded within, and a stimulus for, commodification. By crafting playware that not only appeals to the needs and desires of postindustrial kids but also tethers the latter to a New Age capitalist imagination, Japan is emerging as a toy maker and toy marketer of millennial times.[18]

More than anything, according to Nakazawa, two qualities in Japanese play goods like *Pokémon* account for their admixture of popularity and profitability. One is what he calls their potential to "heal"; the other is their portability (as in games played on Game Boys), so in sync with today's mobile lifestyles. But joined to these and spurring the capitalist imagination that Nakazawa intuits (but leaves unexamined in his own work) is a third quality I call the addictive frenzy fed by Japanese toys. As imaginary playscapes that polymorphously change form and perversely go on forever, they incite a consumer appetite to play more and more, and to buy more and more of the merchandise sold in the marketplace.

By "healing," Nakazawa (and multiple others in what is a central trope in the Japanese discourse surrounding made-in-Japan playtoys) means that *Pokémon* and other Japanese kids' products offer children a way of imaginatively engaging a world beyond that dictated by the rules and rationality they must usually abide by.[19] Here kids play with make-believe, test new territories, have thrilling adventures, and meet fantastic beings. Such a magical space is not merely at odds with the orderly, sanitized, and disciplined lives kids normally inhabit; it is especially scarce today at a time when "play" for children has become cannibalized by the demands of school and the hyperregimentation of daily schedules (Nakazawa 1998:22–30). Populated by hordes of creatures polymorphously perverse in the shapes, powers, and identities they assume (a common feature of Japanese play properties, including *Urutoraman, Digiman, Yu-Gi-Oh!,* and *Pokémon*), this imaginary universe also harkens to an era preceding modernization. In these times—particularly before the country opened up to the West (triggered by Perry's invasion in 1853) and the onset of its intensely rapid period of industrialization in the late nineteenth century (when attempts were made to repudiate the country's traditional belief systems)—Japan/ese indulged an animist worldview where gods, ghosts, and monsters were as viable as any other life-form. It is such a mind-set that is both retained and reinvented in the postmodern playcraft Japanese creators are producing today, as Nakazawa sees it. Following Lévi-Strauss, he calls this the "primitive unconscious" and believes it offers a soothing counterpoint to what has been lost and extracted by the motors of industrialist capitalism undergirding contemporary Japan (157). But, as I would add here, the loss of cultural traditions is not merely an effect of postindustrialization but is actively produced and shaped by it as well. Claiming a solitarism in Japanese today feeds the interests and products of an industry trying to sell companionship as a means to suture over this supposed lack.[20] In this sense, what Nakazawa refers to as a "primitive unconscious" is as much conscious and consciously manufactured.

Japanese play products are noteworthy for a second reason. Plugging into and feeding the world of the unconscious for kids, they also tend to come packaged in a portable form that makes access to its fantasy making both constant and personal. Children can carry a *tamagotchi* or Game Boy everywhere, making of it a fantasy world that travels with its user. Like the Walkman, these electronic game systems are technological machines that transport the user (via sound waves, play waves, or visual waves) to an alternative space of his or her own choosing. As a subset within cultural technology, nomadic technology has proliferated in the postindustrial world. It is also a field in which Japan has been a leading force, in both production and consumption (as in consumer styles and trends). But the concept of nomadicism (as defined, for example, by Deleuze and Guattari 1987 and Hosokawa Shūhei 1984) also defines something more critical about the postmodern world of the late twentieth and early twenty-first centuries. Lyotard has written of the postmodern self that it is "small but not isolated, and held in a texture of relations which are more complex and mobile than ever before" (1984:31). A portable device like the Walkman not only plays music events that are "unique, mobile, and singular" (Hosokawa 1984:169) but also allows its user to experience a "singularity" that interlaces with other singularities to form what there is of the "self." Rather than a whole of parts that unifies such a self, there are just "emissions of singularities" that proliferate into "nomadic multiplicities" (Deleuze and Guattari 1987; Shaviro 2003). This is all to say that fantasy properties like *tamagotchi* and *Pokémon*, with a technological interface to nomadic fantasy waves as well as a nomadicism of a deeper, more all-encompassing kind, resonate at many levels with today's postmodern child.

For these two qualities of healing and portability, according to Nakazawa, a play product such as *Pokémon* both mimics and exceeds the world in which it is used. It embodies (and enhances) the nomadic lifestyle of a postindustrial subject but also magically "heals" the stresses of living in an environment with little time or space for the imagination. And, ironically (or not), the form this takes—a commodity that is bought and sold in the marketplace—is highly addictive. Not only are these play creations promoted with all the savvy of the most current marketing strategies (where what is au courant is the very latest—and most changeable—in fashion style), but the very logic of fantasy itself is one of endless possibility. As in *Mighty Morphin Power Rangers*, characters continually alter/enhance/remake the parameters of their bodies/powers/identities by appropriating a range of weapons/outfits/spirits/tools. Everything is at once fluid and boundless in this imaginary universe: one constituted by a host of particles and elements that, by being rearranged or replaced, generate ever new entities and relationships. And the desire this feeds is to expand the possibilities even further, whether the commodity/play form is *Yu-Gi-Oh!* trading cards, *Sailor Moon* comic books, or *Pokémon* Game Boy games.

Enchantment is continual here, but so is the impulse to keep changing and acquiring more and more of whatever it is that constitutes the core of the fantasy—whether more pocket monsters (to win the game in *Pokémon*), more action figures (as in the newest version of the heroes in *Power Rangers* or *Sailor Moon*), or more virtual pets (as in purchasing a different *tamagotchi* or resetting the original to "birth" a new pet). Players become addicted to the rush of transformation, and this itself feeds a capitalist imagination, one dressed in commodities of limitless play and possibility. But, true to the principle of capitalism, the desire to expand further (by acquiring more powers, more *pokémon*, more wins in battle) eludes ultimate closure or satisfaction (there is always more—of whatever—to obtain/attain). In this way, playing with a Japanese fantasy good both replicates and reproduces the very conditions of postindustrial capitalism (fragmentation, speed, flux, flexibility), with its effects on subjectivity (anxiety, atomism, and alienation).

Yet there is another side to this frenzied addiction. As I was told often (by children, parents, marketers, child experts, and scholars of play) in the course of fieldwork for this project, the sensation that is also produced in the course of immersion in a Japanese playscape like *Sailor Moon* or *tamagotchi* is one of titillation, mastery, and abundance. There is an array of separate and endlessly proliferating parts (swords, skirts, eyeglasses, tulips, pots, big lips) into which entities are disassembled but also reassembled in a plethora of ways. And it is by mastering these codes and also personalizing them (at each point in *Pokémon* games, for example, players have several options for proceeding) that children gain a sense of deep attachment to, and control of, this imaginary space. For even though this is a world of boundless fragmentation, kids continually make connections—both between different particles (as in joining the individual robots of five Rangers into a megarobot on *Power Rangers*) and between themselves and different parts or entities in the playscape (as in playing *Pokémon* and acquiring different pocket monsters but trading others away). And like the repetitive nature of the fort/da game that Freud observed played by his grandson, entities continually come apart (often through violence, as does the boy who dies and is remade as a robot in *Tetsuwan Atomu*) yet are continually reconstituted.[21] Stitching together and animating what would otherwise be inanimate, discrete objects (a virtual blob on the screen whose octopus head and periscoped beret add up to a "pet" on the *tamagotchi*) is what makes play in these fantasy-scapes seem "healing." It is also what evokes the otherworldly spirits of a bygone era: an enchanted space inhabited by a mélange of beings, creatures, and entities whose "lifeform," not conforming to that of the phenomenal world, invites a special kind of (imaginary) connectedness for humans.

The entwining of culture and capitalism, and past traditions with contemporary technologies, is hardly unique to the industry of Japanese play products or to the postmodern times in which virtualized and commodified *yōkai* circulate today. Japan's transition to modernity at the end of the nineteenth century, in fact, was haunted by the same ghosts of the past—otherworldly spirits. Such beings and beliefs were considered a sign of Japan's (primitive) traditions when the country embarked upon modernization, accompanied as this was by reverence for the new gods of science, technology, and rationality (that came dressed, at this point, in Western costume). Efforts were thus made by Japan's new forward-looking leadership to eradicate belief in such entities. Yet a fascination with monsters *(bakemono)* and other "strange"—supernatural, mysterious, and fantastic—things *(fushigi)* endured into the twentieth century, stimulated by the very endeavors intended to contain it.

A preoccupation with "things that change form" (the literal translation of *bakemono*) is not surprising in a country itself undergoing such radical transformations (Figal 1999)—and it is true as much for the millennial crossover today as of Japan's crossover into modernity. But interest in "intangible otherworldliness" also kept alive a familiar worldview and sensitivity: something that, by *not* changing form, reflected what many thought was the essence of cultural (in contrast to modern or Westernized) identity. Committed to salvaging what he assumed would soon be anachronistic, Yanagita Kunio (Japan's "father" of ethnography) spent years (from 1908 to the early 1930s) researching and recording local sightings, customs, and folklore involving the supernatural. Yanagita's work provoked deep interest and passion across the country, and his volumes were consumed avidly by Japanese of all walks of life: rural and urban, the middle class as well as peasants and farmers. Rather than documenting beliefs that were quickly fossilizing then, Yanagita (and other scholars of *yōkaigaku*—the study of *yōkai*—native beliefs, ethnology) directed his efforts, and the discursive forms they took, toward actively inspiring, and keeping alive, interest in the otherworldly. According to Gerald Figal, a historian who has written a book on the subject, this obsession marked, as much as anything, Japan's transition into modernity, investing it with an attachment to cultural roots. Thus, not only did the supernatural fail to be dislodged by modernity, but the discourse of *fushigi* was itself actively constitutive of Japan's modern transformation:

> The fantastic as I conceive it is the constant condition of Japanese modernity in all its contradictions and fluidity. I would even extend this argument to suggest that to some degree modernity in general is born of fantasy and that any "doubling" perceived within it is between modernity as "reality" and modernity as "imaginary." Whether configured as negative impediment to national-cultural consolidation or as positive site of alternative new worlds, the fantastic allows the modern to be thought. In a sense, modernity itself is phantasmagoric; it ceaselessly generates that which is a la mode by consciously imagining difference from things past. Embodying transformation, a change of modes, modernity is akin to the root definition of *bakemono*, a "thing that changes form." (Figal 1999:14)

Dialectical Fairy Scenes

Writing about the same time period, the second half of the nineteenth century in Europe, Walter Benjamin described a similar process of encasing contemporary change within traditional mythology. His Arcades Project depicted an urban metropolis at the dawn of modernity transformed simultaneously by both the drudgery of industrialization and the enchantments of a burgeoning consumer culture (Buck-Morss 1997). Technology, particularly in moments of radical change and transformation, becomes entangled in the mythology of a previous age. As Benjamin also believed, the very forces fragmenting people's lives—the spread of technology and jobs that split people's bodies and labor into discrete units—contain the potential for recouping their "capacity for experience." Whereas other scholars such as Max Weber argued that modernity brought rationalization, Benjamin thought that under the surface of rationality the urban-industrial world had become reenchanted on an unconscious level. Mythology did not disappear in this age of technology but, rather, became rooted within technology itself. This phenomenon resulted from what he believed to be a creative potential within industrial production, as well as the imaginative effect on consumers of the spectacular display of goods (as in the Parisian arcades) as a kind of phantasmagoric "dreamworld" (Benjamin 1999; Buck-Morss 1997).

Benjamin observed this effect in the way that industry and technology were presented as if they were new gods, capable alone of producing peace, progress, and happiness. New department stores arranged goods in carnivalesque dream form, and urban space became transformed by (and into) markets for selling dreams. While such mystification drew people into a system of industrial capitalism that also exploited, isolated, and alienated them, Benjamin (unlike Marx or Adorno, his constant critic) thought there was, or could be, something redemptive in the capacity shown here to hold on to the imagination. An example of this creative potential from Benjamin's time, nearly a century ago, is the mimetic capability he saw accruing to the new technologies of photography and film. Just as young children "mimic" the world as a means of exploring (through creatively replaying) it but lose this ability as they develop language-based cognition, so, too, does industrialization, with its fixation on "objective" science and facts, weed out mimetic play. Yet film and photography offer a means of recouping this doubly lost quality: of mimicking the fragmentation, for example, of bodies and space brought on by new labor regimes by showing it in slow motion, close-up visual detail on the screen. Seeing the effects of industrialization replayed for them in a photo or film (such as Charlie Chaplin's routines in silent films) opened the possibility not only for humor but also for recognition, reflection, even political critique. In such ways, technical reproduction can give back to humanity that capacity for experience that technical production threatens to take away (Benjamin 1999; Buck-Morss 1997).

Benjamin, writing at the beginning of the twentieth century, aimed to tap into the fantasy energy encapsulated in commodities and new technologies, transforming what it said and did for people from mere enchantment to political and metaphysical illumination. His project used modern myths dialectically, retooling them into "dialectical fairy scenes" that "wake people up" from the slumber of everyday labors and mesmerizing commodity spectacles. Borrowing from Benjamin, my own objective in this book is to treat Japanese play goods as dialectical fairy scenes: to analyze their power to enchant, stimulate, and soothe the imaginations of players but to also dissect how such fantasies come embedded in—and help reproduce or alter—relations of capitalism, cultural geopolitics, and techno-communication. In all this I will attempt to take play seriously: to ask how, why, and under what (historical/economic/cultural) conditions such fantasy-scapes as *tamagotchi* and *Mighty Morphin Power Rangers* become so meaningful and pleasurable for their fans (in the two sites I have designated here, Japan and the United States). But, like Benjamin, I also see the imagination as a tool situated within the machinery of, in this case, mobile commodities that circulate the globe in a flow of merchandise, New Age technology, and cultural power. Without merely reducing play here to the media (machines/commodities/cultural capital/popular culture) within which it is set, I will examine here the "work" that Japanese play products performs at multiple levels: the desires, subjectivities, and connections that are produced in playing a *tamagotchi* or *Pokémon* game, and how the players are thus situated to resist, conform to, or modify particular worldviews (such as the hegemony of American pop culture) and worldly relations (such as the rigid academic expectations in Japan to study hard for entrance exams).

As for the politics of these capitalistic playtoys, this is an issue that, quite frankly, I have struggled with ever since embarking upon this project. In the end, *is* there anything redemptive for kids here as Benjamin saw in the new technologies of consumerism a century ago? Or are these toys so deeply entangled in circuits of commodities that the imaginative play they evoke is always, and inevitably, channeled to desires and relations of consumption? Over the years, I have gone back and forth on my own position. Shocked, on the one hand, at the commercialism embedded in these perpetually spreading, morphing, and growing playscapes, I am struck, on the other, by the intensity and profusion of attachments children make to and through these virtual worlds. I have seen lonely kids find electronic companionship in their *tamagotchi* and groups of children work for hours assembling information and strategies to hone their competitive strengths in *Pokémon*. As it has evolved, then, my current view on the subject is that, while grafted on to and actively inciting a commercialism of runaway (and possibly new) proportions, these playtoys also speak to children in powerful ways that scholars—and adults in general, so often clueless about the imaginary worlds their youth inhabit—must, in my opinion, better understand.

In the end, I *do* see a redemptive potential here not only in the power with which these goods capture kids' imaginations but also in particular capacities these play technologies accord youth for interacting with, connecting to, and (re)imagining the world today. More than anything, these toys engage in a continual breakdown and recombination of multiple bodies, powers, and parts. This is the logic of play that not only reproduces a lived world of flux, fragmentation, and mobility but also gives kids the opportunity to both mimic and reweave such particle-ization. The *tamagotchi* does this more through a trope of biological reproduction (hatching one's own pet and raising it to adulthood), *Pokémon* through discovery and conquest (catching hordes of monsters, which are also exchanged along with information between kids), and the team superheroes (Sailor Moon, Power Rangers) through morphing and collective battle scenes. Though the strategies differ, all these playscapes operate through technologies—portable electronics, televisual storytelling, virtual game consoles—that, like (and also unlike) cinema, reenvision the volatility of bodily/familial/spatial borders that come unfixed and are realigned at such frenetic speed today. Kids have continually told me that, in this realm of play, they feel a certain sense of control and also comfort: that this space is their own—to generate pets, friends, or card decks but also to destroy and rearrange as they see fit. This, too, then, is a form of mimetic play where youth explore the world by creatively replaying it—by duplicating breakdown (with potentially destructive, even violent, implications) but also by producing connections. It is in the latter I see the seeds of a dialectical fairy scene: the potential for postindustrial play technologies to give back to youth that capacity for experience that late-stage capitalism threatens to take away.

The structure of the rest of the book is organized mainly through an analysis of four separate waves of Japanese play properties: one chapter each for *Mighty Morphin Power Rangers, Sailor Moon,* and *tamagotchi* and two for *Pokémon,* reflecting both the magnitude of the latter fad and the greater length of fieldwork I devoted to it. In chapters 2 and 3, I precede the discussion of the individual case studies with two historical chapters intended to serve as background for the period during which Japan's postmodern play industry rose so successfully. The first encompasses the years immediately after the war when, in such figures as Gojira and Tetsuwan Atomu, technofantasy became a popular fixture in the mass imaginary of Japan/ese. This constitutes one bookend to the postwar period. The other consists of the years of the late 1990s and millennial crossover: a time when Japan's currency in the world marketplace of play products increased astronomically just as Japan was plunged into national malaise following the burst of the Bubble economy. Both these times have been marked and marred by upheaval at home; they have also been characterized by a flush in fantasy production whose reception overseas has been vitally important to Japan. Setting up here the relationship between fantasy, capitalism, and global/cultural power (in terms of Japanese play goods, a changing form of advanced capitalism, and United States–Japan relations), this is the rubric around which my discussions of specific play products in the rest of the book will unfold.

Methodology:
Ethnography of the Global/Millennial/Capitalist Imagination

I end this chapter with a word about methodology. Given my subject—the globalized flow of Japanese character goods into the U.S. market and their capitalistic spread as playscapes marked by portability, flexibility, and techno-animism—I deploy here a range of methodological techniques and theoretical paradigms. I remain committed to ethnography—the method of my discipline—but as anthropology and ethnography have moved away from the bounded village into the global ecumene, it has had to confront challenges that are quite new to its objects of study and to the contemporary moment.

How does one do ethnography without the false comfort of imagined local boundaries? Certainly, in my own case, the object of study here—toys that travel in a global marketplace and project fantasies of endless morphing and reconstruction—is unwieldy, mobile, and multiedged. Despite its slipperiness, however, I have sought to bring to this project what has always been the premise and promise of ethnography: getting to know a subject inside and outside its skin—what Malinowski long ago referred to as the "imponderabilia" of everyday life. Here it is critical to approach a subject not only through a body of literature and analytic guidelines but also by gaining understanding into its lived and discursive nature—how it is actually experienced, conceptualized, and talked about in the field. The latter applies particularly well to popular culture, in my opinion: a field that is most often studied through cultural studies, with its proclivity for textual analysis, theoretical acrobatics, and what has sometimes been characterized as drive-by ethnography. What a grounded ethnographic study can add to this is examining a popular phenomenon more from the perspective of those living it: a terrain—involving emotions, desires, bodily sensations, otherworldly spirits—that not only is messy itself but often muddies the categories of a more academy-directed approach.

My own project is deeply concerned with matters of the imagination. I am looking at toys that feed and construct the imagination in particular ways that are shaped by the global, millennial, and capitalistic nature of their current traffic. All these parts of the puzzle are important, but paramount is understanding the logic of the fantasy: why and how these goods work so powerfully on kids' minds and in the marketplace today. I call my book *Millennial Monsters* because monsters, both literal and figurative, figure so prominently here: border crossers with identities culled from a (monstrous) blend of the familiar and unfamiliar—normal teenagers who morph into cyborgian superheroes, electronic icons that assemble into virtual pets. By definition, monsters live between two worlds and threaten to collapse or break down the mediating border. Why is this such a compelling fantasy structure for kids in today's postindustrial world, and how significant is it that Japan currently is the cultural producer of such globally faddish monsters: goods that, as they make their way into a market like the United States, do so with the marker of the monstrous—both familiar to humans and radically other (Rony 1996)? Consider Peter in North Carolina. He plays *Yu-Gi-Oh!* cards that are deeply familiar to him but also, in some sense, foreign (and feel much more foreign to his dad). To understand how this imaginary world makes sense to fans like Peter and how the fantasy shifts in different contexts and for different actors in the play scene is my ethnographic objective here.

This is a daunting challenge nonetheless, considering that I am neither a child nor an adoring fan of these properties. So, I have immersed myself in the play culture—watching countless movies and cartoons, reading guidebooks and comics, and endlessly playing electronic games—but also employed other strategies such as observing children as they play, interviewing parents and marketers (ethnographers themselves) about the appeal of particular toys, and studying new waves of merchandise at toy stores and toy shows. Interested as well in the production, marketing, and ideological and historical circulation of these toys as their logic of fantasy, I have adopted a multiperspectival approach for studying my subject, itself not only mobile but also multifaceted. Conducting multisited fieldwork (both in the United States, during summers and spring breaks starting in 1995, and in Japan, for short stints and a full year in 1999–2000), I utilized a range of methodological techniques.[22] These included interviewing executives, designers, and advertisers at (in the United States) Saban Entertainment, Warner Brothers, 4Kids Entertainment, Hasbro, Nintendo, Wizards of the Coast, Bandai America, and Mattel and (in Japan) Shōgakukan Inc., ShoPro, Tomy, and Bandai; conducting an Internet survey of fans of *Sailor Moon;* visiting classes in a U.S. middle school on Japanese pop culture; doing an internship at the advertising firm launching the early *Pokémon* ads for Hasbro; following and analyzing mass media coverage and commentary in both countries; reading scholarship (on cognate toy and kids' trends); interviewing child experts and scholars who have written on characters/toys/global merchandise (particularly in Japan); studying the historical periods (particularly in Japan) of both the 1950s and the 1990s; and reading what is a vast literature and discourse in Japan on children's entertainment, including books written by the creator of *tamagotchi* and the producer of *Pokémon.* My research plan was more flexible than religious in the techniques used to study each wave of toy merchandise. This was for reasons both of serendipity (different opportunities and contacts presented themselves in each case) and of purposely trying to mix up and vary the strategies employed. So, while I conducted an Internet survey with fans of *Sailor Moon* in the States and played *tamagotchi* alongside kids in North Carolina, for example, I studied the seasonal changes of Ranger television shows at the Bandai Museum in Tokyo and interviewed a host of producers and executives involved with *Pokémon* in both Japan and the United States.

In the end, I have examined the toys in my study from multiple angles: as commodities in an ever-cascading empire of addictive consumerism (using theories of political economy and global capitalism), as signs of cultural power (as expressed in local discourses in Japan), as fantasies that elicit pleasure and intimacy (according to players and marketers), and as symptoms of postindustrial youth culture marked by techno-animism, nomadic subjectivity, and anxiety (read through the lens of behavioral trends and socioeconomic conditions). This range of perspective has added complexity if not always clarity to my subject matter; contradictions and tensions abound here in how toy culture is articulated by different voices and positions. But my aim in being multiperspectival is not so much to present an array of viewpoints (that, treated as neutral and transparent, add up to a social fact) as to understand the logic by which these complicated objects circulate in a marketplace of soft power and fantasy capital. Thus, I take it as a given that each position has its own bias that comes ensconced in its own interpretive framework. Marketers of toys are looking to sell their product no matter how eloquently they speak of its redemptive or imaginative potential for kids. And fans are so enamored they rarely can see the hook with which these products also feed an addiction to consume.

Millennial Monsters: Japanese Toys and the Global Imagination is a book about entertainment goods that, produced in Japan and out of specific conditions, are shaping—and being shaped by—the global/millennial/capitalist imagination for postindustrial youth in profound ways. Ultimately, *Millennial Monsters* is about not any static object but interlocking relationships: between global capitalism and Japanese capitalism, fantasies and commodities, techno-animism and polymorphous commercialism, Japan and the United States. Not bounded or grounded units but relations that move and shift, this is how I see the "millennial monsters" in the title: enchantments and commodities that hover between reality and the imagination with the power to both unsettle and entice.

So, with methodology behind us, on to flows of toys and goods, currencies of culture and money, and trades in fantasies and powers.

2 From Ashes to Cyborgs

The Era of Reconstruction (1945–1960)

Toys for Food:
A Tale of Tin Cans

The war ended on August 15, 1945. It was a fiercely hot day in the heart of summer. Bombs had burned everything and all that remained of Japan was scorched land. Particularly hard hit were the cities. Tokyo was reduced to burnt fields and, in the midst of this, sat the toy industry. The "made in Japan" labels produced here had once roared successfully all over the world. Now this was part of what had been lost: Japan's industrial district.

Kitahara 2000:62

Fire and ashes were recurrent tropes in the accounts of Japan's defeat at the hands of the Allies in World War II. By the time of its surrender, the country lay, literally and figuratively, in ruins. American air raids, running relentlessly in the last fourteen months of war, rendered huge civilian losses (seventy thousand alone in the attack on Tokyo in March 1945) and vast urban destruction (half the country, concentrated in urban cities and small adjacent cities: 40 percent of Tokyo, 58 percent of Yokohama, 56 percent of Kobe, 38 percent of Osaka). The national transportation system was crippled; a majority of ports and factories had been destroyed; entire industries were crushed or wiped out (aircraft manufacturing, textiles, iron and steel, cement); and little remained of investment capital. Losing their homes, millions of urbanites fled to the countryside. Even here, though, hunger and homelessness were acute, and the struggle for food and shelter drove people's lives for almost a decade. Following the horror of continuous air raids came the most searing wartime event of all: the atomic bombs dropped by the United States over Hiroshima on August 6, 1945, and, three days later, onto Nagasaki.

With this New Age weaponry was launched a different kind of horror: the mushroom spectacle of wholesale destruction (killing more than one hundred thousand in Hiroshima and forty thousand in Nagasaki) that eviscerated and melted flesh, extinguished physical objects often to literal shadows, and triggered lingering and unknown effects from radiation exposure. The first country to be victimized by nuclear warfare, Japan has been forever marked by the events of Hiroshima and Nagasaki. Producing the awaited national surrender (announced by the emperor in a curious understatement: "The war has not necessarily gone in our favor"), the atomic blasts signaled both the end of the war and the end of an era in Japan.

Burdened by tremendous losses and possessing little in the way of resources, infrastructure, or harvests with which to sustain its populace or commence reconstruction, Japan also faced the despair of defeat in 1945 and the erosion of national identity. Along with the "burnt fields" (yaki nohara) came a dismantling of what had once grounded the state: the emperor's divinity, a body politic tied to militarism, and a citizenry trained to believe in the sacredness and certainty of an East Asian empire to be led by Japan. The familiar was now replaced by the tremors of the unknown: a new atomic bomb, a new occupying force (an unprecedented event in a country never previously occupied by a foreign army), and a new democratic constitution. Times were uneasy, yet the end of the war also meant the disassembling of the military machine that had dictated the country and subsumed national energies for more than a decade. The areas suppressed by the war effort included the subjects that interest me most in this book—the realms of play and the imagination. The movie industry, for example, had been heavily channeled toward the war effort, and Tōhō Studios produced a number of patriotic tales undergirding Japan's militarism with inspirational tales of victory, heroism, and sacrifice. And the toy industry came to a complete halt, stymied by an official proclamation in July 1940 that forbade the use of precious materials (specifically metal) in the production of anything lacking immediate "utility" to the state. This meant fulfilling the only national agenda of the moment: defeating Japan's enemies and erecting an Asian empire (the Greater East Asia Co-Prosperity Sphere).

Prior to this edict, however, the toy industry had been a vital part of the national economy, valued for its worldwide reputation as a top-ranked producer of children's playthings. Known best for the high quality, low price, and detailed design of its metallic toys, the industry was given a vital boost, interestingly enough, by the exigencies of the previous world war. When Germany, then the world leader in toys, was forced to reduce manufacturing, Japan filled the lacuna in production, more than tripling its overseas sales between 1914 and 1918 from 8 to 25 million yen. Shaped by the modernization taking over the country, the toy industry was filled by onetime artisans of metal ornaments for temples and shrines who, finding their skills displaced by new technology coming from Europe and the United States, had retooled their craft from religion to entertainment at the turn of the century. For this reason, the toy district emerged in the Asakusa neighborhood of Tokyo, known as a repository of Japanese traditions of all sorts—major festivals, shrines, temples, and (in the Tokugawa period), the pleasures of the red-light district. Here, where the traditional intermixed with the industrial (in a dynamic that has persisted in today's millennial era of cyberwarriors and digital spirits), Japanese toy making became a modern-day business. With the invention of the handpress machine, imported from abroad shortly after the Sino-Japanese War in 1905, handmade toys shifted to mass production (Toyama 2000).

After its efflorescence during World War I, the Japanese toy industry ebbed briefly with the decline of exports and the destruction of many factories in Tokyo's earthquake of 1923. Stimulated, however, by new interest in children and children's culture at the start of the Shōwa period (beginning in 1925), it quickly rebuilt and was thriving and world famous when, by the mid-1930s, events leading to World War II were well under way. Not allowed to utilize precious resources (metal and also paper) in the construction of "nonvital" playtoys during wartime, the industry found the situation little improved once the war finally ended. Widespread scarcity, including raw materials, had only intensified now, and the sole abundance in the country came from the well-fed occupying army (mainly American GIs) patrolling the streets in their jeeps and military fatigues as Japan's new ruling force. Authorized to rule, these onetime enemies policed the populace, administered the country, and remade the state—installing an American school system of 6–3–3, divesting the *zaibatsu* (large conglomerates of family-owned corporations), and imposing democracy (in a constitution instituting individual rights, female suffrage, separation of church and state, and a ban against rearmament except for self-defense). The presence of the Supreme Command Allied Powers (SCAP), though resented, was not unqualifiedly despised. For along with their authority, the Americans rebuilt schools, factories, industry, and civil services, thereby helping establish the infrastructure for Japan's reconstruction.

At a more banal level, SCAP forces also consumed food and generated garbage. And, ironically enough, it was here—in the refuse of the occupier's everyday existence—that the toy industry found a resource with which to rekindle business in these dire times following the war. Lacking anything else, Japanese toy makers used the only substance they could find—discarded tin cans from SCAP food rations. Modeling these toys after the jeeps being driven by American soldiers (figure 6), the Japanese toy industry recycled, both literally and figuratively, the U.S. occupation as fodder for its postwar reconstruction. The Kosuga jeep is the first recorded toy made in Japan after the war. Inspired by a metal shop owner (Kosuga Matsuzō) whose factory—relocated from Tokyo to Ōtsu during the war and reconverted to military production—had survived the air raids, the toys used tin cans for the car frame and a rubber band for the motor. Priced at ten yen at Kyoto's Marubutsu Department Store the first Christmas following the war, these toys could be purchased even by impoverished Japanese; hundreds were sold the first hour. Enlisting the help of local women, Kosuga increased production; ten thousand toy jeeps were sold between December and January, and the price was raised to thirty yen. And as rumors of his success spread to Tokyo, others were spurred to start up toy manufacturing as well (Toyama 2000:61). Though flimsy in substance, the Kosuga jeep and its imitators were cleverly designed, living up to the reputation Japan's toy industry had enjoyed before the war.

American soldiers found these playthings amusing. So did officials at SCAP, who, already aware of the prewar stature of the Japanese toy industry, called its representatives into General Headquarters (GHQ) and ordered them to manufacture their ware for American children. Told that "from the long war . . . American children are hungry for toys" (Saitō 1989:116), Japanese toy makers were commanded to send a portion of their goods to the United States. A form of exchange was also contracted; in return for cleaning up the SCAP forces' garbage, toy makers could keep the discarded tin cans and use them to produce more toys (Saitō 1989). Dictated by the authority and desires of the occupying forces in the early years following the war, toy production was also the first Japanese business allowed to reenter the "free marketplace" of export sale. On August 15, 1947 (precisely two years after the end of the war), SCAP officially decreed that toys could now be legally exported as commodities. As such, they constituted the first export, and primary impetus, for Japan's postwar economy. There was a condition, however; the words "Made in Occupied Japan" were to be imprinted on the bottom of each toy. Bearing this logo, more than half of all the toys produced in Japan during occupation were sold overseas, mainly in the United States (Kitahara 2000).

As Kitahara Teruhisa (2000) has noted, the influence of export greatly shaped the early designs of postwar toys. For example, Newsboy, a doll made by Nikkō Toys in the late 1940s with a celluloid head and a body built from

Figure 6. Recycling the occupation: toy jeep made out of tin cans and modeled on American military vehicles. (Courtesy of Kōdansha Publishers.)

tin cans, was clearly designed for an American audience. All the written script (on the package and the newspaper held in Newsboy's hand) was in English, and the doll's torso was draped in the Stars and Stripes. Similarly, Atomic Robot, also made from recycled tin cans, came in a package printed not only in English but also—and far more disturbingly—with an image of the blossoming mushroom cloud of the atomic bomb. Parlaying the tragedy of Hiroshima and Nagasaki into a playtoy for American kids is a bitter indication of how Japanese toy making of this era was driven by an "occupied mentality." As observed by Kitahara, the focus was on appealing to the imaginations of children not at home (for whom bare necessities were more pressing and toys were still *mada mada*—in the future) but abroad: kids whose fathers had defeated Japan.

Produced under conditions of subjugation, toys nonetheless provided much-needed business for the Japanese state, and the play industry generated precious revenues. It also yielded something even more basic to the needs of Japanese children at the time: food. When a lunch program was instituted in 1947 along with educational reforms to the schools (modeled after the American system), supplies from the United States were exchanged for the only Japanese commodities (besides silk) then found desirable by American consumers: toys. So while Japanese toys fed the imaginations of kids overseas, the goods they were exchanged for fed the stomachs of schoolchildren at home. Further, once the American food had been eaten, the now-empty cans it came in were recycled to make ever more tin toys. Thus, like the school system itself, these playthings were crafted with the imprint of a distinctively foreign culture—the canned pineapple, baked beans, and sardines on the underside of tin jeeps and Atomic Robots. Put through a complete course of recycling—from the occupier's empty ration cans to the lunches of Japanese schoolchildren and back to cans again— Japan's toy industry rebuilt itself after the war by transforming waste into play products to be enjoyed by kids in another country.

Thanks, in large part, to the access and popularity it had with its principal export market, the United States, the Japanese toy industry also played a major role in rebuilding the national economy. Leading the rise of industry in the early postwar period, export revenues in the toy industry came to 322 million yen in 1948, more than tripled by 1949 (to 1 billion yen), and reached 8 billion yen by 1955. The American marketplace was critically important here, and the currency of play it enabled fed the Japanese economy and Japanese themselves in more ways than one after the war.

Gojira:
The Terrors and Thrills of an Atomic Mutant

> One of the appeals of the 1954 *Gojira* (Godzilla) movie was that it
> expressed Japanese fears of the moment. For people finally
> experiencing economic recovery after a war that decimated the country
> to burnt land, the spectacle of Gojira's urban destructions was
> exceedingly realistic. Without doubt, this was one of its major charms.
>
> Kobayashi 1992:177

By 1954, nine years had passed since Japan surrendered to the Allies; the occupation had been over for only two years. Times were still hard and, with a per capita annual income of ninety-seven dollars, people remained plagued by insecurities of the everyday—making ends meet, having enough food, and living in cramped housing. Yet, stimulated by the outbreak of the Korean War in 1950, which spurred a demand for heavy industry by the U.S. military, Japan's economy not only was starting to recover but even was in an expansionary mode (leading to the "high growth period" that culminated in 1973).[1] By 1955, many arenas of economic performance had returned to prewar levels, and one year later the government officially announced that the postwar period was over. Basic needs were now being met, the white paper declared, and from here on out national goals were to be high levels of production and consumption (Ivy 1993:246). Replacing the wartime agendas of militarism and empire building were the pacifist ones of achieving material prosperity through the joint pillars of a managed society *(kanri shakai)* and technological advances. And though the Japanese economy at the end of the war had been blasted into what one scholar has called "a sort of dark age" (Allinson 1997:75), the "miracle" of its postwar recovery was not far off. The 1950s would be a period of disjuncture. Juxtaposed against the heaviness of daily survival and the residue of wartime disaster was what has sometimes been called a "vitality" (Partner 1999:47) brought on by the newness of the times and hopes for a better future. As Maruyama Masao has noted about a similar period of urban destruction during and after the Great Kantō Earthquake of 1923 (marked, as well, by fierce fires that burned city dwellings to the ground), emerging in the aftermath was an effloresc-ing culture fueled by technological advances: "In this burnt-out field the in-carnation of speed, i.e., automobiles, appeared to wander the streets, soon followed by the monster called radio; then the model of birds, the air-plane. . . . All of these embodiments of modern science, coming forth in Japan one by one immediately after the earthquake disaster" (quoted in Partner 1999:18–19).

In the postwar period, the United States exerted a major influence in the burgeoning mass culture as well as technological culture in Japan. During its seven-year occupation of the country, America directly affected national policies: everything from sanctioning the production of toys (as one of the eleven "necessities of life" [Saitō 1989:116]) and workers' rights to strike to enforcing purges and reforms (against anything thought to have under-written the militaristic state, from the school system to martial arts). It also promoted the spread of radio ownership and broadcasting in the belief, up-held by the Japanese government's Ministry of International Trade and In-dustry (MITI) as well, that quickly developing an advanced network of media culture in Japan would greatly benefit postwar reconstruction (in the direction of what Morris-Suzuki [1988] has called information capitalism). Much in the way of technology (such as transistors adopted by Morita Akio into Sony's highly successful transistor radio) and management techniques (like the concept of quality circles, introduced by W. Edwards Deming) was imported or appropriated directly from Americans. On a more indirect level, the fantasies and dreams of postwar Japanese were deeply aroused by images of American prosperity—spread first by the presence of well-fed American GIs during occupation and, later, by the circulation of American consumer products and popular culture (with its scenes of middle-class abundance projected in Hollywood movies and television shows like *Father Knows Best* so popular in postwar Japan).

Into, and out of, this mix lurched the phenomenon that was *Gojira:* the first cinematic blockbuster of the postwar era, featuring a spectacle of terror—a mutant prehistoric beast ravaging Tokyo with its atomic powers. Released by Tōhō Studios in 1954 (followed by the U.S. remake, with Raymond Burr, titled *Godzilla, King of the Monsters* in 1956), *Gojira* is the story of a four-hundred-foot-tall amphibious monster awakened from his four-hundred-million-year hibernation at the bottom of the sea by nuclear testing conducted by Americans (as they did in real life) on nearby Bikini Atoll.[2] The blasts both enrage and mutate Gojira, turning him into a monstrous hybrid that is part dinosaur, part nuclear weapon (figure 7). Surfacing at Tokyo Bay, the atomic hulk now stalks the metropolis with a vengeful fury. Thrashing his tail and growling fiercely as he discharges nuclear rays, Gojira crumples buildings and crushes people in an orgy of destruction.

Gojira represented a return to popular entertainment on a grand scale after the movie industry's long servitude to the state in the interests of militarism during wartime. Starting in 1897, Japanese cinema was birthed in the shadow of war. The events of the Russo-Japanese War in 1904 were captured by both Japanese and foreign film crews and, shown as newsreels in theaters, inspired public interest in the new medium of cinema. As Peter High has written in his book on Japanese film culture between 1931 and 1945, these early newsreels opened viewers up to a world beyond Japan itself, thereby kindling a sense of "world citizenship" and creating a "true Japanese 'viewing public' in the modern sense of the word" (2003:6, 7). War footage also inspired patriotism, of course, though until the 1930s modern war stories were produced alongside other genres including *jidaigeki*—period pieces showcasing the spiritual fortitude and superior swordsmanship of samurai and other warriors. With the Manchurian Incident of 1931 triggering the events that would culminate in the Pacific War, however, Japanese cinema became dominated by militaristic storytelling and dictated by the policies and agendas of Japan's totalitarian state (High 2003).

Even though about half of all movie theaters had been destroyed during the war, most of the studios survived (Ivy 1993). Enlisted now to entertain

Figure 7. Gojira: a mythological monster for the atomic age, from *Gojira Millennium*. (Courtesy of Tōhō Studios.)

the masses with escapist pleasure (and purged, by SCAP, of any wartime predilections toward militarism, superpatriotism, and "feudal loyalty" that might be "anti-democratic" [High 2003:505]), production rose quickly after 1945.[3] As he related to me in an interview in summer 1997, Ōshita Eiji (the author of a book on the global boom in Japanese mass characters today) sees a distinctively Japanese aesthetic in the mass mythmaking of the early post-war era that has flourished to the present day. Measured less by the realism, flashy effects, or happy endings of Hollywood and Disney, made-in-Japan tales (in film, television, comic books, animation) grip their audiences with an emotional power that registers as "true" while still remaining a fantasy. The mythological composition is crucial: how the story and characters weave an alternative world that evokes deep responses in the audience—yearning, fears, anxieties, desires. The same quality that would later make *Mighty Morphin Power Rangers* so popular around the world—namely, its myth of transformation *(henshin)* that, while fanciful in the form given it on the screen, realizes a universal kid fantasy of being able to morph into an upgraded version of the self—is also key to what Ōshita considers the grounding myth of Japan's postwar imaginary, *Gojira*, a movie featuring a primitive creature forever transformed by New Age technology in the form of exposure to nuclear fallout. Seeing themselves in Gojira, audiences also saw this entity as a deathly force that would destroy their country unless constrained. The ambiguity of these emotions configured the beast as well. Powerful and strong but lumbering, victimized, and solitary, Gojira was a monster that Japanese viewers of the 1950s and afterward could not only fear but also identify with: a monstrosity straddling the border between past and future, destruction and transformation, self and other. Indeed, the monster's name itself is a hybrid: the Japanese word for "whale" *(kujira)* coupled with the American word for "gorilla"—a fitting symbol of America's effect, both good and bad, on Japan's postwar imaginary.

The spectacle of *Gojira* was a defining moment in the postwar recovery of Japan. Unlike the tin toys, which had a currency that directly contributed to the rebuilding of the Japanese economy after the war, this was a movie in an industry important but not critical to national finances in the 1950s. Of more consequence was the blockbuster nature of this production and the fact that it was made, though also for export to the United States, for the enjoyment of Japanese. This was spectacular entertainment targeted (at least initially) to the domestic marketplace. Tōhō Studios conceptualized *Gojira* as a hit from the beginning, giving it a budget (63 million yen) approximately three times that of other films (making it the most expensive Japanese movie to date) and assigning top guns to its production. Overseen by producer Tanaka Tomoyuki, the screenplay was written by science fiction author Kayama Shigeru. Honda Ishirō was the director, Tsuburaya Eiji masterminded the special effects, Ifukube Akira (an internationally acclaimed composer) orchestrated the score, and major actors were cast (including Shimura Takashi and two well-known stunt actors to play Gojira). Opening on November 3, 1954, *Gojira* brought in 9.6 million viewers during its Japanese run, yielding 152 million yen ($2.25 million) in profits (Ryfle 1998). While this made it only twelfth on the list of Japan's box-office hits for 1954 (Tōhō Studios also came out with Kurosawa Akira's *Seven Samurai* the same year), *Gojira* immediately registered as a landmark, launching an era of "monster films" *(kaijū eiga)*.

Because of its subject and the special effects used, *Gojira* also belonged to the genre known in those days as "scientific fantasy movies." Despite the imaginary nature of the beast, however, it was conjured out of historical events that were deeply real and painfully remembered in Japan: the destruction of Tokyo during the war and the atomic bombs that have victimized only Japan, to date, as the target of wartime aggression. Manifestly, though, the creative impulse for *Gojira* came from an occurrence closer in time. On March 1, 1954, the United States secretly detonated a fifteen-megaton hydrogen bomb (750 times the atomic power of the bombs dropped on Hiroshima and Nagasaki) near Bikini Atoll in Micronesia. A Japanese trawler, the *Daigo Fukuryū Maru* (Lucky Dragon), fishing in nearby waters, was exposed to the fallout, and six members of the twenty-three-man crew died shortly afterward. Returning from Indonesia after a canceled movie deal at about the same time, Tanaka Tomoyuki was looking for a replacement film and found his inspiration in the Bikini incident.

A longtime fan of American westerns and Japanese *chanbara* (samurai action films), Tanaka had been most deeply affected by the movie *King Kong,* which he had seen as a young man. Looking back on his accomplishment with *Gojira,* he was proud that others took to this creature with the intensity of "affection" *(aichaku)* and "yearning" *(akogare)* he earlier felt toward King Kong. Of the setting in which his idea was born, Tanaka has said: "The times were somber; the army had been crushed. Born of a nuclear episode, the monster is even stronger than an atomic weapon. With all that strength, he has the capacity to wipe out the civilization built by humans. Audiences hugely applauded Gojira. This is because in everyday life, people have to suppress their anger, and Gojira is a substitution for this. It satisfies everyone's desire for destruction" (Tanaka 1993:22).

Indeed, the movie dramatizes what Susan Sontag has called an aesthetics of destruction. Right from the beginning, viewers are bombarded with scenes of dead bodies, the rubble of fallen buildings, and the despair of Japanese gripped by loss, fear, and the uncertainty of a future threatened by alien intrusion. These images of disaster are omnipresent in the film, and the portrayal of a city under attack whose population is terrorized, weakened, and besieged was certainly a replaying of wartime memories. The story of Gojira, however, is a retelling of the war with a twist. In Tanaka's version, the Japanese bear no responsibility for the destruction wreaked upon their land. Rather, the aggressions in the tale rest entirely with the monster and with the nuclear fallout provoking his transformation and rage. Gojira signifies World War II as a travesty of nature brought on by the atomic blasts of the Americans. For Japanese audiences, then, *Gojira* provided a vehicle for reliving the terrors of the war relieved of any guilt or responsibility—solely, that is, from the perspective of victim. In this sense, *Gojira* was a fantasy. Crafted, as were tin-can toy jeeps, out of the shards of real-life experience borne by Japanese in the aftermath of a devastating war, it also rewove wartime events to efface Japan's role as aggressor: a victimized version of their war role that has gained dominance throughout the postwar period (much to the outrage of countries like Korea and China that were brutalized by Japanese military aggression).

The figure of the monster in *Gojira* is a symptom of its times—the underside of Japan's defeat in the war and, out of the ashes of atomic victimization, its subsequent reinvention as a nation devoted to pacifism instead of militarism and techno-fetishism in both industry and consumer culture. As

Freud uses this word, a *symptom* is a behavior arising out of a set of (traumatic) circumstances that it both bears witness to and is an attempt to survive. In this sense, Gojira is symptomatically marked; he is scarred yet empowered by a particular historical event—a nuclear blast that disturbs his home but also rewires him as an atomic cyborg. The emotions he engenders are accordingly ambivalent, according to a number of Japanese I have spoken to. He is pitied for being a victim, feared for being inhumanly fierce, and envied for being technologically empowered.[4] As the director of the Japanese sequel, *Gojira Millennium* (released in 2000), has remarked, audiences see both an enemy and themselves in Gojira and want to flee him as well as become him. Since the time he first entered the circuits of the popular imaginary in the 1950s, then, Gojira would seem to have embodied the very essence of monstrosity—something caught between different worlds, time periods, and natures. A monster, he symbolizes the monstrosity Japan was reduced to by war but also the transformations Japan had to undergo to survive and rebuild in the postwar era.

Technology, as mentioned earlier, lay at the very heart of Japan's rebuilding: what many (including Emperor Hirohito) believed was America's superior strength during the war and, for being comparatively weaker, the ultimate reason for Japan's defeat. Out of the scars of war, Japan was to rebuild itself by becoming embedded, like Gojira, with new technologies that would forever alter national identity, state policies, and subjectivity. Postwar reconstruction has been a process of cyborgization, defining *cyborg* here less in Donna Haraway's terms (a fusion of organism and machine) than as the everyday intimacy humans acquire with mechanical apparatuses (Clark 2003:6). Geared now to generating consumerism rather than defending the homeland, technology was to infuse the daily lives, habits, and desires of Japanese as never before (in the form more of washing machines and televisions than of airplanes and guns). But it was also tied, at least in the beginning, to trauma and loss—standard in tales of cyborgs that, once they become organisms, are mechanically remade following an injury or death.[5] Technology also brought with it an ever greater reliance on the importation of foreign know-how—a move away from the strictly "domestic production" policy of the wartime era bringing with it an intimacy with the (American) "other" at once exciting and unnerving.[6] How Japanese would and should handle such transformation is part of the story given to the endless proliferation of monsters and superheroes produced by Japan's entertainment industry in the half century following the war. Fittingly, it was also the technological prowess of special-effects director Tsuburaya Eiji in crafting the movie with stunning technique that made *Gojira* a milestone in rebuilding Japan's stock in its own

imagination. One-third of the movie's budget was expended on special effects, and Tsuburaya became famous for the "suitmation" device he initiated:
using actors in rubber monster suits trampling miniature city scenes to play
the role of Gojira. Like Tanaka, he was deeply inspired by the movie *King
Kong*, which when it came out in 1933 impressed Tsuburaya with its sophisticated special effects that contrasted with the rather crude trick photography
still being used then in Japanese moviemaking. By 1954, Tsuburaya had
greatly developed his own craft, and he is still heralded as the guru of special
effects, or *tokusatsu*, which became the name of a genre in both film and television shows in Japan.

For *Gojira*, however, Tsuburaya opted for the less advanced expedient of
"suitmation" rather than American moviemakers' preferred technique
since *King Kong*—stop-motion animation. Used primarily for reasons of
time and money, the low-tech suitmation was nonetheless instrumental in
defining Gojira's cinematic performance. As I was often told in doing research for this project, fantasy is far more valued than realism as the creative aesthetic of popular entertainment in Japan. But fantasy needs to reach
people at a deeply emotional, mythic level, and this is precisely what the
movie's Japanese audience, including critics at the time, has said about *Gojira*. In part *because* real people were used, the monster's movements and
destructive nature seem somehow more powerful, even "strangely humanlike," as a commentator wrote in 1954 (Takeuchi and Yamamoto 2001:90).
Like the character of Gojira itself, then, borders are blurred in production—
between monster and human, technology and actor—that are kept more
distinct in the Hollywood brand of moviemaking.

Indeed, audiences abroad (especially in the United States) often had a
very different reaction to *Godzilla's* production level, regarding the suited
monster as a sign of crudity and "cheesiness." In Japan, however, the fact
that Japanese filmmakers could produce a movie judged to be of superior
quality became a source of national pride.[7] The following comments are
taken from reviews of the film that appeared in the Japanese press in 1954:

- "The trick special effects were great. This really advances the
  dreams of Japanese moviemaking."
- "With trick movies, we always feel bested by the United States. But
  Gojira is the 'real thing *[honmono]*.' "
- "With this kind of movie, we usually feel that America has the monopoly. That we can produce such a fine film in our country too is
  a real joy."

- "In this kind of film genre, we think of American films as out-standing. But *Gojira* makes me proud that Japan can produce something of this quality." (Takeuchi and Yamamoto 2001:90–91)

Given its immediate success, it is not surprising that *Gojira* became an institution, spawning a total of twenty-eight movies produced by Tōhō Studios over a course of fifty years (the last and supposed final one being *Godzilla: Final Wars,* released in December 2004). Approximately two to three million viewers have seen each of these productions in Japan even though, over time, the targeted audience switched to children rather than adults and the monster became more of a lovable superhero fighting to save rather than destroy the human world.

It was not only the size of the movie, of course, but also that of the monster that, in a conflation of production and myth, made *Gojira* the epoch film that it was. As Tanaka Tomoyuki said at the end of his career, reflecting on the importance of *Gojira* after having made more than two hundred films: "My close associates and I were touched to see the shape of a monster *[kaijū]* again in this remarkable movie that we became so attached to. It's a strong thing, one toward which we felt an undeniable yearning." This sentiment has been shared by younger generations of postwar Japanese as well. Takahashi Toshio, a professor of literature and a baby boomer born in the 1950s who had not been a fan of *Gojira* and its sequels as a child, developed a strong interest in a new series that started in 1984 (when he was thirty-two years old).[8] In his words (2001), the story moved him in his body, not his head; he experienced a "tense feeling" generated by something more basic than the quality of production or the catharsis of reliving wartime trauma. A monster, after all, represents the unknown: the edges of human existence beyond which all "knowledge and common sense disappear." In terms of monsters, "Gojira is top rank" because he remains unknowable and indestructible, according to Takahashi. Unlike a monster such as King Kong (or the Tri-Star Pictures' version of Godzilla), Gojira does not die, and what he wants is unclear to humans. The mystery of his motives makes whatever he is both vague and ongoing: something scary but also fascinating, as much for adults as for children. The real secret of *Gojira*'s long-lasting impact, in Takahashi's mind, is its mythic construction. And this, as was the general assessment in Japan, is precisely what the U.S. version (Tri-Star's *Godzilla* that came out in May 1998) so grossly distorted.[9] Instead of a lumbering beast radically (dis)joined between an archaic past and an atomic future, the U.S. monster is a sleekly efficient killing machine whose brutal rationality engenders no other emotion in moviegoers than pure revulsion. As one of the Gojira suitmation actors said of this film, walking out midway through when viewing it at a Godzilla convention in Chicago, "It's not Godzilla. It doesn't have his spirit" (Satsuma Kenpachiro, cited in Ryfle 1998:344).

As important to its business as serialization and franchise merchandise has been the marketing of *Gojira* overseas. Exporting started with the original movie when a low-budget filmmaker, Dick Kay, bought U.S. rights and remade the film by splicing in footage shot of Raymond Burr as the American reporter. Entitled *Godzilla, King of the Monsters* (figure 8), it debuted at Loew's State Theater on April 4, 1956, and proved to be a hit, grossing more than $2 million in its initial run. Kay, who made his living churning out exploitation films, had paid a mere $30,000 for the Japanese footage. Filming Raymond Burr in a small soundstage in Los Angeles in a single day, he kept total production costs under $100,000. Kay and his colleagues (including the East Coast distributor Joseph E. Levine of Trans World Films, who had greater stature in the industry) earned more than $200,000 in the endeavor: eight to ten times what modest hits were yielding at the time. Interviewed recently in the media blitz accompanying the megaproduction of *Godzilla* in 1998, Kay said of his own involvement with *Godzilla* that it was only "business." For the times, his business move—importing a film from a country whose movies were considered to be technologically inferior—was extremely bold. But Kay figured he could turn a profit despite the fact that, in his own opinion, the Japanese production was "hokey." The theme fit into a 1950s craze of atomic monsters that included movies like *The Beast from 20,000 Fathoms*. And *Godzilla* turned into a horror film legend, launching, in the words of the man who brokered the deal, "scores of cheesy sequels" (Ryfle 1998).

There has been no dearth of avid *Godzilla* fans in the United States, however, many of whom, like Steven Spielberg, regard the film as a work of art. And the popularity of the Japanese beast spawned a slew of follow-up creatures, such as Mothra, Ghidra, Mechagodzilla, and Minya (Godzilla's offspring), as well as reproduction across a range of media and pop culture—comic books (Marvel Comics came out with a Godzilla series in the late 1970s), cartoons (Hanna-Barbera developed a Saturday-morning cartoon in 1978 that, although short-lived, also replayed as reruns), and fanzines (like *G-FAN*). Yet as serious lovers of *Godzilla* have also pointed out, Americanization changed and devalued the original cachet these monsters had for their Japanese audiences. In the United States, *Godzilla* took off in large part for the differences it posed from Hollywood productions: differences—an actor dressed up in a monster suit instead of high-tech animation, a foreign language dubbed into English, Tokyo and its Japanese population getting

Figure 8. Remade for the United States: a poster for
Godzilla, King of the Monsters. (From *Sci-Fi Entertainment* 5, no. 2 [July 1993]; courtesy of Sovereign Media
Company, Inc.)

creamed—whose effect was viscerally exciting yet judged (often enough) to
be technically unconvincing and cheap. Few histories of U.S. moviemaking,
for example, list the *Godzilla* films. Yet as three American authors of recent
books on the subject argue (Kalat 1997; Ryfle 1998; Tsutsui 2004), the retooling of these movies for U.S. release is itself to blame for much of the
crudity attributed to this new genre in America. In general, little money or

care was expended on modifying these films for U.S. transmission. The technique of translation in particular was poorly executed (less so in the first movie, however, where entire sequences in Japanese were left undubbed, and Raymond Burr's English-speaking role was spliced in). With the actors' mouths running askew of the words being spoken, the effect of bad dubbing is to make the movies seem unintentionally funny. Rather than being appreciated as an aesthetically different kind of monster movie, then, *Godzilla* and its offspring have been viewed as a camp phenomenon by many Americans—an "other" to the standards of flashy production and realistic moviemaking maintained by Hollywood.

Like the tin toys that preceded it, these Japanese exports entertained U.S. consumers but were still regarded as cheap trinkets: a sign, particularly in the early decades following the war, of the low stature of Japan (and Japanese goods) in the eyes of Americans. Despite this devaluing of a cultural product whose symbolic cachet is much higher at home, however, the Americanizing of Godzilla was the key to its globalization. It was the U.S. version, *Godzilla, King of the Monsters*, that circulated successfully in Europe (and Japan as well, where it was reimported). As was true of the sequels as well, plugging Gojira into the U.S. entertainment industry of distribution expanded this monster's sphere of marketability and recognition around the world. In the words of Sato Kenji, author of two books on Gojira's cultural impact, "He's the greatest star the Japanese movie industry has produced." Ironically, however, its status as global icon has been routed through a country where the Japanese monster and its movies have been regarded as something of a joke.

Tetsuwan Atomu:
The Era of Comic Culture, Robot Heroes, and Mass Characters

> Crowds will cheer you, You're a hero,
> As you go, go, GO ASTRO BOY!!!!!
>
> Theme song for the U.S. version of
> *Astro Boy*, copyright 1963 Suzuki
> Associates; reprinted in Yang, Can,
> and Hong 1997:65

The 1950s in Japan, marked by rawness and reconstruction, spawned teeming hordes of new or mutant life-forms in the popular imagination. At one end of the spectrum was Gojira—the mean-spirited hulk menacing Tokyo and jolting movie audiences with spectacular special effects. At the other end was Tetsuwan Atomu—a lovable boy-robot who was as gentle-hearted and reassuring a superhero as he was futuristic and scientifically advanced. Created by Tezuka Osamu, the revered pioneer of Japanese animation, the character first appeared as a *manga* in 1951 and continued running in the series *Tetsuwan Atomu* for seventeen years. Made into an animated cartoon under the same name, it became the first serialized program on Japanese TV in 1962 (as a black-and-white cartoon on Fuji Television) and was exported to a number of countries overseas, including the United States. And though its tenure as a comic book and cartoon has been generally short-lived outside Japan, *Mighty Atom* is making a comeback in the twenty-first century, spurred by the global popularity now enjoyed by far more recent Japanese pop creations like *Pokémon*. Plans for a live-action, feature-length movie produced by Disney, for example, have been percolating in the United States since 2002, and a new cartoon series was launched in Japan in 2004.

Tezuka Osamu was eighteen years old when the war ended. A medical student at the time—a career he eventually abandoned—Tezuka was more interested in the craft of visual storytelling, specifically comic artistry and film. Experimenting with a two-hundred-page comic he created in 1947 called *Shintakarajima* (New Treasure Island), Tezuka immediately made a name for himself with his innovative style, employing a playful use of sounds and drawing out single images or scenes across multiple frames. Influenced by European cinema and the animation techniques of Walt Disney and Max Fleisher, Tezuka incorporated these into the medium of *manga*, a presage of the creative force with which *manga* would develop in postwar Japan.

Unlike the film and toy industries during this period, where, particularly in the latter, production was affected by and geared toward the export marketplace, *manga* was—and remains to this day—created almost exclusively for a domestic audience. This genre has ancient historical roots; the earliest traces (745 A.D.) are comic self-portraits done by Buddhist monks as a form of relaxation found on the back of a temple in Nara. The first cartoonist also comes from the ranks of Buddhism—an abbot (Toba, 1053–1140) known for his comic representation of animals *(Scroll of Frolicking Animals)* and the everyday struggle of people facing hunger *(Origin of Shigisan)*. Tsurumi Shunsuke has called the perspective in the latter scroll "cinematographic" (giving a bird's-eye view of the people on the ground drawn from a rice silo flying in the sky to rescue them), suggesting that Walt Disney may have seen it and been influenced in his own art by this premodern Japanese cartoonist (Tsurumi 1987:31). Japanese script, done traditionally with brush and with an eye to visual beauty, lends itself to the art of cartooning, and in both there is a play with borders; writing turns to imagery, characters to caricatures, and words to scenes.

In 1919, a Japanese newspaper reporter returned from the United States with samples of comic strips, thereby launching this pen-based art in Japan. From then until after the war, *manga* appeared as newspaper comic strips, serialized comics in magazines, and military propaganda. Not until the 1950s, however, did *manga* blossom into a cultural industry and mass medium, instrumental in the emergence in Japan of what Kurihara Akira calls a "mass culture" during this decade—a particular historical formation associated with advanced industrial societies (Ivy 1993:247). Given its plasticity, which can accommodate a range of audiences (young and old), subjects (from baseball to erotica), and genres (that inform as well as entertain), *manga* was used by early postwar artists to both relive and transcend the everyday struggles Japanese people were facing. Coupling the mundane with the fantastic has remained a characteristic of *manga* storytelling to the present. As Frederik Schodt describes it: "One of their greatest accomplishments is to render visually fascinating the most improbable subjects—such as mah jongg, chopping vegetables, and even school examinations" (1988a:16). The popular comic strip *Sazae-san*, penned by Hasegawa Machiko (a woman), which ran from 1946 to 1975 (and spread to cartoons, comics, songs, and a live-action movie), adopted this model by portraying the everyday dramas of a character named Sazae Isono in her role as caretaker for an extended family. Along somewhat different lines, *Sanpei, the Kappa*—a four-volume work published in 1962 by *kami shibai* (paper-plays)–turned–*manga* artist Mizuki Shigeru—recounted the fantastic adventures of a boy, Sanpei, who filled his days in the mountains playing with a badger and a *kappa*, an imaginary creature that lives underwater (Tsurumi 1987). In such ways, the normal and real are exaggerated, caricaturized, tweaked, and transformed in *manga*, blurring the edges between the everyday and the absurd. For their melodrama yet emotional realness and humanness, Japanese comics are referred to as "wet" as opposed to "dry" (as in an art form that works within a far more limited or emotional register—realistic drama, for example) (Schodt 1988a:16).

In the late 1940s, materials remained scarce in the country, and entertainment needed to be cheap to be affordable for most Japanese. Disrupted by the war, the large publishing companies in Tokyo had yet to regain control of the field. In this moment of poverty yet promise, Tezuka joined a fledgling group of artists and small-time publishers in Osaka working under conditions of limited resources but creative freedom. One of their products was a cheap comic book that, made with red ink and rough paper, sold on the streets. The streets were also where *kami shibai* took place: stories told through large cards painted with visual scenes and narrated by storytellers.

Until it was stamped out by television and *manga* in the 1950s, *kami shibai* was one of the most popular forms of entertainment after the war. Between 1945 and 1953, about ten thousand people made their living by selling candy before and after the performances, and approximately five million Japanese watched these shows daily (Schodt 1988a). Many of these *kami shibai* writers later turned to *manga*. And, for Tezuka, his craft soon led him to Tokyo, where, as publishing houses reappeared, a new genre of publication started taking off: children's magazines featuring serialized comics.

Manga Shōnen was one of these magazines.[10] Founded in 1947 and targeted at boys, it was the place where two of Tezuka's most popular comics first appeared: *Jungle Taitei* (later made into the cartoon *Kimba, the Lion*, which inspired, some say, Disney's *Lion King*) and *Atomu Taishi*. The latter debuted in 1951, becoming a fuller comic *(Tetsuwan Atomu)* the following year in a serialization that lasted almost two full decades (until 1969). This was the period, the 1950s and '60s, when *manga* began their dramatic rise as both an industry and a cultural phenomenon, leading to their present dominance as the format of almost half of all Japanese publications.

The 1950s were the years of *manga*'s creative genesis in the hands of such artists as Fujio-Fujiko, Matsumoto Reiji, Mizuno Hideko, and Ishimori Shōtarō (all of whose work appeared in *Manga Shōnen*). *Gekiga* (dramatic comics oriented to adults) sprouted during this time alongside kids' comics. The latter remained the primary venue for Tezuka, whose work appeared in the children's magazines that were rapidly growing in size and circulation. By the 1960s, there were seven weekly magazines (two for girls and five for boys, including Kōdansha's *Shōnen*, which started in 1959). This type of three-hundred- to five-hundred-page publication featuring a number of serialized comics remains a major force within kids' popular culture today in Japan. When the marketers of *Pokémon* wanted to expand it beyond a Game Boy game in 1996, for example, they created a *manga* version and printed it in *Korokoro Komikku*, a magazine read by more than half of Japanese boys between the ages of ten and fourteen. Then as now, popular comics like *Tetsuwan Atomu* also are printed in their own volumes in which stories are collected and expanded and, over time, generate endless new volumes.

The basic story of *Tetsuwan Atomu* runs as follows. It is 2003 in a big urban center with high skyscrapers when a crash occurs; the son of the Ministry of Science is killed in a turbocar accident. Distraught, Dr. Temma spends one year of national resources and energy in rebuilding his son as Atomu, a high-tech machine (figure 9). The sweet-looking boy robot with big saucer eyes and a distinctive hairdo (a jet-black bob with two points) is outfitted with the latest in technology—an atomic generator that fuels him

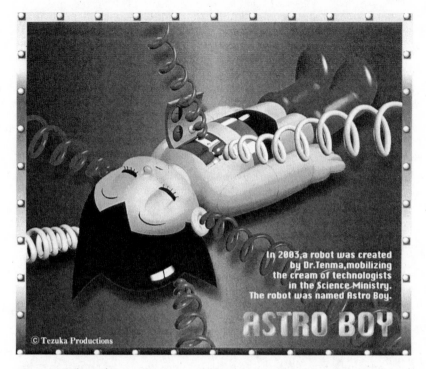

In 2003, a robot was created by Dr. Tenma, mobilizing the cream of technologists in the Science Ministry. The robot was named Astro Boy.

ASTRO BOY

© Tezuka Productions

Figure 9. Robotic futures: Tetsuwan Atomu as cute machine. (Courtesy of Tezuka Productions.)

(at 100,000 horsepower), a computer for a brain (with which he learns sixty languages and every kind of math function), rocket jets in his feet that allow him to fly, index fingers that turn into lasers, a machine gun in his hips, powerful searchlights for eyes, and a hearing ability one thousand times that of humans. Superendowed, Tetsuwan Atomu nevertheless disappoints his "father" over time by never growing larger as would a human boy. Sold henceforth by Dr. Temma to a greedy circus owner who draws in nightly crowds by pitting this superrobot against weaker ones, Atomu finally rebels and, leading the robot rebellion, succeeds in achieving a robot bills of rights. Thereafter Atomu spends his time fighting enemies of various sorts—corrupt politicians, destructive robots, devious schemers—and building his community, of humans and robots alike (with a new father figure, stand-in human parents, a robot sister, and assorted personages—teachers, police, soldiers, scientists, workers, leaders, kids).

The story of Tetsuwan Atomu was birthed during Japan's foreign occupation and period of national reconstruction, when *gijutsu rikkoku*—build-

ing the state through technology—was at the center of national policy to remake the country as an industrial power. Faced (even in good times) by a
scarcity of raw materials, Japan could succeed as a trading nation only if it
could manufacture goods that were desirable and competitive in the export
marketplace. At the heart of these products and the industrial process
erected to produce them was technology. In the 1970s the word *mechatronics* (the fusion of electronics and machines) came to be used to describe what
is now, and considered to be for the future, Japan's key industry: "intelligent" goods produced by an equally smart production system.[11] Today, as
Frederik Schodt (1988b:43) puts it, Japan is a mechatronic empire whose un-
rivaled flagships are robots. Developing and utilizing robots started after the
war as soon as industries could afford them. By 1986 Japan housed as much
as 60 percent of the world's entire population of industrial robots: more than
four times (116,000) the number in the United States (25,000) even though
the later had invented them.[12] Robots are used by practically every industry
today in Japan, and, in contrast to other countries where the majority are
used in auto industries and owned by huge corporations, they are commonplace in small ("mom-and-pop") businesses as well. There is widespread interest in the latest robotic technology disseminated through endless magazines, Internet sites, pop culture, industrial newspapers, and robot fairs.
Unsurprisingly, the turnout was massive when the International Sympo-
sium on Industrial Robots took place in Tokyo in 1985 (223,351 people), approximately eighteen times the number (12,398) who attended the fair in
Chicago in 1987 (Schodt 1988b:25–26).

What Donna Haraway has said about cyborgs—that they are both tools
and myths—pertains to robots as well. As machines were used to rebuild
the nation after the devastation of war, robots also became the tropes and
fantasies of the postwar era by which Japanese crafted a new imaginary of
the state and themselves. Atomu was the mythic robot, ushering in a new
era of technonationalism for both the country and its people. Unlike *Gojira*,
the tale here was forward-looking, and the protagonist, a hero rather than
hostile hulk, invited identification instead of fear from audiences. Like *Gojira*, however, *Tetsuwan Atomu* captured the tenor of the moment: the tentativeness of the times laced with not only the pains of defeat and atomic injury but also the anticipation of an unknown future. In both works, a
high-tech accident starts off the story (the crash of a turbo flying machine,
nuclear testing on nearby Bikini Atoll), leading to a new species of being fueled by atomic energy (an atomic robot, an atomically mutated beast). Both
tales ruminate on the parameters of a postatomic world: How will the dangers of the atom bomb be managed? Who will police and benefit from its

HE JUST WANTED TO BE A REAL BOY... INSTEAD HE DISCOVERED HE WAS DIFFERENT... A PRODUCT OF METAL AND PLASTIC.

Figure 10. Identity confusion: the robot wishes he were a boy. (From the U.S. comic book *Astro Boy* 1, no. 6 [February 1988]; courtesy of Sony Corporation.)

usage? What changes will it inflict on humanity, the earth, Japan? And with a nonhuman as the lead character, the anxiety of identity haunts each text (figure 10). The question of how to define and treat this new being is continually posed, mirroring the fragility of Japan's own (and mutated) identity on the world stage after the war. Yet the same plot point—a rupture to the status quo by an incident involving technology—is played to different effect in the two stories. In *Gojira*, history is configured dystopically into a horror tale chronicling the destruction and victimization of Japan(ese). By contrast, *Tetsuwan Atomu* writes the future utopically in an upbeat fable about national rebirth, reconstruction, and reindustrialization.

It is significant that Atomu is shaped as a young boy who, as his father notes, will never grow into a man. His powers as a posthuman techno-hero are thus tamed by a cuteness and innocence that forever identify him as a kid. Atomu is also a child who has been abandoned and betrayed by his father, just as many in Japan felt they had been sacrificed by military leaders who led the country callously (and shortsightedly) into war. In the comic, the patriarch has a sharply chiseled face and is a stern taskmaster both at home and at the Ministry of Science. After coldly selling his son into a life of servitude and fighting, he has a mental breakdown and is forcibly dislodged from his job, a position of great authority. Scientists and engineers will be a mainstay in the postwar imaginary of Japanese mass entertainment—*manga, anime,* television, games—particularly that targeted to youth. Invariably middle-aged men, often in lab coats, these are the figures on whom the peace and future of the land are seen to ultimately depend. Not military or political leaders, they derive their authority from technical knowledge: building, repairing, and manipulating machines. In the case of Atomu, the technocrat is also a "father"—a not uncommon coupling in what has been another fixation of the popular since the war: artificial life-forms (robots, cyborgs, androids).

On both fronts, however—at home and at work—this father/boss is a failure who loses his place in the narrative (and the world it imagines). Thereafter, Atomu will find new forms of kinship: a robot community, an avuncular mentor, a virtual family. Just as blood does not moor his relationships, neither does hierarchy backed by tradition. Continually, Atomu urges robots controlled by evil humans to resist their claims of superiority. In the father who slips from the picture, then, patriarchy as the grounding authority of family and state erodes as well. It was, in fact, removed from Japan's new ("democratic") constitution instituted in 1947 just as postwar fathers, in the realm of the home, felt the pinch of diminished respect. It is Atomu, the robot forever a boy, who must assume leadership in these "supermodern" times. This is both because he is genuinely kind, a "friend" of all people, and because he is endowed with the best features that technology can offer. On this score, at least, Dr. Temma did well, crafting the robot with "100,000 horsepower and seven distinct kinds of powers" (as described on the package of a newly minted Atomu toy I bought in Tokyo in 2000—almost fifty years after the character first appeared in Japan).[13] Such *mecha* is state-of-the-art robotics: a foreshadowing of the status Japan would assume by the 1970s as the leader of the world in R & D and industrial application of robots.

Intense focus is placed on Atomu's mechanical prowess, not only in the story created by Tezuka but also in Atomu's wider status as a mass idol. Even today, pictures of the robot (sketches at art shows, cartoons in children's magazines, illustrations in books) are diagrammed to show off all his powers. Sometimes he is portrayed in a cutaway displaying half of his humanoid exterior and half of his machine insides, exposed so viewers can see into his body and its mechanical wiring. It is a quasi-scientific rendering that resembles an anatomical picture in a medical text or a mechanical diagram for engineering. This fetishization of the mechanical (or *mecha* fetishism, as I will call it throughout the book) is also fashioned as playful and cute: a sensibility that has pervaded children's media, particularly that targeted to boys, during the entire postwar period down to the present.

From the robotic Doraemon (another pop icon stemming from a comic by Fujio-Fujiko in 1970, featuring a robotic cat who continually helps the boy he lives with out of jams by drawing from his kangaroo pouch of futuristic gadgets) to the virtual pocket monsters, these are imaginary characters with techno-powers that are excessively examined, spectacularized, and praised. The tendency also, however, is to blend the mechanical with the human. As my toy package goes on in its characterization of Atomu, he "most important of all, has a heart as kind *[yasashii]* as that of humans." As if urging Japanese to believe that they, too, could introject technology into their subjectivity and still remain human, this *mecha* ideology was coupled with another that the state promoted as part of its national reconstruction policy in this early postwar period: hard work. Industriousness—whether as worker, mother, or student in what was becoming an incredibly rigorous education system—was a national mantra. It was what, along with advanced technology, was to make up for a scarcity in natural resources and the severe setbacks the country had suffered from war. Atomu was nothing if not a hard worker, diligently using his powers to remake the world as a better, kinder, and more roboticized (and robot-friendly) place. And in him, many saw an image (of a humanized machine/mechanical human) that they comfortably embraced as a "national idol" (Tezuka Purodakushōn 1998:9).

Tezuka was also becoming a national idol in his own right. Like the pride felt for the quality of moviemaking Tōhō Studios achieved with films like *Gojira,* the nation derived a sense of worth in regarding Tezuka as a homegrown genius of his craft. He is widely regarded as the father of Japanese comic/cartoon artistry for the power of his creative imagination, which, considered distinctly different from the Disney products, became associated with postwar Japanese popular culture itself (now called J-pop)—a sign of Japanese cultural power. From the beginning, Tezuka had harbored desires of moving into what was at the time the new technological medium of television. Because the country was still poor, the development of this industry was just taking off in the mid-1950s. Believing, however, that television watching would help regenerate national pride and would abet the process of reconstruction (toward advanced capitalism heavily reliant on consumerism), the government (MITI) actively supported development. And, though MITI still adhered to the prewar goal of domestic production, it approved of foreign imports of TVs, concluding that American technology was superior at the moment and that its importation would benefit Japanese consumers (Partner 1999)

Launched in 1947 in the United States, television debuted in Japan in 1953; NHK (the national TV station) started broadcasting in February, followed by the first public station (Nihon TV Hōsōmō) in August. Triggering what soon became known as "mass communication" (*masukomyu-nikēshōn*—written in the syllabary used for foreign words) and *masukomi* for short (Saitō 1989), television sets were a highly desired consumer good: one in a wave of electric appliances now shaping people's dreams for a new lifestyle. Alongside what came to be called the three "treasures" of the 1950s (fans, washing machines, and electric rice cookers),[14] televisions were so popular that, despite their limited means, almost 50 percent of Japanese households owned them in 1960, from less than 1 percent in 1956 (Ivy 1993). Spurred by live broadcasts of national events (the royal wedding in 1959 and the Tokyo Olympics in 1964), television quickly rose as a mass medium, overtaking film, which, peaking in 1959, started to decline in the early 1960s. It also forced the cultural industry of *manga* to keep pace. In 1959 a number of *manga* magazines became weekly rather than monthly publications in a move that radically affected the impact of comics on both consumers and producers.[15]

Based on the comic, an animated version of *Tetsuwan Atomu* began broadcasting as the first animated serial on Japanese television. Overseen by Tezuka, who had started his own production company in 1962 (Mushi Productions, which unfortunately went bankrupt in 1973), the cartoon was a hit. Triggering a new trend in kids' culture—cartoons culled from preexisting comics that also became lines of toy merchandise—*Tetsuwan Atomu* was exported overseas as well. Cartoon rights were sold to more than twenty countries (including Peru, Venezuela, and Argentina) and bought by NBC for the United States. Under the guidance of veteran animation producer Fred Ladd, the cartoons were dubbed, colorized, and edited for U.S. release. Released under the name *Astro Boy*, the show was considered a modest success and generated many American fans, yet it was canceled after only two seasons and 104 episodes in 1963–64, largely for reasons of content. Though the fighting scenes seem tame by today's standards, they were deemed too excessive by national television guidelines that had grown stricter in the 1950s, particularly for children's programming. Tezuka was personally approached and asked to soften the battle component, but he refused to do anything, beyond superficial alterations, that would affect the artistic integrity of the cartoon. Consequently, the show did not remain on the air long enough to touch or become a part of the popular imagination in the States.

The popularity of *Tetsuwan Atomu* and other comics by Tezuka *(Trea-sure Island; Rose of Versailles; Kimba, the Lion; Princess Knight)* and other Japanese artists inspired *manga* publishing to even greater efforts. By the late 1950s and early 1960s, many popular comic books were being animated for television in what would become increasingly a synergy between these two major industries—*manga* and television—in the mass (kids') culture burgeoning now in postwar Japan. For the most part, these shows were targeted to children in programming that also included live action, mainly superheroes *(Starman, Jiraiya, Rainbowman, Ganbaron, Gekkō Kamen).* A specimen of this genre was *Tetsujin 28gō* (Iron Man No. 28), a comic by Yokoyama Mitsuteru made into a television cartoon in 1956 featuring a giant metal monster that a boy-cum-detective operates by a remote-control device (much like a toy). So was Nagai Gō's comic (turned cartoon) *Mazinger Z* (1969), whose hero, a young man, pilots a hovercraft that becomes the control center for a giant robot by docking in its head. A tale about a man who turns into a giant android—dressed all in red and with a pointy head—to save the earth from attack was the sensational kid hit of the 1960s, *Urutoraman* (literally, Ultra Man). *Gojira* mastermind Tsuburaya Eiji, whose creative energies were now turned to television, designed the special effects (and costumes) for this live-action, cyberwarrior fantasy. And, like *Tetsuwan Atomu, Urutoraman* was a "humanistic" superhero (Ikeda and Takahashi 2001:38) that, piquing the popular imagination of its times, has retained a place and following in popular culture through the decades.

Starting in the late 1950s but growing exponentially in the 1960s and '70s was a third tier within the television/*manga* edifice of kids' mass culture: the production of media characters into toy merchandise. A phenomenon referred to as *masukomi gangu* (mass communication toys) and *masukyarā* (mass characters), it was stimulated by shows like *Urutoraman* with the spectacle of its special effects and also the cascading number of characters involved. Each week, the protagonist battled a new set of enemies, stylized as Godzillian beasts *(kaijū)* distinguished and differentiated by a dizzying array of body parts, powers, and tools. The elaborateness of this imaginary universe filled with multiple beings sporting a host of distinguishing parts/powers became the model of and for toy culture in postwar Japan. Even today, there are specialty *Urutoraman* shops in Tokyo filled with an assortment of character goods (pencils, T-shirts, backpacks, water bottles) and, as the main feature, bins of plastic figures sorted by (the huge number of) *kaijū* and the seasonal variations of Urutoraman (marked by differences in costume, color, eyes, accessories, body protrusions). Such an aesthetic style of bodily detail embedded with transbodily powers (eyes that are lasers, a dorsal fin that shoots out nuclear thunderbolts, a tail that doubles as a knife) was a signature first of *Tetsuwan Atomu*, of course. And in the *mecha* fetishism inaugurated by this robotic hero and mass cultural icon, an imaginary of both cyborgs and (kids') consumerism took shape.

Shifts in Toys/The Shifting Imaginary, 1945–1960

Tokyo's thriving electronics district, Akihabara, is packed with modest-sized high-rises all stocked with the latest in Japanese consumer technology—digital cameras, laptop computers, high-resolution television sets, wireless communication systems—the high-quality "intelligent" goods of which Japan has become recognized as a world-class producer since the late 1960s. Out of this currency, more than any other, the country rebuilt its economy after the war and its image (as an industrial power) in the eyes of the rest of the world. Today Japan is known globally for its technological craftsmanship, creativity, and design: machinery that looks to the future with cutting-edge stylishness and utility. This is why consumers, both locals and foreign visitors, flock to Akihabara to buy the newest in personal electronics.

How appropriate, then, that this marketplace of postmodern technology should also be the home of a museum and specialty shop for Tetsuwan Atomu: the fantasy robot that, for half a century, has served as a durable symbol of and for cyber Japan. On a hot day in the summer of 1998, I visited the museum. As a friend and I entered the building, we encountered first the gift shop: a consumerist sign of the times selling a range of Tetsuwan Atomu goods—everything from T-shirts and pajamas to posters, postcards, and scholarly works on Tezuka. On the walls were photos documenting Tetsuwan Atomu's history in the annals of Japanese mass culture. Upstairs, the only other room in the building, was a small alcove showing a movie on the character: his creation, pop cultural life span, various iterations. The main space offered the feature attraction: a simulated lab bed bearing a life-size reproduction of Tetsuwan Atomu, the mechanical robot. Every thirty minutes a "performance" was scheduled. At the flip of a switch, Atomu would come alive from the construction he had received in the Ministry of Science and, sitting up, be ready to receive visitors on the stage for souvenir photos. As we trooped up individually to bask in the spotlight with this metal icon, all of us showed visible signs of affection (broad smiles, arms around the robot's shoulder, twittering). I, too, behaved like a fan, feeling strangely excited to be part of what also seemed pretty campy: the artificial staging of an artificial hero (that had delighted me for years nonetheless).

This genesis scene reminded me of a similar one in a cyborg myth that had been as intensely monumental for the Euro-American imagination: *Frankenstein* by Mary Shelley (originally written in 1818). In this story, also about a man-made creature built in the lab of a scientist that comes to life at the flip of a switch, the contrasts are much more striking. Seen as a monster, Frankenstein is an outsider, threat, and eventually killer of humanity: a bleak warning about the dangers of transgressing the human-machine border.[16] Atomu, with his boy body and sweet nature, is radically different. With a goodness as superlative as his strengths, he personifies the cyberfrontier as nonthreatening, uplifting, and bright.

In writing this chapter, I spent a number of evenings watching and re-watching cassettes of the *Astro Boy* cartoon (the U.S. version, but composed from Tezuka's original images and story lines). The energy is kinetic; the characters are drawn with excessive caricature (a predominance of huge noses, angular faces, Caucasian flesh, and saucer eyes—the latter two influences from Disney); the transition between scenes is more jagged than smooth; the stories teem with an assortment of cultural references, both Western and Japanese; and the entire effect is carnivalesque in its phantasmic blend of the natural, atomic, and mechanic.[17] Cross-speciation suffuses the screen: animal with human, human with machine, machine with nature. There are flying mechanical crabs, turbo police cars shaped like dog heads (figure 11), "vegetable people" who reside in a time warp, and a dolphin civilization complete with its own army under the sea. All borders between life and machine seem to have gone haywire here, and mechanization has taken over the entire landscape, not just the human body (as with *Frankenstein*, where the crossing of borders between what is naturally human and what is man-made is an abomination). Robots are everywhere, and in familiar shapes: bees, ants, dogs, and cars. This is *mecha* animated by Shinto, Japan's religion of animism in which everything is endowed with a spirit and spirituality imbues the whole universe from boulders to ants. Not particular to the main character, roboticization has seeped into the very fabric of life itself here, expressed as a universal principle where the fusing of the natural and mechanic is akin to a spiritual truth. Thus, in contrast to *Superman*, the 1950s U.S. television show also featuring a transhuman superhero, the entire scene has been cyborgized versus only the body and powers of the main character (who, as Clark Kent/Superman, resides in the most normal and

Figure 11. Cross-speciation: dog's head as flying turbo car. (From the U.S. comic book *Astro Boy 1*, no. 10 [July 1988]; courtesy of Sony Corporation.)

everyday of American settings: the farmlands of Kansas and the midwestern city of Metropolis). The logic here is techno-animism (as laid out in the introduction): what *Tetsuwan Atomu* inspired in the 1950s and '60s.

Yet dark elements, such as atomic energy, emerge as well. In the episode "Deadly Flies," for example, a mushroom cloud starts off the story with a voice-over pondering the effects this discovery will have on nature and noting the recent proliferation of mutations. Enter a mutant fly, the source of poisonous attacks that have been terrorizing the city. Abetting him is another fly, this one a robot, that lives inside another one, and so on until five (all horseflies, though the biggest one looks like a warrior beetle) nestle inside each other like Russian dolls. Needless to say, Atomu figures out what is happening and cures the deadly flies of their evil (they were manipulated, as always, by bad humans). In the end, the robotic horseflies fly away, freed now from human bondage, and the mutant horsefly is dead. The story conveys a message about the dangers of atomic energy and the human abuse of robots (which, by implication, is a technology that is morally neutral in and of itself, becoming "good" or "bad" depending on how humans use it).

Not until the 1990s would the J-pop brand of imaginary play creations epitomized by *Tetsuwan Atomu* enter the U.S. marketplace with anything approaching a serious impact. Though properties like *Godzilla*, *Astro Boy*, *Speed Racer*, and *Star Blazers* had played here since the 1950s and cultivated their separate fandoms, "made-in-Japan" entertainment did not go mainstream in the States, or globally, for another forty years.[18] If Japan's postwar period runs roughly from 1945 to the new millennium (and the end, as many have proclaimed in Japan, of the "postwar"), this chapter has covered the early years—1945 to the early 1960s.

Toys started out, after the war, as metal playthings built from the recycled tin cans of American GIs and intended for children overseas. By the mid-1950s, however, higher-quality materials (vinyl, plastic, and battery-run electronics) were used in their construction, and the designs—robots, monsters, cyborgs—were crafted more for the tastes of a burgeoning consumer population at home whose youth were being raised on *manga*, *anime*, and TV action heroes. Throughout, toys and other media of entertainment (*kami shibai*, movies, *manga*, television) were inspired not only by the desire to create fantasies but also by the pressing need to build business. And on both scores the entertainment industries played a vital role in Japan's postwar reconstruction, spurring the economy (particularly true of the toy and publishing industries with *manga*, and the film industry throughout the 1950s) and fostering new idols and icons with which the nation and its people began to reimagine themselves.[19] Out of the ashes of war came cyborgs: a new regime of mechatronics fusing robotic technology, consumer electronics, and industrial-strength (as in hardworking) humans.

Millennial Japan

Intimate Alienation and New Age Intimacies

> What I liked most about the Aum books was that they clearly stated
> that the world is evil. I was happy when I read that. I'd always
> thought that the world was unfair and might as well be destroyed,
> and here it was all laid out in black and white. Instead of simply
> destroying the world, though, Asahara Shōkō said: "If one trains and
> is liberated, then one can change the world." I was fired up reading
> this. "I want to be this man's disciple and devote myself to him," I
> decided. If I could do that, I wouldn't mind abandoning all the
> dreams, desires, and hopes of this world.
>
> **Shin'ichi Hosoi,** a onetime member of Aum Shinrikyō, quoted in
> Murakami 2001:320

Japan's Postwar Reconstruction:
Disciplined Lives, Materialist Fantasies

It is September 1999, and I am in Japan for a year researching the production
and culture of "made in Japan" children's play goods that are achieving unprecedented popularity in the global marketplace of kids' trends and faddish
fantasies today. As an anthropologist, I study this subject in the field. And,
given the nature of even the Japan end of this study, my field site is dispersed—spread across the urban metropolis of Tokyo, the twelfth-largest
city in the world. Here I go from toy fairs, game conventions, production studios, bookstores, and amusement parks to interviews with children and parents conducted in homes, teenagers and scholars in restaurants or bars, and
producers and child experts in their offices. Unlike the older model of anthropology, which required the anthropologist to enter a village, take up residence in a homestead, and stay there for months, if not years, fieldwork for
me entails daily travel. Moving among multiple sites stretched across a ra-
dius of forty or fifty miles, I spend endless time in transit—whether by taxi-
cab, subway, bus, bike, or foot. In this regard, I am no different from the average Tokyoite, for whom commuting is the very condition of everyday life,
consuming as much as three to five hours daily. In Tokyo, people move as
much as they stay in place, in routines routed (rather than rooted) through
scattered locations (home–school–workplace–cram school–store–bar–ar-

cade–restaurant). Nomadicism—what characterizes the postmodern world more than anything, according to Deleuze—is the trope of everyday life in Tokyo. So how fitting, I thought at the time, that I should be a nomadic field-worker with a research project set by and in the new millennium.

If the early postwar years were marked by loss and the urgency of re-building—a period spent crafting new edifices and goals for a nation dis-membered and defeated in war—the landscape had radically changed a half century later. Crisscrossing the city on the routes of an urban commuter in 1999–2000, I am struck by how excessive if also mundane are the signs of material abundance surrounding me. Drawing heavily on brand-name goods—Vuitton handbags, Gucci scarves, and Prada shoes—passengers are well dressed and well accessorized with a surfeit of high-priced possessions. This is one of the most visible, if superficial, markers of Japan at the other end of its postwar period—a national obsession with material things. A "fantasy of abundance," in the words of Yoshimi Shunya, infused the coun-try during the early years following the war as well, of course. But then it was more of an "ideal" *(risō)*, patterned after a style and level of con-sumerism modeled by the United States (Yoshimi 2000). At a time when as much as 70 percent of household budgets went to food, and scarcity re-mained an ever-present reality, the desirability of particular goods—electric fans, washing machines, TVs—acquired an ethos all its own, remaking the nation and the everyday. Even the imperial family was repackaged using the images of a typical American lifestyle. Emperor Hirohito was shown (in magazines, in newsreels, and eventually on television) relaxing in the palace and joking with Mickey Mouse during his visit to Disneyland, and the wed-ding of the prince and princess in 1959 was given television coverage befit-ting a Hollywood couple. Once shown to the public only in formal poses, the imperial family now became something of a consumable product in an era when nationalism conflated with Americanism, a yearning for newness and richness symbolized by America (Yoshimi 2000).[1]

In the intervening years between the 1950s and the new millennium, the country underwent the "Japanese miracle": a period of high-speed growth in which the economy expanded at a phenomenal rate (doubling in size every seven years). By the mid-1970s, Japan's GNP was the second largest in the world (surpassed only by that of the United States) after experienc-ing a growth that averaged 7.0 percent between 1954 and 1958, 10.8 percent between 1959 and 1964, 10.9 percent between 1965 and 1968, and 9.6 per-cent between 1969 and 1973 (McCreery 2000:17). Production increased ex-ponentially in almost all industries between 1955 and 1975: five times in commercial shipping, 13 times in steel production, 39 times in machine production, and 139 times in auto making (Allinson 1997:105). The two industries that prospered the most, becoming identified on the global marketplace with high-quality Japanese goods, were electrical manufacturing (with Hitachi and Toshiba as the two largest companies in a long list that includes Matsushita, Fujitsu, Sony, and Mitsubishi) and auto manufacturing (Toyota and Nissan led the pack), the latter making Japan the number one leader in vehicle production in 1980. As is generally agreed, a number of domestic and international factors were responsible for the high-speed growth undergone by Japan after the war: a skilled (and disciplined) labor force, managerial experience, the need to completely rebuild industry (and an occupying force that supported this effort), the early demand created by the Korean War, a stable currency (and cheap exchange rate with the dollar), access to world markets, low-cost raw materials, rapid technologization, and institutional resources that channeled capital and investment. The sheer desire to rebuild the country and realize national goals now targeted far more at the personal level of lifestyle and material consumption also fueled reconstruction.

Where and how people lived, worked, and organized households radically changed in these years. Whereas in 1955 half of the labor force were self-employed farmers, 70 percent were wage laborers by 1975, with 34 percent involved in manufacturing and construction, 52 percent in the tertiary sector, and only 14 percent in agriculture (Allinson 1997:111). Not surprisingly, urbanization quickly took root in the postwar years, and though the cities had been emptied during the war, 72 percent of the population lived in urban centers by 1970 (roughly the same percentage as in the United States). Along with industrial expansion and geographic mobility came an increase in family incomes (the average monthly salary of urban households increased more than sixteen times between 1955 and 1989). Accompanying this growth was a corresponding downturn in family size (from an average of 5 members in 1955 to 3.19 in 1987, a phenomenon of "reduction in children" highly troubling to the government today), as well as a shift in living arrangements; extended families were the norm in prewar days, but nuclear families accounted for 60.5 percent of all households by 1987 (Buckley 1993:348). Though the first oil crisis tempered the growth of the economy in 1973, Japan's makeover into an industrial leader and one of the most affluent countries in the world continued in full force.

The 1970s were the era when Japan became fully established as a *kigyō shakai* (enterprise society). Big business, organized around a vast network of corporations of large and small companies directly connected to the government *(keiretsu)*, became the template for the country. The methods and principles of labor management guiding big business percolated throughout the nation, building the image of Japan (both at home and abroad) as a singular corporate entity: Japan, Inc. Meanwhile, public protests, not uncommon throughout the 1960s—including those against the U.S.-Japan Security Treaty by radical student movements in the late 1960s and by workers seeking better representation in unions—started to ebb. National consciousness now became heavily shaped by the corporate model of high performance and—as reward and incentive—material consumption. Pushed by what came to be known as the principles of "Japanese management" ("quality-control" circles, all-company unions, raises based on seniority rather than merit, lifetime employment), workers were expected to give their all to companies to which—in terms of time, commitment, and social identity—they essentially "belonged."[2] Idealized, as both fantasy and norm, was the position of *sararīman:* that of white-collar worker, which, if situated at the largest, most prestigious companies, accorded both security and status. Elevated as well by the same corporate ideology were other laboring subjects: first, children—put through an educational system geared toward highly competitive exams that would determine, almost exclusively, their future careers, including that of *sararīman*—and second, mothers, who, in the postwar role of *kyōiku mama* (education mothers), were to socialize kids into worker bees on the home front by encasing them in a regimen of discipline flavored by treats.[3]

At the time I was riding the trains in Tokyo, during the crossover year of the new millennium, the boom years of the Bubble economy, with its high growth and accompanying extravagances, had been burst for almost a decade. Peaking in the late 1980s and popping in 1991, this was a period marked by high rates of investment, annual gains of close to 6 percent (compared with the 1 to 2 percent experienced by other industrialized countries, including the United States), hefty trade surpluses, and large sales overseas (Allinson 1997). Tokyo property became among the highest priced in the world, but when the stock market plummeted, a deflationary environment emerged, and the news was filled with stories of layoffs, closures, and defaults on loans for speculative purchases made during the Bubble era. Even in this recessionary environment, however, department stores remain packed, and there seems no shortage of money being spent on leisure activities (karaoke, drinking, overseas trips, golf) and consumer goods whose prices are among the highest in the world ("vintage" jeans, for example, that go for as much as a thousand dollars). The materialist "ideals" of the country in the 1950s—repairing Japan's infrastructure and overcoming the insecurities of everyday subsistence—seem to have been realized in spades. If prosperity was once measured in air conditioners, automobiles, and private homes, the signs of good living are upgraded now to electronic toilets, fancier residences, and multiplex personal technology (such as computers with a Sony PlayStation and karaoke system built in). And on the trains—where I, like most Tokyoites, do the bulk of my urban commuting—the degree of trendy fashion, designer accessories, and brand-name goods (in everything from briefcases and handbags to cell phones and Palm Pilots) is spectacular.

The frenzy of fashion I see around me at the dawn of the twenty-first century stands out as a major shift from the earlier postwar period. My fellow passengers are overwhelmingly well dressed—pressed suits and shined shoes for the *sararīman*, designer dresses or jeans for middle-aged women, faddish collages (platform shoes, miniskirts, character goods, jean jackets) for teenagers, the most fashion hungry of all, for whom "consuming is a crucial part of national identity" (Mead 2002:104).[4] Appearances are sharply attended to, orchestrated according to a logic of commodity fetishism that, over the years, has come to reside ever more at the level of the person. Increasingly, the unit of consumption has shifted away from the family or household, as in earlier postwar years, and to the individual. Writing in *Brain* magazine, a reporter notes this trend in terms of the television, that object of such keen materialist fantasy in the 1950s that, once purchased, was typically placed in the family room, the *chanoma* in traditional households, where the place once held by flowers or scrolls was now taken up by a television set (Kelly 1993:84):

One family, one TV has become one person, one TV. One family, one telephone has become one person, one telephone. The living room where the telephone and the TV were the center of the household is buried in dust. The household's members are in their own rooms each watching their own TVs. They communicate with the outside world using their portable phones. To begin the day, each gets up when he or she has to, heats up some ready-to-eat food, or stops by a fast-food restaurant to eat a "breakfast set." The family core of the household is now fragmented in time and space to a shocking degree. (Tomie and Ōzawa 1997:5, quoted in McCreery 2000:255)

The press and cultural critics have devoted much commentary to this feature of millennial Japan. Japanese people are said to spend more and more time alone, to be ever more focused on their own needs and desires rather than those of others, and to be socially detached from the kinds of relationships and commitments that are thought to have once grounded the culture (family, community, nation). According to a report prepared in 1993 by the advertising firm Hakuhōdō, such a trend toward individualism can be tracked through successive stages of consumer behavior in postwar Japan. The first generation of "corporate warriors" (who grew up in the 1940s and worked hard) bought sensibly; baby boomers (the "worker bees" raised in the 1950s) sought safety and glamour rather than glitz; and *shinjinrui* (the "new breed" who, coming of age in the 1980s, grew up in an affluent society of national confidence) shopped for identity. More recently there are the *dantai* ("baby boomer juniors," who, becoming young adults in the 1990s, stay detached from others, "graze" in their consumption tastes, and think of the self as a "fenced-in paradise") and *"amenbo* kids," youth in the 1990s who, like water spiders, have multiple but superficial attachments to both people and things (McCreery 2000). While opinions vary on the escalating materialism and individualism of postwar Japan/ese, there was a certain exuberance in the very depthlessness and transparency of the culture in the 1980s. This was seen by some as a sign that Japan had finally arrived and, having bred its own brand of modernity (or gone beyond modernity altogether), was at the "cutting edge of postmodern capitalism" (Yoda 2000:646).[5]

Atomism or "orphanism" *(kojinshugi)*, as the individuated nature of millennial Japanese is sometimes described (Takeda 1998:38), can certainly be read from behavior observed on trains. Given the length and necessity of commutes, many people spend hours of each day riding to, and between, what are often multiple destinations in busy itineraries. This travel constitutes what James Fujii (1999), writing of the time when trains first started to colonize metropolitan space in 1920s Japan, has called "mediated transitions." Involving movement between places that, built into the ground, anchor identities and bonds (such as work, school, and home), commuting becomes an experience of liminality when travelers are betwixt and between destinations. For most commuters, most of the time, this trekking is done alone these days. There are exceptions, of course; one sees pairs of students, clusters of teenagers, groups of suited men, couples holding hands, and mothers with children. Mainly, though, commuters are solo—even children as young as six, headed to *juku* (cram school) or school with rucksacks on their backs. The atmosphere is one of "intimate alienation" (Fujii 1999) in that, even though people are solitary and anonymous, it is also a space that is familiar, habitual, and shared. Even when they transit alone, that is, passengers are both linked and homogenized by the routine of train travel: a daily practice of disconnected connectedness that not merely accompanies but also defines the postmodern lifestyle and subjectivity of millennial Japanese.

Here people are disciplined into/by a logic of the everyday transacted through commodity exchange and flexible, fragmented subjectivity. Paying the fare, one is transported from family and home to sites of production and consumption. Technologies of mobility (like trains) perform and enable these transitions, detaching commuters from one set of relations and reattaching them to others. Or, as Bruno Latour suggests, the train itself emblemizes the type of connectedness people have to the world in this era of fractured identities, intensified mobility, and catapulting speed of all sorts, apparent as much in the turnover of consumer fashions as in the output demanded of workers (Latour 1993). In constant movement from and toward specific locales, train travel is situated within a network of locations in an age when "network" better characterizes the relationship between individual and geography than does "place" (with its modernist implications of fixed temporal and spatial boundaries). This phenomenon is akin to what Deleuze and Guattari (1987) call "deterritorialization": the effect, in part, of global capitalism with its flows of images, finance, ideas, people, and goods across geographic borders and of New Age technologies that enable high-speed travel, global communication, and virtual reality (leading to the compression, as well as fictionalization, of time and space). If a more territorialized notion of place once anchored people (to neighborhoods, villages, a nation graphed by its rice fields, Mount Fuji, and island status), how, we might ask, do postindustrial Japanese connect to one another and claim identity when they spend ever more time on the move?

Certainly, the connected disconnectedness of Tokyo train travel breeds intimacies all its own. The density and proximity of flesh alone, for example, can be intense. Trains become incredibly, almost inhumanly, packed at times; during rush hour people take running dives from platforms onto crowded trains, and white-gloved train attendants push passengers into cars at each station. Though I myself feel a tinge of terror on trains crammed like sardine cans, I have never seen a fight break out and only rarely heard angry words exchanged or complaints voiced, even when a crowded train was stalled on the tracks for as much as an hour. People tend to endure their commutes in silence, and talk between strangers rarely occurs, even when (or precisely because) bodies are jammed next to one another for long stretches. Yet, boundaries of other kinds are more fluid. When commuters sleep, which is commonplace, flopping heads often come to rest on neighbors' shoulders; a punk teenager may be slumped over a neatly dressed woman, or a schoolgirl might bear the head of a weary *sarariman*. Though not everyone is so indulgent, the grammar of bodies and space here is noteworthy; physical proximity to strangers is tolerated far more than contact by words or even glances. It is often said that there is a tacit understanding about the rules governing public intercourse in Japan. I witnessed this in practice one night when, coming home late on the train, a drunken *sarariman*, sitting next to me, rolled around for a few stops and finally threw up. No one on the entire car registered any reaction, including the older Japanese woman dressed in a stylish kimono sitting next to me. Yet, while never taking her eyes from the book she was reading, this woman gently opened her purse and, pulling out a tissue, walked across the aisle and dropped it over the vomit. As if erasing the act or at least its offense, the woman returned to her seat. Whether this was done for the benefit of the man, the rest of the passengers, or the woman herself, I am not sure, but the gesture was faintly intimate yet all the while studiously disengaged.

Far less benign, however, is something every bit as commonplace (and all too "tacitly" understood): groping, known as *chikan*, the surreptitious touching of girls and women who often have no idea which man standing next to them is the culprit. Here, the mixture of anonymity and proximity promotes a form of intimate alienation that is both sexual and aggressive: indulgences that arouse one party at the expense of violating another. I have heard it said that virtually every woman (over the age of about twelve and until the age of maybe fifty) experiences *chikan* multiple times while riding the trains and sometimes daily. The burden of this behavior still rests with women, for whom such acts are considered shameful. Textbooks for middle school students put out by the Ministry of Education, for example, routinely print warnings targeted exclusively to girls, announcing that it is their responsibility to protect themselves against *chikan* given that (any and all) males are naturally inclined toward such behavior. Public awareness of this phenomenon has risen somewhat in recent years, as have measures instituted to curb it; a few subway lines since 2000, for example, have established female-only cars at rush hours, and feminist groups have urged victims to hold up the arm of the offender and yell, "Whose arm is this?" (which, given the rules of silence and invisibility operating on the trains, shocks everyone and particularly the offender). It is important to keep in mind, however, what *chikan* signifies about the vulnerabilities and violence that are also a part of everyday life in millennial Japan. And reading the prosperity (and atomism) brought on by postwar reconstruction from this angle provides a different picture altogether.

"Ordinary Criminals" and Monstrous Acts:
The Revolt against Transparent Materialism

> The 17-year-olds who become delinquents these days are not the same as the 17-year-olds about fifty years ago. Most don't even look dangerous. One day they seem indifferent and steady—just like pet dogs—and then, the next day, they start attacking people. It's just like in horror movies.
>
> Abe 2000:102

The riches of the 1980s Bubble economy inspired a widespread complacency and national confidence that quenched self-reflection. Indeed, little criticism was launched at Japan's advanced consumer society *(kōdo shōhi shakai)* and the "transparency" (as in the title of Murakami Ryū's famous 1980s novel *Transparent Blue*) of a materialism fetishistically driven by fashionable trends, religiously cataloged in books, magazines, and even best-selling novels such as *Somehow, Crystal* (1980), by Tanaka Yasuo, and earned by intensive labors at school, work, and home.[6] Ever since the Bubble burst in 1991, however, triggering a debilitating and nagging recession that has persisted well over a decade, a deep sense of unease *(fuan)* has permeated the environment. Doubts have been raised not only about the infrastructure shouldering Japan's postwar economy but also about the personal and ideological costs of a nation so single-mindedly fixated on productivity, performance, and individual wealth. Financial and banking institutions have been scrutinized, and in the wake of multiple scandals, so have political leaders and government operations. The mechanisms that once shored up Japan's materialist success have also come under attack. These include the intense demands placed on people to work and study hard, demands that, while ensuring a nation of skilled and industrious workers, have had damaging effects: high stress, death by overwork, bullying and burnout at school, and an individualism untethered, as many believe these days, to the codes of collective moral beliefs that once glued "Japan" together, an opinion held by neoconservatives like Fukuda Kazuya but also leftist cultural critics like Miyadai Shinji and Murakami Ryū (Yoda 2000).[7]

The 1990s and the early new millennium have been a time of national anxiety. Unemployment and layoffs, once unheard of, rose dramatically during this period. So did suicides, many committed—as I can attest from my own stay in Tokyo—by people jumping in front of trains; 228 deaths were reported this way in eastern Japan alone in 1998, when the national suicide rate jumped 26 percent (Efron 2000:10). The premise of an earlier age—the guarantee of lifetime security and employment for those who succeed at school (*gakureki shakai*, literally "educational pedigree society") and are loyal and hardworking at their jobs *(kigyō shakai)*—had been swiftly destabilized. A majority (68 percent) of respondents to a survey done by Hakuhōdō in 1998 reported that they were often worried or anxious (up from 38 percent in 1990), and an even greater number (74 percent) admitted to frequent feelings of anger or irritation (up from 46 percent in 1990). Everyone seems stressed, those with jobs as much as those without. *Karōshi* (death by overwork, which reportedly kills ten thousand Japanese men every year) is often in the news, particularly since Prime Minister Obuchi's death in April 2000 from a stroke brought on, as it was largely assumed, by the fact that he had taken only three days off in the twenty months he had been in office. This is a national pattern that recessionary times have only aggravated (workers took an average of 9.1 out of 17 paid vacation days in 1998, down from 9.5 in 1995). No wonder that so many Japanese are tired these days (according to a recent study, 59 percent of respondents said they were tired—versus 15 percent in Europe and 30 percent in the States—and, of these, 36 percent said they had been tired for six months). And no wonder that students, as saturated by work as their parents, share this fatigue. In a 1997 survey of Osaka high school students, 80 percent said that they felt stressed, and 86 percent that they were not sleeping enough, with 40 percent sleeping less than six hours a night (Efron 2000).

Children, it could be said, are particularly burdened by the uncertainties of the moment because, overtaxed by the dictates of the "academic pedigree society," they can no longer be assured of either the meaning or rewards of hyperperformativity. As they can see in the struggles of their parents (for whom the "managed society" delivers unemployment, restructuring, and layoffs instead of stable jobs these days), the future is unknown. Not only does this lack of stability cloud their own sense of well-being—making youth today feel disconnected from the world of their parents and rooted more to the immediacy of the present than to clear goals or visions of/for the future—but it also haunts the national mood given that children, by very definition, *are* the future.[8] As in the 1950s, there is a sense of rupture from the past. Similarly, this dissonance produces stories of monstrosity and alien attack in the popular imagination. Then the primary source of inspiration was the atomic bombs dropped over Hiroshima and Nagasaki by American planes that ultimately crushed the militaristic state of Japan and its goal of erecting and ruling an East Asian empire. Gojira was modeled on this attack: a prehistoric beast mutated by nuclear exposure into an atomic monster that assaults the nation.

Since the 1990s, Japan has once again been under attack, but this time the assault comes from inside rather than outside the country: not from foreigners but from native Japanese, a product of the very platform of national reconstruction established to remake the country after the war through economic prosperity. Abundance has turned inside out, and Japan is being eaten up now by inner demons, a situation epitomized by a new phenomenon in *shōnen hanzai* (youth crime), widely depicted both in the news and in imaginary venues (such as in *Battle Royale*, the sensationally violent movie by director Fukusaku Kinji that, debuting in 2000 with a sequel in 2002, is a tale about a class of ninth-grade students who are ordered to play a "game" of survival on a deserted island by killing one another off).[9] Given their connection to the future and how precipitous this pathway is at the new millennium, it is not surprising that youth figure heavily in these stories (and moral panics) of villains attacking national security. For their monstrous disruption of the normal, I call these youth criminals (and other disturbing actors/acts of antisociality these days) millennial monsters.[10] And while these "monsters" may seem more real than the imaginary type on which this book is primarily focused—morphing Rangers, virtual pets, and phantasmatic *pokémon* that, mass commodified, attract fans with their techno-animism of exploding/recombinant body parts—the two are intimately connected, as I lay out at the end of the chapter. It is for the latter as well—fantasy creatures—that I use the term *millennial monsters*, interested, as I am, in how this mass-produced variant intersects with criminal youth, and how both are monstrosities (as defined by entities that defy the borders of "normalcy") created under the conditions of millennial Japan/capitalism.

One of the most salient characteristics of the newest wave in youth crime is how *futsū* (ordinary) are the perpetrators. Paradigmatic of this new brand of criminal were the members of the Buddhist cult Aum Shinrikyō, who, attacking the Tokyo subway system with sarin gas on March 20, 1995, killed twelve people and wounded hundreds. Arguably the most traumatic event of the decade (though this period was littered with spectacular crises, including the Kobe earthquake two months earlier that killed fifty-five hundred people and incurred more than $147 billion in direct damage), the target was the train system—that epicenter of Tokyo life on which millions ride daily, depending for their very, and varied, existence. Few people have the choice not to ride the subways, and until the gas attacks, there was little worry in general about the safety of everyday movement here. This was a point of great national pride, in fact: the country's low incidence of crime and violence in the public and civic arena—something Japanese people I meet for the first time often point to in contrast to the rampant crime they associate with the United States. Accepting everyday life in Japan *as* safe, however, also means overlooking or enduring what passage to and through a normal/normative lifestyle entails: groping on trains for women; the fatigue and stress of high performativity for practically everyone; and the fear of bullying in the school system for kids, a behavior so rampant these days that 26 percent of children have been victims and 16 percent perpetuators themselves, according to a recent study (Hakuhōdō 1997).

It was this illusion of security—in both the daily quotidian and the ideological construct of normalcy—that was shattered by the poison gas attacks of Aum Shinrikyō. In terms of deaths, the scale was nothing like that caused by the atomic bombs a half century earlier, yet the sense of violation was searing and deep. This was a result not only of the site where the attacks occurred—a terrain as ordinary and familiar as one's own home, for most urbanites—but also of who the attackers were: a religious cult whose most prominent members came from the highest level of Japanese society. Among the bombers were graduates from Japan's most prestigious universities: young men who had not only adopted but achieved the standard of *gakureki shakai* that has been the cornerstone of postwar reconstruction. To be this successful, they would have spent years of labor and discipline in a study regime culminating in entrance exams so competitive that some people must retake them for years before passing. But just at the point of reaping their rewards, these members of the elite class walked away from high-status careers as medical doctors, corporate executives, and government officials and joined Aum Shinrikyō instead.

Under the mastership of Asahara Shōkō, the agenda of this religious cult was to sever ties with a society overly enamored of materialism and worldly preoccupations, training its members to perform in the service of the organization and acquire spirituality and enlightenment according to its (own version of) Buddhist premises. But at some point what was a monastic mind-set (cutting oneself off from society) became aggressive and terroristic: eliminating society itself. Carefully calculated to create massive horror and death, the sarin gas bombs were deposited by five cult members on three separate subway lines—Hibiya, Chiyoda, and Marunouchi—at about eight o'clock on a Monday morning. In this and also the regime of control by which it demanded absolute subordination from members, Aum Shinrikyō upheld not so much an alternative to postwar corporatization as an extreme manifestation of it, as Marilyn Ivy has pointed out. "Aum pushed the logic of Toyotism and Japanese nationalism to its limit, replicating with a hypermachinic intensity the production of loyal subjects and workers devoted to the corporate endeavors of Asahara Shōkō" (Ivy 2001:824). Not only were Japanese deeply shocked by the savagery of the poison gas attacks, but most also found the philosophy of the cult and the nihilism of their goals to be utterly incomprehensible. Even more unnerving was the fact that the terrorists were not foreign aliens or native-born "deviants" (who defied or failed the system). Rather, they were the putative "best" of Japan, the very embodiment of the ideal postwar subject now turned monstrous and deadly.

During the millennial year I spent in Japan (1999–2000), the news media were inundated with cases of other seemingly ordinary Japanese committing acts of brutal violence in the course of everyday life. Echoing a pattern that had riveted and repulsed Americans only a year earlier—school shootings by middle-class kids that peaked in the Columbine high school massacre—these criminals were typically adolescents who had passed as normal kids prior to committing their violent acts. Even as these acts were sensationalized in the press as a social phenomenon that was dubbed "youth crime," the numbers of youth arrested for murder rose (though inconsistently) throughout the late 1990s. In 1997, they were the highest since 1975, and in 2000 they doubled in the first six months over those for 1999 (from twenty-seven to fifty-three). Though these figures have also been challenged by critics (Kondō Motohiro, for example, argues that they are much lower and have been hyped by the press to produce a moral panic [2000]), they are part and parcel of a public perception that once-normal kids are becoming "strange" these days.[11]

This strangeness has been emphasized by a number of separate but interrelated behaviors. One is the dress and sexual behavior of schoolgirls, which will be explored in more detail in chapter 5. The popular practice of enjo kōsai—"assisting" older men with dates for money—resembles prostitution, and teenage girl fashions (such as those of the kogyaru, also called yamamba or mountain witch, popular in 1999–2000: tanned faces, eyes orbited with white makeup, dyed hair, and platform shoes) are often jarring to adults. Other disturbing behaviors include the rise in bullying (ijime); children refusing to go to school (tōkōkyohi), a pattern that usually starts at about age thirteen or fourteen, the time that bullying picks up and entrance exams to upper school approach; increasing chaos in the schoolroom that prevents teachers from maintaining order (now considered a social phenomenon—gakkyū hōkai, or schoolroom collapse—that has generated intense scrutiny and attempts at intervention); and the spectacular(ized) acts of criminal youth. And, consistent with the elites who carried out the sarin gas attacks for Aum Shinrikyō, criminal acts are increasingly carried out by (once) seemingly normal kids. Since 1996, in fact, this has become a new pattern in youth crime: a rise in criminals with good school records. As Ōgi Naoki, an educational commentator (and once a schoolteacher), observes, such delinquents used to be burdened by handicaps of one sort or another. Particularly since the January 1998 killing of a teacher, however, the key-words of youth crime have become "*futsū no ko, kireru*—normal children are rending [Japan] asunder" (*Yomiuri Shinbun* 2000:17).

In 1999, two of the most publicized crimes were committed by seventeen-year-old boys: one hijacked a bus, killing a woman during the hours he held it hostage; the other murdered an old woman for the "experience" of killing. The busjacker was a boy who, once a good, industrious student, became the victim of *ijime* in middle school, jumping off a high flight of stairs at the command of his tormenters (which led to a two-month hospitalization) when he was a third-year student. The next year he started upper school but quit within days (joining the swelling ranks of refuse-to-go-to-schoolers) and, beginning to display violence at home, was institutionalized by his parents a few months before the incident. Promising to "never forget" what he took as their betrayal, the boy was on his first overnight visit home when, carrying a boxed lunch *(obentō)* from his mother to take on what he said was a planned hike, he got onto an intercity bus with the intention of killing everyone aboard, including himself (Ishidō 2000). The second boy, who lived in Toyokawa, was universally described as a "good child" *(iiko)*. A student at a private high school, he had test scores that were always among the highest in his class; on mock entrance exams, he ranked sixteenth out of two thousand students. Aiming to enter a high-ranked private university (such as Waseda), he lived with his father and paternal grandparents (his parents divorced when he was young). As one news report characterized him, he "fulfilled his father's ambitions to be a good student," though he also repressed his emotions (*Shūkan Posuto* 2000:33). The only motive that he clearly articulated for his actions—the cold-blooded murder of an elderly woman in his neighborhood—was his desire to experience subjectively the act of killing and to observe, on another person, the "natural" process of death.

Alongside these crimes were others that year that similarly troubled the waters of normalcy. Many involved children as the perpetuators, the victims, or both. In November, Yamada Mitsuko, a seemingly average Japanese mother, killed a five-year-old girl who had attended the same nursery school as her daughter. The victim, but not the killer's daughter, had just been accepted into a prestigious kindergarten near the vicinity of Tokyo University, but Yamada claims that her rage stemmed not from jealousy but from dislike of Haruna's mother. Apparently, they had once been friends and socialized around playdates with their children, but in the process and pressure of applying to kindergarten, the friendship had ruptured. After killing Haruna, Yamada buried the child, then joined a search party looking for the girl. At the urging of her husband, she confessed shortly afterward (*Keizai Shinbun* 1999).

In May 2000 came the discovery that a thirty-seven-year-old Nīgatu man had been holding a girl captive in his room for an incredible nine years, having abducted her when she was nine years old as she walked home from school. The man kept the girl confined in his bedroom under conditions that varied over time (at first her legs and arms were tied with adhesive tape; she was also beaten and minimally fed to keep her from having enough energy to flee or make sounds). The man said he had been lonely and wanted a companion fleshier than the virtual ones he had stocked his room with (from video games and *manga*)—a place he had inhabited almost exclusively for years. Apparently a "social recluse" who had found it impossible to hold down a job, the man lived alone with his mother, who claimed never to have been aware of the girl's presence. Obviously frightened of her son, whom she had avoided as much as possible, the mother had been left alone in the home with him for years after her husband, fearing that their daughter might be injured, fled with the second child. The abduction was discovered when the man's violence increased and his mother finally sought outside assistance. Now nineteen, the victim survived, though she left the house unable to walk, weakened from years of enforced immobility (*Asahi Shinbun* 2000).

Other monstrous events percolated as well throughout the millennial year (and in the excessive press coverage these received), all involving close social relations (family members, friends, teachers and students) and sharing the element of rage. Resentful of the way he had been treated years earlier by his teachers, a twenty-one-year-old killed a seven-year-old boy on the grounds of an elementary school. Angry when she caught him pricking himself with a knife (in an attempt to see what suicide might feel like), an eleven-year-old boy killed his mother. Worried about her father's rage when he discovered that she and her boyfriend had played hooky from school, a sixteen-year-old girl murdered the man. Fearful that their increasingly aggressive fifteen-year-old might become another "criminal youth," a couple willingly killed their oldest son to ensure he would not hurt anyone else. Angry at being told not to read *manga* during class, a seventeen-year-old stabbed his high school teacher. Annoyed at his upper-class teammates who ordered the first-year players on the baseball team to crop their hair, a seventeen-year-old struck four of them savagely with a bat (and returned home to beat his mother to death with the same bat). In the outpouring of commentary that accompanied these crimes, a number of opinions were offered, particularly about "criminal youth." In a debate on the subject run by the *Yomiuri Shinbun*, it was said that Japanese kids lack hope or dreams today, and a sense of emptiness rubs up against pent-up emotions that are not released or expressed (at home, at school, or with friends). The hearts and spirits of children are "buried" today in study, says Ōgi Naoki. And even "good students" feel irritated and impatient, eaten up by a workload whose payoff is no longer secure: "It used to be that, if a child could study, s/he wouldn't be picked on and could enter a good university and, in these senses, be happy. But this social structure has recently collapsed and there is no longer the security that once came from studying hard" (*Yomiuri Shinbun* 2000:17).

Increasingly Japan has become an "abstract society" where everything is done by pushing buttons. For kids socialized into this environment, video games are an appropriate form of play. No wonder they constitute not only a popular pastime but, for more and more children, their "biggest friend." As Ikeda Yoshihiko (a clinical psychologist) puts this, "We've never had an age like this, when people can live without contact with others." Children are growing up with fathers rarely home, mothers (con)fusing discipline with love, neighborhoods leached of any community, and teachers who "don't see the hearts of their students." "Closeness" has become ever more elusive today, it is repeatedly said (*Yomiuri Shinbun* 2000:17). In the opinion of Wada Hideki, "Japan as a whole is suffering the problem of inability to communicate." Children are no longer learning how to read each other nonverbally, develop empathy for others, or express their "true" feelings. Ill equipped to converse, Japanese are retreating into themselves (Wada 2000:35–38). As the preceding cases indicate, they are also feeling more and more irritation, which sometimes flares into violence against others. According to one recent study of 1,916 Japanese students in lower and middle school, 65.5 percent said they occasionally or frequently became irritated with friends (and almost as often with parents and teachers). Further, in answer to the question of whether they could control their anger, almost 40 percent answered "never" or "rarely" (*Asahi Shinbun* 1999:1).

Recluses and Nomads:
More "Ordinary" Monsters

Symptomatic of the more general trend toward solitarism or orphanism is the rise in what is considered a new disease in Japan: the condition of being a social "shut-in" (hikikomori or tojikomori-ha). Numbering a reported one million (overwhelmingly male) in the year of the new millennium, hikikomori are people who literally never leave their rooms. For many, this starts in middle school when, overwhelmed by the intensifying pressures around studying, entrance exams, and bullying, they stop attending school (which, under the name tōkōkyohi, is another pathology of the times and also on the rise). Analyzing four of these criminal cases (the abductor, the busjacker, the mother who killed a toddler, the twenty-one-year-old who stabbed a child at an elementary school), Wada Hideki (2000) notes that all were, in some sense, social recluses. After dropping out of school, the busjacker, for example, had been cocooned in his room for more than two years before being committed to a psychiatric ward—and, as with the others, his solitarism bled into violence. Unwilling or unable to "communicate," they all spoke, in the end, by hurting or killing someone else.

Tomita Fujiya, head of Friend Space, which opened in 1990 as one of the first and only counseling centers for hikikomori in Japan, defines this condition as going longer than one year without communicating with family or friends. The case of "Shin" is paradigmatic. At the time his story was recorded, in a book filled with case studies of the phenomenon called Shut-In Youth (Hikikomoru Wakatachi by Shiokura Yutaka, 1999), Shin was twenty-one years old and had been a hikikomori since the time he would have entered high school. A good student until his second year of middle school, he suddenly stopped studying. Joining a gang of rough kids, Shin became violent at home and dropped out of school. After coming home bruised one day, he stopped taking phone calls from friends and withdrew to his room. For the past four years, he has communicated to his parents only through memos he leaves outside his door.

Like most parents Tomita sees at his center, Shin's father is bewildered by his son's condition. What Tomita hears more than anything from these parents is "He was a good kid yet this still happened." Like most of the subjects profiled in Shut-In Youth (gleaned from a number of counselors, psychologists, and psychiatrists working with hikikomori), Shin had been, according to the calculus of middle-class norms, a "good kid." He studied hard, did well in school, and abided by the rules of a gakureki shakai—a personal history that eerily echoes that of the model student who killed an old woman.

Hauntingly, the issue of "dreams" often comes up in the stories of *hikiko-mori*. Always the reference is to a lack—lives and futures devoid of any-thing meaningful or bright—which, in the case of youth, is connected to school, study, and parents. A twenty-six-year-old man self-identifying as a *hikikomori*, for example, traces his progress through school with a growing sense of deep despair. Pushed by his parents to enter a first-tier university, "Suzuki" worked hard to please them. In the process, however, "I killed my-self to keep going; I had no dreams as a human" (Shiokura 1999:39). He was a good student until upper school, which was when he first realized he had no friends. Losing concentration and abandoning the piano he had loved, Suzuki retreated into himself. Scolded by his parents for poor grades, the boy still tried to "play the part" of good kid and model student. Managing to get into only a third-tier university, Suzuki enrolled anyway, even though he went with "no dreams." At the time his story was recorded, Suzuki had been bound to his apartment (which he leaves only once or twice a month) for three years. In his mind, he has been a *hikikomori* for a decade.

Experts on the condition say that *hikikomori* are characteristically sad, stressed, and without hope (lacking the will to live). A study by the Ministry of Education on school refusers points out, concerning this related syn-drome, that children who retreat to their rooms are not necessarily doing so because they want to stay home. Rather, they cannot find a "space of their own" in the world outside—the environment of school, *juku*, and postin-dustrial performativity (the regimen of endless study, endless memoriza-tion, endless exams) that exacts and extracts such expenditures of body and soul. For Shin, playing guitar seems to have been such a personal "space" or "dream" that fueled his passions as he labored dutifully at school. But, as in many of the other accounts in *Shut-In Youth*, when Shin entered high school, his parents forced him to give up the one thing he loved, the guitar, to devote himself single-mindedly to study. As another *hikikomori* related: "My parents always asked me: Are you working hard at school? They never asked whether I was enjoying school. My parents just ordered me to sleep, eat, and study. And, if I didn't answer them, they'd ask, 'Don't you under-stand our love?' " (Shiokura 1999:59–60).

Using the all-encompassing trope for the malaise of these millennial times, Tomita of Friend Space says the root of this problem is "communica-tion": "These kids want to communicate but can't." By communication he means something both personal and interpersonal: an ability to form inti-macies with others and with(in) the self as well. *Hikikomori* are socially constipated, a condition that comes less from any deficit or predisposition in the child than from an environment railroading them into a single mode of identity or engagement. Tomita concludes, "It is better to say, not that these kids have shut themselves in, but that they have been shut out by society" (Shiokura 1999:23).

As the accounts of *hikikomori* make painfully clear, what this means is feeling not only overregulated by society but also wiped out—either because there is no place or recognition for anything they do besides schoolwork or because, in terms of the latter, they are deemed failures. When asked what his happiest moment was "as a person," one *hikikomori* replied that it was being praised by his parents, a rare event (Shiokura 1999:47). In answer to the question of what he would like from his parents, another said he would like them to not be so "dark" (60). In some real sense, *hikikomori* lead lives of nonexistence and are themselves not really "alive." As the recluse in Murakami Ryū's novel *Kyōseichū* (2000) declares, being a *hikikomori* is worse than death. Indeed, since confining himself to home, the main character (a twenty-four-year-old man) has changed his name and identifies himself as a worm (whose history he traces to the hospital room where his grandfather died when the young man was a kid and where he spent long and happy hours visiting). What a commentary this is on the tensions and fractures in millennial Japan, and on how youth today not only are turning to violence but are being "rent asunder" by the violent undertow of the national platform put in place to remake the country after the war.

How different is the state of the *hikikomori*, I wondered during my year in Japan, from that of the "normal" Japanese subject, who, though nomadic rather than reclusive, journeys on the trains encapsulated in a bubble of brand-name goods and personal electronics? And where is the line drawn between "good kids" and shut-ins—an increasingly murky divide, given that each is contributing more and more these days to the latest scourge of "criminal youth," a new (and "ordinary") breed of monster? The term James Fujii uses to describe train travel in the 1920s, at the dawn of Japan's modernity—intimate alienation—seems both apt and exacerbated here. Life, in this millennial Japan, occasions an even greater degree of solitarism, atomism, and disconnection from support systems (such as family or community, at least as they are nostalgically remembered). Further, not only is more time spent in "mediated transitions," but more of everyday life is mediated by constructed realities that are increasingly engaged as a solitary activity. This is just as true for the child studying for exams (poring over books and practice exams at her desk) and the train commuter (plugged into music, e-mail, or games) as for the *hikikomori* (playing video games and reading *manga* in his room). Indeed, the word *otaku*, signaling someone so immersed in the virtual world of video games, *manga*, or role-playing that he has lost touch with "reality," can have both a negative and a positive valence in Japan. On the one hand, Japan is a nation of *otaku*, given the national obsession with techno-constructed realities (from simulated fish in aquariums—the latest in stress-release devices—to artificial ski slopes, ocean beaches, and "foreign" towns). On the other hand, ever since stacks of *rorikon* ("Lolita") comic books and videos were discovered in the home of Miyazaki Tsutomu, the murderer of four children in 1989, *otaku* has also been associated with pathology and violence.

But what is the geometry of intimate alienation here? Does the intimate override alienation (as would seem the case for the wired commuter, who can ease the loneliness of a long train ride by communicating with friends on a cell phone)? Or does alienation intrude ever more into the realm of the intimate (as is seemingly true of the *hikikomori*, who, finding the world painfully alien, retreats to a space that is as imprisoning as it is comforting)? For Marx, alienation is always provoked by an estrangement in the labor process. By working under conditions one-sidedly fixated on producing profits, the worker, as well as his world, is reduced to the abstract currency of a money economy. In the case of postwar Japan, productivity has also been measured, and fed, by academic performance: an extreme value placed on admission into prestigious schools that has been the ruling ideology of and for middle-class kids. In this fetishization of test scores and academic records, children are treated as machines. Programmed in one register, they are far less schooled, or encouraged, in the development of other human capacities (such as interpersonal communication with others or the cultivation of personal hobbies).

But the 1990s were a time of instability and shock, when the riches reaped from postwar reconstruction (and on the backs of Japanese workers, students, and "education mothers") started to crumble. Though they provoked anxiety, the disruptures of this decade—rising unemployment, increases in both layoffs and suicide, the Kobe earthquake followed by the sarin gas attacks, a proliferation of social pathologies and "ordinary" criminals—have also led to more questioning of postwar institutions, including the school system. Out of these current agonies may come shifts in the alignments of value and labor, thereby defusing the ongoing expectation that Japanese will continue to commit excessively and one-sidedly to the same old pressurized spheres (school for children, home for married women, company for white-collar male workers). In post-Bubble times, Japanese women are resisting marriage and motherhood in far greater numbers than ever before (as the government laments), and the ranks of *freeta* workers (who move freely from job to job rather than roosting, as in the *sararīman* model, at one company for life) and "parasite singles" (unmarried adults who live with, and off, parents) are growing among young Japanese. Through such changes, alienation, to the degree it is fostered through estrangement in labor, may start to ease.

But even today, the world of millennial Japan is hardly dominated by estrangement alone. Or, to put this differently, intimacies and enchantments also abound, often appearing in the very circuits of atomistic existence that seemingly promote alienation. This is the world of personal electronics, designer fashions, and character "cuteness": a plethora of things, machines, and fantasies that, closely affixed to people's bodies and interwoven into the fabric of their everyday lives, has an animating effect on consumers. This is the allure of commodity fetishism, Marx would have said: attributing to goods the "life" that has been extracted from the laborer. But dismissing the fascination held by such new-wave products as Game Boys and wireless multisystems (cameras/phones/e-mail/Internet) as no more than false consciousness—the ruse of capitalism to disguise its exploitation under the cover of seductive commodities—can only take us so far here. As Benjamin more persuasively argued, the enchantments held by consumer/techno goods work on people in specific ways, even if (or precisely because) they come linked to a socioeconomic system that is also alienating. This, surely, is the case in Japan, where, in an environment of intense work demands, individualization, and materialism, the reification of life is extreme.

It is not surprising, then, that people increasingly seek "life" in material things: objects that become the conduit for various forms of communication, intimate relationships, and arousals. Integral as it is to millennial capitalism, this passion for material goods that are invested with the power to animate the lives, identities, and communication networks of their possessors must be examined seriously. For it signals not only New Age commodity fetishism but also what Harry Garuba (2003), speaking of Africa, has called "animist materialism": the reenchantment of a darkly empty and rationally modernist world with the animism of spirituality. Infusing the material world with a "life" leeched by corporatist institutions, commodity animism seems as much a culture as a consumer taste and both a corrective to, and extension of, capitalism in a new direction. Following Max Weber, we can call this the "spirit" of capitalism in the age of millennial Japan.

Commodity Animism and the Spirit of Brand-Name Capitalism

The new issues around personal identity and material possessions in millennial Japan have even emerged in psychosomatic symptomatology. In the era that spawned the new wave of social "diseases" ("school refusal," social withdrawal, young criminals with good school records), Ōhira Ken, a Japanese psychiatrist, noticed a new kind of patient visiting his office. Not really "sick" compared with his other patients, these people came in complaining of rather minor complications involving coworkers or family members. While none of these problems prevented these people from being socially functional, the patients were nonetheless inept in communicating with others. By contrast, all displayed amazing eloquence in talking volubly and assuredly about their material possessions. Calling this new type of patient "a person who talks about things [mono no katari no hitobito]," Ōhira (1998) found their numbers proliferating in the 1990s and the syndrome itself a symptom of the times.

A typical case is that of a twenty-two-year-old woman who came to Ōhira troubled by poor relations with her fellow workers, particularly one older woman. Extremely stylish herself, the woman (an OL, or office lady) expounded at length about her personal possessions: a wealth of brand-name goods that she recited in lists and genealogies of categories. When it came to the issue with her coworker, however, the patient was clueless except for saying that, unlike herself, the other woman had a poor feeling for material goods (mono), and there was tension between the two of them. The case of a twenty-five-year-old male office worker in an electric company was similar. Suffering from diarrhea at work, he found that what troubled him the most about his job was the cheap suit he had to wear because he could not afford anything better on his salary. Unable to establish good social relations or feel comfortable at work, the man spent much of his free time poring over consumer magazines with his wealthy girlfriend, picking out the goods they would like to buy. A third patient described herself, and the Japanese nation as a whole, entirely in terms of brand-name commodities: "We go to brand-name universities, enter brand-name companies, and wear brand-name goods. And this isn't just on the outside. On the inside, too, we're 'brand-name people' [burando ningen]" (Ōhira 1998:51).

As Ōhira points out, the mono no katari no hitobito is concerned with her place in the world and aims to elevate it by acquiring brand-name goods. Acquisition gives the person a sense of control, as does a propensity to classify everything. Life is managed by scrupulous cataloging: shoes, kitchenware, meishi (business cards), and phone friends. If something does not fit this pigeonholing, it either is gotten rid of or else provokes a problem—such as the difficulties experienced with real people, some of whom lack the passion for material goods of the mono no katari no hitobito. With the logic that buying and assembling goods will make one happy, things are used to "power up" and concretize the inner self. This mind-set is commonplace today in Japan, where a consuming public borrows the language of commodities to describe everything from personal identity and worth to companionship, intimacy, and interpersonal relationships. As Ōhira notes, material wealth was the "Japanese dream" for postwar reconstruction. But the "treasures" of these earlier years (refrigerators, washing machines, color TVs) have long been realized, and the "dream" has nowhere else to go (1998:230–36). What Japan is now experiencing is a "pathology of abundance" (the title of his book on the subject, *Yutakasa no Seishinbyō*), generating the condition of "people who talk about things." Its symptoms are an intimacy with goods coupled with a deficit in interpersonal closeness.

As evidenced by the *mono no katari no hitobito* who seek out psychiatric assistance, this is not an altogether comfortable state. According to Ōhira, these people do not enjoy being solitary and are actually seeking a way to communicate, albeit through the only language they can speak—that of material goods. Their dilemma echoes, if in reverse, the findings of the Ministry of Education about the "school refusers" who retreat to their homes not because they want to but because the outside world has no meaning or "space" for them. In both cases, the issue at hand is a variant of intimate alienation: alienation from a social world of people and labor (work and school), and intimacy formed with constructed realities (brand-name goods, video games) that are engaged while alone. Of course, "people who talk about things" move about in the world, whereas social shut-ins are marooned at home. But what does it say about millennial Japan that both these conditions not only proliferate today but are "pathologies" that blur into (or even constitute) the norm? And what does this suggest about the languages and conditions for "talking" these days, when children lock themselves in their rooms and adults communicate through material things?

In a 1987 study on consumer trends by Hakuhōdō, the advertising agency, respondents were asked to draw their "dream house." Many did so by sketching single rooms or enclosed spaces that were obviously intended to be inhabited alone: images the researchers found to be "autistic" yet, notably, bright rather than dark. Seeing in this the contemporary mind-set—viewing the self as a "fenced-in paradise" and wanting to protect one's own space while not interfering with others—they have tracked how this trend was played out in consumer desires throughout the 1990s. Strikingly, a high number of Japanese value goods that provide a sense of security, privacy, and warmth; both baths and cell phones, for example, are regarded as "private heavens" and "private resorts" (McCreery 2000:217–43). It is no wonder, perhaps, that Japan is the place that birthed the Walkman—Sony's mobile tape player that enables owners to stay plugged into their own aural worlds (of music/audio tapes/radio) literally wherever they go. Most of my fellow commuters on the trains I rode during my year in Japan were hooked up to such electronic devices: Walkmen, Palm Pilots, Game Boys, and cell phones (which, in many cases, now have multiple functions, from e-mail to digital cameras). The scene reflected what Raymond Williams (1975) has called "mobile privatization" and Kogawa Tetsuo (1984), speaking specifically about Japan, described as "electronic individualism." As Iain Chambers (1990) has noted about the Walkman, the cultural activity fostered is ambivalent, swaying between "autism and autonomy." And one wonders about the grammar of intimacy and alienation here: whether such dependence on private electronics/dreams assuages or merely intensifies the atomism so deep-seated in millennial lifestyles.

According to the engineer who designed the PHS (personal handyphone system—a low-powered wireless phone technology developed in Japan) for Motorola in Japan, 85 percent of Japanese owners are personal users who carry their cell phones wherever they go and conceptualize them also as play devices, fashion wear, and companions. Since phones, in a manner of speaking, are so sutured to the body, *wearability* is a keyword for Japanese consumers, driving fashions that stress compactness and style, along with the latest in technology. As Nakakawa states: "It's your own culture; you make it beautiful and users want to show this to others as well as to themselves" (*Nikkei Dezain* 1998:28). But what is private fashion here also translates into a communication device with which to maintain human connections. Kids these days have as many as three hundred names in their banks of cell-phone pals: up from the average of twenty-four held by the generation of "baby boomer juniors" (McCreery 2000:185).[12] This, in itself, can be a form of addiction, and the "friends" one calls on a cell phone may never be met in the flesh (*Nikkei Dezain* 1998:25). The line between communication and commodity, electronic individualism and *ningenkankei* (human relationships), is increasingly hard to discern.

This is also true of a fad that, blooming along with Japan's postwar prosperity in the 1970s, has peaked again (since 1997) in the millennial years of post-Bubble distress—a craving for "cuteness" as well as cute characters (Kitty-chan, Pikachu, Doraemon, Miffy) that adorn everything from backpacks, toy figures, and comic books to phone straps, key chains, and adult-targeted fashion. Emerging from the children's entertainment industry that, in the 1970s, produced toys out of mass-media characters (cartoons, comic books, television shows), the character business started taking off on its own when Sanrio came up with its Hello Kitty line in the 1970s. Bred, in this case, not from a media production but as an entire line of adorable consumer goods (stationery, hair clips, tea cups, lunch boxes, pajamas, umbrellas), the mouthless kitty cat triggered a fashion in both characters and cuteness (generically referred to by the adjective *kawaii*, for cute). Although it was initially targeted to young girls *(shōjo)*—and fostered by them in such fads as *hentai shōjo moji* (a round, girlish form of handwriting)—cuteness exploded into a national obsession. In the 1980s, commercial businesses started adopting cute characters in promotional advertising. ANA airlines, for example, turned around a lagging ski campaign by employing the American character Snoopy, and JAL followed suit by using the character Popeye to target young women for tour packages. By the late 1980s, banks had adopted the practice of utilizing characters as a type of company logo and insignia on bankbooks (Dentsū 1999), and by the 1990s, personalizing cell phones with character straps (for adult men, the favorite is Doraemon, the blue robotic cat of the long-running *anime* and *manga* series) had become a common practice.

Character branding has become trendy, even fetishistic, in Japan today. In part, according to a book on the character business put out by the Japanese advertising agency Dentsū (1999), this is because cute characters are appropriated as symbols for personal, corporate, group, and national identity. The "essence" of character merchandising, Dentsū states, is that it "glues society at its root. A character accompanies the development of a group and becomes part of, and a symbol for, that identity." Characters, it continues, are a "device for self-realization" *(jikojitsugen)*. Certainly, the images of cute characters are as omnipresent today as animist spirits; indeed, I have a picture sitting in front of me of a *jizo* statue in the shape of Doraemon.[13] Besides commercial goods (hand towels, cooking pans, book bags, pencils), characters also embellish posters for public events or neighborhood fairs, show up on government notices or service announcements, and are stamped onto computers, Xerox machines, and even bulldozers. Cuteness is generally associated with childhood and childlike experiences: innocence, dependence, and freedom from the pressures of an adult world (though, as we have seen, the experience of childhood is quite different in reality). These are grafted from and onto the "play" of fantasy and dreams; the character of Doraemon, for example, whose fanciful concoctions such as the "door that goes anywhere" *(dokodemo doa)* keeps his own imagination open, as one adult fan put it, during the long days and nights he works in the unimaginative space of a *sararīman* (Fujimi 1998).

Speaking of the recent craze in character/cute goods, an advertising executive describes the relationships formed as both kinlike and (inter)personal.

Whether a Kitty-chan key chain, Doraemon cell phone strap, or Pikachu backpack, these commodity spirits are "shadow families": constant and reliable companions that are soothing in these postindustrial times of nomadicism, orphanism, and stress. Someone else in the business states this more sharply: "Parents die, but characters remain forever" (Riri Furanki, cited in *Burēn* 2000:15). Concurring, the authors of a recent book on the character business state that characters are the "lifeline of human relationships" in today's high-growth information society and serve as the totems, protectors *(omamori)*, and "utility symbols" of its citizens (Hashino and Miyashita 2001:4–5). With seeming pride, they label Japan a "character empire," noting that no country in the world has become as thoroughly inundated—both economically and culturally—with character merchandise as it has.

Yet another book (an anthology entitled *The Reasons Why 87 Percent of Japanese Like Characters*) links the vibrancy of the Japanese character business (one of the few successes in these recessionary times) to the unease of contemporary times. Pressured by bullying, academic hurdles, and economic instability, children find relief in characters that offer them a love at once absolute and personal ("they love you alone"; Aoyama and Bandai Kyarakutā Kenkyūjō 2001:17). A psychiatrist calls this the "character therapy age," where characters relieve stress and also reflect the "inner self" (12–13). Chronicling the history of character trends in postwar Japan, he characterizes the present as an era where contemporary citizens "communicate" with character commodities. This is the "route" for relating to friends, and communication has now become the object of character consumption. Speaking of Sony's robotic dog, AIBO, the book concludes that such intimate play goods serve as friends and that these friends assume the role of pets (194).

As I argued in the introduction, the appeal of Japanese play goods can be characterized by two main qualities—polymorphous perversity and techno-animism—that help explain their cachet as the cutting edge of trendy "cool" on the marketplace of kids' entertainment today. This is fantasy-ware with a mass array of spirits and parts (techno-animism) that continually transform, come apart, and recombine in a variety of ways (polymorphous perversity). Further, such a logic of play has been packaged in forms that suit the tempo and lifestyle of these postindustrial times. Gameware is portable (making access convenient and continual) and adjustable for personal use (anything can be listened to on a Walkman), while the fantasy making conjures up playmates that "heal" the ills of materialism, all the while generating an addictive frenzy that literally buys into the same thing, of playing, wanting, and buying more and more commodified stuff. In this chapter I have laid out some of the socioeconomic factors and events that have shaped the national mood in Japan at this moment of the millennial crossover and can be traced not only in the "pathologies" of the era—Aum Shinrikyō, social shut-ins, criminal youth—but also in the trends in producing, accumulating, and bonding with "cute" play commodities that define the subject of this book.

As I have tried to suggest, there is a thin line between the "monstrous" behavior of children who, once "good," retreat into their rooms or act out in random violence and that of so-called normal kids who fetishistically consume brand-name goods and compulsively play with the fantasy monsters that are so popular in (and whose profits are so important to) the Japanese marketplace today. In the discourse surrounding both phenomena today in Japan, reference is made to the same set of conditions: a pressurized school system (of constant tests and rampant bullying), increasing amount of time spent alone, disconnection from others and the inability of Japanese these days to "communicate," and the transparency and superficiality of a materialist society. Keeping in mind these issues (and how Japanese play goods are situated contradictorily as both part of, and—imagined, imaginary—antidote to, millennial capitalism), I now move on to the specifics of four waves of made-in-Japan kids' play that became popular and profitable in the global marketplace in the 1990s. The first of these is the genre of live-action morphin team heroes that, beginning in Japan in 1973, took off as the *Mighty Morphin Power Rangers* on U.S. television screens in 1993.

4 *Mighty Morphin Power Rangers*

The First Crossover Superheroes

In summer 1997, an episode of the children's live-action show *Chōriki Sentai Ōrenjā (Superpower Team Force King Rangers)*, broadcast by Tōei Studios in Tokyo, portrays a hot summer day in downtown Tokyo on which a power outage suddenly halts urban traffic. From commuters stalled on escalators and in subways and street crossings, the camera pans to a huge beast hovering over the city Godzilla-style. Standing on two feet, with a body whose pointy protrusions, we soon learn, are filled with deadly radiation, this monster is named—as written on the bottom of the screen—Mashinjyū Barabirudā (Machine Beast Barabirudā). Threatening to cause even more earthly destruction, Machine Beast is taken on by a defender robot that, gigantic as well, looks like a samurai with helmet and pointy shoulder-pads. Called Sentai Robo (Team Force Robot), it marches determinedly forward and makes martial-arts movements with its arms, all driven, we see shortly, by a crew of five humans (the *sentai* Rangers, team force Rangers) seated in the cockpit located in the robot's head. Fighting hard, Sentai Robo activates a variety of powers. In the end, though, the good robot is trumped by the evil beast and shuts down.

Back at the sentai control room, filled with computers and operated by the "chairman"—a middle-aged man dressed in a military-style uniform who designed the robot—the Rangers are distressed to learn that Sentai Robo will take a long time to repair. Meanwhile, Machine Beast's threats to Tokyo (and, by implication, the entire world) are mounting, and the Rangers are without a defender robot. Turning to the computer system to see if he can find anything, Red Ranger, the obvious leader of the bunch, discovers the presence of a robot buried in the vicinity. This turns out to be Redo Punchā (Red Puncher), a giant robot built by the chairman two years ago that, due to a malfunction, wound up killing the previous Red Ranger.

Because the glitch has not been fixed, the chairman forbids Red Ranger from operating the robot. But, given that there is no alternative and the security of the world is in danger, Red Ranger says that he "believes" in the chairman's invention, and starts it up anyway.

As his comrades—now trapped by the Machine Beast in his huge palm—look on in anticipation, the robot cranks up and sputters into action. But, starting out strong, Red Puncher soon goes haywire, jolting Red Ranger inside. Plaintively asking the machine, *"Naze, naze?"* (Why, why?), Red Ranger knocks his head against the controls and dies just as the robot conks out as well. In the cockpit, the spirit of the previous Ranger materializes and, taking the hand of his dead comrade, transports him to a point above the earth. From there he shows him a natural panorama (the sea, mountains, a ladybug on a leaf) and says: "This is what we must defend." Back in the cockpit, Red Ranger has been reborn, and saying, "We'll do this together," rekindles the robot. This time it gears up with surety and force and then, to the swell of upbeat music, marches forward and starts attacking Barabirudā. Taken by surprise, Machine Beast is quickly trounced and explodes into pieces. As the Rangers cheer and the chairman smiles in relief, Red Ranger claims victory (*"yatto!"*).

In the final scene, everyone has gathered in front of the stacked stones marking the grave of the fallen Ranger. Addressing the younger sister of the latter, Red Ranger tells her it was the spirit of her brother who guided him in his victorious mission. They all then turn to Red Puncher, standing erect in the distance. Paying it their final respects, the group stands solemnly as the camera pans in on Red Puncher, shot against the backdrop of a red setting sun.

Blending Superheroes with Heroic Machines: Japan's Postwar Mythology

The myth of the superhero is as timeless as it is universal. An exceptional being who defies the odds to save the world from danger—it is as if the very frailty and unpredictability of the human condition elicit this fantasy. But as Freud has said about dreams, wish fulfillment also rehearses the boundaries of the familiar world(s) in which we actually live. Superheroes transcend the limits of human normalcy, yet at the same time they work to restore what was once normal (and disturbed by aliens, enemies, natural calamities) at home. The superhero myth, then, is about borders: about extending them in one place only to reassert them somewhere else. And as a fantasy as much about normalcy as about exceptionalism, it is not only mythically universal but also concretely shaped by the times and places in which it circulates as popular culture. The superhero Tetsuwan Atomu, for example, was very much a product of its times: a *mecha* wonder boy who was model citizen and futuristic robot combined. In this fusion of the real with the imaginary were crystallized not only the hopes and anxieties of the recently defeated Japan but also the norms and policies by which the state intended to reconstruct it (a hardworking citizenry willing to sacrifice to their jobs and welcome technology into their workplace, consumer lifestyle, and subjectivity).

Collapsing fantasy into ideology, this mythic superhero stood for an imaginary Japan/ese that, as Benedict Anderson (1983) has argued about the role played by mass media in producing the nation through an image collectively shared, was a product of the burgeoning mass culture arising through the channels of television, *manga*, and animation in Japan's early postwar years. A sign of the future, *Tetsuwan Atomu* also incorporated something of Japan's preindustrial traditions: an animistic belief system in which the border between human and nonhuman is viewed as far more porous than fixed. A legacy of Japanese folklore—filled with tales of hybrid, morphing, and strange beings (human cranes, warriors born from peach pits, snakes that turn into women)—and Shinto-inspired animism, where everything has a spirit from the air and the wind to rocks, rivers, and humans, the amalgamation of robot and humanness here is a sign of both Japan's future and its past.

In 1973, a new genre of live-action superheroes was inaugurated on Japanese television. Called *Himitsu Sentai Go Renjā* (Secret Team Force of Five Rangers) and broadcast by Tōei Studios, this series followed in the tradition of live-action (*tokusatsu*, or special effects) superheroes popularized by shows like *Urutoraman*. The latter, launched in 1966 with spectacular special effects designed by Tsuburaya Eiji (of *Gojira* fame), popularized the dynamic of a cyborgian superhero, in this case, a human morphed into a giant cybernetically empowered, red-costumed hero, who battles an endless cycle of mechanized beasts. These beasts, generically called *kaijū*, became a fad in boys' action shows that still appear on Japanese television today. The story line is always some version of a battle. The *kaijū*, threatening to destroy the earth and kill off humanity, is opposed by a heroic warrior who ultimately (and always) wins, thereby eliminating the enemy—until a new one reappears for the next show (and battle). And, while the hero is the polar opposite of the *kaijū* in that her or his mission is to save rather than attack humanity/the earth, there is also a resemblance: both are different, in powers and constitution, from "normal" humans. Whether they are cyborgs, androids, robots, or host spirits (fueled by the spirits/powers of animals, for example), superheroes are as strange a species as the *kaijū*—mixtures of machinery, electricity, and bestiality. This very strangeness is also of central importance in both the text of the media story lines (on the television program, in comic books or children's magazines) and the children's merchandise that accompanies them (action figures, warrior robots). How precisely the body is composed and what powers are aligned with what physical features is a fascination directed as much to *kaijū* as to heroes, with one crucial difference—only the latter can also pass as human by transforming between one modality (everyday and normal) to another (costumed and empowered).

Go Renjā signaled a major shift in the genre. Instead of a single hero, there was now a team (from three to six members) who fought physically and robotically together as a "team force" of cyberwarriors. Working cooperatively as a unit, they also acquired a collective battle mode of conjoining their high-tech *mecha*: creating a mega-tool out of their separate weapons or fusing their individual flying machines into a giant robot. There were other changes as well. Females were cast as heroes (one out of three, or two out of five, usually), and the overall tone became brighter *(akarui)*—the result, some say, of the addition of women, as well as the colorizing of the show with bubblegum-hued morphing suits (red, pink, yellow, blue, and green). Along with these innovations, the tenor of the battle scenes became more consistently victorious and upbeat. While winning was less assured in the 1950s and 1960s era of fantasy battles—Gojira was never definitively killed, for example, and Atomu faced many obstacles in his battles fought for humanity, including his own for acceptance—this "strain of ambiguity" eased with *Go Renjā* (*Kaijū VOW* 1993). Finally, emphasis was placed on teamwork, not surprising given that the heroes now came in teams, and also on cultivating spiritual fortitude that is literally and figuratively transformative.

In the words of an American fan, *Go Renjā* represented a new concept in superheroism organized around two principles: (1) a team force composed of ordinary people whose positive spirit sets them apart, and (2) Rangers who have individual powers but who work together to achieve superheroic goals (Cirronella 1996:10). The concept proved so popular that Tōei's Ranger series has endured for more than a quarter of a century. Still playing today, the show succeeds, in large part, by doing its own form of morphing every season. Each year it reappears with a new team of Rangers (Car Rangers, Turbo Rangers, Dinosaur Rangers, King Rangers) refitted with different powers, costumes, and tools. Moreover, exported to the United States in 1993 and—following the *Gojira/Godzilla* route—taken up in that Americanized form to the rest of the world, the *Power Rangers* (as the U.S. version is called) turned into a wildly popular, and global, "Morphinomenon."

Why such a concept of superheroism would be so popular in the last quarter of the twentieth century has something to do with the times, needless to say. This was an era marked by global capitalism and proliferating technologies that is often described in terms of flexibility, fragmentation, and fluctuation. As noted by Arjun Appadurai (1996), flows (of people, goods, money, ideas, and images) move between geographic and geopolitical borders of various kinds (nations, economies, cultures), making this an age of deterritorialization as much as reterritorialization. Production shifted away from the previous "Fordist" model (Harvey 1990) of a rationalized labor force in which core workers stay in one place and earn enough wages to consume what they produce: the televisions, automobiles, and washing machines that, mass-produced, embed both the desires and the discipline of a modern lifestyle. By the 1970s, production was becoming based more on a post-Fordist model of flexible accumulation, a situation geared to quick turnover and a constantly changing market in which companies downsized their core workers, diversified their holdings and product lines, and relied on subcontractors, peripheral workers, and outsourcing.

Power Rangers, as we will see, is the embodiment of post-Fordism and a postmodern aesthetics in the realm of children's mass culture. Its characters are flexible transformers who move back and forth between a mix of modalities: martial arts, dinosaurs, high-tech machines, and collectivities. Their pastiche of powers similarly marks the jumble of worlds in which events take place: an otherworld of intergalactic beings and the everyday world of "normal" teenagers attending school, hanging out with friends, and troubled by pimples and jealousies. The pace is speedy, characters teleport across multiple borders of time and space, and life is experienced schizophrenically: as disjointed, incoherent, and lacking linear continuity (Jameson 1984). Identities shift, moving among those of normal teenager, costumed superhero, armed warrior, and conjoined "megazord" (one season's version of the Rangers' megamachine). While there is a modernist narrative of good versus evil, the story is postmodernist in lacking any single hero, essence, or transformation that centers the plot.

Cyberheroes and the Ethics of Lean Production

The early 1970s, when *Go Renjā* first hit the screen, were a period of earnest rebuilding in Japan, an effort shored up by the first postwar economic boost in 1968.[1] More than twenty years after it had been vanquished, Japan was beginning to get back on its feet, remade as a nation devoted to pacifism and material productivity. The optimism reflected in *Go Renjā* is a sign of resurging national confidence, reflected in warriors whose identity as cyber-humans is secure, unlike the robot-boy Tetsuwan Atomu in the 1950s. The story here fits that of the standard superhero myth. According to Richard Reynolds (1994), this myth involves heroes who, living as disguised humans in the "normal" world, transform to superbeings, with special powers and costumes, to fight intruding aliens and save the world from destruction. In the end, the heroes revert to their human form and return to the world they have restored to normalcy. As Reynolds has argued, the superhero myth with its heroic protagonist and evil antagonists is a perfect modernist tale. As such, it has been used to promote national patriotism in various countries, as when the U.S. government sent GIs into World War II (where they fought, among other enemies, the Japanese) laden with *Superman* comics. The story of the wimpish Clark Kent, who transforms into a bold fighting machine to defeat evil foes, replayed a worldview of clearly defined enemies, heroes who begin as normal citizens (coded as white and male), and the urgency of preserving the status quo. Significantly, the original *Superman* story, crafted by Jerry Siegler and Joe Schuster, was far less upbeat: a darker tale focused more on the threats posed to American society by an evil misanthrope (an anti-Semite reminiscent of Hitler). Once it was picked up by DC Comics in 1938 and began publication as its own comic book, however, *Superman* shifted focus and tone, now centering its attentions on the Herculean hero and his transitions in and out of mainstream society.

Created in the 1970s in a country that was relishing its first successes with reconstruction, *Go Renjā* embedded a somewhat different national(ist) subtext than the heroic loners so popular in American comic books (which, despite the occasional team heroes like X-Men, still thrive in U.S. pop culture, as seen in the recent craze of cinematic remakes of yesteryear's comic-book heroes like the Hulk and Spider-Man). Certainly, the American model of superhero individualist not only was popular in Japan after the war (*Superman* circulated widely there, both in comic-book form and in the live-action television show of the late 1950s) but also influenced the construction of Japanese superheroes (in live-action shows, for example, which were popular in this period of early TV). By the 1970s, however, this was no longer nearly as true, as more and more of the shows broadcast on television, for example, were being produced in Japan, and fashions—both in children's entertainment and in mass/consumer culture generally—were being designed more in accordance with Japanese (versus foreign, i.e., American) styles and tastes. One can see this effect, for example, in the difference paid to the everyday between the television shows *Superman* and *Go Renjā*. In the latter, the scenes before and after attack are downplayed, as if what constitutes daily normalcy in society is still in the process of getting established. In *Superman*, by contrast, Clark Kent is repeatedly seen at the *Daily Planet* offices interacting with Jimmy Olsen and Lois Lane or returning home to Kansas to visit his mom: a telling sign of a national imaginary sutured to such scenarios of a 1950s America at once stable, secure, and mundane.

The real focus in *Go Renjā* is less on the human incarnation of the Rangers than on the endless processes these ordinary teenagers undergo when transforming into superheroes. Morphing is a far more intricate procedure here than the simple costume change and offstage upgrade performed by Superman (who, after ducking into a phone booth, reemerges caped and charged). Powers in *Go Renjā* are dispersed among a team of heroes and diffused across a span of spirits, weapons, and bodily strengths (figure 12). This spread of traits makes heroism not only more collective and multisited (decentered from the type of the lone hero with a muscular torso embodied by Superman), but also, in some sense, more democratic. Relying on a combination of hard work, team spirit, and good *mecha*, empowerment is a feat open to anyone, including women. The emphasis in this version of the superhero myth dovetails with that of the state: retooling normal citizens into high-performing peace warriors equipped with (intangible) spirits and (tangible) tools. And, just like the recycling that was done of GI ration tins into tin jeeps by Japanese toy makers in the early months following the war, *Go Renjā* appropriated yet remade what had been a popular American myth/show *(Superman)* that played in postwar Japan during the 1960s.

Performance—exerting oneself for the nation—was demanded of citizens in the 1970s as it had been during the war years. But the focus had shifted from conquering others to build a Japanese empire (the Greater East Asia Co-Prosperity Sphere) to fortifying the self to guarantee security and peace at home. The new law of the land was the democratic constitution of 1947, written by the Americans during their occupation. Under its strictures, the emperor was demoted from god to symbol of the state, and citizens went from subjects of the emperor to individuals with equal rights. Under Article 9 of this constitution, Japan was further forbidden from bearing arms for anything other than self-defense. During the occupation, when this constitution was instituted, anything that smacked of militarism or patriotism was initially removed from public life; this included classes in martial arts (karate, *kendō*, *ki-aikidō*) at school and the display of the national flag and singing of the national anthem in public spaces. It is not coinciden-

Figure 12. Team warriors: the post-Fordist model of superheroism. (From a *Chōsentai Raibuman* illustrated book for children; courtesy of Tōei Company Ltd.)

tal, of course, that warriorship in the venue of imaginary Rangers is directed against hyperfantastical beasts *(kaijū)* and always in the interests of self-defense. In this guise (a return of the repressed, perhaps), it is also striking that warriorship remained such a persistent and popular motif in this national folklore of a "pacifist" Japan.

Reflected as well in *sentai* mythology is the new industrial model of postwar Japan. Directing its national energies after the war to industrial and consumer production (mainly, manufacturing and service), much of which needed to be rebuilt from scratch, the Japanese government encouraged the development of business along innovative new lines (largely borrowed, at least at first, from the United States). Intended to heighten productivity as well as thwart the union activism that had blossomed after the war, a new model of production emerged that was variously called Toyotism, Sonyism, lean production, and flexible production. Fordism—that is, the standardized, large-scale production ushered in by Henry Ford's first car plant in Michigan in 1913—spread internationally after 1945, forming mass markets and absorbing the mass of the world's population (outside the communist world) into the global dynamics of a new kind of capitalism hegemonized by the United States. By the 1960s, however, this hegemony was being challenged by the recoveries of West Germany and Japan, the saturation of America's internal market, and the intensification of international competition. According to David Harvey, 1973 marks the watershed year when the political economy of late twentieth-century capitalism was radically transformed from Fordism to post-Fordism, or what he calls "flexible accumulation." As Harvey (1989) puts it, the rigidity of Fordism made it increasingly less able to sustain the inherent contradictions of capitalism. What was needed instead was a system with greater flexibility to match the uncertainties of the labor market.

Moving away from the Fordist model of mass production, production was now geared to the vagaries of demand (by means of the *kanban*—just in time—system), with workers trained to move between tasks. Thanks to multiple skills and job rotation, employees became increasingly identified more by the company they worked for than by a specific job. Group identity was fostered in other ways as well: all workers at Toyota, Nissan, or other big companies now wore the same uniform and badge no matter what their rank, for example, and separate cafeterias and reserved parking for management were abolished (thereby reducing the gap—so striking in U.S. companies, particularly in salaries—between workers and management). In addition, corporate principles of lifetime employment and all-company unions (in which management and labor work together) became popular, as an ideal if not always a reality, in medium-sized and large companies starting in the 1950s.

As in *Go Renjā*, the stars of the lean production ethos are flexible workers who, though replaceable, are keenly valued for the exceptional service they give to their unit (this is true of the two Red Rangers in the episode that opens this chapter—one Red Ranger is replaced by another, but each has his own identity as well). Team spirit is cultivated, but so is individual initiative (through "quality circles" in the workplace—a concept adopted from the United States), and performance intermixes hard work, spirituality, and high-tech science. Japan's productivity rose astronomically in the period that also produced *Go Renjā*. In the automobile industry alone, car production increased eighteen times during the second half of the 1960s; by the early 1970s, the output per worker surpassed that in all other industrialized countries (Watanabe 1987). The labor extracted from workers under lean production, it should be noted, is so high that critics call it "management by stress" (Price 1995). Ideologically, however, value is placed on working for something higher than the self that pushes and rewards the superhuman efforts workers put out. In all this, robotic technology both supplements and analogizes human labor. Today the number of industrial robots (350,000) utilized by Japan is the highest in the world (Williams 2003).

Robotic technology, however, is not only physically but also psychically more integral to Japanese industry.

In the long period of Japan's postwar reconstruction, cyborgs have populated the landscape both as laborers in the workplace and as mythic characters of New Age dreams. Their omnipresence in mass culture is striking. Tales of atomic mutants, "ghosts in the shell," reconstructed humans, and cyberwarriors or cops pervade television, *anime, manga,* and film. And while certainly not all these cyborgs are heroes, the human-machine interface is boldly, often utopically, conceived, unlike what seems the greater tendency in Euro-America, where the *Frankenstein* tradition is still being replayed (with stories of rebuilt humans who turn on their creators or become otherwise monstrous, as in the popular movies *RoboCop* and *Terminator*). Indeed, even in the more recent cyberhit *The Matrix* (and its two sequels), there is a clear dichotomy—and antipathy—between humans and machines, in which the only hope for humanity comes from religiously encoded heroes (Trinity and "the chosen one," Neo) who are trying to break out of the virtual world (the Matrix) that, imprisoning and literally killing them, has been implanted in their heads by machines.

How different is the vision of the cyberborder in the Japanese postwar imaginary as fashioned in children's entertainment like the Rangers? The episode from the 1995–96 season of *Chōriki Sentai Ōrenjā* is illustrative. The symbolism of the story seems blatantly obvious. In this tale of overcoming adversity, all points along the way are hyperbolically overplayed: the earth is threatened by total destruction, the would-be rescuer dies in a replay of heroic self-sacrifice, and humanity is saved in the end by the hero's return from death to rekindle and merge with a master machine. The melodramatic story line is propelled by impotencies (power outage in Tokyo, broken-down robots, dead and endangered Rangers) that are overturned by a megaperformance (the joining together of mechanical, spiritual, and collective resources). Each element operates both metaphorically (machines stand for humans, human-machines stand for the nation) and metonymically (each robot and Ranger is a part of the cyberwhole). And in both these ways, the interdependence and interchangeability of machine and human are repeatedly expressed. Red Ranger/Red Puncher analogize each other: the man defies mortality as a machine would, and the machine is rekindled by human spirituality and determination. They also merge: physically the two look alike (both are red—the Ranger from a red uniform, and the robot from his red metallic overlay), move as a unit (Red Ranger, seated inside the robot and operating it, is literally a part of Red Puncher), and undergo death and rebirth together (ratcheting the symbolism up even further). In the end, the message is clear: humans are deficient on their own, machines need humanity to be good (unlike the enemy robot) as well as functional (like Red Puncher), and only when they work as coordinated teams—humans and machines, cyborg as tool and myth—is the viability of the world assured.

Transformation and the Aesthetics/Marketing of Detail

> Ōrenjā wa hitorizutsu betsubetsu no buki o motte irunda. Gonin no buki o gattaisaseru to sūpā hisatsubuki ni mo narundayo. Muteki no senshi da Ōrenjā!
>
> [Each O-Ranger has her/his own weapon. And, when the tools of these five people are joined together, one superweapon emerges. The O-Rangers are matchless warriors!]
>
> From a children's picture book of O-Rangers published by Kōdansha: *Chōriki Sentai Ōrenjā* 1995:3

The center of attention in *Go Renjā* as well as *sentai* and cognate genres involving the interface between machine and hero is the body and how it performs armed with powers, machinery, and collective consciousness. As Linda Williams has written about the "frenzy of the visible" in Western pornography (1989:56), the bodily zones most spectacularized (as in made into a spectacle) are those audiences most likely associate with holding secrets. To "see," then, is to "know": a desire both heightened and organized by technologies of visuality—the camera, cinema, video machines, television, virtual reality. In pornography these sites/sights are staged by sexuality: filming bodies in such a way as to make graphically visible what is usually hidden and private—certain flesh zones and interbodily acts that viewers find arousing. Arousal is what sells in this marketplace, and those scenes/sites that are most popular with consumers are called the "money shot." Showing the man's orgasm as it is visibly sprayed on some part of the woman's body (preferably her face) has been the standard, at least in straight porn, since the 1960s in the United States. Using both the Marxian and Freudian definitions of fetish, Williams argues that this "money shot" fetishizes what is valued—and what substitutes or compensates for its lack—both in the political and (heteronormative) sexual economies of American capitalism. Namely, this is performance: a yield in the way of productivity, phallicism, and wealth. Collapsed in this sign of a man's ejaculate—shooting out majestically and captured in its trajectory across space and onto the flesh of an other—is proof of viability, identity, worth. With this, a man believes he has solved the secret of what women want and how to satisfy them;[2] he also has proved himself to be a "man"—the incitement to arousal here which, in its combination of money and sexual pleasure in the money shot, also "perfectly embodies the profound alienation of contemporary consumer society" (Williams 1989:107).

Starting even before *Go Renjā*, there has been a fetishization of metallic bodies and their crossover to and from humans in kids' mass entertainment in Japan, from *anime* and live-action shows on television to *manga*, children's magazines, toy merchandise, and movies. Like the caress of the pornographic camera that lingers, lovingly, over the body parts and activities of greatest exposure, the gaze in these *mecha* fictions fixates on the details of the metallic-human interface. Staging these sites/sights is not sexuality, in this case, but warfare. Fighting is the raison d'être for possessing cyberbodies, and displaying these bodies (in all their intimate detail) is occasioned by a battle: in preparation for, wounded from, or in the very heat of attack.

This is true, for example, of *Tetsujin 28gō* (Iron Man No. 28), a comic created by Yokoyama Mitsuteru in 1956 that later was made into a television show (exported to the United States under the name *Gigantor*). The main character is a giant metal monster operated by a remote-control device usually in the hands of Kintō Shotarō, a young boy "private detective" who, in partnership with the machine, thwarts many evil plots by nasty humans. The main power of this *mecha*, not autonomous like Atomu nor as technologically advanced, was brute force, yet great energy was put into constructing, staging, and displaying his machinery. Yokoyama has said that three things influenced his creation: "One was the sight I saw when the war ended and I returned to [my home] Kobe from my rural evacuation site. Everything as far as I could see had been transformed into scorched earth and piles of rubble. . . . I was . . . stunned by the destructive power of war. Second was the V1 and V2 missiles that the German Nazis developed. I had heard that Hitler tried to use these as an ace in the hole to reverse his waning fortunes. The third influence was from the American movie *Frankenstein*" (quoted in Schodt 1988b:78).

In the story, Tetsujin 28gō was designed by the Japanese military during the war to be their "ace in the hole," but because all the previous models failed and the war came to an end, the machine became a civilian robot. *Tetsujin 28gō* triggered a fad in warrior robots, many of which were similarly fashioned as giants. A somewhat different style in *mecha* fetishism came from *Mazinger Z*, Nagai Gō's comic that started in 1969 (and later was animated for TV) featuring a young hero, Kōji Kabuto, who is the pilot of a hovercraft that docks in the head of a giant robot, serving as both its cockpit and its control center. Melding vehicle with robot and weaponry with cutting-edge technology, *Mazinger Z* also initiated a new style in robotic fashion: samurai chic (intermixed with an insect motif) of brightly colored surfaces, a knight's visor, and both wing and horn protrusions on its helmet. Plots were standard: battles between Mazinger Z and various monsters, including robots. But it is his fusion of hero and machine that defines the genius and legacy of Nagai Gō in the *mecha* imaginary of postwar Japan, as Frederik Schodt notes: "The man-robot symbiosis that Mazinger Z symbolized helped solve an old problem in robot fiction—the problem of personifying the machine while still preserving its mechanical identity. When the robot became, like a car, a machine that could be jumped in and driven, it had a powerful appeal to young boys" (1988b:83).

One might recall here the movie *Gojira* and how Tsuburaya Eiji's suitmation special effect (having an actor play the monster dressed up in a rubber suit) was also regarded, particularly in Japan, where this technique was praised, as a "humanization" of, in this case, a monster. While this is a different order of "merging" than the robot-human symbiosis in *Mazinger Z*, it does involve a blending or crossing of bodily borders (human-machine-beast-vehicle) that mass storytelling in other countries (namely Hollywood) has been far less keen or quick to engage. How precisely bodies—of cyberwarriors as much as warrior robots—are constructed is obsessively deconstructed in what I call the "money shot" in an array of children's entertainment in Japan's postwar period. Movement is a central component here (from one state of being to another), as are power and performance upgrading to a higher level, that is, graphically and visually, marked by precise changes to the physical constitution. This is the logic of transformation (*henshin*), a central feature in the superhero myth and one excessively played up in *mecha* kids' culture.[3] Again, the trigger is always battle; alien attack triggers morphing, which itself is the trigger for the intricate and intimate display of mechanized bodies. While these stories foreground destruction, then, this theme is coupled with, and is the condition for, the staging of construction—how machines are built and humans transform into superheroic cyborgs.

In the plethora of books and magazines that publishers put out to accompany (and capitalize on) children's shows, the superheroes' special powers (*chikara*) are presented as "bodily secrets" (*karada no himitsu*) that are endlessly sketched, diagrammed, and displayed.[4] For example, this is the case for a book, published by Shōgakukan in its "television picture book" series, on *Kamen Raidā Burakku* (Masked Rider Black), a live-action show that debuted in 1971 on TBS. Based on the *manga* series by Ishimori Shōtaro, it features a teenage boy who, killed in a motorcycle accident, is reconstructed as a cyborg. (As is typical of popular shows, *Kamen Raidā* ran for many seasons, and was even reprised in 2000, by continually morphing—changing costumes, weapons, vehicles, characters.) After being introduced as a "new hero" and *kaizō senshi* (artificial warrior) who transforms from a boy named Minami Kotarō into a cybergrasshopper, he is shown in his *henshin pōzu* (morphing poses): eight stances culled from martial arts. At stage eight, a power belt emerges seamlessly from inside the boy's body, immediately encasing the hero in a *mecha* armature that fits his flesh as if it were a second skin. As his body fuses with this machinery, the boy morphs into a warrior whose *mecha* suit has both transformed and empowered him. The analogy with those superheroes of lean production, the Japanese corporate workers who don the same uniform at the start of every day, is noteworthy.

On the next foldout page is a huge picture of Kamen Raidā charting his "bodily secrets": superpowerful arms used in the "rider chop," the *henshin beruto* (morphing belt) that releases his energies, legs so strong he can jump ten times his height (called the "rider jump"), the squiggly mark on his chest that holds a mysterious secret, and eyes that can see even in pitch dark (figure 13). The descriptor "inside the body" refers here as much to the morphing belt as to legs, arms, and eyes, an indicator of how muddied the border between nature and cybernetics has become in the popular imaginary. On the following page, likewise, Kamen Raidā's main riding machine, the *batoru hōpa* (battle hopper), is a "supermachine," a *mecha* that can think, move, and live on its own. This talking motorcycle is simultaneously the warrior's sidekick and his wheels; it also has the look of a naturalistic grasshopper (green, with insect legs off the back and, in the front, antennae and red laser eyes like its master's). Here, too, all the supermachine's powers are carefully charted. The book concludes by detailing Kamen Raidā's fighting skills (the Raidā punch and kick), as well as outlining specifics about his enemies and his group of closest friends *(nakama)*. In other accounts, weaponry *(buki)* figures as well: tools like the "beam gun" and "bio blade," hybrids like everything else in this fantasy world. Graphing New Age powers (lasers, atomic rays) into old-style weaponry (swords, guns), cyber-*buki* also possess the ability to morph into totally different bodies (Kamen Raidā RX, for example, shifts into Robo Raidā and Bio Raidā).

The fascination with bodies and their reconstruction into fusions of insect/machine, human/tool, nature/technology proceeds along two axes in the genre of team warriors that began with *Go Renjā* in the 1970s. The first is transformation *(henshin)*, and the second is union *(gattai)*: assembling

Figure 13. The cyborgian "money shot": revealing the "bodily secrets" of a mecha-hero. (From a *Kamen Raidā* illustrated book for children; courtesy of Tōei Company Ltd.)

the individual bodies, robots, and weapons of the Rangers into superconglomerates. A similar logic is at work in both: power parts that detach and come together according to a calculus that can be charted, studied, and copied with toy goods at home. In a book featuring the "superpowerful team warriors" (*Chōriki Sentai Ōrenjā*), the subtitle is "five-parted weaponry." Shown first are the individual weapons of the Rangers: Red Ranger's "star

Figure 14. Joining arms: five weapons combine into one—the principle of *gattai*. (From a *Choriki Ōrenjā* illustrated book for children; courtesy of Tōei Company Ltd.)

riser" (supersharp knife), Green Ranger's "square crusher" (a pair of splicers), Blue Ranger's "delta tonfua" (a triangular knife), Yellow Ranger's "twin baton" (a pair of sticks), and Pink Ranger's "circular defenser" (a high-powered shield). How all five pieces join together to form a megafirearm—the *"bīgu ban burasutā"* (big baton blaster)—is laid out next (figure 14). The delta tonfua goes on top, one baton on either side, the splicers in back, the shield behind, and the sword underneath. On the last two pages, the team of five is grouped together, jointly holding the supermachine (figures 15 and 16). According to Akira, an eight-year-old boy I talked to about *Ōrenjā*, the intricacies of *gattai* are as exciting as those of morphing (*"Sugoi yo, ryōhō"*—They're both great!). As he showed me with his piles of Ranger merchandise, this is a play universe bursting with body parts whose grammar of empowerment and assemblage is as flexible as it is complex. Akira could recite all the different constellations of this Ranger series, as well as those of the two previous seasons. Though he delighted in staging battles with his toys, the thrill of attaching, shifting, and rearranging *mecha*/body parts seemed every bit as great. And, in his play, transformation differed little from combination.

Figure 15. Fusing forces: the team with its conglomerate tool. (From a *Masukuman* illustrated book for children; courtesy of Tōei Company Ltd.)

Figure 16. *Sūpa mashin* (supermachine): teaming machines and Rangers in the "live cougar." (From a *Chōsentai Raibuman* illustrated book for children; courtesy of Tōei Company Ltd.)

My own introduction to Japanese cybermorphers came in 1987–88, when I spent fifteen months in Japan with my family conducting research on Japanese motherhood and domesticity in Tokyo. My children were young, two and five, and my older son attended a Buddhist nursery school. Every Sunday morning my boys were parked in front of the television set watching the weekly slew of kids' shows that included two favorites, *Metaldar* (a red-suited morpher with a dog) and *Kamen Raidā Burakku*. The shows fascinated them, particularly my younger son, who developed a passion for superheroes and action figures that lasted more than ten years. At this age, he would race around the apartment in his Kamen Raidā helmet and power belt, slashing imaginary beasts with his trusty play sword. Over time, though, I noticed a far more subtle and sophisticated aesthetic sensibility at work. Adam would spend hours with action figures whose every stylistic detail he studied and knew: which weapons and musculature went with which figures, and how different versions were distinctly fashioned (by color, texture, costume, bulk, face, hair). While this particular sensitivity may not have come from the time he spent in Japan, a distinctive feature of Japanese toys is attentiveness to bodily detail.[5] This is a signature of transformers, for example, which were a breakthrough hit of Japanese toys in the U.S. marketplace (though made-in-Japan tin jeeps and robots were popular after the war and through the 1950s, they always bore the cachet of cheap trinkets and were not nearly as trendsetting as the transformers). Launched jointly by Takara and by Hasbro-Bradley in the States in 1983 (and, in a similar though less popular toy line, as Gobots by Bandai and the American company Tonka in 1984), transformers were robots that morphed into vehicles. The idea of transformation, and its successful execution in a toy-body issuing multiple forms, parts, and changes, made transformers a kid craze (and produced more than $100 million in sales for Hasbro in the first year alone).

The aesthetics of a profusion of small parts intricately arranged was something I observed frequently in the everyday environment of Japanese kids. For *oyatsu* (afternoon snacks, doled out daily at three), the stores sell a mesmerizing array of treats, packaged appealingly in tiny boxes that include not only a food substance (cookies, candies, crackers) but often a small toy. These *oyatsu* are like miniature Happy Meals, so affordable that kids can enjoy piles of them every day. Similarly, the monthly magazines popular with Japanese children come with a multistepped do-it-yourself toy: a big baton blaster, for example, with materials and instructions attached at the back. Assembly is complicated (as many as a hundred steps that must be studiously followed—a task that I, rather than my kids, routinely performed), but the end result is ingenious and cute. In the less commercialized realm of nursery school, there were lunch boxes *(obentō)* to be made every day; these boxes, with movable borders or supplementary containers, are an effusion of bite-sized foods.[6]

Taken to the realm of kid toys, these aesthetics materialize in a parade of pieces with subtle differences, distinctions, and articulations. The *Ranger* series (and *mecha* shows like them) generate an endless quantity of stuff (figures, weapons, vehicles, robots), and each of these individual objects is further marked by its own set of (sometimes movable and detachable) parts. The kids I know who have been fans of such television fare, both in Japan and in the States (and going in between, as Adam did), almost invariably are fetishists of the consumer toys, craving as many goods as they can afford and also the latest editions. In Japan, the government imposes even fewer restrictions on commercial advertising for children than does the United States. Kids' consumer appetites are whetted by the fact that the *Rangers* TV show, for example, splices in ads for toy goods using the Ranger actors in action scenarios that are barely distinguishable from the program itself. (In the episode of *Ōrenjā* synopsized at the beginning of this chapter, virtually all the commercials—before, during, and after the show—are for products branded by Ōrenjā. These include Ōrenjā candy, a children's magazine featuring Ōrenjā, an amusement park with a live Ōrenjā show, and two sets of toy merchandise by Bandai: the "transformer series" with weapons and the Ōrenjā robot. The Bandai ads are staged as action scenes using the very same actors in the television show using the very same equipment, making the transition from program to commercial virtually seamless.) Further, in media like monthly children's magazines, stories and comics are jump-cut with ads for commercial goods in a manner that effectively grafts the two together.

Consumerism, even that fashioned for young kids, hardly started with the broadcast of *Go Renjā* in 1973, but the 1970s marked the rapid development of a consumer culture in Japan that has increasingly targeted youth. Thus, alongside the principle of flexible production that shows up in the teamwork and cyberheroism of the Rangers, a new consumerism replete with an aesthetics of detail, newness, and high-tech design was fostered as well. These are the same characteristics—miniaturization, attention to detail, and stylish design—that, thanks to companies like Sony, Matsushita, and Nissan, established Japan's postwar reputation as a producer of high-quality consumer technology. On the home front, desire for such qualities in material goods was cultivated as well, of course. And in entertainments like *Go Renjā*, this desire was mapped at the level of the body: bodies whose secrets and powers translate into a host of commodifiable parts that are eagerly consumed by kids—almost as if they would like to bodily incorporate

Figure 17. Toy consumption/fantasy transformation: kids become superheroes in *Kamen Raidā* toy merchandise. (Courtesy of Tōei Company Ltd.)

these goods themselves and, by doing so, thereby acquire the powers they promise (figure 17).

Instilling this appetite in children and (re)producing them as avid and future consumers was driven directly by toy companies like Bandai that, by taking over the sponsorship of children's television shows starting in the 1970s, crafted "money shots" on the screen that would translate, directly and repeatedly, to the desire to buy (their brand of) toy merchandise. Throughout the 1950s and '60s, manufacturers of candy or electric goods were the main sponsors of kids' shows (Ezaki Guriko sponsored *Tetsujin 28gō*, for example), and, given the nature of their products, goods unrelated to the program itself (fans, radios, chocolates) filled the commercials. Toys derived from popular television (and *manga*) characters were being manufactured, of course, but toy companies (even those exporting to the United States) were mainly small and medium-sized ones that lacked the means to advertise much, if at all, on T.V. Further, only rarely did a single company have exclusive rights to a media character; in the case of *Tetsuwan Atomu*, for example, about twenty companies were involved in merchandising, which also led to a proliferation of toy incarnations.

All this changed in 1973 with Tōei Studio's *Go Renjā* when Bandai became the main sponsor and exclusive merchandiser. *Go Renjā* was Bandai's breakthrough hit, in fact, spiraling it into the ranks of one of the largest Japanese toy companies (and it is the largest today). Expanding the hero to a team of five, equipping them with an arsenal of multipart equipment, and reinventing the crew, along with its costumes and arms, each season were strategies intended to maximize the Ranger toy merchandise Bandai could market and also the desire, in kids, to acquire more and more of it (Hori 1996). This was also the start of the *gattai robotto* (joined robots) fad that, heating up in the middle to late 1970s, fueled many television shows (*Getta Robotto* in 1974, *Chōkiji Kon Batora-re* in 1976, and *Sūpa Sentai Shirizu* with its *kyōdai robotto*, giant robots, starting in 1979), accompanied by toys known for their complexity of detail (and high price).[7] And, as Hori Takahiro has shown, there is a direct correlation between the degree and thematic of battle in a children's television show and sponsorship by a toy company. Using battle and transformation scenes as the trigger for toy merchandise—a proliferation of bodies, body parts, costumes, weapons, and vehicular *mecha*—toy companies promote this in programming and are less likely to sponsor those programs without battle scenes (Hori 1996:122–24).

But there is more to this morphing dreamworld. As a pop phenomenon that captured not only the United States but also the global channels of top-ranked television show and worldwide kids' fad for at least three years in the 1990s, its origin from a place other than the United States was historically unprecedented. Unlike what has defined the pathway for global kids' culture and entertainment in the postwar period before the 1990s—emanating from cultural industries centered in Euro-America and particularly the United States—*Power Rangers* comes from a new place (Japan) that decenters (and perhaps recenters) the production of global kids' culture. This, too, is an expression of a newly flexible world in which old mappings of identity and power are rearranged—or maybe not. For though the show originated in Japan, it was radically transformed for broadcast in the States. Once again, as with *Gojira*, the Americanized version rather than the Japanese original became the global kids' hit *Mighty Morphin Power Rangers*. And neither Japan nor Tōei Studios, the producers of the television series that started in 1975 and is still running today, have been given much, if any, credit in the globalization of *Power Rangers*.

Rangers Do the States

It seems ironic that at a time when Congress has mandated more educational programming on television, children are going wild for a show filled with fight scenes and exploding monsters.

Bellafante 1993:88

During a visit to Japan in 1985, Haim Saban, then a newcomer to Hollywood seeking his fortune in entertainment, viewed an episode of *Jyū Renjā*, the 1985–86 season of Rangers with a dinosaur thematic. Struck by the dynamism of the show and the kinetic blend of morphing, live action, and cyberspirituality, Saban bought the rights from Tōei Studios the following year to air the show in the United States. What appealed to Saban as refreshing and new, however, was greeted by the networks he approached with flat-out rejection. Regarded as "silly," "cheesy," and "immature," *Jyū Renjā* seemed too "foreign" to these executives, who predicted that American kids would not like its aesthetics. Compared with the Hollywood fare dominating the channels of children's mass culture in the United States, *Jyū Renjā* was decidedly different. It was reminiscent, to some, of *Godzilla:* fantasy warfare staged to excess by special effects and monsters played by live actors. The tastes of American children were more sophisticated than this, it was thought, and so networks refused to sign *Jyū Renjā* on despite Saban's persistence for eight years. It was only by finding an executive who was seeking something more "outrageous" than typical kid-show fare (Lippman 1997:A13) that Saban scored a deal. A fan herself of Japanese kids' shows as a child, Margaret Loesch of Fox Kids' network contracted *Jyū Renjā* to air in the States.[8] She decided, however, to change the name and reshoot all the scenes of premorphed Rangers with American actors. In its reconstructed form, *Mighty Morphin Power Rangers* was launched by Saban and Loesch in August 1993. Within five weeks, the show became the top-rated children's program on U.S. TV, generating unprecedented revenues for both Fox Network and Saban Entertainment (which subsequently merged, forming

Fox Kids Worldwide Inc. in 1996) and ballooning into a mega-fad with a show that is still airing a decade later.

Prior to the success of (what started at least as) *Jyū Renjā,* other Japanese media products had enjoyed a degree of exposure and fame in the postwar entertainment market of the United States. The televisual cartoon *Astro Boy* was popular enough in the 1960s to run for two seasons and generate a series of comic books. Waves of children's shows followed, including *Speed Racer, Voltron, Robotech, Star Blazers,* and *The Starvengers,* though syndication was never nationwide, limited instead to certain geographic regions such as Hawai`i and the West Coast. Transformer toys were big hits in the 1980s when, at the end of the decade, Japanese video games started selling as well. And *Godzilla,* of course, broke into the ranks of mainstream pop culture. Along with its offspring (*Ghidrah, The Three-Headed Monster, Rodan, Godzilla vs. Megalon,* etc.), Godzilla lasted until 1975, with a new wave in the 1980s and '90s, a final six-film burst starting in 1999 (Tsutsui 2004), and Hollywood's crafting of its own version with TriStar's *Godzilla* in 1998.

Overall, however, Japan figured little in the landscape of American mass culture prior to the 1990s. In part, this state of affairs reflects the hegemony of Euro-American and particularly U.S. cultural industries in both shaping global (pop) culture and dominating U.S. entertainment. Hollywood has been hostile to imports, and foreignness has largely been, and been seen as, an impediment to mass popularization in the United States. Yet Japan's prestige as an economic superpower on the global stage has been in place since the late 1970s. Despite the strength of its economy and its status as the producer of quality consumer technologies (automobiles, electronics) that are popular and travel widely around the world, however, Japan's cultural capital (in ideas, images, the imagination) has lagged behind. In the realm of global culture, that is, Japan has been a minor player. What has accounted for this gap between the economic and cultural currency held by Japan in the global marketplace in the last quarter of the twentieth century? And what significance is there to the fact that, for Americans, Japan's biggest influence on the field of the imagination was embodied for decades in a radioactive lizard that signified, for many, the country's subordinate status as a second-rate power?

It was precisely to dislodge this association between made-in-Japan and chintzy, cheap goods, in fact, that companies like Sony purposely designed and promoted their products in the export marketplace (primarily the United States and Europe when Sony started in the 1950s) as global *(sekai no)* rather than Japanese *(nihonteki).* Using muted colors (gray), a modernist style, and a global-sounding company name, Sony adopted what became a standard policy in postwar Japan of "denationalizing" *(mukokuseki)* its product—or, as the creator of the Walkman, Kuroki Yasuo, puts it, of making goods that "don't promote a particular Japanese look" (1995:12). Iwabuchi Kōichi calls this the "odorless" quality of Japanese exports (2002:33): deodorizing out the "smell" of Japaneseness was considered strategic both for those markets where their Japanese origin connoted inferior quality (Euro-America) and for those where it triggered memories of wartime brutalization (the Philippines, South Korea, and China, for example). Until recently, in fact, selling Japanese products worldwide has worked better in the domain of culturally neutral products: the "hard technology" of machines (televisions, VCRs, tape recorders) rather than the "soft technology" of what is transmitted on those machines (movies, television shows, music, idols).

This is true of the Walkman, Kuroki laments. As a vehicle of pop culture, the machine has had massive success and influence around the world, yet global users are rarely listening to Japanese music, a taste that remains primarily local (Kuroki 1995:13). One could also argue, however, that the Walkman blends, rather than conforms to, a rigid culture-versus-technology dichotomy. Many, including Kuroki himself, acknowledge the worldwide presence of a "Walkman culture," and in the way it reorganizes space/body/machine borders (thereby making reception a much more personal/mobile/customized operation), the Walkman could be called a "cultural technology" and Japan's global influence in this domain, tremendous.[9] A crossing of borders is also at work in the *mecha* fantasies of the Ranger series, as we have amply seen. But bearing in mind the distinction Donna Haraway (1991) has made about cyborgs—they are tools used to make and enhance existence, and also myths by which we give imaginary shape to life in a technological age—we could also say that the traffic in Japanese tools (including cyborgian ones that remap the interface between human and machine) has flowed far more smoothly than that of its myths (including cybermyths) in the global marketplace. Indeed, as Iwabuchi (2002) and others have demonstrated, media products have, until recently, been particularly hard for Japan to market outside its own local borders.

Haim Saban had a singular goal in promoting the broadcast of *Jyū Renjā* on American TV. By reducing costs in producing children's programming, he hoped to build a global entertainment empire that would eventually outdistance Disney (Freeman 1993). The footage he had purchased from Tōei was cheap, and, indeed, production expenses were low for *Mighty Morphin Power Rangers*. By splicing together preshot segments with newly shot scenes from the United States, Saban reputedly spent only $150,000 per episode, compared with about three times that much for big studio productions.[10] Once *Mighty Morphin Power Rangers* became a hit—only five weeks after first airing, it was the highest-ranked kids' show in Fox Network's history and quickly turned into a craze—Saban himself morphed into a major power broker in the field of kids' entertainment. His company, Saban Entertainment, which merged with Fox Kids Network in 1996 (forming Fox Kids Worldwide Inc., which later joined with Murdoch's News Corporation and was sold by Saban to the Walt Disney Co. in 2001), was producing 21 percent of all children's TV programming by 1997 (outranking Disney's 18 percent share and second only to Warner Brothers' 26 percent) and was predicted to make $80 million in licensing fees alone for *Power Rangers*. Saban, the person who greatly facilitated the opening up of U.S. kids' entertainment to the presence of Japanese cultural goods, was motivated by strictly economic reasons. In an era when industrial countries's production was increasingly relocating overseas, Saban treated Japan—itself an industrial power with a healthier economy than that of the United States in the 1980s—as an "outsourcer" in the field of kids' culture. In doing so, he viewed the world, including Japan, in terms not of bounded cultures but of "one big boundaryless marketplace": "We have this picture puzzle of various countries around the world, with each being able to generate a certain amount of money for certain products. And if we can make sense out of production by mixing Korean and Luxembourgish investments that would cover the production costs, then the rest of the world is open for sales" (Saban quoted in Heffley 1993:1).

Interests were different, it should be noted, for those brokering the sale of *Jyū Renjā* on the side of Tōei Studios. Watanabe Yoshinori, a director at Tōei for years, had long held the hope of "penetrating the U.S. market with Japanese popular heroes." Frustrated with Hollywood's xenophobia and its resistance to imports (the United States "thinks it's the best country" and will not "recognize foreign productions"), he wanted to familiarize American audiences with the strengths of Japanese creators by airing *Jyū Renjā* in the States. His dream was that "American kids would get wrapped up in a Japanese type of hero" and, with this base, "made-in-Japan heroes would get established around the world" (Ōshita 1995:297). Disappointingly, for Watanabe at least, the Rangers became more identified as American than Japanese heroes when *Jyū Renjā* morphed into *Power Rangers*. This was Saban's call, however, for in contracting with Tōei, he acquired exclusive rights to all licensing of the product outside Japan and scattered Asia Pacific markets. And Saban was motivated only by what would sell, first to American kids, and then to "global kids" in the international marketplace. For him, what made sense was keeping what he found different and fresh in the show, but delinking this from its Japanese origins and repackaging the Rangers as American. In his mind, this made *Power Rangers* a type of cultural hybrid: a "bridge," as he called it (Cody 1994:1), between the two countries. But its Japanese character, for the most part, fell out. The remade *Power Rangers*, with no references to the original in the credits and promotion, has become, in the words of a Saban executive I interviewed in 1997, "an American classic."

Hitting U.S. airwaves in August 1993, *Mighty Morphin Power Rangers* featured five seemingly normal American teenagers who morph into superheroes to fight alien enemies and restore peace to their California town. Targeted at three- to eleven-year-olds (somewhat older than its target of two- to seven-year-olds in Japan), the program deviated from the norm in children's entertainment by being live action instead of animated cartoon and showcasing a new brand of superheroism. The heroes worked as a team, used martial arts in their transformation, fought hordes of intergalactic foes, and were superheroically wired by an admixture of dinosaur spirits and high-tech machines. Most adults found the effect "cheesy" at best, yet kids were enraptured, catapulting *Power Rangers* to the highest-ranked kids' show almost immediately and cascading into a multidimensioned fad of mythic proportions soon afterward. Reproduced as videotapes, Fruit of the Loom underwear, McDonald's Happy Meal toys, a live show, and Kraft food products, the "Morphinomenon" was well on its way by Christmas, when shortages of the Bandai-produced toys led to huge scrambles at Toys"R"Us and IOUs brought by Santa for goods that would not arrive for weeks. Fiscal third-quarter sales of *Power Ranger* merchandise in the States totaled almost $19 million, six times what had been originally expected. The news channels were filled with stories of fad frenzies, such as the record thirty-five thousand people who swarmed Universal Studios for an appearance of the Rangers, causing a traffic snarl for ten miles (Meyer, Tsiantar, and Schneideb 1994).

The reason for its explosive success, according to an executive at Bandai, was that *Power Rangers* was excitingly new and different and also that it fed into trends—dinosaurs, transformation, martial arts—that were already popular on the American kid scene in the early 1990s (Biederman 1994). The totemic motif of dinosaurs in *Jyū Renjā* (the sixteenth in the Ranger series in Japan) was inspired by the Hollywood movie *Jurassic Park*. In the States, *Jurassic Park* came out in 1993 and generated a dinosaur blitz spread by everything from a McDonald's Happy Meal campaign to Barney, the cuddly purple *Tyrannosaurus* that has been a toddler craze for more than a decade now. Transformation, the keyword of *Power Rangers,* was a motif already gaining popularity in the mythic stories of American mass culture in the 1990s. On the Hollywood screen, there was a boom in recycled superheroes brought back from the comic books and action television shows of American yesteryear (*Superman* alone came out in a series of four movies between 1978 and 1987). Transformer toys were also a fad in the 1980s, helping to create a more generic interest in morphing that characterizes a number of later popular television shows (*Xena, the Warrior Princess* and *Buffy, the Vampire Slayer* are only two). Martial arts was a third trope whose popular currency *Power Rangers* both tapped into and capped further. By the 1990s, it was a sport that had already been mainstreamed in the lives and imaginations of American kids. Karate dojos are now commonplace in strip malls across middle America, where children call their teachers sensei and respond to commands dictated in Japanese. Kung fu has also become a staple on the Hollywood screen. It is the signature of Asian actors like Bruce Lee, Jackie Chan, and Jet Li, picked up by such American headliners as Keanu Reeves in the cyber sci-fi film *The Matrix* and even the gal trio in *Charlie's Angels* (a TV show in the 1970s, recently remade as blockbuster movies).

As can be seen, even before *Power Rangers* settled into the fabric of American kid culture, the latter was already textured by a mélange of elements, some influenced from abroad, including Japan. While such hybridity is certainly a sign of the times, marking the spread between geopolitical borders of various entities, including the fantasies and fictions of pop culture, there was hard-core resistance by American networks to importing this made-in-Japan *mecha* myth. This may have been motivated, in part, by what was a national rash of Japan bashing (as against Sony's buyout of Columbia Studios and Matsushita of Universal in 1989) brought on by an economic slump in the States just when Japan was experiencing the height of its Bubble economy. Overtly, however, rejection of the show was based largely on aesthetic grounds—that it diverged from Hollywood conventions of mythmaking (including standards against violence in kids' fare) and was too "hokey," "cheesy," and "low tech" (Heffley 1993:1). When *Power Rangers* was picked up by Fox Network, then, "localizing" the show to make it adhere more to American standards was considered imperative. The first change was replacing the Japanese actors with Americans for all the scenes shot with Rangers in flesh mode (out of their morphing costumes). Based on the assumption that American viewers would not identify with Asian faces, the new footage also moved the setting from Tokyo to California and de-

picted "normal American kids who shoot baskets, mall-hop and do aero-
bics—when they are not fighting space aliens." The result was a "campier,
California version of the Power Rangers" (Cody 1994:1). The show merged
those elements Saban wanted to keep from the original (good kids trained in
martial arts who work hard together as a team) with additions for the American remake (a multiethnic, gender-blended team with the violence toned
down and the moral message heightened). In his own mind, Saban made
Power Rangers something of a politically correct enterprise in that the team
had more girls (two rather than the one in *Jyū Renjā*), was ethnically diverse (a Latino, a black, an Asian American, and two whites in the first
team), and fought alien invaders as a cooperative collective.

For the toy marketers of *Power Rangers*, the show's success in the States
signaled their entry into the global marketplace (figure 18). Bandai, now
the largest Japanese toy company, has licensed the Ranger property since
the show first aired in 1975 and, as Bandai America, won the license to the
Power Rangers line when American toy companies were initially uninterested. Until its windfall with *Power Rangers*, Bandai's business built from
reproducing movie and television characters into toys had never succeeded
outside the domestic market. Its characters, such as Urutoraman (Ultraman), with his metallic body and laser-beam eyes, were simply "too foreign" for Americans, according to Yamashina Makoto, Bandai's president
(Cody 1994:1). An executive at Bandai America agrees, saying that Japanese
characters needed to be adjusted to the tastes and "psyche" of American kids
before they could be sold in the United States (Peter Dang quoted in Cody
1994: 1). This meant giving American faces and bodies to the unmasked
Rangers and giving more emphasis to the female characters as well as the
everyday lives of the Rangers as "normal teens." In Bandai's company di-
rective for 1997, such localization strategies are referred to as "globalization" ("creating major attractions which transcend national boundaries";
Bandai Kabushikigaisha 1997:6). This is one of the two pillars of corporate
vision (the other is "diversification," meaning commodifying characters beyond mere toys, including "items such as clothing, food products, and other
everyday goods"; 5). If, in the process of glocalization (localizing global
products—for example, McDonald's adding beer to its menu in France and
spicy chicken in China), character merchandise that started off as Japanese is
(re)identified as something else, this does not upset the company at all, I was
told by executives in Tokyo during an interview in 1996. Why should we
care if we are making profits around the world? Blending different cultural
codes is part and parcel of a global marketing strategy, according to these
Bandai officials. And even if the brand goes from being Japanese to Ameri-

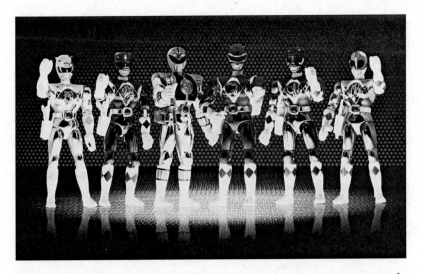

Figure 18. Ranger toys for the United States by Bandai America. (Courtesy of Bandai America Incorporated.)

can, this alteration reflects the flexibility of product marketing in a world marked by global capitalism.

Bandai is on the same page as Saban in its marketing policies. And kids, both in the United States and around the world, have delighted in a show that mixes morphing, monsters, and martial arts and juxtaposes stylized action scenes (shot in Japan) with the everyday dramas of Californian teens (shot in Hollywood). "I think it's cool the way kids transform and fight. And I like the monsters; they're weird but interesting, like the recent kangaroo whatchamacallit beast" (an eight-year-old American girl speaking of the 2003 season *Power Rangers Ninja Storm*). Indeed, by 1995, *Power Rangers* was airing in more than fifty countries (today it is fifty-three) and remained the top-ranked children's television show around the world for three years and, in the United States, through 1995 (in two categories, boys ages two to eleven and overall kids ages two to eleven). When its popularity began fading in 1996 and Saban called a meeting with his top five licensees to decide whether to discontinue it, he decided to invest even more resources into getting "people to believe in it again" because toy sales were still so strong.[11] Thus, as in Japan, the Rangers have been driven both by and for toy marketing. And the investment has paid off; Power Rangers toys were declared the top-ranking "male action toy brand" for both the year 2000 and the decade of the 1990s by the NPD Group Inc (the toy industry's sales-tracking organization), and the television show was proclaimed the "most popular kids' show of the 1990s" by Nielsen Galaxy Explorer. In the process, Saban, who refers to himself as a "cartoon schlepper," has purchased Fox Family, become chairman and CEO of Fox Family Worldwide Inc., and is considered one of the wealthiest and most powerful brokers of kids' entertainment in Hollywood (and the world) today. Bandai (and Bandai America) also has supersized its operation and reputation in a way that would have never been possible without this crossover breakthrough into the mainstream of American pop culture/kids' marketplace.

Mighty Morphin Toyota:
Lean Production Conquers America

> Don't expect to get it. *Power Rangers* is choppy, video-game-paced fare that has the feel of a cheap Japanese monster movie circa 1956. The premise: five teenagers (three boys and two girls) are transmogrified mid-episode into spandex-clad superheroes who battle the evil forces of Rita Repulsa, an intergalactic witch. Through a mix of kung-fu acrobatics, pummeling and pouncing, the Rangers manage to defeat whatever band of clunky, plastic robot-cretins Rita enjoins to cause trouble.
>
> Bellafante 1993:88

Interestingly, what has drawn American kids to *Power Rangers*—the frenetic pace, stitching together of disparate elements, and morphing oscillations between teenage everydayness and fantasy cyberwarriorship—is precisely what adults (particularly when the show first started in the mid-1990s) have found to be bewildering and problematic.[12] A review in *Parents' Magazine*, for example, called its popularity "inexplicable," saying that *Power Rangers* "grafts stories about teen-age do-gooders onto campy Japanese kung-fu fighting footage" (McCormick 1995:231). According to another review, "*Power Rangers* is choppy, video-game-paced fare that has the feel of a cheap Japanese monster movie circa 1956" (Bellafante 1993:88). In *Newsweek*'s account, "Adults are hard pressed to explain the Rangers' appeal. Certainly the plotline is cheesy at best." Similarly, for a special (in December 1994) on the ABC show *20/20*, John Stossel reported: "Why it's so popular isn't clear. From an adult perspective, it's an astonishingly stupid show. Five teens from the suburbs transform themselves—'morph' they call it—into superheroes in Spandex so they can fight Godzilla-like monsters. . . . This is cheap production . . . all the fight scenes are done in Japan. American teens are added later for the American audiences" (December 16, 1994).

The mixing of cultural codes on the show grated on the nerves and sensibilities of American adults. Yet by 1993—the year of *Power Rangers'* debut in the States—Japanese influence in other spheres of American life, most notably industrial production and high-tech consumer goods, was already well established. This was particularly true of what has been widely identified as Japan's model of (lean/flexible) production that had become increasingly assimilated into the workplace and consumer tastes of million of Americans. In car trends, leaner Japanese makes were replacing gasguzzling American behemoths following the oil shock of 1973. And on the factory floor, Toyotism—just-in-time, small-batch production—was overtaking Fordism in the wake of debilitating developments in the U.S. economy, and American industry, starting in the 1960s. The American car industry had been particularly hard hit by massive shutdowns, layoffs, and a declining market (both domestically and internationally) for American-made cars. Imports from Europe and Japan rose rapidly in the 1970s (desirable for their lower cost, higher fuel efficiency, and quality), triggering radical shifts in car design as well as automobile production in the home of Ford(ism).

Innovation came, most notably, from Japan. Japanese methods of flexible, lean production were widely adopted in the U.S. car industry along with what some call a Japanese management style, or "Toyota culture." In some cases, Japanese companies like Nissan and Toyota physically took over failed car plants, becoming, as a number of studies labeled them, "Japanese transplants" on American soil, as in Terry Besser's sociological study entitled *Team Toyota: Transplanting the Toyota Culture to the Camry Plant in Kentucky* (1996). The interbreeding of two distinct production styles and work cultures in car plants across middle America (Ohio, Kentucky, California) was heavily reported in the mass media. It also filtered into pop culture; in the Hollywood movie *Gung Ho* (1988), for example, the story of the Japanese buyout of a shut-down car plant in Pennsylvania was played comedically as the clash of two cultures by Michael Keaton and Watanabe Ken. Driven by the tension of cultural difference, the plotline, in this case, proceeds to a successful resolution; the different strands of work culture are sutured together to produce a functional hybrid—a U.S.-Japanese car plant.

Needless to say, *Mighty Morphin Power Rangers* is a hybrid as well. It literally stitches together two productions—one by Tōei in Japan and the other by Fox Network in the States—each engineered by different production crews, standards, and conventions. From this fact alone, we can see the signs of a postmodern aesthetics: one that, contrasted with the relative stability of Fordist modernity, celebrates difference, ephemerality, spectacle,

Figure 19. "Future-primitive" aesthetic: a vehicular robot as lion. (From a *Chōsentai Raibuman* illustrated book for children; courtesy of Tōei Company Ltd.)

fashion, and the commodification of cultural forms (Harvey 1989). As Fredric Jameson (1984) characterizes the cultural logic of late capitalism, postmodernism revels in a heterogeneity of styles that crossbreeds historicities, cultures, and artifacts in a pastiche aesthetic. Such a coding is evident in *Power Rangers,* with its jump-cutting between stylized action scenes shot in Japan and American teenage dramas filmed in Hollywood. But this aesthetic of fusing styles from different cultures, histories, or genres is also apparent in the Japanese original of the Ranger series. In *Jyū Renjā,* "normal" teenagers move between futuristic transformation and traditional martial arts, and their bodies bleed with prehistoric dinosaur spirits as well as New Age cybermachines.[13] Writing in the *Village Voice,* Erik Davis calls this "future-primitive" (figure 19), an aesthetic strikingly different from that upheld in Hollywood. "Unlike America's reigning ideology, which holds that 'good' effects—like *Terminator 2*'s morphing—are simulacra dependent on the latest technological developments, the Power Rangers present an old-fashioned tacky futurism that is sufficient unto itself" (1994:74). Davis traces the "future-primitive" to *Godzilla,* in which technology figures more prominently in the story itself—transforming a prehistoric beast into a beastly nuclear weapon—than in the high-tech film/television production upheld by Hollywood.

Like other reviewers, Davis is unsettled by what he treats as an alien aesthetic masquerading as American pop culture in *Power Rangers.* Most disturbing of all is the fear that these time-shifting Rangers may in turn transform the identities and consumer tastes of American kids: "But when they morph, the American team doesn't just don costumes, they mutate their core identities. The rough transition and lack of continuity between the Japanese and American footage is a sign of . . . the dreamlike and monstrous scrambling of cultural codes. Our Wonder Bread heroes are not just turning Japanese, they're becoming altered beings in a parallel aesthetic realm, with its own internal logic, myths, and ethics. And maybe their audience is somehow transforming too. . . . The tykes currently addicted to the show may end up becoming a mass market for more mature and vital Japanese popular shows now shrouded in hipster subculture—e.g., anime" (Davis 1994:73).

Besides violating the cultural codes of American aesthetics, there has also been the charge that *Power Rangers* is an excessively violent show that leads to heightened aggression in American kids. In fact, when the show was first becoming a global fad in 1993, a number of countries (Norway, Denmark, Canada, New Zealand) banned it after an incident in Norway in which a five-year-old girl was kicked to death by playmates supposedly mimicking a Ranger warrior stance. According to one U.S. study, *Power Rangers* accrues more acts of violence per show (two hundred per hour) than any children's programming to date in American broadcasting. The two educators who conducted the study, Diane Levin and Nancy Carlsson-Paige, also interviewed primary and nursery school teachers, 97 percent of whom voiced "at least one" concern about the effect *Power Rangers* was having on children in the classroom. As they concluded, what is disturbing about the show is not only its central trope of fighting to resolve problems but also the added, and sanctioned, "realism" this warfare has when the medium is live action, where, it is assumed, kids have a harder time distinguishing fantasy from reality than they would in a cartoon (Levin and Carlsson-Paige 1995:67, 69). As they and others, such as Sissela Bok (1998), have argued, shows like *Mighty Morphin Power Rangers* are promoting increased aggression and a desensitization to violence in American kids these days. Opposing this view, however, is another: that the show and the stylized rituals of play it promotes are also experienced as empowering to kids—a vehicle for confronting, and overcoming, challenges, struggles, and obstacles (whether they be personal or mythical, as the two are often coupled in the shows themselves).

The issue of media violence and its effect on children, in both their real lives and their imaginations, is a complicated one, particularly when dealing with cross-cultural sites.[14] (In Japan, for example, there is less public anxiety about media violence, and it is far more tolerated in venues targeted to kids, yet actual violence—as calculated by criminal acts of homicide, bodily injury, armed robbery, and theft—is vastly less common than in the States, where outcries against violent media have been far more pronounced.) This is an issue I return to in the discussion of *Pokémon,* a playscape that, despite its foregrounding of continual matches among the "pocket monsters"—in which the latter are stunned, blasted, poisoned, whiplashed, and smacked—has generated almost no concern about violence in the United States. To end the current discussion, though, I merely return to my earlier point about the conjoining of battle and body configuration in the *Rangers.* Fetishized here is the dissection of *mecha*/cyberheroes, whether the focus is on the makeup (as in the various weapons/accessories/spirits that constitute the makeup of characters) or breakdown (as in the way these characters repeatedly come undone when attacked) of the subject's parts—a distinction that itself becomes indistinguishable. Hence, an interest in the composition of cyborg bodies and their multiple parts (robots, armor, weapons, computers) bleeds into an interest in the decomposition (smashing, chopping, evisceration, death) that bodies undergo as a consequence of violent fighting. Thus, though coming at it from opposite ends, as it were, both the constructive and the destructive components of *mecha* superheroes are part and parcel of the same geometry: power as it fuses and defuses in bodies with shifting and exploding borders of identity.

This elaborate, interchangeable, and mobile multipartedness is what I see as the appeal of the fantasy; it is what has made the *Rangers* series such a long-lasting fixture in the terrain of postwar Japanese kids' culture and, more recently, such a global craze in the worldwide marketplace of cyber-infected, techno-mobilized, post-Fordist kids. Though *Power Rangers* can be read as a postmodern allegory, it is also a commercial property, and one designed to entertain and sell (to) children. From this perspective, what is decentered and diffuse in the *Rangers* also sells multiple goods: teams of heroes each with their own sets of powers and tools, all of which are seasonally replaced. As a Japanese mother bemoaned, every Christmas she buys her son the biggest and latest Ranger superrobot, which is invariably outdated by March, the start of the new season. Hideki was playing next to us, making battle and flying sounds with the *Ōrenjā chōriki gattai robo* (the super-power collateral robot on the *Ōrenjā* series). Immersed in his fantasy play, the child kept retrieving other equipment from a huge box: a dagger sword, a "king blaster," a Yellow Ranger.

Just as rich as the imaginative world Hideki entered was the abundance of material goods he acquired. A vice president at Bandai America articulated this principle as the cardinal axiom of his business: "The show is the fantasy, and the toy is the material realization of that fantasy for the child to play with on his own."[15] With Rangers, the fantasy is so constructed that it is materialized in a wealth of commodifiable bodies, tools, and "spirits" with a shelf life that is breathlessly short. The principles involved, then, are those of fetishistic consumption as well as flexible production, fulfilling Marx's insight about the constant (re)creation of capitalist desire whose satisfaction is forever deferred. In Benjamin's words, *Power Rangers* is an enchanted "fairy scene" in which commodities are sold as fantasies and myths. And transformation is the key to this postindustrialized dream: a mythic trope that serves the interests of capital and shapes the fantasies of kids at this moment of the twenty-first century.

5 Fierce Flesh

Sexy Schoolgirls in the Action Fantasy of *Sailor Moon*

"Fashion Action":
A Crossover in the Gendered Genres of Children's Shows

In 1994, one year after it had debuted as the top-ranking children's show on
U.S. television, *Mighty Morphin Power Rangers* sold $330 million of toy
merchandise for Bandai America—a spectacular success and major breakthrough into a market (U.S. kids' entertainment, a portal to global kid fads)
long resistant to Japanese properties. Eager to extend its reach in the United
States, Bandai quickly negotiated additional deals: Japanese kids' shows that,
if successful in crossing over to American television, would bring sales of
Bandai licensed merchandise along with them. In 1995, three such Bandai-
sponsored programs debuted on U.S. television: *Masked Rider* (based on
Kamen Raidā, the live-action cyberhero show discussed in chapter 4), *Drag-
onball Z* (a cartoon featuring an alien boy with spiky hair and superior
fighting abilities), and *Sailor Moon* (a cartoon and girls' version of *Power
Rangers* starring five normal teenage girls who morph into butt-kicking
hero-babes). Of the three, *Sailor Moon* carried the most risk but also the
most market potential, and for the very same reason: it targeted girls.
Whereas the other two shows followed the Saturday-morning TV standard
of action plots centering on male heroes, *Sailor Moon* broke this mold not
only with a girls' show but with one whose characters fight and look pretty
at the same time. The concept was considered a crossover in two senses: it
was a Japanese cartoon trying to make it in the United States, and it gender-
blended what tend to be distinct categories in U.S. kids' entertainment—action for boys and fashion/romance/friendship for girls.

Talking to a Mattel executive even before the show was launched in the

United States, I was told that this represented a new model of girl programming (with its carryover to doll merchandise) as "fashion action" (figure 20). Though risky as a new concept in the United States, *Sailor Moon* had already proved to be a big merchandising hit for Bandai back home, with dolls that were outselling *Rangers* action figures and overtaking what had been the leading fashion doll in Japan since the late 1960s, Takara's Riccachan. Thus, by marketing *Sailor Moon* in the United States, Bandai hoped to further "globalize" the reach and popularity of its merchandise by implanting the taste for its morphin fantasies beyond American/global boys (the main consumers of *Rangers* merchandise) in girls as well.

In Japan, *Sailor Moon* (which ran from 1992 to 1997) was not the first show to feature the "pretty soldiers" who characterize the fashion action genre ("Pretty Soldier, Sailor Moon" is the English translation of the Japanese title, *Bishōjo Senshi Sērā Mūn*). Since the 1960s, in fact, fierce but beautiful female warriors (females who are fighters, leaders, heroes, or pilots, and also sexy, cute, attractive, and leggy) have proliferated across *manga, anime,* and television shows. In this genre, generically referred to as *bishōjo hīrō* (beautiful girl heroes), action serves a role similar to that described for *mecha* superheroes in the last chapter. It moves the plot (via battles between good and bad forces to defeat or defend the earth, humanity, and friends) at the same time that it stages the intricate and intimate display of bodies: bodies whose secrets and intricacies become known, seen, and transformed in the course of warfare. Like cyberwarriors, girl heroes transform from a human into a transhuman state through a "morphin" ritual that reassembles their anatomy/circuitry into high-tech fighting machines.[1] In the case of *bishōjo hīrō*, however, the bodies—even as *mecha*—are overtly feminized in ways that could (and are) also read as sexual: skimpy costumes (short skirts, tight bodices, boots or heels) that show off flesh (standardly shaped as long legs, thin waist, rounded breasts). Unlike the Rangers, then, who don similar unisex uniforms when morphed, girl heroes tend to strip down in the course of empowerment, becoming more, rather than less, identified by their flesh.[2]

The girls' market for magazines, *manga,* and television shows has been strong and growing in postwar Japan (and girls' magazines existed in prewar times as well), generating trends such as that of the "beautiful girl heroes" that became even more faddish in the 1980s. Until *Sailor Moon*, however, none of these stories or heroes generated the type of mass circulation or profits of a television series like Tōei's *Rangers*. The latter remained a big moneymaker and an evergreen series (begun in 1975 and still running today) in large part because of the synergy of its operation. Managed by its

Figure 20. Fashion action: Sailor Moon as a fashionable action hero. (Courtesy of Tōei Animation.)

sponsor (the toy company Bandai), the *Rangers* is a multitiered production: a television series that changes characters and themes by season, with toy merchandise that feeds (and is fed by) the show, tie-up commodity lines, movies, videos, a live show at amusement parks, books, and children's magazines. Key here is the fusion of a media drama with toy goods (action figures, robots) that materialize and extend the fantasy. Since this marketing strategy had been so successful with boys, Bandai decided in the early 1990s to adapt it in a vehicle for girls, thereby expanding its consumer base from what had been hitherto mainly boys (as purchasers of *gattai* robots, action figures, and morphers).

Takeuchi Naoko was a young *manga* writer when Bandai executives saw her comic about a klutzy female superhero in the girls' monthly magazine *Nakayoshi*. Imagining this story could be turned into a *Ranger*-like drama for girls, the company contracted with Takeuchi to produce a full-blown comic series (to also be serialized in *Nakayoshi*) that would be released simultaneously as a cartoon on TV.[3] Structurally, the concept was intended to mimic that of the *Rangers:* a group of superheroes who morph from ordinary teenagers, fight alien enemies, and diversify by season (adding new characters, costumes, tools, powers). This was the "action" component, to be made more girl-friendly in a script penned by Takeuchi. Indeed, when *Sailor Moon* appeared in March 1992, it was applauded as a showcase about and for *shōjo* (young females). Increased attention was given here not only to fashion—with lead female characters who spend time on their appearance and are designed to look attractive—but also to making both the characters and the narrative more complex. The protagonists are still fighters who morph to wage war, but battles are overshadowed by the personal and interpersonal lives of the girls in a plotline that moves from a realm of ancient history, secret princesses, and passionate romances to the everyday activities of going to cram school, bickering, and trying to lose weight. The cartoon, broadcast by Tōei for five years, became a huge hit in Japan along with movie versions, videos, a live musical, and the comic, published in endless volumes as well as books and in *Nakayoshi* (which doubled circulation within two years). And, like the Rangers, it was seasonally retooled over five years—*Bishōjo Senshi Sērā Mūn* (1992–93), *Bishōjo Senshi Sērā Mūn-R* (1993–94), *Bishōjo Sērā Mūn-S* (1994–95), *Bishōjo Sērā Mūn-SuperS* (1994–95), and *Bishōjo Senshi Sērā Mūn-Sutāzu* (1996–97)—to keep child fans interested and primed to consume more goods.

As a story, *Sailor Moon* has as its key feature the transformation of five girls (later expanded to ten), each distinct in her own way (one is brainy, another is a "priestess" who lives in a temple, and the main character is a sleepyhead who prefers the arcade to studying), into the Sailor Scouts—celestial-empowered superheroes, each aligned to a separate planet (Sailor Moon, Sailor Mercury, Sailor Mars, Sailor Venus, Sailor Jupiter). In the first comic, now translated into English (by Stuart Levy's Mixx Company, which first brought the story out in its magazine), Tsukino Usagi, called Usagi-chan (Bunny) by her family and friends, receives a test back at school with the low grade—typical of her—of 30. Envious of a friend, whose score of 100 has earned her a shopping spree at a jewelry shop, Usagi decides to compensate by heading off to the arcade to play her favorite video game, *Sailor Moon V.* Musing on her deficits—she loves to eat, shop, and sleep and is bad at punctuality, self-discipline, and studying—Usagi first meets the new girl at school, Mizuno Eimi, who is everything Usagi is not: a genius, studious, and conscientious. Though everyone tells her to shun this brain for being a snob, Usagi—in what is her signature trait—shows kindness to Eimi and invites the lonely girl to the arcade, where, with her computer smarts, she becomes a champion of the *Sailor Moon V* game even though she has never played before. As Eimi runs off to her *juku*, she and Usagi agree to call each other by their first names, thereby starting a friendship that will ground the *Sailor Moon* story to follow. When a crisis occurs shortly thereafter at the *juku*, Usagi morphs into Sailor Moon (in her alter ego as "champion of justice"— the identity of which Usagi just learned the same morning from her moon-empowered talking cat, Luna) to save the day. Shortly thereafter she is assisted by Eimi, who discovers she is Sailor Mercury with superpowers as well.

The plotline that unfolds in subsequent comics and episodes of the cartoon is similarly grounded in the nitty-gritty of the human circumstances and relationships of five teenage girls (figure 21) who ritualistically transform into superheroes to save humans (and each other) from the destruction targeted at them by the Negaverse (a constellation of empowered aliens headed by Queen Beryl). As in *Power Rangers,* the heroes form a team (*nakama* in Japanese, "Scouts" in English) and work both collectively and individually to overcome the evils of a destructive foe. Similarly as well, the heroes double as humans and superpowers, and the transformation each undergoes is highly stylized, marked by a distinct costume and set of individual powers. In the case of Usagi (called Serena and Bunny in the English version), for example, morphing is triggered by the shout of "Moon Power Prism" (in the Japanese version it's the English word "makeup"), which, in a ritual lasting about thirty seconds and accompanied by morphing theme music in the cartoon, goes through the following steps (figure 22): Usagi's nails turn red, her lashes grow long, jewelry sprouts on her neck and ears, red baubles dot her pigtails, a tiara springs forth on her head, and the outfit

Figure 21. Girl morphers in their everyday mode: the Scouts doing homework. (Courtesy of Tōei Animation.)

she wears—a school (sailor) uniform—is first removed (showing the silhouette of a naked Usagi) and then reappears in a miniskirted, sexier version that shows off the cleavage of newly developed breasts.

It is in this guise that (now) Sailor Moon acquires her powers, which, like those of the other Scouts, assume the shape of weapons that are housed in the costume she wears: the tiara on her head becomes a flying Frisbee projectile, and the moon prism she holds in her hand serves as a magic wand. This combination of action hero and "good style" is the reason she is so popular, according to an eight-year-old Japanese girl I spoke to in 1995. This is also the reason given for her fandom among *ojisan-tachi* (older men). With her leggy, slender body, long flowing blond hair, and the miniskirted version of her outfit she acquires after morphing, *Sērā Mūn* is also read as a sex icon—one that feeds and is fed by a general trend in Japan toward the infantalization of female sex objects. The fact that Sailor Moon not only wears a sailor outfit but is also named for it is significant, given that this is the standard uniform worn by girls in middle and upper school in Japan, as well as the clothing sexualized on young females *(shōjo)* to project a nymphet effect. The uniformed schoolgirl is a dominant trope in pornography,

Figure 22. The "money shot," girl-style: the fleshy transformation of a female superhero as Sailor Moon activates her "moon cosmic power makeup." (Courtesy of Tōei Animation.)

comics, and sex culture in general in Japan, as witnessed by the new, frequently reported trend of *enjo kōsai*—the practice of junior and senior high school students engaging in "assisted dating" with *sararīman.* Employing the sailor-uniform motif, then, could be said to stimulate two desires among Japanese. One is to identify with the adolescent girl/hero, an identification (and fantasy) engaged in by girls and also apparently males (boys and men) in a recent *shōjo* fad where "young schoolgirl" carries the connotation of carefree consumer and dreamer. (More on this later.) The other desire is lust for the Sailor Scouts as sex objects, a desire expressed by male and female fans alike (there is a pronounced homoerotic flavor in the Japanese version, all of which was removed for the U.S. broadcast).

The Superhero as Schoolgirl and the *Shōjo* as "Material Girl"

What Fujimoto Yukari (an editor, commentator, and adult Japanese woman) first noticed about *Sailor Moon* was all the chokers the (morphed) Scouts wore on their necks. With these added to their school uniforms along with a bevy of other jewels and accessories—baubles, tiaras, big bows, brooches, heels or high boots—the effect is something out of the *Arabian Nights*. Finding this exciting but also somehow obscene *(inbi)*, Fujimoto notes how sexy the girls appear in the morphin scenes when, temporarily naked, they reemerge made up as babes (and no wonder that Usagi's morphin call is "makeup"—borrowed from the English). But there is more. In the case of Usagi, she is also a reincarnated princess who was married, centuries ago, to Prince Endymion (reincarnated today as the elusive hero Tuxedo, who doubles as the handsome teenage boy, Darien) with whom she had a child, teleported to the present as the pink-haired Chibi-chan (figure 23). Given the time-space compression indulged by the story, Usagi is thus a fourteen-year-old schoolgirl who, at the same time, has a long-standing partner and also a child. And, on top of having a burning romance and good family life (imagined in both the past and the future), Usagi is also a cool fighter, a sexy woman, a princess, and just a normal kid (who can *burikko dekiru*—do everyday things).[4] Isn't this every girl's fantasy—to, if not start out spectacular (like Barbie), go from an ordinary girl to a superstar, all the while retaining one foot in the everyday? This was the template for female idols in the 1990s (like Matsuda Seiko, a singer, idol, and mom) and it is what Sailor Moon still incarnates as the realization of girls' dreams today: to be powerful yet selfish *(wagamama)* in indulging one's earthly desires (Fujimoto 1997:69).

Some Japanese feminists, like commentator Minomiya Kazuko, see in Sailor Moon a reflection not only of girls' fantasies today but also of a positive shift in gender reality. Japanese girls are happier and more satisfied to be born female today than ever before, she notes, a fact that is conveyed in the upbeat characterization of Sailor Moon, who is not only a strong hero but also an ordinary girl who enjoys her indulgences. Her very ordinariness, so different from the typical male hero, makes her a positive role model for girls as well as boys.[5] Using the somewhat odd word *risōkyō* (utopic) to describe the earthbound nature of Usagi, Minomiya applauds the girl's everyday preoccupations with shopping, eating, romance, video games, and general hanging out with her girlfriends. That such a "normal" girl can then become a "champion of justice" makes for a more balanced portrayal of heroism than the standard male scenario, in which the hero, focused and flawless from the beginning, is both willing and expected to sacrifice everything to the job of superhero, just like corporate *sararīman* (Minomiya 1994). Girls, in short, can see themselves equally in the flawed Usagi and the superenhanced Sailor Moon, which will encourage them to be both comfortable as girls and inspired to seek out careers or missions as adults unre-

Figure 23. Teleporting across time and space: Sailor Moon's daughter, Chibi-chan, from the past. (Courtesy of Tōei Animation.)

stricted by their gender. A Japanese career woman, by contrast, sees in the bifurcated nature of *Sailor Moon* a far different, and more regressive, message about gender politics in Japan. Given that powerful women cause such discomfort for men and for society in general, they can only be tolerated by being assigned, or by themselves adopting, a (traditionally) "feminine" masquerade: klutzy, inept, sexy, pretty.

What is confused and also complicated in *Sailor Moon*, as seen from this discussion, is the grammar at work here between dreams, sexuality, power, and the ordinary/everyday. This fable of fierce flesh, as I call it—girls who show off their bodies yet are fierce fighters just like male superheroes—defies easy categorization as either (or simply) a feminist or sexist script. The Sailor Scouts are certainly girls *(shōjo)*, but this gender construction is both excessively performed (particularly in the character Sailor Moon, whose ditziness as a girl and desirability as a woman are both over the top) and rearticulated by adding in new terms. As Judith Butler (1990, 1993) would say, gender is thus rehearsed but also remapped under the rubric of play.[6] The question, then, is who does the playing (are girls in charge or not?) and to what end, interests, or effects is this gender play done in the 1990s fantasy fad of *Sailor Moon*. The story itself, of powerful girl heroes, is not new with this property, or even with the genre of *bishōjo hīrō* in Japan. Even before the era of television, which started in the early years after the war, popular mythmaking in Japan recognized a "boy's country" and a "girl's country," as Saitō Minako (1998) puts it in her book on the subject. The traditional folktale of Momotarō, for example, belongs to boys' territory: the story of a boy who grows from a peach pit into a hero who subjugates monsters and defeats the hateful enemy. The equivalent for girls is the Cinderella-type story, in which a princess or a young woman has a chance meeting with a king that leads to romance and a fantasy marriage.

In a property like *Sailor Moon*, these two worlds blend in a story line that incorporates both fighting and romance. According to Saitō (1998:12–17, 20–31), however, the text still belongs in "girls' country" for the following reasons. Boy stories are organized around the tropes of science, technology, and nationalism. Their male lead characters have powers that are technological/scientific, their weapons are mechanical, they "power up" when transformed, a scientist or engineer designs their equipment, and what they fight for is justice and defense of country or world. By contrast, the "girls' country" features magic, dreams, and interpersonal relations. Girl heroes have powers rooted in magic or otherworldliness, they fight to help friends, their weapons double as fashion accessories, a princess or spirit empowers them, they "make up" when transformed, and "love" is their keyword. As Saito traces in such properties as *Kamen Raidā* and *Urutoraman*, male superheroes mimic the adult world of corporate warriors in their selfless (often coded as patriotic) service to industrial society.[7] These heroes have virtually no personal life; they devote all their energies to their work and rarely take a break, being constantly called upon to fight marauding foes. In this context, transformation is a weapon: shifting and arming one's body to serve a higher goal (sacrifice of self to group, country, planet). When girl heroes morph, however, the process is more a "makeover" than a "power-up." Apart from empowerment, that is, transformation also beautifies girls, fostering personal attractiveness, romance, and dreams (Saitō 1998).

As I explored in the last chapter, kids' mass culture has developed in postwar Japan along channels that promote a fetishization of body dissection: crafting stories and images that fixate on the intricate details of (mecha, robotic, cyber) bodies coming apart and transforming into upgraded models. Whereas battle is typically the nexus of the plot and the staging of bodily display (the "money shot" so promoted by Bandai in television series like the Rangers as a strategy for selling more toy merchandise), there is also an ideological message about performance. Identity, for mecha heroes, comes from working hard and utilizing one's powers to a collective, social end for which a warrior is willing to sacrifice even his life (as both Red Rangers do in the Ōrenjā episode described in chapter 4). And embedded in these kid tales is a national myth that has served as a foundation of postwar reconstruction: building one's body and identity in order to be productive for the state (or at least one's corporation). But if "boys' country" stories have been appropriated and oriented to this end (with a gender politics that assigns males, but not females, to the role of productive, paid worker), how has girls' mass culture articulated national agendas?[8] In Saitō's opinion, female pop culture characters are represented mainly as sexual beings ancillary to those subjects and performances more ideologically central to Japan's "enterprise society": males. As she notes, whereas boy heroes battle to save the world, girl heroes fight to protect "treasured things"—what she sees as a code word for their own sexuality/virginity. Whereas both have the goal of eliminating evil foes to defend the earth from eminent danger, the pursuit crystallizes around precious objects in the case of girls (Saitō 1998:24): something that melds beauty with power much as the heroine does herself. In *Sailor Moon*, for example, the Scouts seek the "phantom gold crystal" that holds the secrets and safety of the universe, a treasure also pursued by the Evil Kingdom to build its own empire.

Saitō also sees the role performed by the increasingly token presence, particularly since the 1970s and *Go Renjā*, of one or two girls on a task force of warrior transformers. The team girl is always pretty and dressed to be schoolgirlishly sexy, serving as a cipher for homosocial bonding, for the crew members on the screen, and masculinist identification, for the boys watching the show (Saitō 1998). Overlooked here, however, is the fact that the schoolgirl has also assumed a much more prominent, and independent, role of her own in the ranks of Japanese mass culture since the 1970s. Generically referred to as *shōjo*, this has been the figure most associated with consumer culture. Assumed to bear the fewest responsibilities and pressures to be socially productive, the *shōjo* (as both subject and object) has come to stand as the counterweight to the enterprise society: a self-indulgent pursuer of fantasies and dreams through consumption of merchandise. In a convergence with the rise of cuteness and character fetishization in the 1970s, girls started becoming major consumers (of fashion, electronic playgoods, cute character goods) and the voice of marketing trends for the society at large.[9] In their embodiment of consumption—the antithesis of productivity on the one hand and equally vital to postwar capitalism on the other—*shōjo* have been given a cultural and national value of their own. The novel *Kitchen*, for example, by the self-identified *shōjo* writer Yoshimoto Banana, not only won a prestigious prize but was also distributed by the Foreign Ministry to its foreign visitors (presumably as a representation of national culture) when Japan hosted the G-7 conference in 1993.

Virtually across the board in mass media from *anime* to *manga* and consumer trends (including the news reportage generated by them), the fascination with—and fetishization of—the schoolgirl has intensified in Japan, particularly since the late 1980s. She is the targeted audience for endless magazines *(Egg, Cawaii, Heart Candy, Street Jam)* and, as what marketers call "bubble juniors," a highly valued consumer base during the post-Bubble recession (the leading bubble-junior apparel maker, Narumiya International, reported profits of $6.2 million in 2000, up from $2.8 million in 1999 [Itoi 2002:19]). In the place she holds in the national imaginary these days as a consummate consumer, the schoolgirl is not only a signifier of and for millennial capitalism but also its symptom:[10] both feared and desired for the "material transparency" with which she is so closely identified.[11] As Sharon Kinsella has observed (from her research on the subject), schoolgirls are continually represented in the mass media these days in terms of their youth, gender, school uniforms, and reputed materialism: a combination that is read and rendered with multivalent meanings. Associated with "earthiness, robustness, exuberance, spontaneity, and refreshing unpredictability," they are also seen, however, as material queens and consumer whores: as persons so fixated on consumption they are willing to turn their own bodies into sexual commodities. Provoking both awe and shock from the press for their "fleshy reality" (Kinsella 2002:19), Japanese schoolgirls are the subject/object of constant interrogation, continually being reported on in stories that focus on the everydayness of their (material) lives: how they spend their days, what they buy and where, how much money they go through in a week, and what the contents of their handbags are.

A fetishized object as much as consumer of material culture, "high school girl" *(joshi kōsei)* has also become an unofficial brand name commonly used to sell consumer goods of all kinds. Schoolgirls who turn this objectification into their own subjective identity call themselves *kogal* (high school gal) or *kogyaru*. Marked by a particular style, the *kogal* wears a school uniform refashioned as anything from supercute *(chō kawaii)* to showy *(oshare)* or lingerie chic *(shitagi-kei)*. In this flashy dress of the *kogal*, the school student, as interpellated by Japan's ideological state apparatus, is remade.[12] From a focus on hard work, self-discipline, and productivity, the schoolgirl turns to fun, fashion, and consumerism. Much like Usagi, whose daily habits are decidedly loose, *kogal* are best known for the "loose socks" (socks worn crumpled rather than neat) they pair with school uniforms. This style, read as boldly lax and sexily cool, is a commentary both on the everyday and the corporate structure of production in postwar Japan that has extracted so much from the bodies and lives of working Japanese. There is little wonder, then, at the emergence in recent years of the new market, previously mentioned, of *sararīman* purchasing the company or clothing (used underwear, called *buru sera*, sold in shops or even vending machines) of schoolgirls in a practice euphemistically called *enjo kōsai*.

Transactions range from talking and eating together to oral or genital sex. What motivates the girls, as endless reportage has claimed, is money to buy brand-name goods: "treasures" more valuable, it is said, to them than their own bodies (which, so treasured by others, however, fetch a high price). Though the prevalence of this behavior is a subject of disagreement, the general consensus is that *enjo kōsai* definitely occurs and may well be spreading in the new millennium—and, as both fad and social phenomenon, is certainly spreading to other countries, such as Hong Kong and Taiwan (Ho 2003). And though the press pays far more attention to the girls than the men engaged in this practice, Kinsella has suggested that the commodity involved is not "simply" sex. Rather, buyers are also interested in capturing other qualities associated with the *shōjo*: her closeness to everyday pleasures and intimate relationships along with the dreamworld she seems to so easily inhabit. Men do not merely want to have schoolgirls, in other words; they also, in some sense, want to *be* them (Kinsella 2002).

Figure 24. The girls unite: all power and legs as ten Scouts join forces. (Courtesy of Tōei Animation.)

    The fantasy of the Japanese schoolgirl is complex and contradictory, as is true of the form given it in the mass genre of "beautiful girl heroes" that is targeted, after all, to girls and not men (figure 24). A striking example comes from *Sailor Moon R* (one in a series of movies primarily for video release that accompanied the television cartoon/comic stories), which, subtitled "Miracle Romance," embeds a tale of girl(y) warriorship within one of friendship and loneliness. The story involves Fiore, a beautiful male alien who tries to woo Darien, Usagi's boyfriend, with a flower meant as a return gift for the one Darien gave him years ago when the two briefly met as boys in a hospital.[13] Darien had just lost both his parents in a traffic accident, but the gesture of kindness he extended to Fiore touched the latter deeply. Having remained on his own ever since (and having lived all alone for centuries before that), Fiore is now hoping to escape his loneliness by (re)kindling a friendship with Darien. Jealous of all Darien's other relationships (particularly the one with Usagi), Fiore has brought a killer flower to earth that will turn the human race into zombies—a fate Darien will be spared by being taken to a distant asteroid (where, however, he will lose life as a human). Realizing the alien's intentions, the Scouts go into warrior mode and, transforming into superheroes, teleport to the asteroid, which, they soon learn, is on a crash course with earth. Despite fighting hard, all but Sailor Moon soon succumb to Fiore's superior powers. What turns the tide is not the girl's warrior skills or superweapons but, rather, the incredible devotion she shows to her friends that, culminating in her willingness to die for them all, so moves Fiore that he stops the deadly asteroid and reawakens Darien. Fiore then gives his would-be friend another flower, but unlike the first gift, this one restores life. And, by breathing in its nectar and passing it to Sailor Moon with a kiss, the princess/superhero is revived.

On the one hand, this story is keyed into romance, magic, and sexy attire: the morphin scenes are staged five times over (showing each girl in naked silhouette, then "made-up" in hot power dress), magical crystals and poisonous flowers are the main weapons, and the lead character is driven to save not only the earth but also her boyfriend. On the other hand, even if this story of superheroism is distinctly gendered as female, its warriors are not diluted of bravery, toughness, or willpower. Indeed, Sailor Moon is as resolute and fierce as any male superhero and—in what is a reversal of the standard rescue scenario—it is the female who triumphs in the end and rescues the whole world, including her prince (who spends most of the plot limp and unconscious). Even more distinctive is the emphasis placed on friendship and interpersonal connectedness in *Sailor Moon R*: a different geometry of warriorship from that at work in *mecha* superheroes (where the mainly boy warriors are fighting less for each other and more for planetary/national/corporate survival). With stress placed on personal loneliness—something said to characterize these postindustrial times in Japan that breed atomism, solitarism, and "orphanism" particularly for kids—the story could be read as a utopic alternative to (and critique of) the enterprise society that has grounded postwar Japan in institutional corporatism. Friendship is valued more highly than anything in the tale and is what, in the end, saves everyone and the earth itself. Yet this does not mean that at the level of image, flesh or flash have been abandoned (given that the Scouts morph early in the plot, becoming skimpily attired). So the two intertwine here: a mythic tale of (precapitalist) solidarity and a commodity spectacle of sexy schoolgirls who combine action with fashion. The former may be a commentary against industrial capitalism, but the latter is certainly an endorsement (pretty, heroic, kindhearted) of capitalist consumerism. And, with this, a dreamy counterculture and consumer culture is given (fantasy) shape.

Doll Fashions:
From Cute to Cool

> In Japan and all over the world, women are more and more assuming positions of power in society. They don't want to be discriminated against as soft or gentle; they want to grow up to be tough and powerful. And Sailor Moon is a role model for that type of girl.
>
> Yamashina Makoto, chairman of Bandai,
> quoted in Reid 1995:16

In 1967, Takara, a Japanese toy company, started producing Ricca-chan, a fashion doll that even today is said by toy scholar Kobayashi Reiji to capture "all the dreams girls have ever wished for" (1998:63). Actually, tastes have also changed over time, and though she reigned as the leading girls' doll for a quarter of a century in postwar Japan (and remains incredibly popular with both young girls and older women today), Ricca was displaced by Bandai's Sailor Moon at the height of the latter's popularity in fall 1992. As many Japanese told me, including three teenage girls I interviewed in Tokyo in 2000 about doll styles and cuteness, Ricca-chan is the embodiment of a Japanese "young refined lady" *(ojōsan)*; she is exceedingly gentle *(yasashii)*, cute *(kawaii)*, Japanese *(nihonteki)*, and—because of all these—a reassuring and comfortable image of and for girldom in Japan. For such an icon of the postwar Japanese *shōjo*, though, it is striking that she has light brown hair and is the biracial, bicultural offspring of mixed parents (her father is French). Indeed, as Kobayashi has argued, "This portrait is a condensation of the dreams Japanese have held toward Western culture since the end of World War II" (1998:63).

Crafted to be perpetually eleven years old and in the fifth grade, Ricca-chan has the body to match: largish head, blue doe eyes, closed mouth, high nose, shoulder-length hair, and a girly figure yet to show signs of pubescence. The story she was given—involving a network of friends and family members (figure 25)—evolved over time and mainly in the interests of creating more dolls to sell (more than fifty in the series to date). Two of the first subsidiary dolls (the third and fourth in the series) were Ricca's best friend, Izumi, and her mother (which Takara felt was a necessity for Ricca's popularity): a thirty-three-year-old Japanese beauty who has a prestigious career as a fashion designer that her daughter dreams about mimicking one day.

Figure 25. Ricca-chan: the "Japanese" doll with her fantasy (and biracial) family. (Courtesy of Takara Toys.)

Ricca was also given six siblings: an older sister, Lisa, who works as an international stewardess; a set of younger twins (Miki and Maki); and a set of triplets (Kako, Gen, and Miku, born later).[14] The father was a mystery for a long time, apart from the fact that he was a Frenchman named Pierre who was an orchestra conductor and lived most of the year in France along with Lisa. When a Pierre doll appeared, in 1989, the story switched so that he was now residing back in Japan with his large family, though it was also learned that his family name came from a castle he received a long time ago from a king. A grandmother, Pierre's mother (Elena), debuted in 1992; identified as a "*sūpa obāsan*" (super grandmother), she has a stunning profile: she speaks five languages, works at the Swiss embassy, lives in Provence, and is married to a big shot at the French Foreign Ministry. Pierre's younger brother, we learn, is a racer, but almost no details are given (nor, interestingly, merchandise made) of the mother's (Japanese) side of the family (Hori 1996).

As for Ricca herself, there have been ample versions and additions over time (figure 26): a pink house, a cabin attendant edition, a computer graphic game ("Idol Ricca-chan," in which she becomes a singing idol), a talking telephone doll, and—to celebrate her thirtieth anniversary—a memory set of six

Figure 26. Ricca remodeled: different models of Japan's most popular postwar doll, until it was trumped by *Sailor Moon* dolls in the 1990s. (Courtesy of Neko Publishing Company.)

Ricca-chan dolls from different time periods, with the thirty-year-old model of Ricca now a career woman, working as a diplomat and enjoying a holiday after giving birth to her first child (Kobayashi 1998). For two of the three teenage girls I interviewed, Ricca was their favorite doll growing up (in the late 1980s and early 1990s). The reasons one gave for this were the following: "I liked her clothes and would wash her hair, bathe her, and make up her face. It felt like she was living in our house, as part of our family. I felt comfortable with her. I also felt I resembled her. She was like me, and me, her."

Curiously, one of the three girls said she did not even realize that Ricca was a biracial child, yet another said that, because her hair and eyes were different than her own, she did not really think Ricca was Japanese. Despite diverging in their reading of her ethnic identity, however, all the girls found Ricca exceedingly familiar: someone with whom they identified, even if she had a "dream life" few of them would ever realize, including a career (only 9 percent of managerial positions are held by women today in Japan in what is ranked to be one of the worst industrial countries—sixty-ninth out of seventy-five member nations in recent rankings by the World Economic Forum—in empowering its women [French 2003:A3]).[15]

Barbie, Mattel's svelte fashion doll, was launched shortly after Ricca in Japan (and after debuting in the States in 1959) and has had a decidedly different reception. Despite selling in more than eighty countries around the world and having a reputation as the global doll par excellence (now localized to reflect different ethnicities and cultural styles from China to India), Barbie has never soared in Japan. Her characteristics—blond, "sharp-eyed," open-mouthed (which seemed vulgar), voluptuous, a young adult with a career (stewardess Barbie, nurse Barbie)—all made her seem too strange, gaudy, and "garish" *(hade)* in the eyes of Japanese girls and, as importantly, their mothers (Masubuchi 1995:115; Kobayashi 1998:62). Only one girl in my interview group had played with a Barbie when she was younger (a black Barbie, she recalled), and all found her "foreign." Masubuchi Sōichi, in his book on the discourse of girls' dolls, argues that Japan and the United States are at opposite ends of doll aesthetics. In the United States reality tends to be important, but in Japan, "if it looks too real, people feel uncomfortable. It is better to waffle on the details because the imagination is more sought out" (1995:114). As he points out, there has never been a Ricca doll with any bendable body parts or joints (like legs, shoulders, and wrists) and, if such realism were incorporated, it would be less popular with Japanese girls, in his assessment. Barbie dolls are "real live," he concludes, but Ricca dolls are "cute" (115). Strikingly—given how artificial Barbie's proportions and miniature feet appear to many Americans—this is a view (with its troubling tendency to reify American and Japanese cultural differences here) I ran across often in Japan: that Americans value realism in their dolls and in mass culture more generally, whereas Japanese prefer fantasy. Indeed, as we will see later, this was a serious issue for Bandai in deciding how to retool its Sailor Moon toy line for marketing in the United States.

Given the time when Ricca first appeared on the market, the big doe eyes she sports and that signify cuteness were already a convention in the increasingly popular medium of *manga*. Originally introduced by Tezuka Osamu, the creator of *Tetsuwan Atomu*, it has been said, to mimic Disney characters, this stylization—huge eyes that can be inscribed with a panoply of emotions by adding tears, cloudiness, flickers, narrowing pupils—often accompanies that of Western (Caucasian) bodies, features, and worlds (stories set in England, Europe, Canada, or America). While Japanese themselves (including *manga* artists, marketers in kids' entertainment, and viewers of *manga*, *anime*, and television) repeatedly told me that such Westernization was simply a marker of fantasy (that, given the homogeneity of Japanese bodies, eyes, and black hair, fantasy characters need to be made "non-Japanese-looking"), it is nonetheless telling that fantasy so typically takes a Western/Caucasian form. But, as the difference between Ricca and Barbie illustrates, even a Western body needs to be given a Japanese style; when it is—as with the biracial Ricca-chan—the effect can register as the epitome of Japaneseness. In Ricca's case, she was an idealized figure invested with the postwar dreams of reconstruction; straddling two societies, France and Japan, this is a cosmopolitan girl who lives in a big house, travels abroad, attends private school, is bilingual, and looks foreign even though she identifies as Japanese. With this profile and her big, cute eyes, Ricca embodied a fantasy about an imaginary postwar Japan: making its way confidently and comfortably in the rest of the (Westernized) world. Barbie, by contrast, was too strikingly and garishly foreign to do anything of the sort.

Taken off the market, Barbie returned in an altered form when Mattel teamed up with Takara in the early 1980s. In this "softer" version, she came with a rounder face, bigger eyes, a closed mouth, and lighter skin tone, and she was packaged in family settings (pushing her baby sister in a stroller, for example, rather than featured as the rollerblading Barbie or the various career Barbies). When the partnership broke up, Takara retained the license and renamed the doll Jenny, which became the second-highest-selling doll after Ricca-chan. Mattel returned to Japan again in 1991 and, after replacing its entire management team in 1995, reported that sales were up 70 percent (a year that Takara, recovering from the Sailor Moon boom, also reported increased sales of Ricca and Jenny). It has subsequently (2000) signed an alliance with Bandai in which the latter will handle all "localization" in selling and marketing Mattel products in Japan. Now targeting largely the collector crowd in Japan, Mattel specializes in dolls like the "Burberry Barbie," sold exclusively in Japan; this doll, dressed and accessorized entirely in the Burberry brand name, sells for 23,000 yen, or approximately $240. From being too foreign, Barbie is now—in this branded incarnation—only too "Japanese": a sign of what Yoshimi Shunya has described as the shift from yearning for the West, specifically America, as a symbol of newness and wealth during the 1950s and '60s (when the "fantasy of abundance" was modeled after America and American consumer goods) to incorporating American things and goods at a deep systematic level of everyday consumption experienced as Japanese. Writing about Tokyo Disneyland (built in the early 1980s and Disney's most successful and lucrative park in the world), Yoshimi argues that while it is maintained as fetishistically authentic (everything is an exact, or near-exact, duplication of the U.S. original), Japanese derive pleasure and meaning from going to Tokyo Disneyland not as would-be Americans but more as proud and confident "Japanese," materially prosperous enough to own their own Disneyland close to home (Yoshimi 2000).

While never a huge seller in Japan, Barbie—with her siren's body and flashy womanliness—has captured the global marketplace like no other doll in the world. By contrast, the girly Ricca-chan—gently soft and cutely Japanese—has remained strictly local.[16] Yet the same has not been true of the Sailor Moon dolls, called "figures" and "adventure figures" in their export version, which galvanized a fad in many countries outside Japan (including Canada, France, Spain, and Hong Kong). No longer a model of cuteness, Sailor Moon is "cool" *(kakko ii)*, as my three teenage interviewees put it.[17] As one added, "It was the first time I had ever seen a girl on the television screen transform *[henshin]* like that into a warrior *[senshi]*. I thought that was cool." Yet as another observed, some of her friends were also made uncomfortable by the sexiness of the girls: their short skirts, long legs, exposed cleavage, and glittery morphin style (their battle mode). A radical shift from Ricca-chan (who, at eleven, is only three years younger than the fourteen-year-old Scouts), Sailor Moon is certainly flashier: the very quality that damned Barbie, particularly when she first appeared in Japan in the 1960s. But brilliantly—if one thinks of Bandai trying to come up with a global product that would also appeal to Japanese girls keen to stick with, yet go beyond, Ricca—the Sailor Scouts double as both ordinary girls and superbabes. It is this continual fluctuation between different modes (displaying flexibility and multipartedness) that is key to their popularity, both at home and abroad.

Teleporting the Pretty Soldiers to America

> We think American girls might move toward Sailor Moon. Barbie is
> an excellent doll. But she has no story. Sailor Moon is a warrior on the
> side of justice. I mean, the girl is a superhero.
>
> Bandai president Yamashina Makoto,
> quoted in Reid 1995:16

> Fighting evil by moonlight
> Winning love by daylight
> Never running from a real fight
> She is the one called Sailor Moon.
>
> English lyrics for the theme
> song from *Sailor Moon*

A Mattel executive with whom I spoke weeks before the debut of *Sailor Moon* in the States recognized the pioneering new concept in the marketing of girl(y) superheroes. "Fashion action," he said, was in keeping with the times: girls who are active like boys these days (in sports, school, career aspirations) but still gender-identify by body and dress (fashion). This combination made good marketing sense; it was a way to add a new wrinkle to two different genres—the (traditionally male) genre of action heroes and the (traditionally female) genre of fashion dolls/girls. Given the paucity of female heroes in American pop culture even in the 1990s, such a new breed of girl/heroine offered a new taste in—what this executive was most interested in—doll fashions. A year later, I noticed that Mattel's own Barbie doll had a new action look with "superhero Barbie." Two years after that, the company used a similar idea to penetrate what had long been considered a boy's domain—the "action" sphere of video games—with a video game tailor-made for girls—Barbie's Fashion Design.[18] By 2002, two of Mattel's most recent and successful dolls employed the same logic of active fashion. Diva Starzz is a series of four dolls, each with her own dress and action motif (from a hippie naturalist in green overalls to a skateboarder in sporty dress and tiger-print hat). And What's Her Face? is labeled a "fashion activity doll" that, packaged with markers, stampers, and stencils, has fluid looks that are custom-made (and remade) by the doll's owner.

As he spoke to me in 1995, the Mattel executive recognized the potential of the fashion action heroes *Sailor Moon* was bringing to the States that fall. He also saw this trend as an advance over what had seemed so progressive in *The Mighty Morphin Power Rangers:* adding girls to the Ranger team. This move had been popular with children of both genders and was applauded by many adults for its feminist politics: girls as tough fighters. In the course of transformation, however, the Rangers become indistinguishable from guys; they wear unisex power suits and adopt fighting stances just like the boys. To this marketer of fashion dolls, the Ranger girls lose their girliness when they morph to action heroes—precisely what *Sailor Moon* added back in. If the Rangers mask their gender in battle mode, the Scouts perform it excessively in frilly, girly fashion. This was a brilliant touch, given that girls of the age targeted by *Sailor Moon* (two to ten) express their identity in terms of gender, the Mattel executive noted. Offering them the fantasy of action hero is novel in its own right, but how much better to code this role as "female." By this he meant the body designs fed by consumerist feminine fashion: boots, jewels, clingy bodices, and short skirts. Far more interested in selling fashion to girls than in gender/feminist politics, he liked this new girly model for both its "femininity" and the newness of its action.

But fashion is exceedingly fickle, shaped as it is by styles and trends that tend to be both short-lived and market specific. In clothing, global fashion has been set by very few places: Paris, Italy, Britain, and the United States. In recent years, Japanese fashion has also gained world renown through designers like Issey Miyake and Yohji Yamamoto. Even here, though, as Dorinne Kondo (1997) has astutely observed, the worldwide appeal of Japanese fashion rests, in part, on what is read as an orientalist difference. Japanese design is known for qualities that are treated as stylistically and culturally different: free-flowing shapes, aesthetic mélange, mix and quality of fabric, subtle colors. And this is its defining feature: not fashion that a Japanese person happened to design, but "Japanese" (or, as it is commonly called, "Oriental") fashion.

Orientalism may be a chic flavor in the market of high fashion, but it was not in the circuits of kids' entertainment in the early 1990s, and particularly not in the United States when *Sailor Moon* was first launched here in 1995. Given a mass culture that, at the time, was almost exclusively made-in-the United States (with American faces, places, and sensibilities), the introduction of anything foreign was risky. Adjusting to this marketplace was fairly easy in the case of *Power Rangers*. With heroes who literally are masked when they transform into action mode, all the fighting footage could run as it was originally shot. The scenes with unmasked Rangers were then reshot in the United States using American actors. When the two sets of footage were spliced together, the end product had been transformed from a Japanese into an American show. And though it was recognized as excitingly different (for its live-action format and cyborgian transformations), these differences were disassociated from the show's origins in Japan.

To alter *Sailor Moon* similarly would be more difficult given its medium of animation rather than live action. Anticipating this problem, the executive from Mattel predicted that winning over American girls would be hard for *Sailor Moon* unless its distributors could find some way to effectively localize it. For the show to catch on, U.S. viewers would need to identify with the characters. But could they do this with the story and imagery of Japanese schoolgirls given *Sailor Moon* by its comic-book writer, Takeuchi Naoko? Indeed, little alteration was made to the visual imagery of the show for U.S. broadcast. One technique available for animation—and used aggressively by Warner Brothers for its U.S. run of the Japanese cartoon version (starting in 1998) of *Pokémon*—was made little use of by DIC Entertainment (a much smaller operation with less capital than WB) for *Sailor Moon*. Called rotoscoping, this procedure involves airbrushing out certain details in an image. In *Pokémon*, telltale signs of cultural difference have been overtly removed or replaced; rice balls become doughnuts, for example, and Japanese script is studiously effaced. In this case, the aim of the U.S. producer, as he told me in interview, was not to Americanize the show per se but to culturally neutralize it. Kids are absorbed in a fantasy world when they watch entertainment like *Pokémon*, he explained, and the flow is disrupted if anything too jarringly unfamiliar appears on the screen.[19]

The concept of flow, which has had much currency in television studies, was originally introduced by Raymond Williams (1975) to refer to the immersive everyday experience of this medium, in contrast to the experience engendered by other media such as film. In the case of *Pokémon*, the assumption is that if American kids are to be drawn into a television show, they cannot be made to feel "not at home" with any particular image. Needless to say, plenty of American shows have flowed quite easily around the world, and children of diverse places and faces have enjoyed them immensely. And as both Erica Rand (1995) and Elizabeth Chin (2001) have shown in the case of the Barbie doll, identity may be much more flexible than fixed in the way girls play with the doll. Many girls read their own identities or desires into the doll ("queering" her heterosexuality, for example, or "seeing" a white Barbie as black) rather than simply accepting the raced/gendered/sexual identity she comes packaged with. But I am also talking about power here: packaging in a way that sutures particular places and faces (American, white, male) to what is accepted, and expected, as standard. Counting on seeing "oneself" reflected in mass culture is the chauvinism of the empowered. And when the only identity available is different from one's own, viewers must either find a way to position themselves in the fantasy or be excluded. Gender is a case in point. Given the dominance of boy shows and male heroes in kids' entertainment in the United States, girls routinely gender-cross in their viewing, often identifying with the male-gendered lead characters. The reverse is far less true, of course, since crossing gender in the other direction entails a downgrade rather than an upgrade of power. Needless to say, networks favor boy over girl programming, given that the former will draw in more viewers.

In the end, *Sailor Moon* was marketed in the United States quite differently than *Power Rangers*, both because it was a cartoon instead of live action and because it was broadcast by a much smaller operation (DIC Network rather than Fox Network). As an animated cartoon, *Sailor Moon* presented almost insurmountable technical problems as far as localization was concerned. Hence, apart from dubbing and some adjusting of "problem" elements (violence, nudity, and homoeroticism between the Scouts and other characters, which were totally removed for U.S. broadcast), the television show remained largely intact, undergoing little "Americanization," making identity and identification a key concern. In anticipation of the show's debut in the United States, experts on both sides of the ocean wondered whether American kids could relate to a show in which the lead characters so obviously lived somewhere else—attending cram school, eating with chopsticks, frequenting temples, and dreaming of being a sushi delivery girl.

In fact, this was the reason—insufficient localization—that the show failed to generate high enough ratings to constitute a success, I was repeatedly told by people in the kids' entertainment business (both in Japan and in the States). After *Sailor Moon* was launched in August 1995 on local networks (through DIC), the ratings never rose to a significant level. The fact that it did not receive a slot on Saturday morning TV (*Sailor Moon* aired weekdays, early in the morning or early in the afternoon, in most places), as *Power Rangers* had, did not help in establishing its popularity. But the general consensus for its failure here was that the property had been insufficiently "Americanized" to work in this America-centric marketplace. American girls are not receptive to Japanese *anime*, Bandai officials told me in Tokyo. And executives in the field I spoke with, both in Japan and in the United States, said simply that marketing had not paid enough attention to localization. In spring 1996, DIC took *Sailor Moon* off the air, judging it to be a commercial flop.

When I visited Tokyo in the summer of 1996, I met with a group of executives from Bandai, the toy company that had engineered the *Sailor Moon* operation in Japan as a way of gaining a foothold in the girls' market there. In their assessment, the show's failure in the United States was due not merely to inadequate localization but to the very medium in which it was transmitted—Japanese animation. As one man put it, "American girls don't like Japanese *anime*." I found this rationale interesting because *anime* developed cult popularity across the world (including the United States) in the 1990s, and fans tend to like it precisely for its differences from, rather than accommodations to, Western conventions of visual storytelling as displayed in Disney cartoons and Hollywood movies. It is also true, however, that most *anime* fans (in the States, at least) are male (though this is changing with popular *anime*, like *Spirited Away*, that girls have loved as well as boys). According to the Bandai officials, the construction of stories, images, and even fashion in the medium of *anime* was simply too alien for the mainstream tastes of young American girls. They cannot get into the fantasy, was the assessment. This was not because the Scouts looked particularly Asian (the reason Japanese actors were replaced with American ones in *Power Rangers*). Indeed, as is typical in Japanese *anime* artistry, the characters were designed to have a fantasy rather than a realistic ("Asian") appearance and to look Western. Physically, with their pale flesh, long-legged bodies, Caucasian hair color (bright blond on Sailor Moon), and non-Asian

Figure 27. *Sailor Moon* dolls for the United States: toning down the fantasy and adding Barbie. (© 1996 Bandai America Incorporated. Sailor Moon © 1996 Naoko Takeuchi/Kōdansha, Tōei Animation. All rights reserved. Sailor Moon, the Sailor Moon characters, and their respective names and likenesses are trademarks of Tōei Animation. Used under license.)

eyelids, the Scouts could pass as Anglo-Americans. Worried that something "different" still came across in the style of the Scouts, however, Bandai attempted to modify this feature in the one realm where they could make significant changes for U.S. marketing: doll merchandise.

Discussions had apparently been heated in 1995 over what precisely the U.S. market demanded and to what extent Bandai, a Japanese company, should accede to it. Delaying the release of the doll merchandise until after the debut of the cartoon in the States—a factor that, some say, contributed to the failure of *Sailor Moon* to take off—the company finally instituted the following changes. The U.S. dolls were given bigger breasts, rounder eyes, toned-down accessories, and "realistic" hair coloring rather than the fantasy hues—pink, blue, green—favored in Japan (figure 27). Making them less like *anime* characters and "more like real humans"—how a Japanese newspaper reporting on the changes described Mattel's Barbie ("Amerika Shiyō ni Henshin yo," 1995:1)—Bandai effectively tried to Americanize the doll version of *Sailor Moon* for the United States. This was not a sufficient antidote, however, to spur popularity for a show deemed too Japanese for American girls to meaningfully relate to. The "smell" of cultural difference still clung to the vehicle of storytelling: a Japanese cartoon barely modified for U.S. transmission.

Performative Identities:
The Fans React

"Even crybabies can be heroes."
"It is an emotional story juxtaposed with action and adventure."
"It is more realistic [than other superhero shows]."
"The girls use heart and not just weapons."
"Serena/Sailor Moon is an average human girl."
"It turns unpretentious teens into protectors of the universe."

Respondents to Internet survey conducted
by author among U.S. fans in 1988[20]

Despite the judgment calls on both sides of the Pacific, however, in reality *Sailor Moon* had already acquired a sizable and impassioned cult following in the United States by the time DIC pulled the plug. Fans even launched a campaign—called S.O.S. ("Save Our Sailors")—to keep *Sailor Moon* on the air. Thanks in part to their efforts, *Sailor Moon* returned to the screen in 1997 on USA Network and was picked up by Cartoon Network in 1998. *Sailor Moon* was still being broadcast in 2002 (and, though temporarily suspended, started rebroadcast in June 2003 by Cartoon Network) in a run now being assessed as at least reasonably successful. Bandai-made Sailor Moon dolls returned to the shelves of American toy stores (Toys"R"Us had them stocked through 2002). And the English translations of the comic books (published by Mixx Production Co., starting in 1999, as both books and picture-laden comic books) have sold exceedingly well in a marketplace far less attuned to comic books than is Japan.

Not surprisingly, perhaps (though confounding the perception of American kids held by DIC), fans of *Sailor Moon* have been drawn to the very differences it poses between both American programming and the gendering of the latter: the prevalence of boy shows and the construction given (male) superheroes. Fans have praised not only the presence of female action heroes in *Sailor Moon* but also their portrayal in complicated story lines that weave together a host of elements without privileging or sacrificing any particular one. What is valued here is something both flexible and performative that pertains to the form of storytelling, as well as the fleshing out (both literally and figuratively) of its main characters: girl(y) superheroes.

On a cool winter day in 1998, I talked with two fifteen-year-olds about the fascination they had with *Sailor Moon*. At the time, this Japanese cartoon show was playing on cable TV in the United States, three years after it had commercially bombed when DIC Entertainment launched it on major American networks. Part of a cult following that rose up in this country around *Sailor Moon,* these two American girls were drawn to the story of female transformers: ordinary teenagers who morph into and out of the identities of heroic fighters. One of my interviewees was particularly impassioned. She loved the intricacy of the drama and the fact that there are five separate girls, all of whom have their own personalities, weapons, and styles. Each is celestially empowered and fights like a warrior when morphed. As critical to the narrative, however, are the interpersonal dynamics of the Scouts and the everydayness of lives spent eating ice cream, playing video games, and shopping for clothes.

For the other girl, Jen, there was something almost bodily about her attachment to *Sailor Moon.* Coming to the interview armed with a pile of fan goods she had accumulated, Jen continued to play absentmindedly with the fashion action doll as we talked: stroking her hair, adjusting the skirt, touching the legs. Because this was a fifteen-year-old girl, far beyond the age of playing with dolls and much older than the targeted audience for *Sailor Moon* (two to eight in this country), Jen's fixation surprised me.[21] Yet as we chatted about the enticements of *Sailor Moon*—a story featuring girl leads who combine toughness with beauty and superheroism with the blips of normal adolescence—I came to see what Jen was "playing" with was as much her own sense of self as fantasy creations. And for her as well as the Sailor Scouts, identity is deeply entwined with the body. A serious student, budding feminist, and fan of fantasy novels, Jen was also a teenage girl who enjoyed experimenting with and changing her appearance. Dressed androgynously the first day I saw her, the next time she was in a short leather skirt with high boots and fringed vest. When asked what she thought of the long-legged femmy look of New Age women who kick ass, she answered that the two features were not contradictory; if the Scouts were not attractive, they would be far less appealing or convincing as heroes. "Hey, who would want to watch the show if the main characters didn't look cool?" Fingering the doll in her lap with hands that spent hours a week on her own appearance (so her mother told me), Jen said she identified most with Sailor Mars. For her friend, it was Sailor Moon. And for neither, in answer to my question, did the fact that the property came from Japan affect their reception of the show or their identification with its characters.

The most striking feature of this fan group, as I have examined it through surveys, discussions, and interviews, is how it confounds the demographics originally targeted for the show: namely, girls ages two to ten.[22]

Sailor Moon fans include males as well as females and adults through middle age. The atypical gender-crossing of boys here is one of the reasons, in fact, that the show was brought back in 1997. And for them, the conspicuous "girliness" of the story is not a detraction; rather, it contributes many of the features they like best about *Sailor Moon*. In this reaction, males differ little from females. "The Scouts are girls in short skirts with lots of emotion," said one ten-year-old fan. "*Sailor Moon* deals with issues like death and true love; it works at many levels" (a twenty-five-year-old male). Many fans (the three hundred respondents to my survey: females and males from Canada and the United States, aged ten to twenty-seven) described the appeal of *Sailor Moon* in terms of how it differs both from male superheroes and from American programming:

- "Japanese *anime* is much more complex that American cartoons. Emotions are better described."

- "*Sailor Moon* is different from the American cartoon superhero thing. It is full of mythology and kind of like a soap opera."

- "The Scouts aren't invincible like many North American characters."

- "Americans couldn't make anything like this."

- "The Scouts are more clumsy than male superheroes. But this gives another perspective; the Scouts are also girls."

Repeatedly, fans praise the juxtapositions at work in *Sailor Moon*— fighting and romance, friendship and adventure, modern life and premodern magic and spirits. By fleshing out the story and characters with multiple layers, *Sailor Moon* is said to be more "real" and emotionally satisfying than other superhero fictions. Differences are also flaunted here, produced in a cacophony of alternative modes that do not blend seamlessly but retain their distinctive yet pliable edge. The lead character, for example, is a jumble of contradictions, and her persona as an ordinary girl is as notably, even excessively, performed as that of superhero. The two sides come together, of course, but in a character whose differences are (jarringly) maintained rather than (neatly) dissolved.

The identity of this girly superhero, then, is less a hybrid, in which multiple traits and girls fuse, than it is mutable and performative. Indeed, this is one of the show's major appeals for fans: its host of strikingly different characters who themselves shift between multiple modalities. Borders are unstable, and new aspects or dimensions of the Scouts are always being revealed. In the cartoon episode "Driven Dreamer" (in the *Sailor Moon Su-*

pers series), for example, Amy (Sailor Mars)—the genius Scout who studies hard to realize her dream of becoming a doctor—dons a mechanic's outfit to help a friend fix up an old car. Both her appearance and her newfound obsession confound the other Scouts, who are far more used to seeing Amy at cram school or plugged into her computer. When they learn, however, that Amy's motive is to help Natsumi, a woman in her twenties, realize her own dream (the repair of a car she was working on when her husband died four years ago), the Scouts understand and pitch in to help. In a series devoted to the thematic of dreams (this is one of the overarching tropes in *Sailor Moon* at large, but in this series it is highlighted even more), this episode weaves dreaming into various subplots. The studious Amy is portrayed in an alternative light in a story that also plays with the stereotype of girls and car mechanics.

Both in interviews and in survey responses, viewers of *Sailor Moon* often mentioned identifying with particular characters. Sometimes these identifications were shared among friends—with each person linking to a different character—and sometimes each fan liked all the characters for different reasons:

- "I identify with Serena the most because I tend to trip over stuff and get confused."
- "I like all the characters for different reasons."
- "I like Amy's intelligence, Rei's fire, Makoto's consideration and friendship."

Besides appreciating the Scouts' versatility in the range and nuance of identities they assume, kids also like their versatile body parts: the makeup of their bodies/identities and also the breakdown of these bodies in the heat of battle. Many children cited the specific weapons/accessories/fashions/body parts they liked (Serena's brooch, Rei's green-skirted outfit). Observing these children actually watching episodes of the cartoon, however, I noticed how attentive they were to the action scenes—the moments of battle when, threatened by destruction, the girls upgrade their powers and shape-shift to zap, blast, cream, or otherwise eviscerate their foes.

When I asked whether any of the kids had found these battles to be "violent," one twelve-year-old boy shouted, "Yes," adding that this was his favorite part of *Sailor Moon*. Becoming highly animated, he described this and other attack scenes from the show in which bodies break apart, disintegrate in midair, and mutate (an arm changes into a blade, or what looks a human transmutes into a monster, for example). Only one other member of this group (a girl) agreed with the characterization of *Sailor Moon* as violent (a factor she similarly liked); the rest, in a far more typical reaction, thought the show was better described as "cute" or "soft." Yet for all these viewers, and for fans in general, *Sailor Moon* is appealing for the shifting identities of the characters: girls/monsters who transform in both directions and are, at either end, a complex of attributes. And the fashion mode is little different from the action mode in this respect; the characters change shapes as easily as they change clothes. Whether they are morphing into superheroes or fighting evil monsters, what is centered here is the fact that the (de)composition of bodies comes about through the manipulation of armor/fashion/body parts.

Given that Americans who like *Sailor Moon* appreciate its concatenation of differences and flexibility of mutation, few fans complain about its being too Japanese. More complaints are made, in fact, about changing the show too much (rather than too little) for American transmission.[23] Of course, included among the admirers of *Sailor Moon* are fans of *anime* more generally who came to this show having already developed an appreciation for and understanding of the Japanese genre. Still, what were obstacles to the show's gaining popularity with American kids when it first aired in 1995—its *anime* aesthetics and overt signs of cultural difference in the images and story line—have become much more acceptable in U.S. kids' entertainment in recent years. Bandai Entertainment, for example, released about seventy-five *anime* television shows and movies in American markets in 2001, a tenfold increase over a decade ago (McKinley 2002) and a sign of how mainstream Japanese imports have become in U.S. kids' media. Becoming increasingly *anime*-friendly these days, U.S. television has hosted a plethora of Japanese cartoons across a number of networks in recent years—these include *Cardcaptors* and *Pokémon* by Warner Brothers, *Digimon* by Fox, and *Dragon Ball Z* and *Sailor Moon* by Cartoon Network. This assessment was confirmed by an executive at Saban International involved with the production of *Digimon* with whom I spoke in 2000. According to him, having the show register as Japanese (overt signs of Japaneseness on the screen, from Japanese script to images of kimonos, samurai, and temples) was a plus rather than a detriment with viewers. And this cachet of coolness has only increased with even more Japanese programming on U.S. television today: *Yu Hakusho, Kikaider, Hamtaro, Kenshin, G Gundam, Kirby,* and *Yu-Gi-Oh!*

In one of the most recent and spectacular homegrown hits on U.S. kids' TV—*Powerpuff Girls*—one sees the influence of *Sailor Moon* in the bending of not only genre but also gender. The creator, in this case, is an American who, in a reversal of the masked identity assumed by *Power Rangers,* is often presumed to be Japanese. An admirer of *anime,* Craig McCracken purposely adopted what he calls an "iconic" style in this story of three little girls (who, in their creation by Professor Utonium, mistakenly had Chemical X added to their sugar and spice, infusing them with superpowers). Of his characters he says, "They're like graphic representations of a cute girl, like a symbol. I mean, they don't really look like real humans" (McCracken 1999:2). This could be a description of *anime* aesthetics, whose characters, like those of *Sailor Moon,* are not drawn with realism but instead display a playfulness meant to be funny, unexpected, and dissonant. Says McCracken: "I wanted to do a superhero film. . . . But I didn't want to do the big muscled guy thing 'cause it's been played out. . . . And I had happened to draw these little girls and just accidentally I went 'Wait!' What if they were the superheroes? I mean it would make them look even tougher because they're so cute. It's just that simple contrast of one idea opposed to another one. And it just was a funny idea to me, I found it cool" (2).

Calling the visual motif a mixture of *Underdog* (an American cartoon) and Hello Kitty, McCracken says the story line of *Powerpuff Girls* is moved by the personalities of the characters in a way meant to appeal to both children and adults. Indeed, because of its mix of action, girlishness, and parody, this show's crossover success has been remarkable. Boys watch it as well as girls, and *Powerpuff Girls* is popular with teenagers, college students, adult women, and gay men.

Fragmentation of Demand:
The Globalization of *Sailor Moon*

The model of "fashion action" developed by the product(ion) of *Sailor Moon* and trafficked as kids'/girls' mass culture in the global marketplace in the 1990s did exceedingly well in a number of places—Singapore, Hong Kong, Taiwan, Malaysia, Mexico, Spain, France, Canada, and Switzerland—in a business as lucrative as it is quixotic, given its play in the territory of desire and the imagination. Trading in toys, television shows, morphing, and superheroes, Bandai calls its business that of "fashion": the popularization and commodification of styles, tastes, and fads. Since its worldwide success with *Power Rangers,* Bandai has attempted to deterritorialize this business away from Japan. Going "beyond national boundaries" to become, as it now identifies itself, "a global entertainment enterprise" (Bandai Kabushiki-gaisha 1999:1, 3), Bandai aims to create character merchandise that will appeal to kids around the world. In the case of *Sailor Moon,* the product involved characters that moved beyond a number of national borders into the marketplaces and imaginations of millions of non-Japanese hosts. Its failure to do this in the United States at the mass level (thereby constituting a commercial success) is significant. But so is the fact that, in the aftermath of this "flop," *Sailor Moon* generated an active cult following among American kids.

While *Sailor Moon* received a mixed reception in the U.S. marketplace, it has achieved global popularity unlike any other product in girls' mass culture outside the fashion doll Barbie. Even in the United States, as we have seen, the show made greater inroads into the territory of the imagination (linked as this is to the slippery borders of body, identity, and desire) than was thought possible for a Japanese-made fantasy/product. Why did this property manage to take off around the world, becoming the type of (action/fashion) "girl" that once was Barbie's sole prerogative? Its appeal, I have argued, rests in the way action is articulated with and as fashion, changing both the type of "girl" who is (re)presented and the type of "girl" (which includes many boys) who consumes, and identifies with, these characters. This new "girl" is highly flexible: multiple characters who shift in space and time, alternate between heroism and watching their weight, and have bodies with (inter)changeable parts (tiaras that double as decoration and projectile weapons, for example). Action propels these girls into their fashionable display of multiplicity; their powers are activated and their bodies shape-shift as a preparation for battle. Identity is decentered from any one modality/body and is fragmented into multiple pieces that girls around the world can mix and match when they "play" *Sailor Moon*. This feature is a major factor in *Sailor Moon's* global appeal. It also makes play and identification a pursuit ever more linked to consumerism. Choosing from the plethora of body and character styles in this show resembles nothing so much as shopping at a mall.

Sailor Moon embodies the cultural logic of post-Fordism: fragmentation, flexibility, customization (just-in-time demand). As a global commodity/culture, then, it carries a different fantasy and a different politics than the more Fordist model. Coca-Cola, for example, built its empire around a primary product. A brown, sweetened syrup added to carbonated water and sold in glass bottles, this drink has galvanized worldwide tastes and profits to the point of "coca-colonizing" the global market. For decades, though, people have been drinking Coca-Cola for more than the taste. Embedded in the product's aura is the allure of other things. For many consumers around the world, this aura—of modernity, escape, wealth, satisfaction—gets associated with the country producing Coke: the United States. Thus, in what is also called cultural imperialism, "America" is sought in the purchase of a Coca-Cola, and (a fantasy) Americana is spread throughout the world via the medium of U.S.-made commodities. Increasingly, however, the Coca-Cola Company has needed to localize as well as diversify its product for different audiences. Coke ads are tweaked now for local marketplaces, and the company sells a range of drinks to appeal to diverse tastes. As consumer habits undergo what is called a "fragmentation of demand," the ability (of Coca-Cola or the United States) to dictate world tastes through singular products is fissuring as well.

Indeed, sales of Coke Classic are decreasing around the world, as are sales of carbonated soft drinks generally—what has been the essence of Coca-Cola's business. As an article titled "The New New Coke" in the *New York Times Magazine* put it: "Above all, the world's consumers are getting choosier. It is truer in richer nations than in poor ones, but almost everywhere consumers are becoming more sophisticated and demanding. We want more options. We want bottled water. We want health drinks. We want a brand new thing we have never seen before, and three months later we want another one" (Stevenson 2002:40).

Japan figures heavily in this article, described as a nation on the cutting edge of today's new market mentality. Japanese consumers demand continual (re)invention of commodities, and producers respond with innovations in design and style that are off the charts. In Tokyo, for example, people can buy drinks from vending machines by using cell phones, an innovation piloted by Coca-Cola. The company also keeps about two hundred brands of drinks on the market in Japan at any one time (in the United States it is less than one-fifth that number), 23 percent of which are always new. Recent fad drinks include Water Salad (a health drink), Love-Body (an herbal tea), and Real Gold (a hangover cure), and the biggest Coke brand in the country is not Coke Classic but Georgia Coffee, a coffee drink that comes in more than ten varieties. Unlike Coke Classic, the very "body" of Sailor Moon is grounded on the principles of morphing and multiplicity from the get-go. And following Japan's lead, this model of fragmentation of demand is spreading around the world. Noting how global consumerism is rapidly becoming dictated by the tastes of teenagers in Japan, the *New York Times* article says it all: "In short, we are all becoming Japanese teenagers" (Stevenson 2002:40).

Sailor Moon is a harbinger of a consumer demand/product based on transformation, fragmentation, and polymorphous perversity. And, in the mix-and-match aesthetic it inspires, there are shifts not only to the gender and genre of superheroism (mixed traits, assorted bodies and parts) but also to the identity of its cultural producer (Japan making it in a market hitherto dominated by the United States: global kids' trends). In the next chapter, I move to another Bandai toy property, *tamagotchi,* that sold profitably and popularly around the world in the late 1990s. Similarly constructed around a principle of transformation, this one featured not humans, however, but virtual pets that engender a play of interaction and attendance (as in raising a pet) rather than identification. How, why, and with what implications such a fantasy construction from Japan became a global fad on the eve of the millennium are the questions I ask there.

6 *Tamagotchi*

The Prosthetics of Presence

> Congratulations! This is a very special day for you because you now
> have your very own Tamagotchi! And just like you, your
> Tamagotchi needs some very special care to grow up into something
> you can be proud of—something that's nice and well behaved and
> won't embarrass you in front of your friends. That would be
> terrible. . . .
>
> One thing to remember, more than anything else, is to pay close,
> close attention to your Tamagotchi. The more you do what's right
> for it, the better it will grow up and the longer it will stay with you.
> Being a caretaker to your Tamagotchi is an adventure you're going
> to remember for the rest of your life.
>
> From *Tamagotchi: The Official Care Guide and Record Book*
> (Betz 1997:7, 8)

From Heroes to Pets:
Raising a Portable Plaything

At the peak of its popularity in the late 1990s, the *tamagotchi* was called
"the world's most popular toy" (Berfield 1997:33), a "sensation around the
world" (WuDunn 1997:17), the "current craze" (Clyde 1998:34), and the
"next Japanese gadget to sweep the continent" (Pollack 1997:37).[1] An egg-
shaped device that hangs on a key holder, the *tamagotchi* is a portable game
with a liquid crystal screen whose purpose is to raise virtual pets. Targeted
first to eight-year-olds, the electronic play pal took off with teenage girls
and adults when it was launched in Japan in December 1996. With its
crossover appeal and multiple functions—a toy that is simultaneously pet,
gadget, game, fashion accessory, and virtual reality—the *tamagotchi* sold
out in Japanese stores only days after hitting the market. Saving Bandai, its
manufacturer, from a slump in toy sales, the product became a hit both at
home and abroad, where it was exported much more quickly than earlier
waves of Japanese kid properties had been.[2] (The lag time was only five
months for its debut in the United States, for example, in contrast to three
years for *Sailor Moon* and eight years for *Power Rangers.*) Hitting the U.S.

marketplace at FAO Schwartz in May 1997, thirty thousand *tamagotchi* items were sold in three days, and three million were sold in three months.[3] By May of the following year, the game was selling in more than eighty countries and had produced revenues of more than $160 million.

The *tamagotchi* also generated a craze of virtual spin-offs: "pets" in a range of shapes—from dinosaurs, gods, and babies to fish, chimps, and dogs—marketed by a host of companies (Fujitsu, Tiger Electronics, Sega, Casio, Playmates, PF Magic). The medium migrated as well; from handheld toys, digital petdom spread to computer software, television games, and cell phones (the *tamapitchi,* for example, is a cross between a PHS cell phone and a regular *tamagotchi* that, for 45,000 yen, or $500, allows callers to send digital images of their virtual pets over the phone to friends). In what became a global fad on the eve of the new millennium, the *tamagotchi* is regarded as the ur-form. If not the first virtual pet of all time, it is the form in which this cyborgian fantasy was popularized and (re)produced as mass culture.

Simulating petdom—sprouting a lifelike image of a pet that users interact with as if it were alive—was Yokoi Akihiro's aim in creating the *tamagotchi.*[4] As he relates in his book (1997) on "birthing" the virtual pet, Yokoi was inspired by a television commercial he saw in which a young boy, packing to go away on vacation, puts his pet turtle in the suitcase. As an animal lover himself (with an apartment and office stocked with "real" pets), Yokoi says two aspects of the scene touched him: the boy's attachment to his pet and the limited mobility of flesh-and-blood animals. Yokoi's story of creating a "pet" that could travel everywhere with kids is reminiscent of Morita Akio's reputed inspiration for the Sony Walkman. Walking the streets of New York and wishing he could listen to music the way he could at home on a radio, record player, or hi-fi, Morita was possessed by a vision of mobile music. Like Yokoi, he was driven to create a machine that could move along with its owner.[5] Portability was key in both cases, as reflected in the product names that resulted: "walk" in Walkman and "watch" in *tamagotchi* (the original idea was that the pets would hatch from eggs, *tamago*, that would be carried on *watches = tamagotchi*). But movement, in this age of flux and mobility, was only one concern. Equally important to both men was what their nomadic machines would do for their users: namely, expand personal access to something—music, pets, intimate attachments—that would otherwise be limited to specific places and times. In the case of virtual petdom, access moves out of the home into a space that is more fluid yet, coincidentally, more grounded as well—a handheld egg with a digital screen that is carried in the pocket or backpack or on the key chain of its owner.

As Mitsui and Hosokawa (1998) have written about karaoke, one of the greatest innovations in what they call the cultural technology produced by postwar Japan is its (re)organization of space and body. Blurring the distinction often made between technology and culture, they see in the invention of karaoke a mechanical system that also becomes the conduit for cultural production. As a technology, it allows for not only the reproduction of music but also the (re)staging of songs popularized by well-known stars, whose voices are deleted and replaced by that of the karaoke singer. And, as a global pastime, karaoke has traveled around the world from Nepal and Columbia to Italy and the United States (where even a McDonald's in Ohio features karaoke). Given its interactivity, karaoke is engaged differently in different places, often incorporating (and remaking) very local traditions of participatory singing. In this sense, the globalized practice of karaoke does not produce a homogeneous culture, and neither Japan nor Japanese music may be explicitly referenced in karaoke clubs outside Japan.

Still, karaoke is far more than a "hard" technology. It is not only a medium for expressive culture (the personal and interpersonal staging of songs), but also a technological advance that enacts, embodies, and spatially expresses this culture. The word means empty *(kara)* orchestra *(oke)*. In practice, though, karaoke empties the "orchestra" of certain bodies as much as it fills this space up with new ones. Giving an elasticity to the borders of musical performer/performance, karaoke allows anyone to be a singer and the stage to be a restaurant, bar, or family room. Body and space are both malleable, reshaping the experience and production of performative singing. The same is true of the Walkman, writes Hosokawa, as music becomes part of the everyday "walk act" (deCerteau quoted in Hosokawa 1984:175–76) and sound comes from a system wired to the body itself. As the person holding the Walkman moves through the course of her everyday routines, she listens to music that at once decontextualizes the outside world and recontextualizes it according to her own customized tastes. The activity is both private and personal—situating it ambiguously between autonomy and autism (Chambers 1990:2). This effect extends and also mutates the body, turning the music-listening experience and the Walkman itself into a bodily prosthesis. "Whether it is the Walkman that charges the body, or, inversely, the body that charges the Walkman, it is difficult to say. The Walkman works not as a prolongation of the body . . . but as a built-in part or, because of its intimacy, as an intrusion-like prosthesis. The Walkman holder plays the music and listens to the sound come from his own body" (Hosokawa 1984:176).

The realignment of the intimacies of music onto the geography of body and place is the great innovation of the Walkman and karaoke. It suggests a reconfiguration of not only body and space but also subjectivity: what Deleuze has called the "singularity" of the postmodern subject that, distinct from the individual, is "anonymous, impersonal, pre-individual, and no-madic." Plugged into technology like the Walkman, "singular" subjects con-nect to their environment (and others) in a relationship at once distant and intimate, akin to the "intimate alienation" I discussed in chapter 3 and what Deleuze labels "positive distance" (Hosokawa 1984:169–70).

The same is true of the *tamagotchi*, though a different aspect of life is re-aligned here. Whereas music is an experience or performance, a pet, at least as it is conventionally conceived, is a living organism—usually an animal. One of the most noted characteristics of the *tamagotchi*, however, and one that contributes to its popular and global appeal, is the uncanny sense of presence it generates in players. Owners repeatedly comment on how their *tamagotchi* feel "real" and how they interact with these pixilated images as if they were "actual pets." Much like music, in fact, it is the experience (in this case, of having a pet) that Yokoi Aki emphasizes in his descriptions of crafting *tamagotchi*. The physical appearance of the pet is less important than the personal relationship one forms with it. As Yokoi claims from his own experience, cuteness matters most when a person first buys a pet. After that, a bond is formed mainly by taking care of the organism: endless chores and duties *(mendō)* that Yokoi implanted in a game sequence meant to mimic those involved in the raising of a flesh-and-blood pet (Yokoi 1997:70). By manipulating buttons on the toy and icons on the screen, a player attends to her *tamagotchi*'s needs and desires (for food, play, disci-pline, medicine, attention, and poop cleanup). According to how attentively the player follows this script, the *tamagotchi* "grows up," assuming one of several possible forms (some more desirable than others, according to the information that accompanies the toy). But the player needs to be con-stantly vigilant. And these menial labors constitute play in the context of the *tamagotchi*: what gives "life" to the virtual pet and intimacy to the bonds formed between people and their machines/*tamagotchi*.

This playscape differs from the imaginary realms I have been exploring in the two previous chapters: stories of superheroes who look human and fight as moral warriors against evil that are enscripted in mass-media pro-ductions (television shows, children's magazines, comic books). With *tama-gotchi*, we are dealing with a toy whose characters are not recycled from a popular kids' show or comic—what Bandai exploited with such success in kid hits like the *Power Ranger* series and *Sailor Moon*, and a marketing strategy whose payoff was beginning to diminish by 1996. Yokoi Akihiro set out to design a new kind of toy, and, indeed, the corporeality of the *tamagotchi* characters is different altogether from the *mecha* (male) Rangers and fleshy (female) Scouts. After an initial empty screen, the *tamagotchi*'s image fills in gradually, as in karaoke, in response to a player's input. The likeness is sketchy even when the pet has fully matured: a smiling amoeba, a head on two feet, a flower, with eyes and beak, in a pot.[6] The *tamagotchi* are neither humans nor heroes, and the shapes they assume are meant to be weird. This makes them more interesting to children, according to Yokoi (1997:83), who aimed to design "strange living beings" *(henna ikimono):* a queer (and postgender) subset, as it were, of phenomenal life.

This is the cyborgian frontier that we have encountered already in morphing superheroes who shift from human to machine mode with bodies that transform and translate into weapons/vehicles/robots/jewels. With the *tamagotchi,* though, the interface has shifted. Because the cyborgs here are pets rather than heroic humans, they invite an imaginary relationship other than identification. Further, the materiality of the image is different. Rather than being pregiven forms projected onto a television screen or comic book page, the *tamagotchi* result from an interactive game held and adjusted by the player herself (who has various options, including "killing" the pet). In that cyborgs are both tools and myths, the mythology given their use-value shifts here as well. Superheroes are cyberweapons programmed to serve collective interests: defending the homeland (and friends) by destroying aliens bent on conquest and change. *Tamagotchi,* by contrast, are a strange new life-form designed to be the virtual pets of their owners. The mytho-play dynamics move here from the grandiose (saving others) to the personal (raising cute pets), and from humanism (protecting earth and humanity) to the posthuman (suturing attachments to digital icons). A different logic— and fetishization—of bodies, powers, and the human-nonhuman contact zone is at work in the *tamagotchi,* reflecting, and refracting, something different in the world, the imagination (with which to play and escape "reality"), and global marketability. For the child player, the characters invite a relationship not of mimesis (mimicking the morphin stances and performativity/sexiness of the superheroes) but of ownership, caregiving, and petdom.

Permeable Borders:
Widening the Fan Base

The *tamagotchi* is a fitting toy for the post–cold war era of the new millennium. This is a world in which clear-cut divisions between friend and enemy no longer exist. Borders are more permeable than permanent, and identity —whether of nation, gender, or race—is difficult to anchor in any one spot. As reflected in the *tamagotchi* game, forging alliances between self and other is emphasized over distinguishing (and defending) these as bounded entities. And this interface becomes a play zone: one that represents postindustrial confusion as much as fusion in connections between organism and machine, human and pet, labor and leisure. Accordingly, the *tamagotchi* are represented according to the rules of fantasy, not realism. Drawn as ironic, iconic sketches, the lines are recognizable but assembled with a syntax that is both disorienting and enchanting—a rose with eyes and feet, a head with poochy lips and a tail. As Haraway (1991) has written about cyborgs, there is a progressive potential to liberating bodies from nature when nature is used ideologically to assign power and privilege to bodies of only certain types (white and male, for example). As if trying to assure such liberation in a global marketplace long dominated by the United States, Bandai came up with a toy that featured neither humans nor the realistic style long held to be Hollywood's cachet in entertainment (particularly film, but also television).

As will be recalled, Bandai's experiences with marketing *Power Rangers* and *Sailor Moon* in the United States were fraught with difficulties. Networks refused to take on *Jyū Renjā* for eight years, and when Fox Network did make an alliance with Tōei Studios, the condition for acceptance was radical reconstruction. Only after all the sequences of the Rangers in their human, premorphed forms had been reshot with American actors in California (and then spliced together with the action footage from Japan) was *Power Rangers* reborn in hybrid form. The assumption, by the Americans managing the property, was that American children would not identify with Asian heroes on-screen. Any sign of cultural difference, including the show's origins in Japan, was effaced for U.S. transmission. As we have seen, this remade version—with its American rather than Japanese identity and actors—is the form in which *Power Rangers* traveled around the world as a global hit. *Sailor Moon* was a somewhat different case, given that its medium was animation rather than live action, a fact that made alteration of the images more difficult even though, in appearance at least, the cartoon characters could pass as Anglo-Americans. But in the portrayal of lifestyle and dramatic intrigue, the show—as is commonly assessed by those in the business—was too little altered for American audiences to succeed in the channels of mainstream kids' TV, though it did fine in other countries like France, Spain, and Hong Kong and generated plenty of American fans when it was broadcast on Cartoon Network. (This discrepancy is an issue I return to in the following chapters on *Pokémon*.) In either case, launching these properties in a global marketplace has been dictated by American productions and tastes and involves major issues around cultural translation/transformation.

Such has not been the case, however, with the *tamagotchi*, a toy that configures body and place very differently. *Tamagotchi* are not only something other than human; they grow up in a world deterritorialized from any geographic place. The only context here is that of cyber interactions that mimic the biological rhythms involved in the care of a flesh-and-blood pet. This "biology" is itself a (cultural) construction, of course, since cleaning up poop or turning off lights is hardly hardwired into the care of animals around the world. Yet whatever of "culture" is at work here is far less overt than it is in the case of morphing superheroes. Virtually biologic (or biologically virtual), the *tamagotchi* realizes Bandai's corporate policy for the late 1990s: creating toy merchandise that "transcends time and space, and goes beyond national boundaries" (Bandai Kabushikigaisha 1998:5). The company's aim, both in the products it sells and in the markets it sells to, is to stretch borders. Because its business of character merchandising "depends on knowing to which specific groups a particular character is likely to appeal" (4), the goal is to make characters that will appeal to as broad a consumer base as possible. In its corporate guide for 1997, Bandai uses the *tamagotchi* as an example of this very principle. Targeted first to senior high school girls in Japan, it attracted a much wider fan base in both the domestic and global marketplace than previous products. As Bandai says proudly: "These characters have now become the close friends of many, many people" (4).

In the form of this virtual "friend," Bandai has come up with a toy commodity that has transcended national boundaries with remarkable ease. In doing so, the *tamagotchi* reflects shifts in the way place both figures in and is configured as entertainment in global kids' trends. The place of Japan has greater prestige in the economy of the imagination these days, challenging (as other countries have) the hegemony once held by U.S. culture and its cultural industries. Yet the construction of place itself as it is imaged and imagined in commodified play is changing as well. In an era of space-time compression—intensified speed, movement between borders of various kinds, communication and travel across time—the parameters of place become fuzzy. But this does not mean that place no longer matters in how people experience the world. Rather, homes and intimacies remain important even when their mapping and mooring shift. The proposal by cultural geographer Doreen Massey to redefine place in terms other than rigid boundaries or unique identities is relevant here: "What gives place specificity is not some long internalized history but the fact that it is constructed out of a particular constellation of social relations, meeting and weaving together at a particular locus" (1994:154). Place is both fluid and anchored, held together at both junctures by what Massey calls social relations.

The idea of petdom, even when it amounts to a virtual creation, engenders relations and interactions. In Massey's sense, then, the *tamagotchi* is a new kind of place that produces new sets of relationships—global commodity flows, postindustrial kids' trends, mobile and imaginary attachments. Both its power and its appeal come from combining movement with the groundedness of relationship—a convenient pal, portable intimacy, traveling pet. How does this contradictory mix work in practice?

The Discipline of Play

The *tamagotchi* (or *tamagotch*, as it is also called in Japanese) sold for about eighteen dollars in stores and came in various colors and styles. These included a proliferation of species—angels, dinosaurs, chickens, ocean and forest creatures—and, to tweak this nurturing toy more toward boys, the Digimon version, featuring monsters that can be hooked up to a buddy's *digimonchi* (what the Digimon *tamagotchi* is called) to fight in what is called the "dock 'n rock" function.[7] To start the *tamagotchi*, the player presses the reset button on the back, adjusts the time, and pushes the middle one of three buttons on the bottom (figure 28). Immediately a pulsating egg appears on the liquid crystal screen, which hatches five minutes later as a smiling face, in white or black, named *Bebitchi* (Baby-tchi) or *Shirobebitchi* (white Baby-tchi). Significantly, these Japanese names remain on the toys worldwide. In the English-language official Bandai guide, they are given phonetic rendering in parentheses—for example, *takotchi* (taco-tchee), *tamatchi* (tama-tchee), and *kuchitamachi* (koo-chee-ta-ma-tchee).[8] Lit up on the screen now are the all-important caretaking icons: symbols that, standing for the pet's needs, the player must attend to in order to raise a happy and healthy *tamagotchi*. A fork and knife signifies food, for example, and a rubber ducky stands for cleaning up poop. Altogether the player responds to eight icons by working the buttons at the bottom. These are food (dispensed in both meals and snacks); lights (that must be turned off when the *tamagotchi* is sleeping); play (transacted through games); medicine (given when the *tamagotchi* gets sick); cleaning (the follow-up to a poop, which appears as a Hershey chocolate kiss on the screen); the health meter (a scale that registers how happy and healthy the *tamagotchi* is at any one time); discipline (administered by pushing a button); and attention (lights

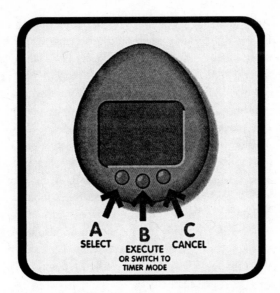

Figure 28. Prosthetic presence: the *tamagotchi* as egg. (TM & © 1997 Bandai Company, Ltd. Tamagotchi and all related logos, names, and distinctive likenesses herein are the exclusive property of Bandai Company, Ltd. and Bandai America Incorporated. Licensed by Bandai Entertainment Incorporated. All rights reserved.)

and beeps from the *tamagotchi* indicating that it needs something or, as the Bandai guide suggests, is just being bratty).

As a game, the basic routine is as follows. After the *tamagotchi* hatches as a baby, the player needs to interact regularly with the toy by keeping the pet happy and healthy. How well the *tamagotchi* is doing can be determined by reading the health meter, which displays its current weight and age (one day in *tamagotchi* time equals one year of earth time), as well as three scales registering how happy, well fed, and disciplined the pet is. Each scale appears on the screen as four hearts that indicate an optimal situation when they are filled and encroaching danger when they are empty. To keep the hearts filled, a player feeds the pet by doling out meals or snacks; disciplines it by simply pressing the discipline icon; and gives love and stimulation by playing games (the player guesses whether the *tamagotchi* is going to turn right or left at the play mode and must win three out of five guesses to earn credits for playtime). In addition to these regular interactions, there are also more intermittent demands. These include remembering to turn off the lights when the *tamagotchi* falls asleep, administering medicine if the sick sign shows up on the screen, cleaning up at the sight of a Hershey poop, and figuring out what the *tamagotchi* needs when it beeps for attention. As Foucault would note, play here is a disciplinary regime in which players become disciplined into assuming the subject position of (virtual) caregiver.

The overall objective, at least if one plays according to the official directions, is to keep the *tamagotchi* alive as long as possible and to raise a pet with socially desirable characteristics. To achieve these goals, a player must constantly interact with the *tamagotchi:* giving it food and love, keeping an eye out for sickness and mess, and being as mindful about discipline and moderation as kindness and devotion. As the instructions on the package for the *tamagotchi* angel clearly state: "It's up to you to raise your Tamagotchi Angel with just the right measure of love and attention. If you're successful, your Tamagotchi Angel will fly home to be rewarded with its wings. If not, well . . . you can always try again!"

In the case of the original *tamagotchi,* successful parenting is measured by the personality the pet assumes in developing through different stages of growth. The infant phase, which occurs about one hour after hatching, is said to be the crucial time for determining a *tamagotchi*'s adult personality. As it says in the English-language version of Bandai's *tamagotchi* official guide that sold in U.S. bookstores for $5.95, "Honey or brat? Nice or nasty? What you do at this stage makes a big difference in how your Tamagotchi turns out" (Betz 1997:35). By the childhood stage (figure 29),three to seven years old (*tamagotchi* time), differences are already apparent; the frisky *tamatchi* and the energetic *tongaritchi* bear the signs of great caretaking, but the sluggish *hashitamachi* and the happy-go-lucky but unattractive *kuchitamatchi* suggest lax parenting. By the adult phase of middle age (appearing after about six or seven days), the range of personality types—fourteen in total—has broadened further. *Masukutchi* is quiet and spies on everyone; *ginjirotchi* is empathetic and independent; *kusatchi* loves nightclubs and heavy metal; *mametchi* is mannered and brilliant; *hashizotchi* has disgusting food habits and little energy; *kuchipatchi* is laid-back and dull-witted; *zukitchi* tends toward meanness and hyperactivity; and *mimitchi* is witty, charming, and a math wizard. The shapes, too, now come in an interesting assortment. Each is an assemblage of physical traits—ears, lips, beaks, tentacles, leaves, feet, eyes, legs, masks—that, familiar on a dog, badger, or rose, come together here in a grammar that remixes the virtual and the real. These pets are, at once, both naturalistic and strange. Takotchi is an octopus (*tako* in Japanese) with a rounded beak, one eye, and a periscope on its head;

Figure 29. The *tamagotchi* grows up: a range of childhood and adulthood stages. (Courtesy of Bandai Company, Ltd.)

Nyorotchi (after *nyoro nyoro* for squirming) is a spermlike blob with a wiggly tail, big lips, and an eye; Bill is a human head with a stylish beret sitting atop a pair of legs.

The general wisdom in *tamagotchi* culture is that certain adult forms are better than others. For players I spoke with, these superior forms were usually the better "behaved," more active, or rarer *tamagotchi* (for example, both Bill and Zachi are "secret characters" that appear as the last, rare stage). According to the official Bandai guide, desirability stems from behavior rather than appearance. Approving of certain characteristics (intelligence, alertness, cheerfulness, and independence), it disapproves of others (laziness, mysteriousness, dullness, and weirdness). And, consistent with the game's play logic, a direct correlation is made between "good" caretaking and positive traits in *tamagotchi*. The guide applauds, for example, the appearance of Mametchi, who boasts an IQ of 250, saying it "shows that you've really paid a lot of attention to your Tamagotchi" (Betz 1997:41). But, for Takarotchi—with smelly feet and a mysterious personality—it notes, "If you have been neglecting your Tamagotchi, it may turn out like this" (38).

This script is most apparent in the Japanese edition of the Bandai guidebook. Entitled *Tamagotchi Boshitechō*, it is designed like the health records—distributed by the ward offices and called *boshitechō*—used by Japanese women for charting the growth of their babies.[9] In the *tamagotchi* edition, advice for raising the pet is clearly articulated in terms of becoming a mother and keeping a "bright *[akarui]* family." These suggestions range from the basics in toy maintenance (feed, play with, and attend to your *tamagotchi* promptly) to the ideological in imaginary family making (maintain your own health as a mother, never intentionally kill your pet no matter how it develops, remember that all *tamagotchi* are brothers and sisters, so never mistreat one). The guidebook concludes with a list of parental ideals whose scope has been broadened even further: raising *tamagotchi* with a social consciousness. As the guide recommends, bring *tamagotchi* up as "members of society" to be individualistic but also cooperative, with a keen appreciation of nature, science, the arts, and morality. The last item on this list sums it all up: "If *tamagotchi* is raised by joining love with goals, it will be able to contribute to human culture and peace as a national citizen" (Bandai Kabushikigaisha 1997:1–9).

One might wonder to what "nation" the *tamagotchi* is to be enjoined in citizenship, given the very global territory Bandai intended for this playscape. The suggestion seems parodically (if playfully) excessive. Indeed, I have never encountered a player of any nationality who conceived the virtual identity of a *tamagotchi* to be anything approaching that of upstanding citizen. Yet the fantasy of a bond developing between *tamagotchi* and player that feels humanlike even if it fails to mimic human life completely is not Bandai's alone. One commentator reporting on the *tamagotchi* craze for *AsiaWeek* attributed some of the intensity *tamagotchi* owners described feeling for their pets to the fact they serve as substitutes for real pets, which few families in crowded living conditions can afford (Berfield 1997). In a related vein, Nagao Takeshi, a Japanese journalist, linked the popularity of toys like *tamagotchi* and games like *Pokémon* to contemporary lifestyles of Japanese children, who are lonely, busy, and pressured by school. A toy they can interact with when they are alone, and one from which they can gain some measure of feedback, response, and—in these senses—life, is highly appealing (Nagao 1998).

A number of psychologists in the United States claimed instead that the popularity of *tamagotchi* arose from the sense of empowerment they gave children in being responsible for the care and fate of their virtual pets (Berfield 1997). This perception also led to a debate about whether these positive feelings outweigh the sense of loss experienced by some children when the *tamagotchi* dies (Lee 1997:264). On both scores the psychologist Andrew Cohen described the *tamagotchi* as "the most powerful product I've ever heard of in terms of what it demands from a child" (cited in Lawson 1997:A18). Others also viewed the *tamagotchi* as a type of breakthrough product that builds on old play forms of mimesis and pretense but propels these kinds of experience into the new dimension of cyberspace. Here the relationship with a virtual pet can be, in some ways, more interactive and more continuous than with flesh-and-blood pets that stay, for the most part, at home. *Tamagotchi* accompanied their owners everywhere—a fact much reported on because of the disruptions caused in the classroom, where the beeps and demands of needy *tamagotchi* led to a widespread ban (in Japan, the United States, and many countries where the toy was a fad) on their presence in school. Even here, though, a number of teachers and parents found the caretaking demanded of the *tamagotchi* and the nurturing it therefore elicits to be positive play qualities encouraged by the toy.

The type of intimacy children formed with a *tamagotchi* was healthy in another way, according to Heather Kelley (1998), director of online development for GirlGames (a company that makes video games for girls). The care taken by children in raising their digital pets encouraged a degree of personalization and emotional closeness with cybertechnology previously unseen with kids. Here the mode of operation is nurturance, in contrast to the more competitive stance demanded by fighting and action that is the prevailing motif in the bulk of video games even today. This focus draws in more girls to an electronic game field still dominated (in the United States, at least) by males.[10] The *tamagotchi* is also a toy that not only stands in for but also bleeds into other social relationships. In the voluminous response Kelley received to a posting about the *tamagotchi* on her Web site for girls, many spoke of the toy in terms of relationships with parents or friends. Whether they were leaving a pet in the care of friend or family, swapping advice, or sharing pet-raising experiences, there were numerous stories about *tamagotchi* as a medium for interpersonal relations between humans.

In the end, no matter how diligent a player has been or what kind of relationship has been formed, the *tamagotchi* is terminated—or, in terms of the life conceit fostered by the game, it dies. In the early period of life, this can occur in less than an hour if a pet is left hungry, unhappy, sick, or not cleaned. As the *tamagotchi* matures, however, it becomes more independent and can be left unattended for longer stretches. Eventually, however, players will ignore their *tamagotchi* long enough that they die. The average life span is about fifteen days; the record, reputedly fifty-nine days, was set by an eleven-year-old schoolboy in England (Clyde 1998). When the end comes, it is signaled by a gravestone and cross in the Japanese version (using Western symbols that may serve to mark the virtual, playful rendering of "death" here).[11] Because virtual death was thought to be too traumatic for American kids, however, this finale was rescripted for the U.S. edition. Instead of passing from life, *tamagotchi* are said to pass to a different world—an alien planet—marked on the screen by an angel with wings (incorporating comfortable allusions to heaven). Despite this change, a *tamagotchi*'s demise is interpreted, even by Americans, as death, and users across the world have "played" with this loss in a variety of ways. There has been a host of virtual memorials—obituaries, graveyards, funerals, and testimonials—printed mainly over the Web but even in obituaries published in regular newspapers. There are reports, as well, of *tamagotchi* mourning counselors. Another twist to the death routine is that some users purposely try to kill off their *tamagotchi*, a practice that has sprouted chat rooms, Web sites, and user groups devoted (both for and against) to the issue of sadism against *tamagotchi* (Berfield 1997).

Resonant with this age of replaceable parts and flexible accumulation, the *tamagotchi* can also be restarted after it has died. If the player pushes the reset button on the back, another egg appears, and the whole life cycle begins again. Until the battery runs out, the *tamagotchi* can be endlessly reborn, though most users I have spoken to say their interest in the pet usually runs out first. Then the *tamagotchi* becomes less a pet than an object: a plastic egg on a key chain that decorates a backpack, holds a key, or is simply shoved to the back of a drawer.

Sociality and the New Work of the Imagination

The *tamagotchi* is a toy that produces a pet whose existence, in visual form at least, is contained on the screen. In this sense, it deals with the realm of the imagination when we define that term, as does the *Random House Dictionary*, as forming mental images of something not actually present, and believing or conjecturing this thing's existence. In the case of the *tama-*

gotchi, of course, the images formed are digital rather than mental, but the game plays with the same borders as does the imagination itself: between an image, not in and of itself materially "alive," and a phenomenal existence that is read into and out of the imagistic form.

The way in which the *tamagotchi* plays with the boundaries of the imaginary is symptomatic of the social reality we inhabit: one in which virtuality is becoming increasingly integrated into everyday life and movement, of both people and things, is rapid and intense. The anthropologist Arjun Appadurai has argued that conditions of deterritorialization and media proliferation have changed, and heightened, the work of the imagination today. I apply this thesis here to the *tamagotchi.* How does a virtual pet both reflect and shape an imagination that not only fits these postindustrial times but also helps kids adjust to a world where the border between the imaginary and the real is shifting so quickly? Because I find Appadurai's argument so useful (though not without its limitations), I take the liberty of laying it out in some detail. Afterward, I apply this model to the *tamagotchi* and its play logic of imaginary life that effects a reimagination of sociality, subjectivity, and space.

In *Modernity at Large* (1996), Arjun Appadurai argues that the world we live in today is characterized by the new role that imagination plays in social life. This state of affairs has been brought about, he says, by a historical rupture in recent times triggered by two separate but interrelated developments. These are the rise of electronic media (technologies that represent and reproduce the world by stories and images) and the increase in migrations (the movement and displacement of people away from "home" to someplace else). Linked together, these changes have produced a new order of instability in the world today because images as well as people are in constant, though not necessarily overlapping, circulation. As Appadurai describes it, the work of the imagination inheres in the social condition itself; societies have always transcended and reframed ordinary life by recourse to mythologies of various kinds. The effect of this work is to imaginatively deform and reform social life, or what Émile Durkheim analyzed in his *Elementary Forms of the Religious Life* (1961)—the rituals that ritualistically rehearse, or perform, to use Judith Butler's word (1990), social norms, tightening the social in the minds and lives of individuals. In the format of a rain dance or initiation ceremony, a community is physically brought together and also symbolically expressed. The expression is less literal than symbolic and articulates the logic of a place in highly imaginative terms: shaved hair, blood-red tattoos, immersion in water. While the meaning is abstract (abstracting society into ritual), the experience is emotionally and sensually intense. Beating drums, chanting cheers, ingesting intoxicants—ceremonies are special, in both time and space, creating an atmosphere dislocated from everyday routines. Given that the ceremonial is also social, carried out by and for members of the community, the feeling of hyperaliveness it triggers helps connect individuals to their society. These flights of the imagination, in fact, are as important for sustaining the social as is the materiality of production, reproduction, and cohabitation as a group. Durkheim's great insight, adopted by Appadurai, was that sociality depends on the imagination as much as it does on anything "real."

For Appadurai, the operation of imagination today is distinguished by the conditions that David Harvey (1989) and Fredric Jameson (1984) attribute to late capitalism and its cultural state of postmodernism. In an economy of continual downsizing, outsourcing, roboticization, and flexible accumulation, people are constantly driven, out of need or desire, to move and remake their jobs, identities, relationships, and communities. Ruptures to self and social networks occur frequently, and distance and alienation are commonplaces of everyday life. Technology, too, is continually altering and reordering the dimensions of human existence, remaking bodies and remapping the ways in which people make a living and experience the world. As machines become embedded ever more deeply into life and even flesh, the line between human and nonhuman increasingly blurs. So does that between material reality and the image making we rely upon to see, know, and interact with our world(s)—cameras, video players, televisions, computers, ultrasound, game systems, movies. It is in the electronic production and reproduction of materiality—what I call virtuality—where Appadurai locates the role played by imagination today. Just as the print media were a prerequisite for imagining the nation at the moment of modernity, as Benedict Anderson (1983) has argued, electronic media produce the images that imagine community, reality, and self in today's postmodern era. Appadurai gives the example of diasporic migrations—how people, displaced from their home communities, will hold on to these places through the imaginaries made available by CNN, photographs, movies, and videotapes. As he points out, these images—of the world, homeland, place, and ethnicity—are shaped as much by desire and longing as they are by anything real. What Appadurai means by imagination, then, is a vision of a life-form—a community, a human, a pet—that feels real and is related to, but is not the equivalent of, material reality.

How does this notion of imaginative "realness" tally with the way Appadurai also depicts the more generic processes of imagination fundamental to any society—the reframing and transcending of ordinary life by means of ritual and myth? Both processes entail reimagining everyday sociality at a distance, but the nature of this distance has shifted. Ritual entails assembling a community in a space that is symbolically distinct from daily routines; the postmodern imaginary involves invoking community across time and space via images that stand (in) for the phenomenally "real." In Appadurai's mind, a historical shift has indeed occurred. Whereas once it was sequestered into special ceremonies, ritualistic events, and sacred objects, imagination is now part and parcel of quotidian life. It still involves an order of play, performance, creativity, and myth, but now these impulses are scattered throughout the everyday, just as the collectives that the imagination is attached to (diasporic communities, for example) are scattered as well.

For Appadurai, place and imagination are directly related; it is the deterritorialization of the world over the past two decades that has led to the diffusion of the imagination into everyday life. That is, as people have physically dispersed, moving out of and between places whose borders were once tighter, they come to rely more on images of place, identity, and sociality that become, or blur into, their experience of the world. But the relationship between place and imagination is limited neither to people who literally migrate nor to images of places that people identify, in whatever sense, as their own home. Deterritorialization refers to a much broader slippage of the local—to a world in which people are encountering difference and dislocation much more frequently than ever before. The places where we materially live, play, and work and the constructed spheres representing and imagining life both feature people, ideas, and things from different, shifting worlds.

The imagination, in my reading of Appadurai, is what captures and recreates a sense of sociality in a world fissured by dispersal and encounters with difference. Sociality—our sense of connectedness to people, communities, humanness, and life—is what centers subjectivity. Today, sociality is in a radical state of fluctuation and change; uprootedness from bonds that constitute home, place, and belonging is a commonplace. But opportunities to form new kinds of ties with distinct, sometimes different, sets of pleasures are also present. This duality lends to sociality a sense of what Appadurai calls schizophrenia (Jameson [1984] uses the same word to refer to postmodernism, as do Deleuze and Guattari [1977] in reference to the lived experience of capitalism today): locating roots, attachments, and identity in places that are familiar and long-standing as well as different, fragmented, and new. Thus imagination, as the mechanism people use to ground themselves in an increasingly ungrounded world, is inherently schizophrenic as well.

Appadurai's theory of the imagination provocatively links deterritorialization to the proliferation of images—two phenomena that indeed characterize conditions of global capitalism—and posits (new) constructions for subjectivity and intersubjectivity: what he collapses under the term *imagination*. There are also problems with his thesis; it is overly schematic, too rigid in its postulation of a historical rupture, and sketchy on the issues of both power and production (how precisely is the imagination produced, by and for whom, in what forms, and with what vested interests?). It is his formulation, nevertheless, of a schizophrenically charged force positioned between groundedness and mobility that I find extremely useful here. For this is the rubric of the *tamagotchi:* a pet that goes virtually anywhere but whose existence is rooted in, and mimetic of, corporeal upkeep.

Evocative Objects and Labor-Intensive Toys

In the *tamagotchi*, imaginary petdom is coupled with the banality of cleaning up poop, dispensing food, and turning off lights. When it came out, observers called it a new kind of toy because of its admixture of virtuality with a caregiving so intense to be unprecedented, according to some, in an era of cybertechnology better known for saving labor and enhancing human powers. *Tamagotchi* require so much work, in fact, that adults have been typically confused as to what is fun about them at all. Indeed, Bandai rejected the concept initially because the pleasures of the toy seemed too overwhelmed by the menial chores it entailed (WuDunn 1997).

Yet *tamagotchi* succeeded and became immensely popular as a playtoy that transforms duty and responsibility into enchantment and entertainment. For whom, how, and why is a toy that doubles as work compelling? Players were children as young as five (more girls than boys the world over), and adults of any age (particularly in Japan, where *tamagotchi*, first targeted to teenage girls, were also popular with young working women and even *sararīman*).[12] What fans said they liked about the *tamagotchi* is that it feels more serious, meaningful, and real to them than other toys do. It "relies on me," one eleven-year-old American boy told me; "it's as if it were really alive," a ten-year-old American girl said. "This play literally changes the player's life," a reporter for the Japanese magazine *Dime* noted after keeping his own *tamagotchi* alive for close to three days. In reporting on the phenomenon, he also quoted a Japanese girl who, when asked to define what a *tamagotchi* was on Japanese TV, answered that it was "life" *(inochi)*, a sensation that came to her after six straight hours of caregiving (*Dime* 1997:110). In his explanation of the toy's magically earthy appeal, the reporter noted that *tamagotchi* players are in a space hovering between the imagination and reality, and that while this is also true of other entertainment media (movies, *anime*, TV), what distinguishes the *tamagotchi* is its mobility.

Imaginary pets go almost everywhere, inserting themselves into a child's everyday routines and continually asserting their presence by demanding, over and over, attention and play. This, of course, can get boring or burdensome. When it does, however, detachment comes as easily as attachment once did. A number of kids I interviewed said they felt little pain in seeing their pets leave the screen. A few, in fact, said this was part of the fun: eliminating a source of work and annoyance even if this was a "pet" to which they had once been deeply attached. One rowdy ten-year-old American boy went further by announcing, "I love killing off my *tamagotchi*"—an admission that seemingly fazed none of the other kids assembled in my interview group.[13] In this sense, *tamagotchi* fluctuate between presence and absence; the player shifts between engaging the virtual pet as if it were alive and disengaging from it as if it were dead, nothing but a machine, a discarded plaything to be put aside in a drawer (and retrieved when the urge to play returns). As Appadurai (1996) has suggested about the schizophrenia characteristic of the imagination these days, *tamagotchi* alternate between different states of being and also between being different things: alive/dead, pet/machine, virtual/organic. This intermixture defines the very (promiscuous and flexible) nature of virtual pets that, by name alone, borrow on two ontological realms—the material world of flesh-and-blood life and the electronic world of cybernetic image making. In shape, *tamagotchi* are reminiscent of, but also not exactly like, pets (such as cats and dogs) and plants. In personality as well, their traits combine behaviors at once humanlike and imaginatively playful: intelligence coupled with smelly feet, hyperactivity along with a craving for café mocha. And in terms of life cycle, virtual pets live and die like organisms but can be reset and restarted as only machines can be.

Significantly, it is human labor of the most mundane and meticulous kind that grounds the life of a virtual pet. Or, to be more accurate, an electronic game set, run by a battery and programmed by digital icons, is wired to be interactive. And the mode of interactivity mimics that of raising a flesh-and-blood pet: an imaginary construction that makes players feel not only *as if* their *tamagotchi* were alive but also that their caregiving has life-and-death implications. At one level, this is nothing more than playing house by mimicking the duties and responsibilities of adults (particularly mothers) in child rearing. Surely this is the earliest and most universal form of children's play (Goldman 1998; Sutton-Smith 1997). But what is "old-fashioned" here is propped onto a New Age media technology. This is a move that resembles what Freud called *anaclisis:* how one activity turns, and is a conduit, into another (such as a baby's nursing on a mother's breast that moves from feeding to also being an interbodily site for pleasure, intimacy, and communication). In the case of the *tamagotchi,* the propping goes both ways; tending to a machine as if it were a dependent child/pet invests it with "life" and warmth but also flavors the latter with hipness and trendy cachet. Indeed, in an age when the Japanese state is anxious about its low birthrate and the increasing reluctance of Japanese women to marry and procreate, the *tamagotchi* could serve as a promotional toy for reproduction (an ideological message encoded in Bandai's *Tamagotchi Boshitechō*). And in Japan, the United States, and other marketplaces where it was a fad, the *tamagotchi* has been praised for the attentiveness (to a dependent other) it enscripts in the play. The demands it places on players and the fact that these demands cannot be ignored at the risk of "killing" one's pet have also made the *tamagotchi* a valuable pedagogical tool for birth control (as it has been used in sex education and social science classes in the United States).

In Appadurai's thesis, the imagination always refers to a social body, imaginary or otherwise. This is true both of the more fundamental type (ritual enchantments in which a community is reimagined at a symbolic distance from everyday life) and of its newer form (recouping and reinventing signs of sociality in an age where people are physically dispersing from geographically anchored homes). What, in the case of the *tamagotchi,* is the social referent, and why is labor (of such a caregiving sort) so critical to its imagination? Making the toy labor-intensive from the minute it hatches was part of Yokoi's design, intended to make players attach immediately to their "pets." Indeed, the first hour of the toy's "existence" was made to be particularly intense, both in the care demanded by the newborn and in the tentativeness of the *tamagotchi*'s life after birth. In this way the interface between human and machine is modeled after birthing/raising a biological organism: *tamagotchi* are "troublesome," instilling "worry" in their owners (Yokoi 1997:72–73). Speaking from my own experience, I became emotionally involved with my *tamagotchi* immediately and panicked that I might kill the thing off before it even grew to childhood. Checking in every five minutes to ensure it was well fed, poop-free, and cheerfully entertained, I became deeply attached to the plastic egg and the constant neediness issuing from it to me as its caregiver.

Yokoi intentionally designed the *tamagotchi* to foster this very sense of intimacy by refusing to install a pause button (which would allow players

temporary relief from the demands of their pets) and insisting that, if neglected, the *tamagotchi* would soon die.[14] On both scores, Yokoi believed a
"tension" would be produced in players that would make them invest in,
and emotionally attach to, their *tamagotchi* as love objects rather than machines. This aspect of the playtoy has been much cited by fans and commentators: how relating to the *tamagotchi as if* it were alive produces a
bond that is deeply personal, intimate, and social (in the Appaduraian sense
of attaching to others, albeit, in this case, an electronic machine). In the case
of the *tamagotchi*, of course, it can be reset multiple times, making the time
line of life and death reversible—something Yokoi himself was adamantly
against precisely because "real pets" cannot be mechanically restarted. Because a reset button could not be easily taken out of the generic game program, however, on this issue technology in virtual petland trumped "nature." Still, as Yokoi (1997:69) notes in his book, the *tamagotchi* was
designed to efface the border between organism and machine by engender-
ing "love" as would a turtle, rabbit, or dog (and "sadness" over its
loss/death). Indeed, his own fantasy is that someday *tamagotchi* will be sold
alongside cats, dogs, and hamsters in pet stores.

Children I spoke with who had been or were *tamagotchi* fans kept men-
tioning the emotional closeness they felt with these toys. Some added that,
unlike a more passive object like a pet rock or action figure, the *tamagotchi*
acts with a mind of its own, as it were, demanding a reaction from its owner.
Sherry Turkle (1994) has called cybertechnology (computers, MUD programs) an "evocative object" because, while it can be distinguished as an object outside the self, it also evokes something deeply personal in users.[15] Besides this inner connection, the *tamagotchi* also evokes the sensation of an
interpersonal relationship, something children told me keeps them company in what, as Appadurai and others have noted, is an age rife with dislo-
catedness, flux, and alienation. Two twelve-year-old American girls—at the
time, players (off and on) of *tamagotchi* for two years who both lived apart
from one parent and spent a great deal of time alone—described the companionship that a *tamagotchi* afforded them. It went with them everywhere
and kept them distracted and plugged into something meaningful, they said,
even when no one else was around. In this way, *tamagotchi* can fill in for the
absence of human contact or relationships just as do other compensatory
objects—flesh-and-blood pets, for example—or what Winnicott calls transitional objects.

But the *tamagotchi* can be used to reimagine sociality in other ways as
well. A virtual companion, the *tamagotchi* is scripted to mimic a particular
kind of social relationship—a hierarchical one between caregiver and cared-

for dependent. Any user will be familiar with this script from, at the very least, her own experience as a child. With the *tamagotchi*, however, roles are reversed; here it is the child doing to another what is usually done to her—turning off lights, administering discipline, injecting shots—producing an aura of control kids so often feel deprived of.[16] This labor of caregiving can remap other social situations as well. Yokoi, for example, mentions the case of a Japanese OL who, oppressed by her work situation and particularly an overbearing boss, relieves her stress by taking *tamagotchi* breaks. As she describes this pattern, periodically throughout the day she will flee her desk and run to the toilet; once there, she pulls out her *tamagotchi* and cleans up its poop. What is metaphorical of her situation at work—feeling like crap—is expressed here in an act that conjoins the bodily wastes of woman and *tamagotchi*. In this ritual—the imaginary limning of the real—the woman feels both needed and "healed." Laughing out loud in her toilet stall, the woman is reanchored, through a fantasy of banality, in what is at once a flight of fancy and a quotidian act of the most basic sort. At the end of the day, she goes home on the train with the pet riding in her pocket. "My *tamagotchi* is with me all the time," she gushes. "It relieves my loneliness" (Yokoi 1997:141).

Body figures prominently here; the imagination is routed through bodily intimacies—of the *tamagotchi* accompanying the woman even into the toilet and of the woman cleaning up the poop of her pet. All this is mediated, of course, through a technology of disembodiment in which digital images are reproduced on the screen (with a tactility limited to the electronic). But virtual reality is an evocative medium, producing the (imaginary) sensation of being elsewhere even as a person stays, physically, in place. Better known for transporting players to vistas less earthy than earthily divine—skiing in the Swiss Alps, deep-sea diving on the Great Barrier Reef—virtuality goes in the other direction here. Rather than traversing imaginary distances to what is (physically and experientially) sublime, the *tamagotchi* retreats to what is most carnally elemental inside the body—sleeping, eating, eliminating. These rudiments of bodily upkeep, though, offer something comforting, familiar, and (seemingly) universal that in turn is commodified into a global playtoy that anyone, anywhere "can get." This returns us to Appadurai's observation about the schizophrenia of the postmodern imaginary. In a world that—because of movement, dispersal, and technologization—is or feels increasingly groundless, there is a desire to find grounding in some semblance of place, community, and relationships.

Walter Benjamin made a similar observation about the changes wrought by modernity; even as we turn to new media and machines to navigate a shifting universe, there is a tendency to return to (or take along with us) the stodgingly familiar in bodies, places, and myths. Thus, in the "attempt to master the new experiences of the city in the frame of the old ones of traditional nature," the first railroad cars were shaped like stagecoaches, and the first electric light bulbs, like gas flames (cited in Buck-Morss 1997:110). Indeed, in the case of the *tamagotchi*, it is almost as if the toy is a reminder of the most basic biology of bodily maintenance: the very needs and demands that, as Freud told us long ago, make us human and represent the juncture between our bodies and the world, and ourselves and others with whom we have relations.[17] And this is at a moment at the cyberfrontier when technology is increasingly liberating humans from the constraints of biological life.

Sandy Stone (1995) has coined the word *tokens* to refer to a similar process in the practice of phone sex, in which workers try to reproduce the sensation of bodily sex acts through the very disembodied medium of the telephone. As she notes, phone sex tends to be intensely graphic precisely because there is a total absence of other bodily props. Bodies are thus imaginatively evoked—described, visualized, narrativized, fantasized—all through tokens that stand in for, but also differ from (because of the very medium in which they are enacted), embodied sexuality. They adhere, in other words, to an embodied construction of sexuality despite the fact that the condition for phone sex is the material absence of bodies altogether. Tokens, then, like fetishes, operate as both an absence and a presence, referring to what is (not) there by imaginary devices that evoke (or construct) the real.[18] This intermingling is what Appadurai would call schizophrenia and what Sherry Turkle (1998), borrowing from Donna Haraway, has labeled "irony"—the holding together of incompatible elements, real and imaginary, that kids become fluent in today through the cybermedia that structure so much of their study and play.[19]

Importantly, what this amounts to is not, as I interpret it, a mere fusing of disparate parts that confuses the discrete identity of any one part—a process of hybridization. Rather, it is more akin to what Jameson (1984) has called the pastiche effect of postmodern culture. Or, to speak from recent trends in children's toys, the logic of transformation consists of a delight taken in things being constantly in flux, transforming from one state into another. Within these chains of body shifting, there is no one, real, or authentic self. Rather, as in *Mighty Morphin Power Rangers*, a human morphs into a Power Ranger, a dinosaur, a flying machine, or a weapon and then morphs back into a human again. What is ironic or schizophrenic in such play is the refusal to locate identity or authenticity in one particular place—the human body over the morphed body, for instance. Both identities are equally present (though not at the same moment), with neither (nature/artifice, mechanical/biological, virtual/real) trumping the other. And what is true of cyberplay is true as well of how subjectivity and sociality are being organized in this moment of flexible accumulation, fragmented demand, and postindustrial capitalism: identities and relationships are as easily assembled as they are disassembled and reassembled.

Besides implanting tokens of biological life into virtual play, the *tamagotchi* does something else with bodies. It becomes embedded within a player's everyday routines: from getting up in the morning and commuting to work or school on the train to shopping for dinner and going to the bathroom. In lives that are becoming increasingly mobile, nomadic machines like the *tamagotchi* become a person's constant companion almost more than anything outside the body itself. They fuse with, and offer distraction from, the intricacies and intimacies of daily existence. In this sense, tending to the "natural" needs of a virtual pet (con)fuses the two kinds of imagination laid out by Appadurai. On the one hand, these are rituals of enchantment that relieve, and reimagine, social everydayness. As kids often told me, playing five minutes with their *tamagotchi* in the midst of studying, school, dinner, or chores was a pleasant, even meaningful, break. (Parents and schoolteachers, by contrast, often viewed these breaks as disruptions.) It could make them feel "relied upon," "important," or "loved" when, otherwise or in other contexts, such emotions were scarce. The social referent here was not so much a community united by common history, traditions, or culture as the child herself plugging into what many commentators (on *tamagotchi* and other toys, like *Pokémon*) have called a "space" of her own. This is an imaginary world that kids can and do use for momentary diversions from the real. It also is one that is shared by an entire fandom of players, making the *tamagotchi* a language or tool that fosters communication, *communitas*, and even identification with others.[20]

On the other hand, the *tamagotchi* not only provides a momentary escape from the ordinary (as do ritual ceremonies demarcated, in time and space, as special) but also becomes part and parcel of the ordinary itself. As Hosokawa (1984) has said about the Walkman, it is a bodily prosthesis. The latter works not as an extension of the human body but as a built-in part (rebuilding the very parameters of the body and how they operate as containers of and for life). The sound comes from inside, not outside, the Walkman user listening to her music. Thus, what is transmitted (in this case, music) penetrates the skin, inverting the (modernist) mapping of body. Pores become portals incorporating, as much as opening toward, the world outside. But unlike the Walkman, the *tamagotchi* is interactive, demanding a response from its owner. In this sense, a player must enter into the screen, filling it up—as does a singer in the "empty orchestra" of karaoke—with her own presence, which merges with that of the machine. This is what Sandy Stone calls the "prosthetics of presence," which, as she rightly points out, is not a mere stand-in for something else more "real" (1995:400). Rather, a prosthetics bleeds into the flesh, becoming part of a (new kind of) entity, body, and social network, no matter how tentative or temporary this connection is. In this case, what is bred is a companion, "partner," and pet: an imaginary creature with which, thanks to its technological simulation of life, a player can both mimic and create a "social" relationship.

Needless to say, this is a strikingly different way of organizing sociality than a community ritual that, participated in by people who share residence or collective identity, performs a symbolic rehearsal of their shared bond. It differs, too, from the New Age communicators (phone, e-mail, video) that Appadurai cites as keeping and producing social connections (among flesh-and-blood people) in this age of heightened diasporas and migrations. With the *tamagotchi*, the social bond is with a virtual construct, and the relationship formed is generated from an electronic egg, activated and played by an individual. In the words of some observers, the *tamagotchi* is like a constant shadow or ghost, attaching to whatever the child is doing and wherever the child is physically present. This is an imagination that spills onto everything, as mobile as the body carrying it and as ordinary as bodily waste. It also involves an interface, a circumstance that invites a different kind of response, and subjectivity, than does mass media/entertainment (film, television, newspapers, books) in which the projected image or story is not affected by the audience's reaction. In our postmodern era of technologized labor and play, people acquire subjectivity not through seeing or thinking of themselves as whole beings (interpellation through mirroring) but through interactive relations (interfaces as in chat rooms, Internet, e-mail) that split and shift. As Joseba Gabilondo and others have noted, identification today is more ghostly than mimetic—the ghostliness that adheres to images not of "us" per se but of interactions in which "we" appear as only a part (1995:429). This is true of the *tamagotchi*, whose "strange" looks can become strangely "cute" and which is dependent on the caregiving it receives from the player. *Mimitchi* bears the marks of a good parent, for example, but *hashizotchi* the signs of a parent who has been lax. As a queer (postgender, posthuman, postmodern) life-form, then, *tamagotchi* are amalgams of not only the real and the imaginary (including flippers, leaves, feet) but also of the player and the machine. This is *mecha* fetishism taken to the realm of the interactive and prosthetically social.

Beyond *Tamagotchi:*
Electronics Go Soft (and Sociality Goes Virtual)

As quickly as it emerged, the *tamagotchi* craze died off. By spring 1998, forty million of the toys had been sold (twenty million in Japan and an almost equal number abroad); by the end of the year, however, sales had fallen off, leaving stocks of unsold merchandise and a loss to Bandai of 6 billion yen. Like many trends, this one had peaked.[21] But the mechanical fantasy it gave form to—techno-intimacy—has only intensified in the years afterward, coming to constitute one of the biggest and hottest fashions in the millennial toy market, both in Japan and in the United States. Furby, for example, came out in September 1998 from Hasbro's Tiger Electronics (marketed by Tomy in Japan): "a soft, loveable, teachable virtual pet" that, chip-enhanced, can respond to human touch as well as talk, giggle, and move (open and close) its eyes. Operating through crude infrared signals, the Furby was relatively cheap ($30) and interactive: a responsive, talking electronic pet.[22] A huge hit, more than thirty million had been sold by January 2000. Equally sensational was Sony's release in 1999 of its high-tech (and high-priced—$2,500) AIBO (figure 30): a walking, talking computer-robot whose various motors, sensors, and circuitry enable it to perform multiple movements, recognize up to forty voice commands, and respond to (as well as exhibit) a range of "emotions." Using highly sophisticated software to program, and mimic, body language, AIBO "does an effective personification of a cute and frisky puppy," from yawning and scratching itself to lifting a leg and responding to praise as well as punishment (Pogue 2001:D1). Its name stands for Artificial Intelligence Robot, according to Sony, but *aibō* also means "pal" in Japanese (the term of affection to which the robot responds when called by its owner). By the new millennium, more than one hundred thousand AIBO had been sold worldwide.

Three years after *tamagotchi* hit the market in 1997, the biggest new trend in the toy industry was electronic companions: what booth after booth of toy manufacturers at the Tokyo Toy Fair in March 2000 advertised as "pet robots" *(petto robotto)*, from Poochi by Sega Toys (Tiger Electronics in the United States—an electronic dog that sings and moves and is called a *robo paru,* "robot pal") and Takara's three "human/thing communication goods" ("pet robot," "home robot," "NEW *hāti*")[23] to Maruka's Robo Inu ("robot dog," a small, inexpensive electronic dog) and Sony Entertainment's *dokodemo isshō* ("everywhere together," a video game apparatus) for PlayStation to Sega Enterprise's Seaman (a TV game from Dreamcast where, via complex software and a microphone attached to the controller

Figure 30. "Entertainment robot AIBO": Sony's advanced cyberdog. (Copyright © 2004 Sony Corporation.)

pad, users can "talk" with the pets hatched on the screen, including Seaman, a fish with a human face that talks about life). The big theme in the toy fair, which I attended, was "communication" *(komyunikēshōn):* mechanized play properties that, often shaped like animals (dogs or cats), are promoted as pets, partners, and pals. Said to be fun and interesting to play with, as well as warm and heartful as companions, this new trend is a morphing of earlier (and still popular) robot fads—the humanoid Tetsuwan Atomu in the 1950s and 1960s, the cyberwarriors who fuse with their robots (the Ranger series, *Mazinger Z, Gundam*) starting in the 1960s, and "beautiful female heroes" like the Sailor Scouts on *Sailor Moon* whose bodies house weapons as well as sexy flesh. And thinking particularly of the "giant robot" and *kyōdai (gattai) robotto* (fused, multipieced robots) fads in boys' shows/toy merchandise starting from the late 1970s,[24] this newest fashion in "communication partner robots" represents a shift, as one observer puts it, from *mecha*-tronics to *"sof*-tronics" *(Toy Journal* 2000:51): from "hard" to "soft" electronic fantasies/goods.

If, in *mecha* superheroes, the fetishistic gaze (what I have called the "money shot") is on the display and detail of body assemblage—showing (off) the bodily "secrets" of the robot/warrior/cyborg/babe's powers—it is the same in sof-tronics, but with a different logic: using *mecha* not to construct the superhuman but to reconstruct the humanlike in "pet robots." Performance is every bit as important here and is similarly mapped by intricate and intimate attention paid to circuitry. But the model of "life" it imagines is not a posthuman warrior (cybernetically endowed to supersede human limitations) but what, going in the other direction, is the mechanical imitation of a biological animal—one that, because it rolls over, wags its tail, or takes a poop, invites humans to bond with it like a pet. As Sony describes one of its newest toy products (*ningenDOG* = human dog), it has a "human smell" (*Toy Journal* 2000:51), an odor less inscribed with the national identity of Japaneseness than other made-in-Japan cultural products, a factor that has hindered (until recently) their globalization, leading Fox Network, for example, to "Americanize" *Power Rangers* for U.S. broadcast (Iwabuchi 2002:28). Indeed, Japan is doing well on the global marketplace exporting robotic petdom, both as actual products and as a trendsetting new play fashion. The New York Toy Fair in 2001, for example, was filled with electronic toys, and sales in the category of virtual robo-pets rose exponentially from a mere $5 million in 2000 to $159 million the following year.

Techno-intimacy is a sign of the times. While *mecha*-tronics was the fantasy as well as national policy for rebuilding Japan after the war—remaking the country as a techno supernation—sof-tronics is the symptom and corrective to this industrial master plan in the new millennium—assuaging the atomism, alienation, and stress of corporatist capitalism with virtual companionship. What performativity exacts and extracts from citizens in the era of speeded-up, "just in time" delivery, soft robo-pals promise to make up for: a "humanness" that, once lost, is to be recouped by mechanical petdom. As Benjamin noted about an earlier stage of industrialization: "It is in this way that technological *reproduction* gives back to humanity that capacity for experience which technological *production* threatens to take away" (quoted in Buck-Morss 1997:268).

This would seem to be the answer, in part, to what kind of "sociality"—in Appadurai's sense—the *tamagotchi* serves to artificially "imagine" for its users; it operates as a fetish bearing both an absence (a loss) and a presence (that masks, stands in place for, and—in this case—also transforms what has been lost and is still desired). Intimate play goods are machines used for play and instruction and also for communication and companionship. Significantly, these devices are also said to be "healing" in rhetoric that assumes players are already wounded: psychically on edge, overworked, stressed out. Being touched by another, albeit a machine, is soothing: the s(t)imulation of social intercourse.

Not surprisingly, adults are increasingly becoming consumers as well as players of sof-tronics. Bandai, for example, has a service that thirty thousand *sararīman* subscribe to called "Love by Mail" that sends messages from make-believe girlfriends to the subscriber's Internet-enabled cellphone. And Takara's Aquaroid, released in 2001 at a price of $750, is a solar-powered robot that—living in an aquarium of water and mimicking the movements of a jellyfish (by moving up and down and side to side)—is a big seller among *sararīman* for its hypnotic and soothing effects. In both these cases, a form of companionship comes from an other that has been artificially/virtually constructed, is a commodity sold in the marketplace, and has been designed to please and heal the individual (as player and consumer).

To see how such intimate play goods are a product of the very conditions of capitalism they are used to assuage, we must turn to the next, and biggest, Japanese contribution to global toydom, the phenomenon known as *Pokémon*. Continuing the trajectory in play goods away from the big mythic themes of good versus evil that devolve upon human (super)heroes, as in *Sailor Moon* and *Power Rangers*, *Pokémon* engenders a fantasy world that, like *tamagotchi*, centers upon nonhuman characters (and the relationships humans form with them). Here, however, these creatures are conceptualized as pocket monsters: a slew of "wild" beings (151 in the first Game Boy game edition) that players track down, battle in matches, and then catch (thereby "pocketing" them), versus the singular *tamagotchi* that players hatch from an egg, attend to like organic animals, and raise as virtual pets. While incorporating an element of the nurturance and companionship fostered in the *mecha* soft (play)ware of a *tamagotchi*, *Pokémon* also shifts and extends its logic of (transformational, animistic, polymorphously perverse) play in significant ways. The consequences of this direction both for the global marketing and marketability of *Pokémon* and for the construction of fantasy it breeds for children at this moment of millennial capitalism are the issues I take up in the next chapter.

Pokémon

Getting Monsters and Communicating Capitalism

Welcome to the world of Pokémon! Once you start this game, you'll find yourself immersed in a world that is as challenging as it is fun. Your mission: To become the world's greatest Pokémon trainer. To do this, you'll have to wander down many streets and through cities, towns, and dungeons—and defeat many Rivals, including the one who used to be your best friend. You also have to find and collect 151 Pokémon and raise them to be your bettermost fighters. It takes skill and determination, not to mention a bit of luck.

From "How to Become a Master Pokémon Trainer," in *Pokémon*: *Prima's Official Strategy Guide* (Hollinger 1998:1)

Empire and Offspring:
New Avenues of Fantasy

When I enter the room, two children (a six-year-old girl and a ten-year-old boy) are glued to their Game Boys. Each is playing the game *Pokémon*, activated on their screens by inserting a cassette. Occasionally the kids whoop with delight or pound their legs in disappointment. For the most part, though, they sit on the edge of their seats, moving the controls on their Game Boys, immersed in their own separate (if parallel) pursuits of scouting out/capturing/battling pocket monsters. When their mother calls them to supper, neither moves. They have been playing for an hour, the limit for predinner play in this household. Only when they are threatened with having their Game Boys physically taken from them for a week do the kids relent (very reluctantly) and move (very slowly) to the dinner table. During the meal, they chat a bit to each other about the games they have been playing, the strategies they've employed, and which "pocket monsters," or *poké-mon*, they are currently trying to capture. Their parents, however, remain clueless about all this talk/play/fantasy. The game world of *Pokémon*, they confess, is alien.[1]

Pokémon is a game of strategy, skill, perseverance, training, and knowledge, and the play activities it is said to promote include collecting, competition, pet raising, mastery, adventures, and role-playing. The world within which it is set, and the bodies, powers, and tools involved in achieving the goal of becoming the "world's greatest *pokémon* master," not only are intricate but also continually shift, expand, and evolve. As I write this in 2005, there have been more than one dozen editions of the *Pokémon* Game Boy game (the latest, Emerald, came out in 2005, increasing the number of *pokémon* now to more than three hundred), and the playscape has spread over multiple media, arena, and merchandising opportunities. *Pokémon, Inc.* has been a huge industry, marketed—in various forms and iterations—in more than 140 countries and producing global profits of more than $15 billion by August 2003.[2] In the words of some Japanese commentators, *Pokémon* is a veritable empire—of imaginary monsters, virtual play, and real revenues.

The millennial moment in Japan was marked by not only a bruising recession and social unease (and diseases) but also resounding triumphs in the fantasy industry. The phenomenal success of the *Pokémon* multimedia products has brought Japan unprecedented profits and acclaim in a domain of cultural production long dominated by Hollywood. The media have proclaimed *Pokémon* a "global character" and a sign of Japan's "cultural power" in a marketplace where, as the *New York Times* reported, Japan is becoming the new "superpower of superheroes." Kubo Masakazu of Shōgakukan Inc., who turned the *Pokémon* Game Boy game into a comic book story (and oversaw the cartoon and movie versions), speaks of this corporate product as if it were his child. Using the Japanese word for child raising *(sodateru)*, he told me: "I raised *Pokémon*, which is why I feel a particular bond with it." Interestingly, children also described their play with *Pokémon* in the same terms. (Yet, telling me they "raise" pocket monsters by developing their strengths over time, children would then speak far more instrumentally, calling their wards "weapons" and "tools" used in a playscape premised on capture.) For Kubo Masakazu, *sodateru* also signified something of a cultural difference: an ability to relate personally, almost spiritually, with a product/mass-produced imaginary that differed from the attitude he encountered among Americans (when negotiating for *Pokémon*'s U.S. release). Whereas Japanese creators crafted and produced *Pokémon* with affection ("raising" it like a child), Americans treated it only as a business. The former represents Japan's genius in the field of fantasy production, Kubo added: an appreciation of cuteness and playfulness (across the human/nonhuman border) that, coupled with smart marketing strategies and flexible merchandising, is the source of the entertainment industry's successes today.

In the accounts of Kubo and others, there is something reminiscent of the general feeling of pride inspired in Japan by *Gojira:* a film that, when released in the early years following the war, fostered national and popular sentiment. Resonating with the fears and wounds of the early postwar generation, *Gojira* aroused people's emotions with its mythic story line as well as its blockbuster production. This was a homegrown monster showcased in a cinematic masterpiece worthy (or so some Japanese thought) of Hollywood. The same is true of the millennial *Pokémon*. Encased in the form of popular culture, it is a vehicle of and for the national imagination transmitted through a currency of superpowers and lovable characters.[3] As reported by *Nikkei Torendi* in 1998, for example, *Pokémon* (and the character business more generally) was called the singular success story in the world of Japanese business during the recessionary times of the post-Bubble. Its profits were a welcome boon to the national economy. As important as the sales it accrued was the influence *Pokémon* exerted in the domain of cultural production. Representing a breakthrough in a marketplace where, "until now, the characters that have been popular around the world have been primarily produced by the giant country, America," Japan's success here is a sign that it is on "the road to becoming a character empire" ("Kyarakutā ōkoku no michi" 1998:91). Kubo agrees. In his five-hundred-page book on the subject of *Pokémon* (cowritten with Hatakeyama Kenji), he states: "There never has been a game that has spread so broadly around the world and gone beyond race, language, values, and religion. In the sense of its international commonness and the spectacular speed as well as breadth of its worldwide circulation, we could say that the phenomenon of *Pokémon* is unprecedented in human history" (Hatakeyama and Kubo 2000:8).

In the 1970s, when Japan began experiencing the comforts of recovery in the wake of the country's first economic boom since the end of the war, a story called *Doraemon* began serialization in the boys' comic magazine *Korokoro Komikku*. Created by the comic team Fujio-Fujiko, *Doraemon* was soon turned into a popular *anime* (a television cartoon and also featurelength movies) that, much like *Pokémon* thirty years later, captured the popular imagination of the nation. In both cases, the lead character is a fantasy creature attached to a singular child (boys about age ten).[4] In *Doraemon*, this is a blue robotic cat: pudgy, with a supersized head, round eyes, whiskered mouth, tiny white pads for hands and feet, and a huge kangaroo pouch on its tummy. Doraemon lives with Nobita, a sweet but incompetent kid who is always getting into jams of various kinds. Nobita's great-greatgrandson, the story line goes, invented this robot and sent it back in time to improve the flawed forefather he grew up hearing about (in a commentary, one might ask, about Japan?).

Doraemon is cuddly and cute, but he is also equipped with an entire storehouse of futuristic machines that can be pulled from his tummy and activated to assist Nobita. The backdrop, as is typical in Japanese kids' shows, is a gang *(nakama)* of friends—the bully (Giant), the smart aleck (Tsuneo), the sweet girl (Shizuka), and Nobita himself—interspersed with adult authority figures (mainly, the kids' schoolteacher and Nobita's mother). A typical episode goes something like this: looking at his messy room, Nobita panics when he hears his mother coming upstairs to give it a cleaning inspection. When he turns to Doraemon for help, the robot pulls out an "absorb-everything" pouch and attaches it to the boy. Throwing toys, clothes, and even the desk into this magic pocket, Nobita cleans up his room in a flash. Given the okay to go outside, he runs into Shizuka, who is sad because her mother is making her throw out all her comic books. Offering to let her store them in his pouch instead, Nobita earns the girl's gratitude. But Giant has seen the device as well and bullies the boy into letting him climb inside to escape his overbearing mother. Soon the whole neighborhood follows suit, and when tensions rise and a huge fight erupts, the magic pouch heats up. Once again Doraemon comes to the rescue. Removing the pouch, he teleports the boy back to the safety of his house. As the robot scolds him for misusing the gadgetry, Nobita is momentarily chagrined. Soon, however, he will be imploring his robot for more assistance (and another gadget), which, when it comes, will provoke another predicament.

The logic of fantasy in *Doraemon* is both like and unlike that in *Pokémon*. Both story lines share the central premise of an ordinary child who can tap into the extraordinary powers of an otherworldly creature wired as a high-tech machine. In both, the bond is a mixture of service and friendship; Pikachu and Doraemon are constant buddies but also genies who realize the fantasies of their master. The creatures are sweet but also practical, and the plots are driven by the transfer and conversion of power from a fantasy source to a human child. The settings of these two stories and their articulation with "reality" are considerably different, however. *Doraemon* is set in a localized Japan that bears many distinctive features of a Japanese world (tatami mats, chopsticks, sliding doors, a Japanese household). The tale also takes place in the mundane setting of school, class assignments, tussles with parents, and scuffles with the local bully. By contrast, *Pokémon* is set in a virtual world: a landscape of cities, zones, forests, and islands whose identity is nonlocalizable (Masara Town, Mount Iwa, Cycling Road, Nibi City) and also not "real."[5] Fantasy is injected into ordinary reality in *Doraemon* (magic is applied to homework and house chores), but fantasy takes over in *Pokémon*. This *is* the world, with no references to another world outside it, and with strictly self-referential goals; the *Pokémon* trigger powers that are used to catch ever more *pokémon*. In *Doraemon*, fantasy is placed into a "realistic" setting where magic is particularistic (there is only one superrobot and only one beneficiary of his powers). In comparison, fantasy is much more fluid, accessible, and universalistic in the *Pokémon* format; anyone can become a *pokémon* trainer like Satoshi (the boy protagonist) and accumulate pocket monsters (that, unlike Doraemon, come in droves). Fantasy empowerment is also more democratic and more easily generalized in *Pokémon*. Satoshi captures his *pokémon* by dint of sheer will and effort. Nobita, by contrast, gets his Doraemon merely as a reverse inheritance, on the basis of the "blood" he shares with his great-great-grandson.

These two models of fantasy attachments can be read as allegories of a Japan that had significantly changed in the nearly thirty years between the release of *Doraemon* and that of *Pokémon*. In the 1970s, Japan, like Nobita, was still viewed by its citizens as riddled with "lacks." The country accordingly pinned its financial viability on mechanical inventions and electronic contraptions, and its cultural identity on markers rooted to the grounded locale and family traditions of "Japan." The story *Doraemon* tells is thus modernistic and teleological; Doraemon fills in Nobita's gaps within the context of a place whose cultural logic is fairly specific (one of the main reasons *Doraemon* has never been exported to the United States, it is said). *Pokémon*, however, allegorizes the world quite differently. Satoshi is a far less flawed protagonist than Nobita and one more actively involved in acquiring the powers he needs to be competent. This posture reflects a far more confident Japan at the millennial moment—one whose goals, more ambitious now, have moved from the domestic (tromping the local bully, pleasing his mother) to the global (becoming the "world's greatest *pokémon* trainer"). Identity has become shifting and mobile in/for Japan, tied less to the geographic boundaries of place (and the customs and bloodlines attached to it) than to the production and circulation of virtual landscapes. The organizing trope here is travel; unlike Nobita, who sticks close to neighborhood and home, the junior *pokémon* trainers are constantly in motion. The tale of *Pokémon* is postmodernist, featuring multiple subjects with flexible attachments who never stay in one place and have goals that, while clear-cut, are open ended and take them in many directions.

Pokémon is a media-mix complex—of electronic game, *manga*, television *anime*, trading cards, movie, and character goods—where the basic concept is an imaginary universe inhabited by wild monsters that children capture, then keep in balls in their pockets. Whether a child is playing the game or following the story through *manga*, *anime*, or movie, the structure of an encounter with wild and fantastic creatures is replayed through the ritual of "pocketing" the Other. In this play world, with its magical topography of towns, forests, and caves, live 151 *pokémon* (now more than 300), and the goal of the game is to capture them all. This process, called *getto suru* ("getting," which was translated into "gotta catch 'em all" in the U.S. ad campaign), is the game's ultimate goal. The *pokémon* are creatures that, over time and given proper training, care, and attention from their owners, will become stronger. This triggers, in some cases, evolution: most *pokémon* change forms as they gain experience, and some will evolve twice before they reach their final form. This is also a state that, as with so much in this game world, has alternative and flexible means of realization. Evolution (for some *pokémon*) can be produced by something called elemental stones and also through trades with friends: exchanges negotiated with other players and transacted by connecting two Game Boys through a cable. The latter is another means of acquiring *pokémon* in general; though matches are the dominant method, trading is encouraged and actually necessary to capture 11 of the total 151 *pokémon*.

While the aim of the game is continual acquisition, the objects one "gets" are both thingified (valued economically) and personalized (cute monsters inspiring affection, attachment, and love). The logic of play here involves a currency of shifting and multiple valences—between spirits and profits, companions and capital, inalienable and alienable goods. Capitalism is thus equally mimicked and (re)constructed in the forms of play/consumption engaged by *Pokémon* (figure 31). Even as it conforms to a preexisting market economy, *Pokémon* also pushes this economy in new directions—what I call here (only half facetiously) *Pokémon* capitalism. This is a millennial dreamworld of enchanting goods and virtual relations in which commodities double as gifts and companions. It is also an arena that features a borrowing and reinvention of a Japanese cultural past (gift exchange, supernatural spirits, otherworldly aestheticism). And with this comes the objective not only of selling goods and making profits but also of mapping Japan's place in the world as the New Age synthesizer of old-style sensitivity and human relationships. How this double intent has evolved in the play world and product empire of *Pokémon* is a story in itself.

Conceiving *Pokémon*:
Communication, Community, Communion

Pokémon (or *Poketto monstā* in its longer version) was originally designed as a software game for Game Boy, the handheld digital game console launched by Nintendo in 1989. Created by a young game designer, Tajiri

(GOT YA!)

Figure 31. *Pokémon* capitalism: a play world where "getting" is cute. "Gotta catch 'em all!" is the slogan from the U.S. promotional campaign. (Courtesy of Nintendo.)

Satoshi, and his staff at Game Freak over a period of six years, *Pokémon* was bought by Nintendo and released in February 1996. Initial predictions were for only modest sales, given that Game Boy and its eight-bit technology was on the wane in an electronic game world now dominated by far more powerful machines (Nintendo 64, Sega Saturn, and Sony PlayStation). Sales were far better than expected, however, in part because the game is simple but fun and the handheld Game Boy fits in with today's *keitai* (portable) culture of cell phones and Palm Pilots even among young kids. (And, thanks to *Pokémon*, Game Boy technology was revived and is still in existence today, having gone through numerous innovations, including Game Boy Advance.) Sensing the start of a fad, its marketers sought to develop *Poké-*

mon across a mix of media venues. In summer 1996, *Pokémon* came out as a serialized comic in *Korokoro Komikku,* one of the most popular young boys' *manga* magazines, read by half of all Japanese boys in grades five to eight.[6] Playing cards, distributed by Media Factory, followed in the fall. The television *anime* produced by Terebi Tokyo debuted in April 1997. Toy merchandise by Tomy appeared in spring 1997, and the first movie hit the screens in the summer of 1997.

Along with these major media products came a cornucopia of tie-in merchandise—pencils and stationery goods by Enikkusu, curry and *furikake* (spices for rice) by Nagatanien, chocolate and other candy by MeijiSeika— as well as a host of highly visible service campaigns, including the launching of the *Pokémon*-painted air carriers by (All Nippon Airways) in summer 1998 and a train promotion by the national railways (JR) the same summer. Starting almost immediately in 1997, *Pokémon* was exported; beginning in East Asia with Taiwan, Hong Kong, and China, it entered the United States in 1998, followed by Australia, Canada, Western Europe, Latin and South America, Israel, parts of the Mideast, and Eastern Europe.

Within months after its launching as a Game Boy game in February 1996, *Pokémon* had gained fame in Japan not only as a commercial sensation but also, and more surprisingly, as what some experts were calling both a new form of play and a "social phenomenon" (Yamato 1998:247). As characterized by Okada Toshio, a University of Tokyo lecturer and expert on mass culture, *Pokémon* is a play that goes beyond the world of the game itself. This characteristic distinguishes it from other electronic games that have become increasingly difficult over the years, demanding intense concentration and single-minded (often solitary) absorption in the alternative worlds they construct. By contrast, *Pokémon*'s software is simple yet fun and uniquely designed to foster communication and exchanges between children (Yamato 1998). Its designer, Tajiri Satoshi (figure 32), purposely crafted the game to feature not only matches *(taisen)*—the competitive trope that is standard, and compulsory, in action games targeted to boys—but also exchanges *(kōkan)* that build communication, interactions, and, in Tajiri's word, "drama" continuing beyond the framework of *Pokémon* itself (Nintendo 1999:12). Its potential for *tsūshin* (communication) and *ningenkankei* (human relationships)—that quality of sociality so ideologically central to Japanese culture—has been much cited in the rhetoric surrounding the *Pokémon* phenomenon in Japan. Indeed, the "newness" of the play form it is credited with stems, in large part, from the "oldness" of social interrelations the game advertises as part of its virtualized, digitalized monster catching.

The immediate impetus for the concept of *Pokémon* was the release of

Figure 32. Tajiri Satoshi, the designer of the *Pokémon* Game Boy game. (Courtesy of Nikkei BP.)

the portable game technology Game Boy. The mobility of the machine intrigued Tajiri, as did one of its functions: an attachment that could be purchased to link two Game Boys together. Called the *tsūshin kēburu* (communication cable), this link enabled two players to compete against each other. Given that competitive fighting (trying to kill, knock out, or otherwise defeat an opponent) was the central motif of video games at the time (and remains so today), this development was unsurprising. But Tajiri had a novel idea: to utilize the *tsūshin kēburu* for "communication" instead—for exchanges between players in which the objective would be to barter with, rather than eliminate, an opponent by trading monsters. Finding this an innovative concept in the world of gaming, Nintendo signed the project on in 1991, when Tajiri met with officials from the company (Kawaguchi Takeshi and the game designer Ishihara Tsunekazu, who subsequently became a producer of *Pokémon* and started his own company, Creatures). Though Nintendo gave Tajiri wide leeway in developing the game (and amazing patience in the six years it took for *Pokémon* to be completed), it insisted that the play not consist entirely of exchanges. Arguing that a game without battles would be considered boring by kids and thus a poor seller, the company demanded that Tajiri include both strategies in the software. *Pokémon* was subsequently built as a game of "getting" based on exchanges *(kōkan)* as well as *taisen*. But to make the former not merely an option but a requirement of play, Tajiri programmed the game so that 11 of the 151 total *pokémon* could be "gotten" only through exchanges (using the communication cable to link up with a friend).

Tajiri has said that he had two major motivations in designing *Pokémon*. One was to create a challenging yet playable game that would pique children's imaginations. The other was to give kids a means of relieving the stresses of growing up in a postindustrial society. Born in 1962, Tajiri shares the opinion of many in his generation that life for children today is hard. In this academic-record society, the pressure to study, compete, and perform starts as early as birth. Space and time for play have diminished. And in an environment where everyone moves fast to accomplish more and more every day, the "human relationships" once so prized in society have begun to unravel. Increasingly, as discussed in chapter 3, Japanese spend more and more time alone, forming intimacies less with one another than with the goods they consume and technologies they rely upon (cell phones, Walkmen, Game Boys). Children are particularly victimized by the "solitarism" of lives spent commuting on trains, studying at cram school, and poring over books at home. Such mobile kids, as we have seen, find intimacy elusive and seek companionship in the "shadow families" of virtual, technomediated worlds.

In Tajiri's mind, the rewards of millennial Japan have come with a loss to humanity. Nostalgic for a world not yet dominated by industrial capitalism, he strove to re-create something from his childhood in the imaginary play world of *Pokémon*. To "tickle" memories of the past, Tajiri borrowed on his own experiences in a town where nature had not yet been overtaken by industrialization. As a boy, his favorite pastime had been collecting insects and crayfish, an activity that involved interactions with both nature (exploration, adventure, observation, gathering) and society (exchanges and information-sharing with other kids). Fascinated by the abundance and diversity of species in his natural environment, Tajiri spent long hours studying, collecting, and exchanging bugs. At once fun and instructive, this play form is what Tajiri aimed to capture and transmit to children today, for whom nature is not a ready-made playground. The format he chose for this New Age insect collecting was virtuality: digitally constructed worlds, activities, and monsters (figure 33). A game junkie *(otaku)* himself since the age of twelve, when a video arcade featuring *Space Invaders* came to town, Tajiri became as hooked on these virtual worlds as he had once been on nature. Here he rediscovered the type of adventure, exploration, and competition he had once found in insect collecting, with one main difference (Hiratsuka 1997:

Figure 33. New Age insect collecting: the virtualized species of *Poké*-world (*pokémon* = pocket monsters). (Courtesy of Shōgakukan Production.)

168–70). Whereas the latter opens up a child to horizons beyond the self, games are often myopic, enclosing kids within their virtual constructions. Since the late 1980s, the trend in game design has been toward greater complexity that demands intense concentration and pulls players into solitary engagements with their virtual game worlds.

Disturbed by this current tendency toward atomism, both in gaming and in society at large, Tajiri designed his game to promote more interactivity. He did this by, first, making the game challenging but doable, even by children as young as four years of age. In contrast to the current trend in gaming, which is targeted to older children and young adults (in the United States, the mean age of video game players is currently twenty-six), *Pokémon* was relatively simple. The rules could be grasped and success achieved as long as a child was persistent in playing and learning the game. Given the surfeit of detail involved in *Pokémon*, however, kids were also encouraged to gather and exchange information with other children, making the game world into something like a language that promotes communication. *Tsūshin*, in fact, was the keyword used by Tajiri and its marketers in the written materials surrounding *Pokémon* in everything from the guidebooks to instructional books that accompany the game. This communication is literalized further in the exchanges that are a central feature of playing the game. Distinguishing *Pokémon* from other action games in which the staple is fighting, exchanges were new here (and were part of the reason that *Pokémon* is usually categorized as a role-playing game rather than action per se). As Tajiri intended it, the necessity for exchange envelops players in webs of social relationships, given that, by the very rules of the game, one cannot play strictly alone. And, as was the hope, exchanges are perpetuated outside the parameters of the game itself and into currencies of other kinds. In a mixing of metaphors, economies, and pleasures, one example given by Tajiri was that a child might exchange one of his *pokémon* for a bowl of ramen or a desired comic book (Nintendo 1999:12). The ideal is a community of friendship built on communicating through *Pokémon*.

Interactivity was crafted into this play world in yet a third way by giving children an imaginary space where relations with pretend beings could be enacted. As I heard repeatedly (from marketers as well as commentators, particularly child experts) in the course of doing fieldwork, *Pokémon* gives children a "space of their own" (Nakazawa 1997:22): a play environment that, although make-believe, is emotionally real and cushions them from the daily grind of studying, taking tests, and commuting. Pocket monsters are the embodiment of this imaginary space. Formatted as digital icons on game technology that children carry wherever they go, these are, literally and figuratively, pocket fantasies. As such, they straddle the border between phantasm (their construction) and everyday life (the context in which they are played—on Game Boys as a child commutes from school to home, for example).

As children conveyed to me when describing their involvements with *Pokémon*, this is a highly interactional play world. One six-year-old told me (in fall 1999) that virtually everyone in his class was a *Pokémon* fan. As his mother elaborated, bringing *Pokémon* cards or Game Boys into the classroom was forbidden, but kids shared stories, information, or chants about *Pokémon* in the schoolyard. Many of these kids also commuted to school on trains or buses alone and would play with their Game Boy games or read comics while en route. During playdates after school or on Sunday, they would often converge in each other's homes, watching *Pokémon* videos, exchanging cards, playing Game Boys together, or mimicking the moves and personalities of specific *pokémon* by enacting minidramas. *Pokémon* was a thriving culture, one a child risked being excluded from if she lacked the means, knowledge, or aptitude to participate. The *Pokémon* that another four-year-old child described was more of a personal (pre)occupation. Not yet in school and somewhat withdrawn, this boy had learned how to play the Game Boy game at an unusually young age and was obsessed with every aspect of this game world. Showing me cardboard boxes filled with *pokémon* play figures, he rattled off the names of endless monsters along with their vital statistics and the stages (of strength and evolution) at which he had captured them on his Game Boy. By his description, this seemed more of a solitary activity, yet, as his mother added, the boy played *Pokémon* with his father every night and had learned how to read (from the script printed on the Game Boy screen) in the process.

A ten-year-old boy whom I interviewed along with his seven-year-old sister stated that he what he liked most about *Pokémon* (which he followed in the three media of Game Boy game, cards, and television *manga*) was definitely the *tatakau* (fighting). He also liked other aspects of this play world: collecting and raising *(sodateru)* specific monsters, and also the *manga* story, particularly the adventures of the three protagonists (Satoshi and his two buddies, Kasumi and Takeshi). But *taisen* were what Hideo considered the most "interesting" part of *Pokémon*. When I questioned him on the exchanges presented by Tajiri (and much of the promotional literature on *Pokémon*) as one of the game's distinctive features, Hideo said he did not take part in many. Because he had more *pokémon* than most of his friends, and not everyone owned a communication cable, there was not much incentive to trade. Still, what he described was hardly a solipsistic engagement. Although he played his Game Boy mainly alone now, Hideo had originally learned about *Pokémon* and how to play it from his friends. He conveyed the sense of a shared world in which he spent a considerable amount of time communicating (passing back and forth information, devising game strategies, playing cards, watching videos). Indeed, Hideo said he did not know a single child (girl or boy) who did not like playing *Pokémon*. His sister Chiori

Figure 34. Toughness and cuteness merge in pocket monsters. Barukī, on left, is categorized as a "fighting-type" *pokémon,* which is the evolved form of Sawamurā, on right, a "kicking" *pokémon.* (Courtesy of Shōgakukan Production.)

agreed, though she was far more intrigued with the cartoon and comic books than with the Game Boy game, and conceptualized *Pokémon* more in terms of specific *pokémon* she found "cute" *(kawaii).* Telling me that her brother preferred *pokémon* he considered strong *(tsuyoi)* and thus useful in battle, Chiori liked those monsters who somehow amused her or seemed endearing (figure 34). My two neighborhood children in Durham, North Carolina, were similar in detailing specific features of *pokémon* they found "interesting," "funny," or "cute" (because of the unusual color, shape, or odd assemblage of parts, such as a flower with lips that can speak). Asked to define what a *pokémon* was, practically all the children I spoke with answered in terms of the relationships they had formed with them. For a ten-year-old boy in Tokyo, for example, *pokémon* are "imaginary partners, creatures that can be your loyal pet if you control them. They're companions until the end, sort of like animals that are real except mutated." To a seven-year-old girl in the United States, they are "like creatures that are made up. The creators took ideas from nature, but they turned nature around. People care a lot for their *pokémon,* but they also use them to fight other *pokémon.*"

Significantly, the *kawaii* trend—cute goods and cute characters—in Japan, which started in the mid-1970s and has been enjoying a resurgence since the late 1990s, inspires similar attachments and emotions. Again and again, cute characters are defined not just by their physical attributes alone (big head, small body, huge eyes, absent nose) but also, and more importantly, by the relationships people form with them. A longtime fan of *Doraemon*, now an adult in his thirties, describes his deep attachment to the character. Inhabiting an imaginary space that mediates between fantasy and reality, Doraemon is what Fujimi calls a "transitional object" (a term coined by the object relations theorist D. W. Winnicott)—something that is both outside and inside the self. This character/space is "part of me," the author states. What makes Doraemon cute is not only the figure he cuts (blue color, pouch-lined tummy, oversized head, cuddly paws) but also the relationship he enables with an imaginary world. For this adult fan, devices like the *dokodemo doa* (door that opens to anywhere) are a reminder of something beyond the reality of his office, cramped housing, and daily commutes. This is what he carries with him from his childhood fascination with *Doraemon*: a mechanism for interacting with the world through the imagination (Fujimi 1998).

The same is true of imaginary play pals in general, of course. Across cultures and time, children take things from their environment—sticks, blankets, dolls—and invest them with personalities, stories, and "life." With these entities, kids develop attachments that help them navigate and survive the bumpy road of growing up. What, on one hand, is an extension of the self is, on the other, a means for interacting imaginatively with the world outside. This type of communion with the imagination is also what Tajiri had in mind when building "communication" into the game design of *Pokémon*.

The *Pokémon* World:
Discourse of Cartographies, Categories, and Charts

As Foucault (1980) defines it, discourse is the cartography by which the world is mapped by values, relationships, and power(s). *Pokémon*, too, I soon learned when I embarked upon fieldwork in Japan in 1999, was a discursively charged subject. Not only did it sprout passionate speech (among kids, parents, teachers, commentators, reporters, psychologists, and economists about its merits, rules, pleasures, and significance), but the product itself came embedded in a hefty range of written texts issued by its manufacturers. As I noticed on my first visit to the Pokémon Center near Tokyo train station (a brand store that, featuring the latest in *Pokémon* goods, was always packed with customers lined up outside, including foreign visitors dragged or sent there by their children), publications—*manga*, game guidebooks, magazines, illustrated texts—were prominent in the selling, consuming, and enculturating of *Pokémon* in Japan. In examining the logic of the *Pokémon* play world, it is therefore key to look at the discourse generated by its producer.

Nintendo, the company holding the rights to the *Pokémon* Game Boy games, has published a number of guidebooks and instructional manuals to help players learn and master the game.[7] As virtually all the child fans I interviewed about *Pokémon* confirmed, these publications are considered useful in developing game skills and strategies. One of these is the *Poketto Monstā Zukan* (Illustrated Book of Pocket Monsters; Asupekuto 1997), a foundational guide that lays out the world of *Pokémon* in terms of levels or layers, each with its own body of information to be processed and mastered by players seeking competence in the game. The organizing trope in this discourse is knowledge, directed to a fantasy world premised far more now on the invisible and unseen—what must be learned and charted through data—than on what is fetishistically known and revealed through bodily sites/sights of *mecha* transformation. The latter, what I have called the money shot, has been a central feature in kids' mass culture in postwar Japan; true as much for the team warriors (Ranger series) and giant robots as for the schoolgirl babes *(Sailor Moon)*—morphers who upgrade their powers and performance to fight evil. Fixating on the human-nonhuman border in terms of specific body parts that are activated for battle, the gaze is on something that can be seen—a "bodily secret" revealed as hardwired circuitry (and also sexy flesh in the case of the girls). As in the Ranger series as well as *Sailor Moon*, these properties are often based on a television show accompanied by a comic book series (or features run in children's magazines) and lines of toy merchandise: Bandai's winning formula. But since the 1990s and reflecting lifestyle trends, the play industry is turning more to other (electronic, mobile, and interactive) media such as Game Boys, *tamagotchi*, video game systems, and trading cards where fantasy worlds are less dependent on preset or stable visual images (as is the case with television and comic books). As the terms of visuality shift and interactivity builds, the rubric of play (and its fetishes) changes as well.

The *Poketto Monstā Zukan* is broken up into six sections, each laying out a different arena of the *Pokémon* world that is identified (in title and image on each section's title page) by an epistemological trope.[8] The book's layout is one of overlapping cartographies, charts, and accounts where the coordinates continually vacillate between phenomena that actually exist (the creators of the game, a nature of rivers and grass) and the imaginary *Poké*-world (monsters who live, evolve, and advance as tools of and for humans). Linking the imaginary playscape of *Pokémon* not only to the seriousness of knowledge but also to Japan's place in the modern (and postmodern) world of advanced powers is part of the official discourse found in the *Poketto Monstā Zukan*. Starting off the first section, this is rendered as an origin myth that goes as follows: pocket monsters first appeared on earth about two million years ago. The first person to study their genealogy was an eighteenth-century French writer, Count Tajirin. Based on his discovery of thirty types of *pokémon*, the school of *Pokémon* studies *(Pokémongaku)* was founded. Spreading to other countries in Europe, this science reached *waga kuni* (our country, Japan) by the end of the eighteenth century. Discovering that *pokémon* evolve, Professor Nitsunomori (the Japanese founder of *Pokémon*ology) greatly advanced the field, and upon the publication of his thesis ("Reflections on Pikachu's Evolution"), Japan has become a *senshinkoku* (advanced country) in *pokémon* research. Since that time, when only eighty *pokémon* types were known, research has progressed further thanks largely to Japan's Ōkido Hakase (Professor Oak), professor at the Tamamushi Daigaku Keitai Jyū Gakubu (Department of Portable Beasts at Scarab Beetle University). Professor Oak has discovered a total of 151 monsters and knows how to categorize them according to their ecological habitat. There are still *pokémon* to be unearthed, however, and Professor Oak asks that all players help him in his research by entering what they learn of *pokémon* into their own *zukan*—databases.

Though whimsical, this story embeds a tale about national identity. The theme of evolution is key; *pokémon* evolve (figure 35), as has Japan's stature as a modern, now postmodern, nation marked by its contributions to (monster) science. "Advanced country" is a revealing word choice here, given that the term was much used at the time of modernization (the end of the nineteenth century) when, by Euro-American standards, Japan was anything but. Yet thanks to eminent Japanese scientists, the *Pokémon* story goes, the country is achieving global stature in the field of mobile fantasy creatures/creations a century later, a status embodied by Professor Oak, the world-renowned researcher of "portable beasts" today. Folded into a tale about imaginary beings, then, is an ideological one about Japan's place in the world, tallied on the basis of a science devoted to playthings: a commentary on Japan's rise to global prominence as producer of ("evolved") kids' goods.

At the end of this origin myth, Professor Oak invites readers/players to step into his place by envisioning *Pokémon* as a frontier of discovery and investigation. This is a world that still retains secrets, mysteries, and gaps in what humans know and have recorded about one of its most fascinating lifeforms. As the professor later notes (in his public lecture in the journal section), the precise nature of pocket monsters is difficult to pin down. They are

カメール

カメックス

ゼニガメ

▲ゼニガメは、カメール、カメックスと しんかするよ。

Figure 35. The three evolutionary stages of a pocket monster: Zenigame, Kame-ru, Kamekkusu. (Courtesy of Shōgakukan Production.)

not a race per se (because, for one thing, they evolve), nor are they merely pets or monsters. What they do share, however, is the quality of entering a monster ball and possessing qualities that "come in handy" for the humans they live alongside (like Pikachu's electric powers, which Professor Oak uses to fuel his house)—a cyborgian interface with humans and their portable machines.[9] Such queer creatures are fascinating because they both resemble and deviate from natural categories and organisms. But what is "good to think" (as Lévi-Strauss said about nature) must also be studied with the rigors and discipline of *Pokémon* science in order to be captured: the objective, after all, of the game.

The two longest sections of the book, those on pocket monsters and the world they inhabit, are filled with information, statistics, and colorful images, all detailing a game environment whose contours are grounded in nature (or "fake nature," as Nakazawa [1998] calls this fantasy version). Laid out, in the first of these, are the eleven basic ecozones that identify, structure, and explain the originary nature of each *pokémon*. Mixing fantasy and reality, the text tells us what *Pokémon*ology has learned to date: for example, grassland *pokémon* have warm personalities (because food is abundant and life easy there),

Figure 36. Virtual geography: a world that is nowhere and everywhere at the same time. This is the region called Kanto. (From a guidebook for the *Pokémon* Game Boy game, Crystal Version; courtesy of Beckett Publishers.)

sea *pokémon* rarely evolve or have high intellects (a result of their relatively unchanging environment), and town *pokémon* have been subjected to industrial pollution. There are also deviations from this scheme and gaps in the knowledge; strange, extinct, and legendary *pokémon* come from habitats that are less "alive," and they have mysterious *(fushigi)* powers that *Pokémonology* cannot yet account for. Each of the 151 *pokémon* has a mini-profile at the bottom of one of these pages.[10] Through such entries, players come to know the individual *pokémon* by learning their origins and nature: facts with multiple components, implications, and values that must be mastered and strategically manipulated when battling *pokémon* (for more *pokémon*).

In the next section, the *Poketto Monstā Zukan* moves from ecozones to the specific geography of the *Pokémon* world (figures 36 and 37). This land-scape is presented via descriptions of each separate locale (Nibi City, Diggers' Hole, Twin Island, Sekiei Highlands), including the tunnels and roads that connect them, distinguishing landmarks (fishing ponds, caves, electric power works), and hidden treasures or traps. Because each region in this

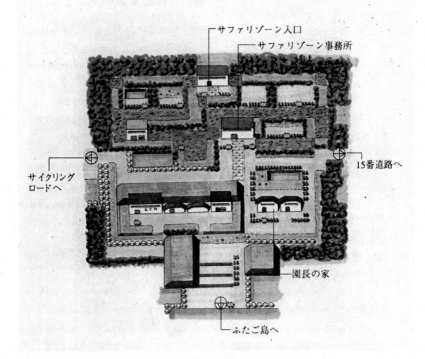

Figure 37. Geography on the grid: "Sekichiku City" as iconized on the Game Boy screen. (Courtesy of Pokémon Company.)

world represents a stage in the game (although, true to the principles of postmodernity, one's path can also be reversed, defying strict linearity), information useful for playing is written into the narrative of place. Like the discourse of imaginary biology/ecology in the previous section, the science of geography here is shaped by utilitarian desire; what one learns about this world is in the form of goods useful to the pursuit of acquisition. Thus, for example, the player is told that in Nibi City old *pokémon* fossils and moonstones (that translate into gaming powers) can be found, and we learn that wild *pokémon* can be caught in the forest adjoining Tokiwa City.

In this, *Pokémon*'s cartography is based on modernist principles—those of new frontiers inviting exploration and conquest. Such a logic informed the worldly expeditions of Euro-Americans in the seventeenth to nineteenth centuries when, driven by burgeoning capitalism (at the stage of "primitive accumulation"), imperialist powers circumnavigated the world looking to discover, then conquer and pillage, new frontiers. As Mary Louise Pratt has noted, these ventures were accompanied by a new expansionist paradigm in science as well. Redrawing the world as an object of knowledge, scientists shifted their focus from landmasses and coastlines (producing geographic maps useful for maritime exploration) to nature—an entity that was at once more elemental and more global. At the forefront of this shift was Linnaeus's *System of Nature* (1735), whose taxonomic grid enabled the classification of all plants on the earth according to their configurations of key reproductive elements. Armed with such a science, Europeans could apprehend more of the planet as a whole (spurring what Pratt calls a "planetary consciousness") and deeper into its interior (1992:15–37).

The principle here of mastering nature by the imposition of scientific order stems from a modernist worldview, one that Japan subsequently adopted as well, where it was similarly tied to the birthing of the modern nation-state and the rise of capital accumulation that fueled the Industrial Revolution: "In the sphere of culture the many forms of collection that were practiced during this period developed in part as the image of that accumulation, and as its legitimation. The systematizing of nature carries this image of accumulation to a totalized extreme and at the same time models the extractive, transformative nature of industrial capitalism and ordering mechanisms that were beginning to shape urban mass society" (Pratt 1992:36).

At the dawn of Japan's modernity, science was turned not only to developing industry and expanding national territory (by launching wars against Russia and China, for example, and embarking upon colonialist conquest) but also to remaking the cultural landscape in conformity with Western standards of modern rationality. Given that folk beliefs in otherworldly creatures like monsters defied such rational norms, a Linnean system of natural history was adopted to study, classify, and record "mysterious" beings (like monsters called *yōkai*, a synonym of *fushigi*, meaning strange). Though the attempt here was to effectively eradicate such so-called irrational beliefs by subjecting them to rational science, the latter also became a means by which the former came to survive modernity. Crisscrossing the country to unearth, investigate, and catalog Japanese folklore of strange beings *(bakemono)* became the lifework of eminent scholars such as Yanagita Kunio. As we know from Foucault (1980), a discourse intended to suppress a particular behavior can actually incite its very production (like sexual repression in the Victoria era, which, spoken about so excessively, produced a greater investment, conscious and unconscious, in sexuality). As Gerald Figal (1997:7) has similarly argued, the Linnean methods of empirical observation and scientific inquiry adopted by Yanagita and others helped to not only reframe but also perpetuate the fantastic in Japanese cultural consciousness as the country transited to a modern nation-state (1999:7).

One century after its move into modernity, Japan has arrived at another transitional moment. Once again, monsters are being invoked, and once again this invocation is taking place within a taxonomic classificatory system steeped in national(ist) ideology and a worldview joining the rational and irrational, seen and unseen, material and immaterial. In *Pokémon*, the object of both knowledge and accumulation has shifted (from nature, folktales, plundered lands) to something whose boundaries are even more expansive. This is virtuality: a world of vistas and creatures that is entirely made up (and therefore limitless). Here, a fictional construct with a labyrinth of habitats, landmarks, and beasts has expanded exponentially over the years from the original Game Boy game to a veritable empire of (ever more) editions, iterations, and forms. Within this world of expanding imaginary creatures/creations, the game can go on forever. "Just because the story is over does not mean the game is over. This game is not that passive. The goal is to record *pokémon* from all over the world in your *zukan*. Which version of the Game Boy game do you have, red or green? You can get the other one now and play that one. There are plenty of *pokémon* left that you don't know about" (from Professor Oak's "public lecture" in *Asupekuto* 1997:32). What is treated like a science (the exploratory activities of discovering and recording more *pokémon*) is also a consumer practice (buying and accumulating more *Poké*-goods: "Which version of the Game Boy game do you have?"). And in this convergence, a new kind of logic is apparent. The world envisioned is not "real" but overtly constructed, inviting claims to classify and accumulate what are now manufactured commodities.

Significantly, a major section in the *Monstā Zukan* consists of interviews with all the creative staff (of Game Freak) who designed the Game Boy game. Forefronting not only the fact that *Pokémon* is a made-up game but the specific way it was put together is a tactic that differs strikingly from the conventions of the public discourse of other fantasy factories. In Disneyland, for example, the illusion of magic is maintained by concealing references to both the outside world and the machinery of production. *Pokémon's* artifice, by contrast, is fully exposed. Tajiri Satoshi, the main

Figure 38. *Pokémon* epistemology: by sight and by statistic. This is an entry for Gōsu—Ghost in English— in a guidebook. (Courtesy of Pokémon Company.)

designer of the game, for example, speaks of how he aimed to create an "interesting new game" that mixed genres: portraying battles (as in action games) but with the "lines" of information and stories favored in role-playing games. The result is that *pokémon* are represented on the game screen both figuratively (bodies with flying sparks, attacking vines, venomous poison) and computationally (by an analytic grid that measures the powers, strengths, and attack strategies of each party). This gives pocket monsters a double epistemology, known to players both through sight (their material appearance out of the *Poké*-ball) and through data, or their statistical profile (figure 38). The latter is what Tajiri sees as *Pokémon*'s "gorgeous implications for communication" because, in contrast to a game based on mere battle, players not only gather information but also exchange it with others. This trade of information is what Tajiri sees as "the most important thing" in the entire game and a "concept easy for players to grasp."

In the last two sections of *Poketto Monstā Zukan* (public lectures and staff interviews), the discourse significantly shifts its emphasis from conquest, discovery, and accumulation to exchange, communication, and caregiving. The objective of getting *pokémon* is played down by the creators of the game, who play up instead the fun of exchanging monsters, trading information, and bonding with *pokémon*. As Watanabe (the programmer) states, the game was designed so players can give their *pokémon* personal names, and "*pokémon* remember the names of the parents who have raised them" (Asupekuto 1997:141). Nishida (the graphic designer) adds: "Battles are interesting, but I'd like you to think not just of winning and losing but also of how to be nice to the *pokémon* you're raising" (142). For his parting words, Tajiri advises children to "carry the monsters you raise around with you everywhere" and "play without any limits to how you play, forming partnerships with many *pokémon* as well as many friends" (143). Mimicking the logic and discourse of *tamagotchi*—a play of raising virtual pets— *Pokémon* takes this to a new level of exchanges, information, and communication with "friends," both virtual and human. This is the essence of "Advice for Battles and Communication Exchanges," the section that lists the following as pointers for conducting trades: "Always exchange with someone; after you've exchanged, you can play by yourself; give or lend what you've raised to another friend; give a *pokémon* that you've personally named to a special friend; try to create dramas apart from the game itself; hang in there until the end of the game; follow the rules; make a lot of friends" (123–28). So acquisition—of knowledge, territory, pocket monsters—moves to communication and friendship: a fusion of capitalism, "soft electronics," and sociality.

The Monster Economy:
Gifts, Commodities, and Spirits

In Marx's classic formulation (1977), capitalism is an economy based on the estrangement of labor. Work is sold for a wage, and the surplus labor extracted from one class feeds the profits of another. Transforming what Marx believed was the essence of human life ("species being")—labor—into a thing used to produce and purchase commodities, this system turns everything into a currency of exchange. Life, including people and the relationships between them, is thingified in the process.

An antithetical economic system is one anthropologists have identified as gift exchange. In his canonical work on the subject, *The Gift* (1967), Marcel Mauss describes communities in which labor congeals into gifts (as opposed to commodities) that are exchanged between individuals and groups rather than being transacted through money. The principle here is not self-interest, accumulating goods for oneself. Rather, the aim is to reciprocate with other goods (rice, beer, wives) and, through this exchange, establish bonds between persons. Whereas in capitalism relations are used to produce things, in gift exchange things are used to produce relations.

Japan today is a country fully embedded in capitalism. Its national goal, as structured by postwar policies, has been material prosperity fueling (and fueled by) personal consumption. Yet Japanese national culture has long been grounded in an orientation toward the collective: groupism, interrelationality, communalism. It is the erosion of precisely these values in recent years that is often linked to Japan's current problems (everything from the economic recession to the social pathologies of schoolroom collapse, refusal-to-go-to school syndrome, the sarin gas attacks of Aum Shinrikyō, youth crime, and "amateur prostitution"). As consumer capitalism escalates, nostalgia appears for what Marilyn Ivy (1995) has called the "vanishing" of traditional culture, invented or not: a time and place in which not material things but human relationships mattered most. Still, traces of what is considered the traditional Japanese cultural fabric are seen in contemporary times, including a rabid engagement in gift exchange: everything from the institutionalized gift-giving seasons twice a year to the ritualistic purchase of *omiyage* (souvenirs) from even one-day outings to local hot springs. Such gifts are exchanged with an assortment of people, including landlords, neighbors, coworkers, and relatives, with whom one has social and economic relationships. I myself have been the beneficiary of endless gifts, including a ten-kilo bag of Japanese rice airmailed to me from a friend in Tokyo as a reminder of our friendship (and the time we spent eating what she was sure I missed in the States, Japanese food).

The transactions of gift exchange reflect the bond they express as well as the giver of the gift. In some sense, one is giving oneself in the exchange: what is materialized in the form of a thing that is also (as in gifts given to a god) a personal sacrifice. As Mauss pointed out, it is this element of gift exchange that makes what is economic (building the social relations on which life depends) also moral, even spiritual. Things given in exchange are inalienable in that the gift retains something of the giver, such as the person's name, as in the *kula* ring studied by Malinowski, even though the giver parts with it.[11] This is the meaning of the gift and the reason its symbolism is so powerful; relations between people are built on exchanges of self. By contrast, in transactions dictated by money, things or goods are alienable from the self (as in selling one's labor for a wage and buying goods at a store) and are traded according to the value of the market rather than that of social relationships. Commodities take on a life of their own, producing a very different type of cultural ethos and logic. It is the individualistic desire to own and accumulate that drives the economy now, and material things are not merely the means to an end (more spiritual and social) but the end itself. Weber called this the iron cage (1987:181), when meaning and enchantment drop out of the capitalist machine. And Mauss decried the loss of morality in modern economies, in which the gift has been displaced by the commodity.

In *Pokémon* one sees the principles of both gift exchange and commodity economy at work. Pocket monsters, the currency of play here, are simultaneously traded and accumulated; they build capital for the player but also relationships with others. *Pokémon* are gifts as well as commodities, and the "communication" Tajiri and Nintendo so self-consciously intended for this playscape evokes a premodern past but also a postmodern future (of virtual relations, animated commodities, spirited "getting"). The "monster economy" laid out by *Pokémon* serves simultaneously as template for, and corrective to, conditions of millennial capitalism in Japan today. And, functioning within this system, it alludes to (but also reinvents) the past: a past of insect collecting, gift exchanges, and a world beyond the materiality of things, humans, and rationality. As mentioned previously, gift exchange is not a practice that is new (or newly revived) with *Pokémon*. Neither is the commodified form in which gift giving has been updated today (during gift-giving season, for example, the stores are stocked with "gift" goods, and shelves are coded by price, a differential by which the "value" of relationships is marked—a 5,000-yen shelf with boxes of soap, tinned fruit, and cookies; a 6,000-yen shelf with coffee, whiskey, and candy). Rather, *Pokémon*'s innovation is the mapping of an almost infinite network of things/ places/monsters/relations that decompose and recompose into an endless array of parts/powers/attributes/weapons. The boundaries between these entities are fluid and flexible, but the agenda driving this game space is to make, out of minuscule parts, an entire world, even an empire, that feels as cozy and warm as it does masterful and empowering. Along with "getting," that is, weaving relationships is the name of the game. And in *Pokémon* these two acts become synonymous, since getting entails and produces relations, even though they are with partners as much virtual (monster) as real (other kids).

The voluminous commentary on *Pokémon* in Japan (by scholars, reporters, child experts, and those in the toy/game/character business) repeatedly assessed this playscape in (seemingly) contradictory terms: as a blend of competition and exchanges, strategy and nurturance, accumulation and communication, premodernity and (post)modernity. In a tone reminiscent of Ruth Benedict's depiction of Japanese culture as anchored in contradiction (*The Chrysanthemum and the Sword*, 1946), these accounts overwhelmingly praised the multisidedness of *Pokémon*, regarding this feature as key not only to the product's market success but also to the "benefits" this play world yields to millennial kids. In an article in the *Asahi Shinbun* (one of Japan's most heavily read newspapers), for example, the reporter used the metaphor of financial circles to describe the transactions kids engage in while playing *Pokémon*. Focusing on the cards, he noted that children enjoy collecting them more than playing them because they are excited by the "cash value," which is readily available in magazines tallying current market values. Value is based on rarity, a feature Nintendo built into the availability of cards and also imprints as one of the attributes differentiating each monster/card. Yet even at the height of the fad, most kids did not wind up actually cashing in on their cards, though there were hobby shops and dealers willing to buy them (as is the case now with *Yu-Gi-Oh!*). Rather, organized play trades, in which "cash value" is the (imaginary) currency of operation, were far more common. Lumping this activity under the category of "collecting," the *Asahi* reporter wondered why children around the world were now atavistically collecting video games and monster packs the way they used to collect baseball cards, insects, and stamps. His answer, in part, was that in the accumulation (and exchange) of monsters/cards, there is an "arousal of *ningenkankei*" (human relationships)—that foundation of traditional culture and also the principle of gift exchange (Takanarita 1999:4). So social bonds here are created by something (also) resembling financial circles.

A researcher of children's games and play sees the dynamics of *Pokémon* somewhat differently. Concerned about the solitary, bleak, alienated life led by kids in the current atmosphere of consumer capitalism and academic competition, she notes the tendency to turn inward: "People feel a lot of darkness today. As a defense, they retreat into solitary capsules. On the trains, everyone is immersed in their Walkman, *manga*, books they buy at kiosks: defense mechanisms used to maintain distance from others. Youth also turn to consumer products that allow them to relate to one another by maintaining the rule of silence" (Watanabe 1999:74). *Pokémon* offers a corrective to this kind of gloomy existence: a "route" (75) out of atomistic isolation to a brighter world beyond the self. Key here is the fact that the game is structured in such a way that players continually win. Whether it is through battles or matches or exchanges, a child keeps acquiring more *pokémon* and, in the process, receives (time and time again) what Watanabe takes to be the main message of the game: "You're great!" (72).

Getting monsters equates with self-confirmation, something Watanabe also refers to as "unconditional love" (and believes is acutely lacking in the lives of Japanese children today). Kids are worked like machines to perform on exams over which they have no control or often any personal interest in. Alienated in their labor at school, and with parents who pressure them to perform academically, kids find a world that is far more meaningful and "loving" in *Pokémon*. Less critical is the nature of this world per se than the "route" by which children navigate it by continually acquiring and winning monsters: what Watanabe calls the "story line" of *Pokémon* (72). These acts of acquisition convert what is alien (wild monsters) and alienated (kids' lives) into the inalienable terrain of the personal and the self. The latter (personal, inalienable things) is reminiscent of gift exchange. But simply taking what is alien/alienable in the outside world and pocketing it as one's own is the logic not of a barter (noncapitalist) economy but of consumer capitalism (and commodity fetishism).

In the mind of *Pokémon*'s designer as well, "getting" is the organizing principle of this game world. But it combines (rather than conflicts) with the principle of exchange, and both processes serve to "open up" children to a world beyond the narrow confines of an atomistic lifestyle (of study, no-madicism, isolation). Many commentators agree, as does the cultural critic Okada Tsuneo, that *Pokémon* is "play that goes beyond the world of the game itself" and is revolutionary for this reason. Because the software is simple yet fun, it allows kids to play either alone or with others. Easy to get into and out of, this is a flexible playscape that can accompany kids wherever they go and also be used to foster relations: "In an age when kids have fixed schedules and are busier than ever before, *Pokémon* provides an opportunity to fit in communication with friends" (Yamato 1998:247). Yet as Tajiri himself has put it, what inspires such communalism is not simply or principally the desire to build friendships, as in gift exchange. Rather, it is the self-interest (consistent with a commodity economy) of, as he gives the example, seeing another child on a train with a monster one wants and negotiating a transaction to "get it" (Nintendo 1999). Kubo Masakazu, one of the producers of *Pokémon*, has said similarly that the genius of *Pokémon* is its "open-endedness," by which kids can take their Game Boys anywhere and, motivated by the desire to "get" a monster from the child standing next to them (on a train, in a line at a supermarket, in the countryside for *obon*, the Buddhist summer ancestor-commemorating festival), start playing/negotiating with new friends (Hatakeyama and Kubo 2000:136).

Figure 39. *Pokémon* ball: a weapon for catching and a technology for containing pocket monsters. (Courtesy of Pokémon Company.)

Conversion:
Mobile Technology/Data-fied Monsters

Monsters are the medium of play, exchange, and "getting" in *Pokémon*. It was important to the game's inventor, therefore, to create a mechanism by which these monsters convert into a currency of equivalence. This mechanism was the monster ball. Monsters start out wild, but once they are captured, they inhabit balls that are owned and controlled by their masters (hence the name "pocket monsters"). The ball (figure 39), which stands for a player's powers, is activated at the time of a match, thereby releasing the pocket monster inside. While the balls and the monsters who live in them function like personal genies, they can also be quantified and, in this respect, resemble money, which converts the qualititative differences of commodities (use values) to a quantitative equivalence (exchange value). Most of the children I spoke with about *Pokémon* took great pride in knowing and comparing their stocks of pocket monsters, measured according to numbers owned, type of *pokémon,* and their strength, type of evolution, and degree of rarity. Treated like private property, the *pokémon* differ from the property in another children's game, Monopoly. In contrast to houses and hotels erected on Monopoly's fixed properties—Park Place, Pennsylvania Railroad, Water Works—*pokémon* are a much more fluid and flexible currency. Composed out of multiple parts that break down and recombine in a complex array of possible constellations, the postmodernist *pokémon* are less stable or reducible to a material thing than the fixed real estate offerings of the more modernist Monopoly. As Tajiri has said about his monster economy, the critical component in *Pokémon* is that monsters convert to balls through what he calls a process of "data-fication": the reconfiguration of value from a material form (monsters) into data that are storable, portable, and transferable (via communication cables on the Game Boy). This, in his mind, is what makes *Pokémon* a kind of play that keeps going beyond the game itself: a mechanism by which what takes place within the game can be (endlessly and polymorphously) communicated/gotten/exchanged with kids outside (Nakazawa 1997:25). Capital becomes communicable: commodities that double as gifts.

But there is more. Originally, the ball was supposed to be a capsule, and the concept Tajiri first floated to Nintendo was a game about "capsule monsters." Wanting to re-create a motif popular in his youth, the capsule toys sold in machines (Nakazawa 1997:93–94), Tajiri also aimed to produce an alternative world different from the prevailing tendency toward social atomism, as in "capsule hotels." As we saw in chapter 3, the recent rise in "social shut-ins" in Japan—people who live literally in their rooms, unable to interact with the society around them—is an example of the latter condition. These *hikikomori*, whose condition usually begins in their teenage years around the time of the rigorous high school entrance examinations, are often described by the word *fujikomeru* (literally, "contain within"), as in persons who are contained within capsule existences. Adopting the same word, Tajiri describes how he designed *Pokémon* to "contain" the experiences of his youth as an avid bug collector in a town not yet depleted of nature or communal pastimes. "Tickling" memories of the past and "transmitting" them to youth today (via New Age capsules inscribed with older cultural values), *Pokémon* serves as a corrective to the postindustrial state of atomistic alienation (quoted in Nintendo 1999:12). Kids will not be so much trapped inside this "space of their own" as routed to the outside world—in the form of communities, communions, and communications.

What makes *Pokémon* at once a container of the past and a medium for millennial relation-building are the pocket monsters themselves: creatures that broker the border between the practical, everyday, capitalistic and the fantastic, extraordinary, communitarian. As Nagao Takeshi notes, they operate both as utilitarian tools (helping players win the game by being acquired in numbers) and as something akin to spirits or companions (1998:132, 134). As he sees it, this attitude is rooted in traditional beliefs—in a worldview that gives value and respect to the nonhuman. In Shinto, for example, humans are no more than one part of nature, and stories of independent animals (not mere useful appendages of humans) abound in folk legends. Japanese also have a "weird sensibility" for mechanized things and have traditionally believed that if a tool or natural thing lives long enough, it becomes a spirit or ghost (*yōkai*, which also translates as "monster"; 137). According to Nagao, such a "Japanese sensitivity *[yasashisa]*" is character-istic of "our spiritual culture" (142), something the creators of *Pokémon* have self-consciously tried to convey to children entering the next century. Like the return of the repressed, spirits of the past reemerge embedded in the nomadic technology and data-ized currency of millennial capitalism.[12] Haunting a postmodern form ("well suited" to the needs of today's kids), the *pokémon* are "nonnormal things" *(igyō no mono)*, a category that in-cludes a whole range of otherworldly beings such as fairies, demons, mon-sters, and ghosts popular in Japanese folklore, legends, and myths: *kaibutsu, yōsei, yōkai* (189). As such, *Pokémon* represents a blend of the old and the new in Japan. And in a view that is widespread in the commentary on *Poké-mon*, Nagao believes that this construct of otherworldliness is a healing force in these contemporary times of hypermateriality and individuated lifestyles (150).

Parents I spoke with in Japan often expressed similar sentiments. Unlike American parents (who, almost without exception, experienced *Pokémon* as alien territory), their Japanese counterparts recognized something familiar here that connected them to their youth. Finding its world gentle and en-couraging of good values (forging relations with other children, nurturing wild creatures), these adults also said *Pokémon* reminded them of their own childhood, specifically, playing cards *(menko)*, collecting things (insects, base-ball cards), and watching *Urutoraman*, a live-action television show popu-lated by monsters. As we saw in chapter 2, *Urutoraman*, designed by the special-effects creator of *Gojira*, was a huge hit in the 1960s. It was recently reprised in Japan and was also launched for the first time in the United States (in the rising presence of Japanese shows on American TV). These *kaijū*, marked by the cold war logic of the show's times, are unilaterally bad and are wiped out time and time again by the hero, a human who morphs into a giant cyborg. Consistent with *Pokémon*, however, are the hordes of monsters that, in their diversity and abundance, evoke the scores of *yōkai* that proliferated in folklore and literature of the seventeenth- and eighteenth-century Edo period (and were similarly cataloged in handbooks) (Foster, n.d.). As one fa-ther told me, he loved this fantasy world far more for the *kaijū* than the hero because they constantly changed, displayed a wealth of different attributes, and were what he and his friends tried to master (by collecting cards, typologizing them, and reading about them in *kaijū zukan*, illustrated monster books). In Lévi-Straussian terms, monsters are "good to think." Even more important for capitalism, they are also good to sell. Easily commodifiable into collectible models, *kaijū* are one of the principal items in *Urutoraman* specialty stores that do good business in Tokyo today.

It is this juncture between fantasy and profits, spirits and goods, gifts and commodities that Nakazawa Shin'ichi sees as the "paradox" of *Poké-mon* as well. An anthropologist trained in religion who has written a book on the subject, *Poketto no naka no yasei* (Wildness in the Pocket, 1997), Nakazawa believes that *Pokémon* captures what he calls, following Lévi-Strauss, the "primitive unconscious" (1997:160). Also, echoing Benjamin, he sees modernization as a process of taming and materializing life: of seeing the world in terms of rational, visible, and commodifiable things. For children, too, growing up entails placing limits on the imagination—producing a disenchantment of reality when one's life is swamped by test scores, daily schedules, and financial transactions. *Pokémon*, according to Nakazawa, is a rich alternative to the concrete and routine. Here children play in a field of infinite possibilities, where borders are something to go beyond rather than be contained within. Pocket monsters anchor this space as entities that hover between the known and unknown, visible and invisible, real and fantastic. Serving as what Lacan calls *petit objet a*, these beings exceed phenomenal existence and fill in, imaginatively, for its lapses and lacks (Nakazawa 1997:90). As such, *pokémon* offer a connection to what has been lost in the materialism of millennial times: a sensitivity to the nonmaterial, otherworldly, and interpersonal that, Nakazawa believes, characterized Japan's premodern past. But, paradoxically, *Pokémon* also yields tremendous monetary profits for the game's corporate owners: a paradox he sees as "encapsulating the direction in which capitalism is headed today" (personal interview, 2000). Indeed, the play industry is the one entity that has managed not only to hold on to Japan's "primitive unconscious" but also to market it as one of the country's leading products and most successful exports. As a newspaper reported in 1999, if Japan could produce *Pokémon* electricity, *Pokémon* houses, and *Pokémon* trains, its financial woes would be eliminated overnight (*Nikkei Entertainment* 1998:49). In its commodity form, then, *Pokémon* is a stimulus to the very capitalism it also serves to imaginatively disassemble. And with its premise of accumulation that is at once enchanting and communitarian, the monster economy spells out Japan's promise for a millennial future.

Cuteness and Friendship:
Expanding the Empire

The success of *Pokémon* was totally unexpected. For Tajiri and Nintendo alike, this was a game that would do reasonably well only in a fairly limited market. Game Boy technology was becoming outdated by the time *Pokémon* was released (February 1996), and the game was not expected to travel beyond its target audience, young Japanese boys. Yet the product did surprisingly well, exceeding original predictions. Believing it had the seeds of a fad on its hands, Nintendo was prompted to expand its horizons. Enlisted to help in the process, Kubo Masakazu, a publisher who had made his career in boys' comics, first proposed a *manga* version of *Pokémon.* Still concentrating on boys, he launched a serialized comic in the magazine *Korokoro Komikku* (a monthly magazine read by half of all Japanese boys between the ages of eight and fourteen) in summer 1996. Capitalizing on Tajiri's theme of exchange, the *Pokémon* comic was launched with a special gift (called a special "exchange") for kids—a trading card of the secretive 151th *pokémon*, Mew Two. Successful in this medium, both the comic and the giveaway card generated further products. *Pokémon* trading cards (managed by Ishihara Tsunekazu for Media Factory) took off in the fall, tie-in merchandise and campaigns were engineered with a host of commercial interests, and Kubo set to work on what would be a television cartoon as well as a series of animated movies (nine to date, the most recent in 2005). As virtually everyone in the children's business, in both Japan and the United States, has confirmed, even a successful toy or video game must be accompanied by a television show or movie version to become a real fad. In the case of *Pokémon*, the venue of storytelling—the adventures told of a trio of kids in their travels to discover, capture, and domesticate ever more *pokémon* (figure 40)—widened and altered the scope of what started out as a mere Game Boy game.

As Kubo explained the empire to me, *Pokémon, Inc.,* is built on three pillars: the electronic game, the movies and television cartoon (serialized also as comics), and the trading cards. Each of these pillars sports a host of elements with wide appeal to a range of audiences. Overarching all the components is a "harmony" that Kubo attributed both to the characters (the *pokémon* as well as the humans in the story versions) and to a quality he referred to as "cuteness" (*kawaisa* or *yasashisa*, "gentleness," as others in the business also labeled it). Speaking specifically of *Pokémon* and its success on the export market (such as becoming the top-ranked children's show on U.S. television when it launched on Warner Brothers Network in fall 1998), Kubo added that cuteness gave Japan "cultural power," something the

Figure 40. The traveling trio in their endless quest to discover more (and more) wild *pokémon:* Kasumi (Misty in English), Satoshi (Ash), and Takeshi (Brock). (Courtesy of Shōgakukan Production.)

Japanese are "polishing" as both capital and prestige overseas. Cuteness, the Japanese cultural critic Okada Tsuneo has argued, is one thing that registers for all people, and in his mind, *Pokémon* defines cuteness: a cuteness that may well be Japan's key to working foreign capital in the twenty-first century (Yamato 1998:244). Others have suggested that Japan's future in influencing, even leading, global culture will come through three industries: video games, *anime,* and *manga.* The market for these industries has surpassed that for the car industry in the last decade, leading some economists to hope that it will pull Japan out of the red. As one economist notes, instead of the Silicon Valley, Japan has the *"anime komikku* game industry," which will be the root of the twenty-first century's culture and recreation industry (*Nihon Keizai Shinbun* 1999:3).

What makes Japan newly successful in its marketing of games, comics, and cartoons is not simply technological or business prowess, but what has been called the "expressive strength" of their Japanese creators (*Nihon Keizai Shinbun* 1999:3). The same portable convenience, data-ized flexibility, and fantastic spirituality that characterize *Pokémon* are part of the wider postmodern play aesthetics I have been tracing in this book. The word used more than any other in Japan to summarize this quality (of technology, play, consumer culture) is "cute(ness)," the very property that, once added to the *Pokémon* machine, helped transform a mere Game Boy game for boys to a kids' craze of global proportions. *Yasashisa*, the "gentle" aspect of cuteness (and also the word used by Nagao Takeshi for the sensitivity at the heart of Japanese culture), is precisely the word Japanese producers I spoke with used to describe the marketing of *Pokémon* in Japan. As they pointed out, however, this was not its original identity when *Pokémon* started out as a role-playing/action game targeted to boys aged eight to fourteen. Cuteness came with the development of the story versions, particularly the *anime* developed by Kubo and his staff for Tokyo television. As he told me in an interview, the overarching objective here was to extend the audience of *Pokémon* to girls, younger children, and even mothers (as important in the marketing of children's entertainment as children themselves). Giving characterization and story lines to what are only sketchy images on a Game Boy screen, the cartoon also came up with a central character: a figure who, like Mario or Mickey Mouse, could ground and iconize the entire phenomenon. Instead of a character with whom audiences could identify—a human or anthropomorphic animal (like Mickey)—they chose a pocket monster. Such a lead character engenders a different type of imaginary bond that is key to the construction of *yasashisa:* feelings of possession, companionship, and attachment in viewers. This was the genesis of Pikachu (figure 41), the cute, yellow, mouselike *pokémon* with electric powers and a squiggly tail. Merely one of 151 monsters in the original Game Boy game, Pikachu subsequently became the lead *pokémon* and a global icon on the order of the Nike swoosh and McDonald's golden arches.

According to Kubo, a checklist was followed in making this selection. The character needed a shape recognizable from a distance (a sharp silhouette and basic color—and yellow would be better than red, which signals competition), a face that could "pleasantly" show a range of emotions (including tears), a catchy name that kids could easily pronounce, an unforgettable refrain ("pika pika chuuuuu," which sounds good and is globalizable without translation), and, most important, overall cuteness. As Kubo sums up Pikachu's phenomenal appeal, this character "grabs" people's emotions. Its huggable look makes children happy and mothers feel safe (Kubo 1999:344). But equally important are the fierce powers Pikachu possesses within its cute frame—much like Japan itself these days, whose "cultural power" comes in the disarming form of character/commodity cuteness.

Needless to say, Pikachu's appeal is based on more than image alone. In

Figure 41. Pikachu: The (cute) genesis of a global icon. (Courtesy of Shōgakukan Production.)

the context of the TV cartoon (movies, comics), this yellowy thunderbolt (a mouse type with electric powers) acquires a definite personality that, significantly, is built up mainly in terms of the bond it shares with a human. A ten-year-old boy aiming to become the "world's greatest *pokémon* master," Satoshi (Ash in the U.S. version) is the lead human character in the story whose travels in *Poké*-world (accompanied by Kasumi, a ten-year-old girl, and Takeshi, a fifteen-year-old boy more interested in studying *pokémon* than in capturing them) constitute the plotline of the cartoon. The boy and monster first meet in the initial episode, where, mimicking the structure of the game, Satoshi acquires his leadoff *pokémon* from Professor Oak. Seeing a cute monster, the boy is initially disappointed with what he assumes will be a weak *pokémon*. Immediately, however, the boy discovers Pikachu's indomitable will. When ordered to enter the monster ball, Pikachu refuses, thereby forcing his master to carry him on his shoulders, like a pet or a child (figure 42). As the only *pokémon* to remain outside a ball in the story—and therefore the currency of equivalence into which all the other monsters are convertible—Pikachu never gets "pocketed." Always appearing more monster than thing, it is forever visible and cute: the material sign of use value

Figure 42. Satoshi with his Pikachu: a relationship both feudalistically old-fashioned and futuristically cyborgian. (Courtesy of Shōgakukan Production.)

in what is (also) a generalizable medium—monsters that, like money, stand for and generate wealth.

Engaged in what Roland Barthes called a "constantly moving turnstile" (1957:123), *pokémon* continually oscillate between meaning and form: full on the one side and empty on the other. In this, Pikachu serves as an alibi: the material sign of use value in what is simultaneously a system of exchange. It is the boy's property, possession, and tool, but also something much more in the story: free agent, loyal pet, personal friend. Such a deep(er) relationship starts in the very first episode of the cartoon. Having refused the monster ball, Pikachu is riding with Satoshi on his bicycle when the two are attacked by killer birds overhead. When the boy is knocked unconscious, Pikachu goes into warrior mode and saves his master from the birds. Impressed when he awakens at the boldness of his *pokémon,* the boy then returns the favor when Pikachu is hurt next and needs to be taken to a *pokémon* center. This sets the scene for what, in the television cartoon, is staged as the model relationship between *pokémon* and trainer. There is the reciprocity of friendship; the two mutually assist one another and work, in some sense, as a team. Yet crosscutting this friendship is a more hierarchical bond not unlike that of feudal servitude. Pikachu is the dependent, continually serving Satoshi whenever ordered into battle ("I choose YOU, Pikachu!"). In return for loyalty and service, Pikachu is taken care of, nurtured, and trained or reared. In essence, these are the basics of the human-monster relationship: something feudalistically old-fashioned yet futuristically cyborgian (a pocket genie, friend, pet) as well. Time and time again in the cartoon, both aspects are played up: scenes of sharing, camaraderie, and kinship juxtaposed with scenes of monsters subjugated to, sacrificed for, and "pocketed" by humans.

Such contradictions lie at the heart of this construction of cuteness. Oozy cuddliness is evoked, but so is a sense of ownership, mastery, and control: the antidote to, but also template of, capitalism. This paradox is embodied in an episode of the cartoon in which acquisitive self-interest ("getting") is displaced, then recontained, by interests more communitarian and nonmaterialist—saving the ecosystem of/for monsters. Like many episodes, this one is set in a natural wonderland: a forest thick with trees, vegetation, and species of wildlife (most of them *pokémon*). Trekking through *Poké*-land in search of new monsters, the triumvirate (Satoshi, Kasumi, Takeshi) enter the forest and come upon a worried-looking naturalist who solicits their help. "You seem to be *pokémon* trainers," he says. " 'Getting' *pokémon* is fine, but first I really want you to help me check out the scene here." Told that what was once a thriving ecosystem is being threatened by invading beetles (figure 43), the kids put aside the thought of capturing *pokémon* and turn to investigating the terrain instead. Accomplishing this goal and thereby restoring ecological order and harmony among the forest community, the team readies to leave without capturing a single new pocket monster. But, touched by Satoshi's kindness, one of the befriended beetles indicates that he wants to join the boy. Though Satoshi urges him to "return to your own," the beetle persists. Shrugging his shoulders, Satoshi throws his monster ball and, upon crawling inside, the beetle becomes, as the narrator announces, the boy's lat-

Figure 43. Eco-blues: restoring friendship among battling beetles. (Courtesy of Shōgakukan Production.)

est "acquisition." So the agenda of "getting" has not been displaced as much as contained within a loftier worldview. As a reward for his kindness, the boy receives another monster—which will be part of his personal stock and also a new breed of (transspeciated, flexible) kin relations.

Conclusion

In the beetle episode, nature collapses into capital (wildness into acquisitions) and capital into culture (a relation of things into interpersonal relations). Such a ploy occurs often in the cartoon series. Touched by the altruism of humans, *pokémon* leave their "own kind" behind to join the human mission—a worldly journey to discover and pocket more monsters. Needless to say, this is a gentler method of acquisition than attacking wild monsters with balls or winning them in battle after they have been whiplashed, pummeled, or stung. It also reimagines the bond(age) formed. Willingly entering into a system that will reduce them to balls, the representation here mimics that of capitalist ideology: how people are "free" laborers willingly contracting work for a wage (in an economic system built on exploitation and reification). Implicitly, the monsters making this choice exchange the "wildness" of natural habitats for something more enticing—worldly travel, nomadic adventures—but also more moral in the Maussian sense. Exchanging a gift (human kindness) for a gift (the monster itself), what results is a storehouse of goods but also New Age intimacies and attachments.

Speaking of the recent craze in not only *Pokémon* but also character/cute goods more generally, an advertising executive describes the relationships formed as both kinlike and (inter)personal. Whether a Kitty-chan key chain, Doraemon cell phone strap, or Pikachu backpack, these commodity spirits are "shadow families": constant and reliable companions that disseminate "unconditional love" in these postindustrial times of nomadicism, orphanism, and stress. Animating what can be the loneliness, anonymity, and dislocation of life at the millennium, such properties also animate capitalism itself: playscapes whose logic (as in *Pokémon*) masters new frontiers by "getting" indigenous creatures and converting them into possessions, powers, and pals. The principle of value here is consistent with what Jean Comaroff and John Comaroff (2001) have called "occult economies": a symptom, they say, of millennial capitalism, in which production is overshadowed by consumption, and acquisition by a means other than labor (producing wealth "magically" by get-rich schemes, gambling, speculation, or venture capitalism) is ever more sought after in times as desperate and unstable as these. Indeed, such speculative pursuits have moved from the illegal or immoral to the mainstream and state-sanctioned (as in the stock market and national lotteries). In the case of *Pokémon*, acquisition certainly defines the modus operandi of the game: the quest to become the "world's greatest *pokémon* master," as assessed by the quantities and qualities of pocket monsters acquired. And while labor certainly plays a part in achieving this goal (through the study, mastery, and manipulation of endless data), so does chance (the luck of the draw, as in which trading cards one acquires when buying them from a store). As I have argued in this chapter, however, what precisely acquisition of *pokémon* signifies in the logic of play culture for kids involves something both complex and contradictory. Because *pokémon* are a fluid currency—cute but powerful, alienable and inalienable, a form of both capital and companionship—they have affective as well as "market" value and mix (up) different economic logics: the communicative spirit of gift exchange and the addictive frenzy of capitalistic acquisition.

Most commentary in Japan has viewed the *Pokémon* empire of play, goods, and techno-animism as basically good both for Japan (in the profits and reputation it is achieving overseas) and for Japanese kids (by encouraging creativity and communication and by providing a space for kids to relieve stress and connect with a world beyond themselves). Throughout this discourse, *Pokémon* has been treated as akin to an occult economy: a capitalist venture that produces riches out of the magic of creative genius (strange monsters, clever game design) and an entertainment form that, for players, embeds practical goals ("getting") in a virtual gamescape that is fanciful and fun. And, at both the corporate/national and the personal/play level, enchantment intertwines with enterprise, and the two together—enchanting goods, animated capitalism—spell out New Age values, intimacies, and relations seen by many to be "healing" in this age of disaffection, disconnectedness, and stress. As discussed in chapter 3, "speaking things" *(mono no katari)* is how the psychiatrist Ōhira Ken assesses the cultural logic of millennial capitalism in Japan today: an era when people map out their identities and relations with others via brand-name goods—a "language" in which they are far more fluent and intimate than they are with flesh-and-blood human beings (Ōhira 1998). Such connectedness to and with intimate commodities bespeaks a sociability (as in the way we live in the social world) that has become ever more dependent on things. But, as Ōhira sees this and as I would agree, this magic of material acquisition cuts two ways. On the one hand, a richness of human experience is extended to the arena of things in an era when people otherwise feel thingified themselves. On the other hand, investing things with "lifelike" attributes, energies, and attachments not only reflects but also perpetuates the tendencies Marx attributed to capitalism at a far earlier stage: increased alienation, atomism, and dehumanization (by projecting onto commodities the power and value of human labor and relationships—what Marx called "commodity fetishism").

I end on a sober note, recalling a news story that aired the day after I left Japan in early July 2000, at the end of my year of fieldwork. Involving one of the "criminal youth" I discuss in chapter 3—adolescents who, hitherto good students and seemingly "normal" kids, suddenly enact a violent crime—this one was a fourteen-year-old boy who, two days previously, had beaten members of his baseball team with a bat, then returned home to kill his mother with the same bat. In what has become a rash of youth violence somewhat akin to the Columbine shootings in the States (and dovetailing in time period), "criminal youth" are often explained as cut off from society and unskilled in both human empathy and interpersonal communication. As Ikeda Yoshihiko has said of this behavior, which he finds symptomatic of millennial

Japan/ese in general, "We are now living in an era when people have lost contact with other people" (quoted in *Yomiuri Shinbun* 2000:17). In the case of this boy, the profile that emerged was of an angry and solitary youth who had been teased by his teammates for a recent haircut and whose domestic situation was not immediately known. Missing for two days after his attacks, he finally was discovered on a bus headed to Hokkaido. As the press—including the news account I read—reported, the boy was traveling alone, accompanied by only a rucksack filled to the brim with hundreds of *Pokémon* cards, a series of *Pokémon* Game Boy games, and a Game Boy set.[13]

I raise this case not to make a causal linkage between the boy's attachment to *Pokémon* and the violent acts he committed, but merely to point out the proximity of these two passions and that something in the boy's lived environment incubated both. Being "friends" with virtual monsters is a relationship premised not only on cuteness but also on ownership and control. This is the other side of the enchantments *Pokémon* offers in an era of millennial capitalism.

8 "Gotta Catch 'Em All"

The *Pokémon*ization of America (and the World)

> To the best of our abilities, we have tried to prevent kids from feeling
> that these are characters coming from Japan. This is on account of
> localization. The reason is not because we want to hide the fact that
> *Pokémon* is made in Japan, but because we want to promote the
> impression that *Pokémon* are global characters.
>
> **Gail Tilden,** *Pokémon* project coordinator, Nintendo of America,
> quoted in Hatakeyama and Kubo 2000:421

In a regular skit shown from fall 1999 to winter 2000 on *Oha Sutā*, a children's program airing early mornings on Japanese television, a cute dimply woman dressed in schoolgirl chic—short red skirt and matching shoes, frilly pink blouse and loose socks—introduces herself as Becky.[1] Asking the television audience, *"Genki?"* she follows this up with the English translation, "How are you doing?" The words HOW ARE YOU DOING? pop up on the screen in capital letters before a backdrop of huge *Pokémon* cards that move up and down against a field of yellow flowers on the ground, scattered trees, and fish suspended in the air. In the midst of this surreal cuteness is Becky, who, moving girlishly like a pop idol, communes with her audience: "I'm fine (I'M FINE). Okay! *Sorede Pokémon* the World *de* (Then let's do *Pokémon* the World)! Get English (GET ENGLISH). Here we go (HERE WE GO)!!" One of the *Pokémon* cards moves down on the screen with an English name written on it: "Growlithe." Becky starts repeating the word very slowly as the camera zooms in on her mouth. Warning the audience about the "th" and "g" sounds, she chastens them not to be embarrassed and urges everyone in the family to try it: "Growlithe. Growlithe." Never letting her smile waver, she does a shimmy and announces: "FUNKY. BECKY. MONKEY. U-KI [written in the Japanese script of *katakana*] *nanoda*." Putting her hands around a *Poké*-ball that appears as animation on the screen, Becky ends the routine by saying, "Check it out. See you! POKÉMON the world!" as the ball morphs into a blue globe. Winking to her audience and kicking a leg in the air, Becky stands for a few seconds with her hand clasping the miniature world.

Like the recycled tin toys that were bartered for food to feed schoolchildren during Japan's occupation, the *Pokémon* phenomenon has been a trade built on commodities of play. In this case, however, the parties seem more equally positioned and the medium of trade is money rather than food. Yet, while fortunes were made on both sides of the Pacific, power and geopolitics still cling to these transactions around playthings. The entire venture has been fraught with tension, but new alliances and relations have emerged as well. And while *Poké*-mania in the United States and elsewhere around the world has been viewed by a number of Japanese as a sign of Japan's new cultural power and the growing potency of Japanese creativity in leading global designs, at the height of the craze its U.S. marketers tended to see the game as "beyond culture" and its success in the States the result as much (if not more) of their own sophisticated efforts to sell it to American kids. The two sides, Japan and the United States, worked from different mythologies in marketing *Pokémon* in the States, and—as we have seen with earlier cultural products originating in Japan—changes were made (in the product and the marketing strategies) to sell *Pokémon* in the States that were tied to considerations of cultural identity and aesthetics. The marketing of *Pokémon* fit in with a preexisting economic and geopolitical dynamic between Japan and the United States at the same time that it broke new ground, particularly in the way that children interact with the virtuality of this imaginary world and the growing influence of Japanese goods and "coolness" in the arena of global kids' culture today.

To understand how the United States and the rest of the world went through *Pokémon*ization, we must look again at the overall development of the Japanese toy industry. In the years immediately after World War II in Japan, as we have seen, a currency of exchange between an occupied country and its occupier was founded on play goods. The situation almost sixty years later, just after the turn of the millennium, is radically different in some ways. Having rebounded from the war and restructured its economy in record time, Japan has been an industrial superpower since the late 1970s. Its reputation around the world has been established, in large part, as a producer of high-quality consumer goods: cars, VCRs, tape recorders, and toys. No longer constructed from materials gleaned from its victor's trash cans, Japan produces goods today that stand at the forefront of advanced technology and superior design. And with the phenomenal successes of *Pokémon* and other globalized kid properties, the toy industry has made Japan a world leader in the field of children's mass entertainment. These millennial-era toys embody New Age play themes and virtual mechanizations: transformers, morphing Rangers, digital pets, and electronic play worlds. A far cry from the crude tin jeeps modeled after the real-life vehicles of an occupying army, sophisticated systems like Sony's PlayStation 2, geared more to the invention of virtual worlds than the mimicking of real ones, exemplify "made in Japan" today.

At the start of the twenty-first century, Japan's play industry is flourishing. Constituted of multiple strands—comics, animation, electronic games, toys, and character merchandising, an industry that earns 2 trillion yen per year—it remains a ray of sunshine amid what has otherwise been a nagging recession. Since the burst of the economic Bubble in the early 1990s, the nation has been plunged into an economic malaise that has produced countless company layoffs, downsizing, and shutdowns. In these hard times, *Pokémon* (along with the play industry more generally) has been called the "single success story": a sphere of productivity that is a boon to an ailing economy much like that directly after the war. And as it also did in the earlier period, the play business relies heavily on foreign trade, since only by extending a relatively limited domestic market can profits significantly increase. Today the sale of Japanese play products has become increasingly global, and globalization is the key to the vibrancy and expansion of the business. Take *Pokémon*, for example: in the year 2000, at the height of the fad, its games were selling in seventy countries, the cartoon was broadcast in fifty-one countries, the movies played in thirty-three countries, and the cards had been translated into eleven languages (Hatakeyama and Kubo 2000). Total worldwide sales as of August 2003 were $15 billion (*Business Wire* 2003).

Echoing the importance it had in the early postwar years of Japan's toy trade, the U.S. market has been specially targeted within the global scope of Japanese play traffic. Penetrating this market has been the driving goal for many Japanese toy companies. On the one hand, this ambition is motivated by sheer economic calculation; the United States represents a huge market because of the size, money, and consumerism of its child population (and though Japanese kids also have significant consumer power, their numbers have fallen sharply with the decrease of the birthrate).[2] Succeeding here ensures big profits (on the order of the billions now registered for *Pokémon*, where revenues from global sales for the movies alone, $91 million, only barely exceeded those from the United States and adjoining North America alone, $85 million).[3] On the other hand is the desire to achieve not only real but symbolic capital in infiltrating the realm of kids' mass/popular culture that, globally, has been dictated up to now by toys, movies, television shows, and characters coming from the United States. To compete in this arena is to disrupt the cultural hegemony of Euro-America embedded in the commodities that have defined worldwide fads and trends. It is also to overcome

Japan's own sense of exclusion in being a player in the cultural marketplace of ideas, lifestyles, and the imagination.

Pokémon has solidified and extended the growing presence (and acceptance) of Japanese children's goods across the world at this millennial moment. The same is true of the United States, where *Pokémon* triggered a craze in pop culture ("*Poké*-mania") carried on the wings of a marketing blitz ("*Pokémon*ization") of intense proportions. The symbolic profits this success has yielded seem as prized back home as anything monetary. Indeed, the release of the first *Pokémon* movie in the States (in November 1999) was front-page news in Japan. This was both because it played on the mainstream circuit (in three thousand theaters) and earned opening-day profits that outranked all films but *Star Wars* in the history of American moviegoing. Before *Pokémon: The Movie* (the first of nine), the only other Japanese film that had even come close to this reception in the States was *Shall We Dance?* which was a modest hit in 1997.[4] Still, its total profits here ($9.5 million) did not even match what *Pokémon: The First Movie* made in one day ($10.1 million, which built to $85 million for overall U.S. sales). For a country riveted to its movie screens and raised on the legacy of Hollywood moviemaking, the success the *Pokémon* movies had in the States is considered a historic breakthrough for Japanese creative industries. With feats such as this, Japan has gained ground in an increasingly changing terrain of global fads, a transnational imaginary, and the cultural marketplace of ideas, images, and virtuality. Once dominated by the place, power, and capital of the United States, global culture is being increasingly influenced and shaped by Japanese entertainment product(ions).

Traveling (Japanese) Power or the Domestication of *Pokémon*ization?

> It was said that the *Pokémon* characters were too cute, too *kawaii* for the U.S. and that in America cute doesn't sell, only "cool" does. . . . This opinion came even from the "character experts." Obviously, their expertise on this matter was totally wrong.
>
> Arakawa Makoto, quoted in Hatakeyama
> and Kubo 2000:407–8

Prominent in *Pokémon*'s trajectory of worldwide marketing and global fantasy making are the tropes of travel and power. This is the logic of the game/story line itself, where children become *pokémon* masters by journeying through *Poké*-world trapping wild monsters inside balls that endow them with power. This, too, is the story of *Pokémon*ization: a humble property that, starting out as a Game Boy game in a single marketplace, territo-rialized the world by seeking ever-new marketing opportunities and, cap-turing them with commodity lines, pocketed profits and powers for the world's "greatest *pokémon* trainers."

How did both the fantasy and the marketing of *Pokémon* work in the United States? In traveling to the States, that is, how was an imaginary playscape originally intended for Japanese boys transmitted, translated, and transformed for American kids? As Yoshimoto Mitsuhiro has observed, de-spite all the current attention paid to globalization, far too little is known about the concrete and distinctive features by which global flows of various kinds actually travel. What precisely are the dominant vehicles of global culture? he enjoins us to ask. Who or what controls them; and how do they affect and alter the ways in which we (as both local and global subjects) per-ceive and interact with the world (Yoshimoto 1994)? This chapter examines *Pokémon* as just such a vehicle of global kids' play culture, focusing on the specifics of how this Japanese property was handled for marketing in the United States—what many (especially in the United States) were still treat-ing as the dominant site of and for global kids' culture. Keeping in mind the lines of power and travel here, the points of interest are the entwinements of fantasy, capitalism, and cultural politics. That is, when this made-in-Japan play product traveled to the United States, what happened to its cultural identity and, in the global culture (of *Poké*-mania/*Pokémon*ization) that en-sued, who were the brokers and beneficiaries of its power?[5]

In February 2000, the official "*Pokémon* lecture tour" kicked off in the United States. A curious concept, it was organized not by the marketers of *Pokémon* but by Japan's Foreign Ministry. On the docket were three main participants, all Japanese who had been central players in negotiating *Poké-mon*'s entry into the U.S. marketplace—Kawaguchi Takashi at Nintendo, Ishihara Tsunekazu at Creatures (the designer of the cards), and Kubo Masakazu at Shōgakukan (a producer who had launched the comic in *Ko-rokoro Komikku* and oversaw cartoon and movie production). Occurring two years after *Pokémon* debuted in the States, triggering national *Poké-*mania, the "*Pokémon* lecture tour" was a public relations endeavor. But the agenda was not to sell *Pokémon* as much as to publicize the story of its re-markable history, starting in Japan and ending up as the global fad of the new millennium. The tour's kickoff took place in San Francisco, where Kawaguchi, addressing the audience first, spoke about the joy he and the others felt at the incredible success *Pokémon* had enjoyed in the States. In polite Japanese, he then thanked the crowd for "the warm welcome you have given these Japanese characters, for which we are deeply appreciative"

(Hatakeyama and Kubo 2000:421). As Kubo noted in the volume he published on *Pokémon* the same year, identifying the pocket monsters as "Japanese" may have disturbed the U.S. marketers in the audience, committed as they had been to localizing *Pokémon* and playing down its origins. One of these people was Gail Tilden, the project manager for *Pokémon* at Nintendo of America (NOA), who told me the following month that the initial aim of the American marketers had been, indeed, to "globalize" *Pokémon* by taking the marker of Japan/Japaneseness out altogether.

Interestingly enough, considering that it became the hottest global property of its times, *Pokémon* was not originally designed for export outside Japan. Tajiri, its creator, as well as all the major marketers who were first involved in the project in Japan, conceived the game as a product strictly for domestic consumption. As Ishihara explained when the *Pokémon* tour continued to New York (where it addressed audiences at both Columbia University and the Japan Society), "We made the *Pokémon* game to be for Japanese only: for Japanese play and with Japanese images" (Hatakeyama and Kubo 2000:435). To the question of whether *Pokémon* had been originally crafted with "international characters," Ishihara answered a resounding "no." When Nintendo bought *Pokémon* from Tajiri, the company did not designate it as a game for export elsewhere, including the United States. This was a departure from Nintendo's usual pattern in recent years of releasing games in the United States and Japan simultaneously. Taking over the microphone from Ishihara, Kubo continued to the New York audience: "If its images could be exported, we thought: Asia perhaps." That despite national differences, kids around the world have come to play *Pokémon* much like Japanese children came as a total surprise to its marketers back home. The impact of this reception has been deep-seated, as Kubo admitted: "I would never have imagined that I would be talking to you all in New York today. Does this mean we have entered the friendship circle of New York?" (436).

The initial negotiations, in fact, were exceedingly tough. The first to become interested was Arakawa Makoto, the CEO and chairman of Nintendo's operation in the United States (the independent NOA). Visiting Japan only months after Tajiri's Game Boy game first came out in February 1996, he noticed the absence of *Pokémon* on the list of games targeted for U.S. release. Piqued by its whirlwind popularity in Japan, he returned with the game to test out on his NOA employees in the United States. But the results were not encouraging. In a game market dominated by action games, the Americans were captivated neither by the role-playing game format of *Pokémon* nor by the fact that the game takes a number of hours of playing time (at least ten, according to Kubo) before it gets interesting. Further, he was not sure the designs of the characters would work as brands because they were "cute" rather than "cool," and it was unclear which quality carried more currency in American pop culture (Kubo 2000:407).

The suggestion was made to change the characters, readjusting them for American tastes. But what Japanese toy manufacturers did willingly in an earlier period (designing tin jeeps and robots according to American trends) they adamantly refused to do now. As Kubo told me in an interview, "I raised these characters," using the word *sodateru*, with its connotation of child raising, that is also used to describe the function of training and raising pocket monsters in the game.[6] By contrast, as he continued, Americans saw *Pokémon* strictly as a business, particularly at the beginning. But an agreement was made that no major alterations would be done to the property itself, including the characters, other than translating their names into English equivalents, which took place for almost all the characters and pocket monsters except Pikachu, whose name remains the same the world over. Having attained what was extremely important to the Japanese side— the promise to uphold the aesthetic integrity given *Pokémon* by its creators—the parties continued their negotiations.

The path continued to be littered with obstructions, however. Arakawa had decided that were NOA to take *Pokémon* on, it would have to be for not only the game but the whole package—games, books, cards, tie-in merchandise. This decision entailed a huge commitment, and he budgeted an unprecedented $50 million to launch the campaign. To do this, he wanted NOA to become the master licensor to all foreign rights outside the territories of Asia and Japan, and to acquire these rights he wanted to deal with only one Japanese broker. But *Pokémon* had already spawned a multilayered network of corporate investors and aggregations in Japan: the game and images were owned by Nintendo, Creatures, and Game Freak; the cartoon show was owned by ShoPro and TV Tokyo; and the card game and character merchandising were owned by Creatures, then Media Factory. NOA refused to barter with this undulating snake of dispersed powers, insisting that it negotiate with a single owner who possessed the rights it desired.

It took until January 1998 for ShoPro to consolidate these rights (becoming the master licensor for sales to the whole world, excluding the region of Asia). By this point, however, the cartoon "disturbance" of episode 38 had occurred in Japan, sending more than seven hundred viewers to hospitals with convulsions. Incendiary reports about the dangers of Japanese mass culture percolated through U.S. press coverage of the incident, threatening a moral panic that would contaminate made-in-Japan play goods in the minds of the American public. NOA took note of this event, but in light of how sales were heating up in Japan (the software alone was selling at four hundred thousand sets per month by this point, and Arakawa figured that *Pokémon* would *have* to do well in the States as well), proceeded with negotiations. In May, NOA's president announced that *Pokémon* would be released in late summer, and on August 25, 1998, *Pokémon* made its debut in the United States.

This event occurred with a splash, given the high hopes and vast sums NOA had committed to the project. Also, echoing the sentiments of the *Pokémon* project coordinator at NOA that *Pokémon* should not evoke feelings of foreignness, it was launched in the heartland of America—Topeka, Kansas, amazingly renamed Topikachu for the day. As a thousand stuffed Pikachus were dropped over the city by air, ten Volkswagen bugs, painted yellow and outfitted with tails, assembled in the center of town. These "*Poké*-bugs," loaded with *Pokémon* paraphernalia, including videos of the cartoon, were dispatched later in the day to ten states across the country, where they served as roaming promotional vans for a month. *Pokémon* was thereby embedded in cutely accessible (parachuting stuffed Pikachus) and culturally familiar (VW bugs) vehicles for its travel across America. And this circuit dovetailed with another: a million promotional videos that had been sent out by NOA earlier in August to the homes of American children, as well as to the toy store Toys"R"Us. In the fifteen-minute promo, clips of the cartoon are shown, highlighting the main characters (renamed Ash, the ten-year-old boy trying to become the world's best *pokémon* master; Misty, the ten-year-old girl who accompanies him on his quest; and Brock, the fifteen-year-old boy who studies *pokémon* instead of chasing them). Made to be jazzy and fast-paced for American tastes, the video also introduced different aspects of *Pokémon* (the cards, game, Pocket Pikachu, strategy) through staged narrations by made-up characters (a quirky woman posing as Ash's Aunt Hillary, an African American man with oversized glasses identified as Ash's teacher, and a protofeminist girl acting as Misty's "best friend").

Given the assessment that the game (the focus of *Pokémon* in Japan) might be a harder sell with American kids, the campaign stressed the story line of the cartoon and the visual psychodynamics of the lead *pokémon*, Pikachu. Reversing the order it was given in Japan (where the game preceded the cartoon by a year), the cartoon was released first (September 7), followed by the game software three weeks later (September 28). This proved to be an effective strategy; on the heels of the cartoon broadcast by Warner Brothers (first by syndication and then by network TV starting in

February), the software was an immediate success. Packaged in the Stars and Stripes colors of red and blue instead of the red and green versions of its first release in Japan, it had sold one million units after just one month (a level it had taken almost nine months to achieve in Japan, with the lessons learned there guiding the U.S. campaign). In the same month Hasbro released toy merchandise, and a tie-in campaign with Kentucky Fried Chicken began shortly thereafter. Playing cards, issued by Wizards of the Coast (bought soon afterward by Hasbro), hit the market in January 1999. The ANA *Pokémon* jets started flying to New York in February; other game software appeared the same year (including Nintendo 64 software, *Pokémon* Snap); a card tournament pitting the United States against Japan took place in August (the "Challenge Road 99 Summer Tropical Mega-Battle" in Hawai`i); and the first movie *(Pokémon: The First Movie)* hit U.S. screens in November, accompanied by a Burger King promotional. By this point, the country was judged to be in the grip of *Poké*-mania. And when the silver and gold versions of the Game Boy software were released in the States one year later, first-week sales broke the all-time *Pokémon* record: 1.4 million units.

The success of this foreign-born fad in the United States was no less than astronomical. Dovetailing with other imported trends—the British-based *Harry Potter* books and television show *Teletubbies,* for example—the craze appeal of this Japanese creation has been an undeniable breakthrough in the homeland of Disney. For this very reason, the course it charted in navigating the territorial waters of American kids' culture and entertainment is symptomatically marked—which is to say, it changed preexisting assumptions about the U.S. marketplace at the same time that it was constantly resisted for deviating from them. According to almost everyone I interviewed who was directly involved with the *Pokémon* campaign in the United States (designers, advertisers, and executives at Warner Brothers, Wizards of the Coast, Hasbro, NOA, 4Kids Entertainment, and Grey Advertising), marketing *Pokémon* in the States presented brand-new challenges. The manufacturers of the toy merchandise, Hasbro, for example, considered that taking on *Pokémon* was a big risk—because it "broke so many rules" of American kids' media, an executive at Hasbro told me.[7] There is no strong heroic character, the pacing of the cartoon is slow, the story line (in the cartoon, movies, and storybooks) is complex, and it is a game-based property. For these reasons, Hasbro itself was reluctant to acquire the property (but, because of Mattel's connection to Disney, Hasbro was the company approached by *Pokémon*'s marketers). Even after it did, the company found that the major "trade" in the toy business here (the three largest toy buyers, Wal-Mart, Toys"R"Us, and Kmart) thought Hasbro was "crazy" to offer it and refused to sign on the *Pokémon* package. Eventually they all did, but the toys were first released through Kaybee Toys stores (and, in a bold move, through the chic toy store FAO Schwarz), where they sold out immediately. Having originally made ten to twelve million items, Hasbro multiplied these sales by twenty times in merely one year. Still, the first few months saw product shortages so severe that the company temporarily stopped advertising until it could restock the items.

In marketing *Pokémon* in the United States, many adjustments were made in both the product and the promotion to ensure localization. The understanding, however, was that all these decisions had to gain the approval of the Japan side (through ShoPro) to guarantee the creative integrity and coherence of the property. In the case of Hasbro, I was told that these negotiations were straightforward but sometimes excessive and onerous. Some proposals on the U.S. side were flat-out rejected; the word came back on one product, for example, that ShoPro would willingly sacrifice the money rather than go ahead with the deal in order to remain faithful to the idea of *Pokémon*. More of a challenge to Hasbro, however, was translating the *Pokémon* concept into something that would work for American kids. Before this time, few Japanese properties had been easily and successfully mainstreamed in the U.S. marketplace, and many members of the Hasbro crew had doubts that *Pokémon* would fare any better.[8] While the characters were cute, it lacked what was considered a key ingredient in kids' fare in the States: a clear-cut theme of good versus evil. This is, in part, why *Power Rangers* (a story in which heroes fight evil enemies) did so well here, as did transformers, toys that change shape as if they were embodying clear-cut shifts, such as good versus evil, a story line given transformers for their U.S. ad campaign precisely to enhance their appeal to American kids. In contrast, *Pokémon* is marked by greater ambiguity, as is Japanese children's entertainment more generally, and by avoidance of conflict. In taking the property on, Hasbro came up with various strategies to work against this perceived defect. For one, it emphasized the human dimension, adding the figures of the human characters to the line. (In Japan, human figures do not sell well, and the toy line has consisted primarily of the pocket monsters themselves.) The themes of mastery and action have also been foregrounded. Whereas in Japan one of the biggest *Pokémon* toy products was a single two-inch collectible figure, for example, here more "play" was added to make it a "higher ticket." A package with two figures plus a power bouncer (bouncing ball) was one of the first *Pokémon* toys sold in the States; another was a three-pack that added a "blaster" that is used to knock over the characters.

Overall, more color and dynamism were added to the *Pokémon* promotional campaign in the States, executives of ShoPro told me in Tokyo.[9] The overall image conjured by *Pokémon* in Japan was one of *yasashisa*—gentleness. In contrast, *Pokémon* was made brighter and more sharp-edged in the United States, as well as bigger and louder ("Everything is big and loud" in the States, an executive at Warner Brothers explained). The concept of mastering all 151 characters (now more than 300) was stressed as well. The slogan "Gotta catch 'em all" was selected by Hasbro to market the toy lines for this reason (Perry Drosos, personal interview). This motto worked so well that it was considered a marketing coup. The phrase not only was catchy (and the effect was heightened by putting it to music in ads) but also miraculously managed to gain approval of Federal Communications Commission censors, who prohibit the usage of injunctions ("You must buy this!") in television ads directed to kids. "Gotta catch 'em all" does enjoin kids to consume, but because it also rehearses the logic of *Pokémon* play—catching all the pocket monsters—the slogan was allowed. The whole concept (of catching, collecting, mastering, consuming) caught on like wildfire, needless to say, spurring the campaign and popularity of *Pokémon* in the States. Despite these early signs, however, it was still assumed that Ash needed to be the central focus of the U.S. campaign and that his heroics needed to be inflated.

In Japan, Pikachu had been the center of the *Pokémon* craze ever since the pocket monster's role was expanded for the cartoon in an attempt to widen the audience base (to include younger children, girls, and mothers) from those drawn to the game (mainly boys aged eight to fourteen). In marketing *Pokémon* in the States, however, it was decided that Ash would work better as the main character. This has not necessarily proved to be the case, however, and whether or not he is central evokes a range of opinions from those who worked on the *Pokémon* campaign in the United States. An executive at Warner Brothers who managed publicity for the *Pokémon* movies, for example, told me that American kids were most excited about Pikachu. Contrary to expectations, kids mobbed the actor dressed as Pikachu at the U.S. premiere of *Pokémon: The First Movie* in Hollywood, ignoring even the movie stars. "I don't think kids here really care about the human characters," she concluded.[10] Massey Rafoni, another executive at Warner Brothers who handled the ad campaigns for the movies, expanded eloquently on this point.[11] Based on a number of focus groups with kids, Warner Brothers concluded that Ash was secondary rather than primary, and that children were more interested in becoming *pokémon* trainers themselves rather than following Ash's adventures in doing the same. All this stems from the fact that *Pokémon* is organized centrally around an interactive game that positions children as players. This focus contrasts with the older media of television and movies in which the audience is more passive, watching the story line as spectators and identifying with particular characters. Of course, in the case of *Pokémon* and its media mix (cards, movie, cartoon, game, toy gear), children are variously positioned to engage the world of *Pokémon*.

Rafoni also agreed that Pikachu was the lead symbol of the *Pokémon* operation in the United States. In taking this position, however, he is tacitly acknowledging that the pocket monster represents a crossover in what constitutes popular appeal in this country. The Disney model traditionally pushes strong males and weak, dependent females. But the Japanese have punched through these stereotypes to come up with imaginary beings that are postgender, nonhuman, and completely apart from a reality-based universe. Because it is so unlike the fare they were raised with, many American parents have a difficult time getting either this concept or the deep attraction *Pokémon* holds for their kids. Adults told me repeatedly how incomprehensible a world they found *Pokémon* to be, a response that became a big factor in the marketing of *Pokémon* in the States. In promoting the movies, for example, Warner Brothers had to determine how much it would try to "explain" *Pokémon* to noncomprehending adults. The company decided to cater to adults very little and to speak almost exclusively to kids. *Pokémon* is different from other WB properties, Rafoni told me, in that the game (and the movies, bred from the games) is hard for parents to understand and has no one-sentence synopsis.[12] Disney movies, in contrast, succeed basically on the cinematic level: epic scenes, good story, musical score, and ethical themes. *Pokémon* is not built on the movie alone and is a far more integrated phenomenon involving game play as well as a new breed of character development: Pikachu, as the archetypal *pokémon*, "crosses all barriers." "When I first saw the movie, I realized how crossover Pikachu can be," Rafoni told me. "Cute here does not translate as weak or wimpy. Mew is the smallest *pokémon* [in the movie], but the most powerful." In the hands of Japanese creators, Rafoni continued, "cute" is becoming a crossover concept in the United States.

Despite the appeal of what many acknowledge was a paradigmatic shift in the construction of play that *Pokémon* offers, it was also shaped to feed preexisting conventions at work in the American marketplace. In the process of localization we have seen repeated over and over again with Japanese cultural goods, American marketers were keen to neutralize the overt signs that *Pokémon* came from Japan. The point, Gail Tilden insisted to me shortly after *Pokémon* hit the United States, was not to hide the property's origins but to go beyond culture so that kids would adopt the fantasy as familiar rather than dismiss it as alien. As Tilden put it, "We want to make *Pokémon* culturally neutral," adding: "We want kids to buy into the mythology as their own."[13] And this goal was attained; American kids do not see *Pokémon* as Japanese, she said, even though most are fully aware that the property originated in Japan.

The biggest changes for achieving cultural neutralization came, unsurprisingly, in the domain where Hollywood and Disney have traditionally brokered their authority in dictating global kid trends—moviemaking and cartoons. The adjustments made here to the product overwhelmed all those mentioned already, and the stakes, on both sides, were the highest—the reason, presumably, that Japanese marketers were willing to bend more here than in other aspects of the property.[14] Japanese storytelling styles do not necessarily travel well, I was told by Norman Grossfeld at 4Kids Entertainment, the person in charge of designing the movies and cartoons for U.S. release. To ensure that *Pokémon* would be well received in the United States, it could not "feel like a foreign experience."[15] Accordingly, a number of strategies were employed to domesticate the story. Some of the characters were changed for both the television show and the movies. James (half of the "evil duo" Rocket Team), for example, was made into a more comic character and something of a bumbler, and Meowth, a cat that is very philosophical in the Japanese version, was made into more of a wisecracker. Grossfeld, working with Michael Haigney, proceeded with caution, however. He showed all the Japanese cartoons to his own kids and their friends and made his adjustments based on their reactions.

Pacing was another problem. The stories unwind slowly in the Japanese version, with little musical accompaniment. Grossfeld added much more (American) music to both the television cartoons and the movies, so much so that the sound tracks are sold separately on music videos, and the music alone is considered "extra value" to the product. Saying, "That's the cultural thing," Grossfeld noted that Ishihara and others involved in the Japanese marketing loved the music and were pleased with these American additions. The other major change in the television shows was rotoscoping everything frame by frame, airbrushing out the Japanese text (and other, if not all, signs of cultural difference such as rice balls, which became doughnuts in the U.S. version—a device no longer deemed necessary in the majority of Japanese cartoons now airing on U.S. television). The aim was not simply to put English on top of the Japanese but to take out the "place" of Japan, thereby making *Pokémon* "placeless," in Grossfeld's term. The fact that the imaginary world originates in Japan is not a bad thing in and of itself, Grossfeld explained, but it is a deterrent "if it takes kids out of the experience. . . . We want kids to stay rooted," he said, and not pondering the presence of rice balls in a scene.

Issuing the *Pokémon* movies in the States presented even more challenges; the alterations made to the first film required a vast outlay of energy (on the American side) and money (by the Japanese). Besides an entirely new musical score pitched to American tastes, the biggest shifts came in making the story line explicit, more black and white, according to Grossfeld, over the "shades of gray" preferred by Japanese in their storytelling. In the Japanese version, details and motives are left unexplained. But as Tilden (at NOA, who worked with Grossfeld in the U.S. production) told me, "American kids need to be hit over the head." This meant clarifying and pinning down what was left ambiguous in the original. In the Japanese movie, for example, Mew-two (named the same in the Japanese and English versions), the cloned *pokémon* seeking to promote internecine fighting among the other *pokémon* and worldwide destruction, is never portrayed as absolutely evil. Further, when it abandons these efforts in the end, neither Mew-two's reasons nor what the creature is thinking is ever articulated (even though this follows the scene in which Ash willingly sacrifices his life to stop the fighting—he is later revived by the mournful tears shed by other *pokémon* in a connection to water that is also made more explicit in the American edition). Mew-two simply says, "It's best this is all forgotten," and flies away. In the U.S. version, a much longer speech is added that delivers not only clarification and closure to the events but also a "moral message" (what Tilden describes as a "feel-good" element). Here Mew-two clearly admits its own wrongdoing and recognizes the moral goodness of a boy willing to sacrifice himself for the welfare of others (which is meant to extend more generally to the "friendship" among humans and *pokémon*). Just as the goodness of Ash is spelled out, so is the evil of Mew-two, concluding on the old theme of good versus evil so commonplace in American pop culture mythology (and yet, counter to the tradition in the United States, the evil character admits wrongdoing).

In short, *Pokémon*'s paradigm-shifting qualities seem to have been tolerated less, and tamed more, in the domain of moviemaking than in the other spheres of its operation (gaming, cards, toy merchandise) in the U.S. marketplace. Indeed, what precisely has driven such extensive efforts to remodel the Japanese movies on and for U.S. territory is the assumption that without such adjustments *Pokémon* could never travel successfully or make it big in the mainstream of American pop culture. And not only the U.S. marketplace but also the global market outside Japan and Asia is involved: the rights that NOA purchased from ShoPro at the beginning of (and as a condition for) its negotiations. Thus, *Pokémon: The First Movie* was released in Europe in its American version just like the *Gojira/Godzilla* phenomenon of a half century earlier, reflecting how certain channels of global movie culture—Europe and America versus the rest of the world—have remained intact since the time of *Godzilla*. This echo of the old days was initially a concern for the Japanese. But as Grossfeld, speaking for 4Kids Entertainment (the exclusive licensing agent for Nintendo-owned properties, including *Pokémon*, in all territories outside of Asia) and as screenwriter and producer of the film explained, "Our thought was that for Western cultures, it was better for them to get our show." This meant that "Europeans are getting it twice removed," even though everyone knew *Pokémon* came from Japan. Still, the editing process was undertaken with great care, and no scenes were cut in the first movie to avoid antagonizing the Japanese.

When the time came to deal with the second movie (*The Power of One*, released in July 2000), just as much effort was expended in removing the distinctively Japanese features, even though the expectation, going in, was that far fewer changes would be required. Again, the main issue was clarifying the story and pinning down motivations. Further, the plot was given an overall focus different from that in Japan, where it centered on the struggles among three "god" *(kami) pokémon* and the intervention of a fourth, the phantom monster Lugia. In the United States, far more emphasis was placed on the human character, Ash, and his heroic efforts to save the day— hence the title *Power of One*, changed from the Japanese title, *Pokémonstā Rugia Bakutan* (The Revelation of the Pocket Monster Lugia). As Kubo, speaking from the Japanese side, summed up the alteration: Americans love heroes.

Assumptions of cultural difference have certainly been at work in the marketing of *Pokémon* in the States. Yet when they attended the *Pokémon* display at the New York Toy Fair at the end of their road show, the members of the "*Pokémon* lecture tour" were greeted by a huge statue not of the human hero, Ash, but of Pikachu. This was the same icon the property is branded by in Japan: a pocket monster carrying an aesthetics of cuteness and ambiguity that has been deemed culturally Japanese by its marketers on both sides of the ocean. And not only was Pikachu the American toy fair's featured fantasy character, but the *Pokémon* display was center stage, relegating that of Hasbro's other major property, *Star Wars*, to a small corner— a reflection of its falling sales (to half that of *Pokémon* the year before). For Kubo and the other tour members, the site/sight of Pikachu's central presence at the New York Toy Fair (displacing the more quintessentially American *Star Wars* to off-center) was symbolic indeed: a sign of how far made-in-Japan play products had penetrated into the ranks of U.S. kids' culture. But, as they also knew, this reception was being spurred by the cold hard facts of the marketplace: the riches *Pokémon* had managed to pocket for virtually all those involved with the property.

These profits have been gargantuan. All the major players have significantly raised their stock and stature: Nintendo, which had fallen to the third-ranked gaming company, returned to first place; NOA showed a 250 percent rise in profits in the year 1999 over 1998; Hasbro rose to the second-ranked toy company after Mattel; 4Kids Entertainment expanded thirty times in revenues thanks to *Pokémon*.[16] Equally conspicuous have been the plethora of small companies fortunate enough to obtain licensing rights for *Pokémon* merchandise. At the fad's height, more than twelve thousand *Pokémon* items were licensed internationally, and more than one thousand applications were coming in a week, seeking licensing for more goods.[17] As Arakawa has said about trying to turn this property into a long-lasting ("evergreen") commodity not only for his own company (NOA) but also, implicitly, for the global prestige of Japanese creations: "I think *Pokémon* is a character that, thanks to [its Japanese creators] Tajiri, Ishihara, and Kubo—will last twenty, thirty years. We all want to keep raising it carefully for a very long time" (quoted in Hatakeyama and Kubo 2000:464).

Casino Capitalism: Market Play

On November 3, 1999, *South Park*—the wryly satirical cartoon show aired by Comedy Central on U.S. television—ran an episode on *Pokémon*. Savvy enough to use a Japanese colloquialism in the title ("Chinpokomon," from *chin* for penis), the screenwriters lampooned not only the addictive frenzy the fad had ignited among American kids, but also their parents' utter cluelessness about its nature and appeal. The story is set in middle America, where, watching a news report on the recent "Chinpokomon" fad, a wife says to her husband, "What *are* those things? Animals? Robots?" He answers, "I don't know, but suddenly I want to own them all." The scene then shifts to a toy store, where the owner discovers that the *pokémon* toys are programmed to say not only "Buy me! Buy me!" but also "Down with America!" Worried that Japan is trying to take over the minds of American kids with this newest fad, he flies over to confront Chinpokomon's manufacturers. There the man is reassured that the Japanese political power he feared is only a chimera (by being told that he and all other American men have huge penises compared with the puny ones of Japanese). Back in the

States, however, the shop owner is confronted by the town's adults, who have become increasingly disturbed by the fanaticism displayed by their kids. From compulsively buying, playing, and mimicking Chinpokomon, the children have now enrolled in summer camp, where, overseen by a Japanese general, they are being instructed in Japanese language, as well as political education about the evils of America and the need to take over their country's government. Fearing that they have lost their youth (and perhaps their country) to foreign influence, the parents contrive to break the Chinpokomon spell. The strategy they come up with—to become seasoned players and fans themselves—is effective. As the adults proudly show off their new game strategies and *Poké*-skills, the children suddenly announce, "Chinpokomon doesn't seem that cool anymore," and, throwing their Game Boys aside, run outside to play with something else.

In this skillful parody of *Poké*-mania in the States, *South Park* captured a certain truth about the social cartography of its popularity, namely, that while this Japanese craze was quickly absorbed by American kids, adults were in the dark about what pocket monsters even were. There is nothing new, of course, about a chasm between parents and their children in the domain of popular tastes. In the case of *Pokémon*, however, this gap was not only profound but also inflected in a particular way. Almost all the adults I spoke to were utterly mystified about the rules of the game or the parameters of the playscape, yet few, in fact, were overly worried or suspicious about the effects it was having either on their kids or on the national polity of the United States. What I encountered instead—an attitude of befuddled acceptance—is strikingly at odds with the portrayal on *South Park:* that by making inroads into the U.S. marketplace of toys and fantasy goods, Japan is taking over the minds, imaginations, and patriotism of American kids. While laughably parodic in 1999, such a mind-set is reminiscent of a (not so) previous era—apparent when Sony bought out Columbia Studios and Matsushita acquired MGM in 1989, for example. It was at work when Fox Kids' Network launched *Mighty Morphin Power Rangers* in 1993; the commentary by adults was overwhelmingly negative, some of it explicitly tied to the show's Japanese origins: "Our Wonder Bread heroes are not just turning Japanese, they're becoming altered beings in a parallel aesthetic realm, with its own internal logic, myths, and ethics. And maybe their audience is transforming too. . . . The tykes currently addicted to the show may end up becoming a mass market for more mature and vital Japanese popular shows now shrouded in hipster subculture—e.g., anime" (Davis 1994:73).

What happened in the last few years, then, to disrupt national anxieties about the rising "Nipponification" of U.S. pop culture, particularly the arena of kids' entertainment? And how should we read the apparent xenophobia in "Chinpokomon"? Is this a retrograde expression of Americana, or is the danger parodied actually less about the cultural identity of the property (that materializes here as a Japanese influence invading the imaginations and political consciousness of American youth) than about the United States itself and its failure to comprehend what kids are up to these days, both at play and in "real" life? The image of (im)potency here is quite revealing, given how closely this episode aired after Columbine, the most spectacular of the school shootings that, striking at what had once been considered a haven from the violence of the inner cities (schools in middle-class neighborhoods and rural countryside), sent shock waves through middle America.

It was the spring after *Pokémon* debuted in August 1998 that the shootings occurred at Columbine High School, killing thirteen and wounding twenty-one. As reported in the press, the two perpetrators had spent months concocting bombs in a family garage under the noses of their unwitting parents. In what became commonplace in the profiles of these school shooters, the youth were ostracized and bullied at school for not being part of the "in" crowd and, partly in reaction perhaps, had been absorbed in their own fantasy subcultures of—in the case of the Columbine killers—Goth. As a large class of undergraduates at Duke University told me the day following the shootings at Columbine, feeling alienated, picked on, and full of rage in high school is a common experience for American teenagers today (even those as privileged as the Duke student body). Turning to forms of popular culture (music, video games, drugs, fandom of various sorts) to assuage the anxiety and stress of growing up is almost universal, they added. So is the fact that parents tend to be uninterested in or judgmental about these fantasy pursuits, thereby missing an important channel for communication with their kids, which, as a number articulated, they wished they had had (Allison 2001). In spring 2000 I interrupted my fieldwork in Japan to return to the States for an intensive two-week stint interviewing all the major players—including kid fans and their parents—involved in *Pokémon*'s U.S. campaign.[18] In the group sessions I organized with the adults, a number mentioned Columbine as a reason for why, despite knowing virtually nothing about the ins and outs of *Pokémon*, they were inclined to find it unobjectionable and benign. In an atmosphere of heightened fear provoked not only by the school shootings but also by the moral panic surrounding it that, in seeking easy targets, pinpointed media and entertainment violence as a probable cause, adults were comforted by the cuteness and innocuousness they associated with *Pokémon*.

Figure 44. Entering American culture: Pikachu as Halloween costume. Emma and Jake wear matching Pikachus made by their mother. (Courtesy of Hal Bogerd.)

Its trademark *pokémon*, Pikachu, is one of the reasons *Pokémon* has come across in the United States as harmless and cute: Pikachu is striking but nonthreatening, with its yellow color, zigzag tail, pet-sized body, perky ears, and sweet face (figure 44). If they read the books or watch the cartoons or movies, parents discover that this primary *pokémon* for Ash, the lead human in the story, cannot even speak (except for "pika pika chuuuuu"), which keeps it from being anthropomorphized like Disney's Mickey Mouse or Donald Duck. With its powers (and cultural identity) packaged in this cutely innocuous form, Pikachu resembles Hello Kitty, Sanrio's mouthless white cat that has traveled successfully around the world (there are now between twelve thousand and fifteen thousand licensed products in the Hello Kitty line of cute goods).

In contrast to the guns, guts, and gore that have proliferated in U.S. media

and that register as iconic of violence in America, the *Pokémon* universe produces no spilled blood, dismembered body parts, or death of any kind. Even
with the most minimal exposure, parents have understood and valued this
quality about *Pokémon,* tending to find nothing troubling about the fact that
competitive matches (to the end of personal accumulation: catching all 151,
now more than 300, *pokémon*) center the plot/game and, in the process, continually wound, if not kill, individual *pokémon.* Given that "getting" also
comes embedded in stories where the kids and *pokémon* variously cooperate
as teams, there was considerable commentary in the U.S. press that even
praised *Pokémon* for its cultural values. For example, the *New York Times*
commended the cartoon for promoting responsibility, cooperation, empathy,
respect for elders, and humility, concluding, "There is something notably
Japanese here in the emphasis on team-building and lending a helping hand,
values that are admired but not always handsomely rewarded in American
society" (Strom 1999:4). Adults have found the *Pokémon* universe to be
"sweet," if utterly incomprehensible. This was true even in the media format
Americans are most used to—the movies—where 80 percent of adults said
they did not like the first *Pokémon* film. Anticipating this reaction—due, in
part, to the fact that the play world is game based, which, coming across even
in the movie rendition, contrasts with the more familiar narrative structure
of Disney films—its U.S. distributor, Warner Brothers, had problems in promoting the film. Because members of the press could not relate to it, they
were not interested in covering the story, and WB had to engage in an educational effort—teaching reporters how to play the game, showing them
footage of mall tournaments, and arranging meetings with fans to convince
them of *Pokémon's* popularity—to elicit coverage. In the end, WB also made
a judgment call to target only kids in their major promotionals rather than
parents, who would not "get it" anyway.[19]

What adults *do* get about *Pokémon* is, if not its content premised on
learning and mastering the highly complex and intricate language of *Pokémonology* (involving endless parts, powers, evolutionary stages, and attacks—kids' fluency in which parents often treat as if it were Greek), are the
goals of collecting and trading. According to Rick Arons, a game designer at
Wizards of the Coast (the U.S. distributor of *Pokémon* trading cards), the
real innovation in *Pokémon* is that the game play is the main part of
the story that kids take away with them. What he calls the "metagame"—
the mind-set that, not explicitly written down as part of the instructions, is
picked up in the course of playing the game—is collectibility, as inscribed in
the U.S. advertising slogan of "gotta catch 'em all."[20] Akin to Gramsci's notion of hegemony and Barthes's of myth (as in the imprinting of particular

political-economic relations into everyday habits, rituals, and play), this metagame has been organized somewhat differently in Japan. What marketers, commentators, and parents have stressed there is "communication"—the ways in which trading/getting/training Pokémon opens kids up to a (social) world beyond the game itself (albeit one mediated through the world and goods of Poké-mania). In the United States, by contrast, more attention has been paid to the stock market mentality and "bad trades" engendered by Pokémon: a myth of transactional economics brought on, in part, by the centrality assumed by trading cards in the U.S. operation (which led to their almost universal ban in schools because children's obsession with the cards proved to be too distracting).[21]

A capitalist frenzy is notable here: of kids buying endless ten-card packs at $3 a pack and, upon assembling them in albums, carting these to school, hobby stores, and card tournaments in the infinite quest to trade duplicates for the ones still needed to "catch 'em all." Rare cards sold for more than $50 (and up to $200) in specialty shops or online auctions at the height of the craze, and some parents wound up spending hundreds of dollars ($2,000 in one reported case) on cards and related merchandise. Kids who made bad deals were teased and called "chumps," and their parents often called each other up, protesting trades made by their children at school. According to psychologists and educators, the financial dimension is what distinguished Pokémon from earlier kid crazes over marbles, yo-yos, or even Beanie Babies. "The thing with the Pokémon cards is that kids are really aware of . . . their value," a psychologist noted, adding that kids tend to bring calculators with them when they trade. A number of news stories described recess at school as being like a "buy and sell bazaar," and kids gathered at malls on Saturday mornings like traders at the New York Stock Exchange (Healy 1999:27). With their collector notebooks tucked snugly under their arms, they appeared to be "miniature salespeople" investing in their own form of pork bellies—in this case, Pokémon trading cards. As a reporter from the Atlanta Journal-Constitution admitted, "Like most grown-ups, I don't understand this latest import from Japan." But the owner of a sports card shop in the mall spelled it out for him; in a mere six weeks he had earned $40,000 from card sales—a boon for this small-time businessman (Houston 1999:3).

Although I encountered few stories about bad trades or violence associated with Pokémon cards or merchandise in Japan, papers in the United States and Canada were filled with them. A fourteen-year-old boy in Quebec was stabbed by a younger boy trying to retrieve stolen Pokémon cards, nine youths were attacked and robbed by thieves in Philadelphia trying to steal Pokémon cards from other kids, an adult customer at a Burger King in

North Carolina punched out a cashier when he did not get a *Pokémon* toy with his meal, and there was a stabbing incident in Toronto over a $45 box of *Pokémon* cards (Cox 1999). The high passions, and money, invested in *Pokémon* cards also generated a number of lawsuits. A boy was awarded $1,500 in a small-claims court when the judge ruled that his school was responsible for his cards being stolen during school hours. In the most publicized of the cases, Alan Hock, a New York lawyer, sued Nintendo for engaging in illegal gambling. His suit (which was eventually settled out of court) contended that the cards were a form of lottery, inciting kids to buy hordes of cards in their quest to find the limited-run (and randomly placed) "chase" cards with the highest value (Halbfinger 1999:5).

It seems ironic that, given the game's aura of apparent sweetness and nonviolence, *Pokémon* has generated such acts of aggression in the way it is played and appropriated in America. Yet the impulse here is akin to the desire for any brand-name good—Nike shoes, for example—that, high-priced and au courant, triggers the dramas and traumas of a consumerist lifestyle. Violence is always the underside of this dreamworld, given that desires are never sated (in an endless quest to "get" more where accumulation confers power[s], if only of a virtual/fantasy kind) and great disparity exists in the means available to consume in America today. But compared with what usually is understood as media violence—acts that destroy or damage the body or property of someone else—*Pokémon* has a plotline in which there are no real enemies and no destruction that is not reversible (when they are hurt in battle, *pokémon* can be healed in *pokémon* centers). The logic of *Pokémon* is not confrontation but accumulation: the never-ending quest to "get" more *pokémon* that, though starting out as opponents, are assimilated into (rather than exterminated by) the self.

The adult reaction to this capitalist metagame has been general approval on the grounds that, despite its commercialism and risks of bad trades or even theft of private property, it teaches kids valuable lessons. As the American craze was reported on by the *Yomiuri* newspaper in Japan (reprinting an article from the *Los Angeles Times*), for example, *Pokémon* is as much about entrepreneurship as fantasy critters and, in its "buy and sell bazaar," teaches kids important skills (Healy 1999:27). In a news report airing on October 7, 1999, on *CBS News,* Dan Rather similarly reported that while *Pokémon* is "gambling pure and simple" (making grade-school kids "fanatics" and their parents "crazed"), there is also something "good" in the lessons it provides children. Parents reiterated the same point. As one mother told me, her seven-year-old-son had been the victim of theft (his cards were stolen at a tournament when he set them down to go buy a candy bar) and a couple of bad trades. But she believed these setbacks would make him more savvy in interactions with others and more responsible in tending to his personal property. These have been "learning experiences," she concluded. "The whole thing seems pretty benign; I'm not against it."

The term *casino capitalism* has been used to describe the way in which luck has come to dictate monetary systems and the international financial system has come to resemble a gambling hall, making "gamblers of us all" (Strange 1986:1–3). As the potential for venture enterprise has expanded along with the growth of globalized markets, electronic media, and finance capital, the gaming room has become "iconic of capital: of its 'natural' capacity to yield value with human input" (Hardt 1995:39). *Pokémon* is the play version of casino capitalism: getting and trading commodities in a market highly dependent on fantasy, luck, and also skill. As my nephew said upon opening a pack of cards I had brought him from Japan, "Hey, Dad, I just got a twenty-five-dollar card." For this eight-year-old, who, unlike other kids, never went to the hobby shop to cash in or barter his fortune, the value of this card was more imaginary than "real": the mere fantasy of pretend transactions and accumulated wealth. Yet Mitch knew the "market value" for each card he owned, as assessed by his unofficial card collector guide that listed going rates according to a complex calculus (involving a host of factors such as the edition of issuance, whether the card was printed in Japanese or English, the card's rarity, and the differential value for specially minted holofoil cards).

Mitch's father also understood the logic of this play because he had collected baseball cards as a kid and knew that the ones that were hardest to get were also the most precious. The layout of the card was similar as well: a picture of a team member identified by name (both personal and group) and game statistics.[22] But baseball cards stand (in) for something not only corporeal (real players who are members of teams and perform in events where their record is public history) but also culturally American—a sport that, while played the world over these days, is still associated with its roots in the United States. *Pokémon* cards, by contrast, refer to a world that is entirely made up: a virtual construction created by Japanese designers and marketers with no referent outside itself.[23] In this sense, *Pokémon* is the play version not only of casino capitalism but also of virtual capitalism, a term that describes the current stage of a market system wired through venture enterprise trading in a currency that is virtual and floating rather than grounded in anything "real" (like gold bullion). Here the kind of play (and economy) of baseball versus *Pokémon* cards differs as well. While the former is located more securely in time, place, and identity—real teams, corporeal bodies, and culturally "American" roots—the latter is more flexible, deterritorialized, and hybridized.

Interestingly, though, given what we could call its mutable identity, there has also been a fetishization of the Japanese originals in U.S. card culture. *Pokémon* cards printed in Japan and enscripted in Japanese have carried much more value for collectors and fans despite (or because of?) the fact that few American kids can actually read them without relying on the translations provided in what is now a host of official and unofficial card collector guides published in the United States, which devote entire pages to the Japanese cards. This seems an amazing change in the currency of coolness since *Power Rangers* only a few years earlier, when its U.S. distributors completely effaced all signs of its origins based on the assessment that American kids would not buy (into) anything overtly Japanese. But six years later, this itself had become a fetish: signs of Japanese origin(al)s as signified by a script that carries its meaning symbolically rather than literally (given that so few Americans can actually read Japanese). This trend has not only continued but has advanced today, when American youth are increasingly exposed to and literate in a range of Japanese cultural goods (from sushi, karate, and karaoke to *manga, anime,* and *Yu-Gi-Oh!*—the newest in Japanese trading cards) that increasingly come packaged in the cultural framework of Japanese language, history, and religion.

Why this fascination with authenticity in an era of casino capitalism whose reigning cultural logic is virtuality—a time, as I have argued in this book, when the diffuseness, multipartedness, and perpetual reconstructibility of Japanese play products are particularly resonant? When I asked twelve American kids, all self-identified *Pokémon* fans, what image they had of Japan, one answered that he and his friends all thought Japan was tremendously cool because it produces cool goods like Nintendo's Game Boy, Sony's PlayStation, and *Pokémon* for American youth. A couple added that their interest in Japanese play products made them want to visit the country one day and also to study the language and culture later in college—a reflection of a nationwide increase in the number of American undergraduates signing up for Japanese classes. But unlike the 1980s, when such students were mainly business majors hoping to make their riches in Japan's Bubble economy, today they are largely pop culture fans *(otaku)* hoping to acquire the skills necessary to read and understand the originals (whether of trading cards, *manga, anime,* or games). Like the fetish for made-in-Japan *Pokémon* cards, there is a sense that the closer a product is to the creative source, the more "real" and hence better the engagement (as is true of fandom in general, of course, where watching a baseball game at the stadium beats out reading an account in the paper). So the quest is not so much for the authentic Japan but for what "made-in-Japan" authenticates—a leading brand name of coolness these days. And for global consumers like these American kids, a Sony PlayStation or a pack of *Yu-Gi-Oh!* cards *is* what stands for Japan today.

Beyond Disneyfication:
A Virtual World That Keeps "Opening Up"

> *Poké*-world is different from the real world. But if our world were like this, it would be good. I like this world because getting is central to it. What is my motive for doing trades? Getting things for myself.
>
> Eleven-year-old Japanese boy

> *Pokémon* aren't real. They're in a different part of the world. Like Pallet Town—we don't know where this is, but it's familiar.
>
> Ten-year-old American girl

When I interned for two weeks during the summer of 1999, under a visiting professorship program at Grey Advertising, a New York firm, I was told that the key to good advertising is stripping a product down to its "core fantasy," then "positioning" this fantasy to a target audience.[24] Instructed in what is called psychographics, I learned that advertisers try to increase the "intimacy" consumers have with the brands that, like Starbucks coffee, are what companies stand for and what advertisers work to "nurture." As distinguished from products that exist on the shelf, brands "exist in people's minds" and thus stand at the interface between product and consumer. Making brands seem special and consumers feel as if they own them is the assignment handed to advertisers. By studying the lifestyles of various consumer bases (questioning how each spends time and money and profiling the psychic makeup as mapped by specific desires, anxieties, and concerns), advertisers use psychographics in crafting portraits for the products they are promoting. By "surrounding them with symbols," advertisers thus give brands a "stage presence." This is the "core fantasy" that, if effective, turns a product into a brand, a brand into an intimate friend, and a consumer into a loyal fan.

Hasbro is a client of Grey Advertising, and during my summer internship the *Pokémon* campaign was one of Grey's assignments. Expectations were high that, as one member of the group working on the project put it, "*Pokémon* will be a brand versus an object." But the kid business is even riskier than most others (because children are young, and their desires are harder to calculate and sustain than those of adults), and the *Pokémon* property was considered a paradigm shifter: a toy concept with a new construction of fantasy. As it was explained to me, toys are always about giving kids a sense of power. But in a property like *Batman*, children transport themselves into the hero, whereas in *Pokémon* players themselves control the action. As in video games, there are continual levels to be mastered in *Pokémon* so that kids are constantly mastering something but also being challenged to proceed to another arena (a new vista, a new *pokémon*, a new battle). This means that the dynamics of interaction and empowerment are continual, and are aligned not to a uniquely endowed superpower but to a generic everykid (Ash, but also a host of humans who appear in the games/cartoon/movies as players aspiring to be the "world's greatest *pokémon* master"). The key to success here is hard work and dedication to learning the game, training one's monsters, and playing a lot. This is why *Pokémon* is so brilliant, someone said; it is about instant gratification but establishing loyalty as well—also the formula of branding, I recalled. Yet the logic of this play also mystified a longtime veteran in the toy and advertising business. For him, other Japanese toy properties seemed more consistent with American fantasy conventions; in *Power Rangers*, the "idea always seemed a classic story to me," and *tamagotchi* "gave kids a proprietary relationship with something" established, in part, by its constant need to be taken care of. By contrast, the *Pokémon* game seemed very cerebral and its success in the United States a complete mystery. But then he added, "Maybe I wasn't giving American kids credit."[25]

What this man perceived as a heady diffuseness has been central to *Pokémon*'s success both as a new form of fantasy/play and as a highly profitable (and ever-expanding) line of merchandise in the global marketplace of kids' entertainment today. Although it is set—like so much of mass fantasy—in an alternative, imaginary world, *Pokémon* is also, as Tajiri (its creator) has said, a play that doesn't close and a game/property that opens up in various directions (Nintendo 1999). Together, these two factors make for a fantasy play quite different from the Disney model, which, based in spectacles of animated or theme park storytelling, has circulated the world, dominating the channels and tastes of global kids' culture since at least the 1950s (marking the broadcast of *The Mickey Mouse Show* on TV and the erection of Disneyland in Anaheim, California). The Disney impulse has been to create a closed rather than open world: a fantasy space that, autonomous and utopian, is cut off from the rest of society (as in the theme parks, where all signs of the outside world are concealed). The artifice of production here is both elaborate and hidden (employees at Disneyland are called by their first names and dress in underground changing rooms so they always appear in character). The fictional wonderland that is constructed is also micromanaged and rigidly set by Disney; customers are guided through the theme parks by controlled routes that limit choice and affix preset narratives to the experience (Yoshimi 2000; Yoshimoto 1994). And in all this, Disney is cinematic both literally on the screen and figuratively in its full-bodied amusement worlds.

As Disney's magic and empire have globally spread, Disneyfication has been both despaired of as cultural imperialism (by the French, for example, when Disneyland was erected near Paris) and popularly embraced as a marker of modernization, prosperity, and the American dream (as Tokyo Disneyland has been in Japan).[26] But whatever its reception, the influence of Disneyfication has begun to erode today, challenged by what some say has been both its biggest threat and the clearest sign of future trends in the global marketplace of kids' play: *Pokémonization*. Played on a handheld Game Boy set or arranged in an album of trading cards, *Pokémon* is a far more interactive, portable, and fluid playscape than Disney fare, accessed primarily through the highly crafted and self-contained fantasy lands of cartoons, videos, movies, and theme parks. As a "vehicle" of and for global culture, *Pokémonization* also wears the signature of its cultural origins quite differently from Disney(ification), whose brand of fantasy making has been clearly identified the world over as American (as a cultural flow emanating from and associated with American power).

By contrast, *Pokémon*, whose Japanese origins are generally known by its global fans, is more "placeless," and not just as a result of the localization exacted on it by American marketers. Decentered from Disney's more modernist model of heroism, spectacle, and neatly contained make-believe, it invites a different kind of fantasy play that "opens up" to a world less anchored to singular locale or stable identities. As the fan quoted at the beginning of this section said about Pallet Town (one of the sites in the original Game Boy game), "We don't know where this is, but it's familiar." What is at once anywhere and everywhere is a game setting that extends endlessly outward: to new zones, further interactions, additional conquests. "The blanks are filled in gradually," is how an executive at Warner Brothers articulated the logic of fantasy at work in *Pokémon* (and Japanese entertainment in general), contrasting this with the more story-based and contained lines preferred by Hollywood.[27] Similarly, Tajiri has said that he designed *Pokémon* with a sense of place at once grounded and elastic: "If I got on my bike in Kanagawa [close to his home in the suburbs of Tokyo] and rode hard,

I'd get to a new place. This is similar to *Pokémon*; you get to a faraway world by working hard *[ganbaru]*. This is how you can go a little beyond the place where you live with your friends and find a world that is deeper than reality but also accessible every day" (quoted in Hatakeyama and Kubo 2000:511).

Many U.S. parents first dismissed *Pokémon* as cheap Japanese animation, and even those involved in its American marketing campaign generally agree that its visuals are not especially sophisticated. The imagery of a Disney cartoon is more technologically advanced, I heard often. But the appeal of *Pokémon* comes from somewhere else: from what Al Kahn, head of 4Kids Entertainment, referred to as its "gaming essence"—a creative impulse in which Japan, he believes, is leading the world today. *Pokémon* is based on a role-playing game that is very textual, but in the United States—which Kahn calls a visual culture—"we usually start with the character, whereas in Japan gaming comes first." *Pokémon* works more on the imagination than the eyes, as Massey Rafoni at Warner Brothers, a veteran in the American film business, put it. It draws kids in by the architectonics of a world that they enter not as passive spectators or by identifying with the lead hero but as active players who insert themselves into the game/story/journey—as does a singer in karaoke—moving it along through their own input and interactions.

The organizing trope here is evolution: as the pocket monsters gradually change their identity and develop new powers, so do the players and the game world itself (figure 45). This differs from transformation—the motif of superheroism so central in American mythmaking and in the cyber epics so successfully globalized by Japan (such as *Power Rangers* and *Sailor Moon*).[28] In transforming, the protagonist upgrades from one mode to another, and the shift, at once radical, is also transitory and fantastic (marked, as it is, by costume change); superheroes fluctuate between two distinct worlds and states of being (one of mundane humanness, the other of transhuman powers, spirits, and fancy). The fantasy of empowerment is different in *Pokémon*. There is only one universe here and no other or outside to *Poké*-world. And, rather than replacing or splitting their identities with (phantasmatic) alter egos, humans gradually build and expand their powers by traveling through virtual space, mastering its landscape by study and training, and capturing the wild monsters hidden there. The "core fantasy" in *Pokémon*, then, is accretion instead of morphin—a power of having rather than being, and of capital rather than identity.[29] This is the logic of its U.S. ad campaign—"Gotta catch 'em all!"—which reflects not only the position assumed by consumers but also the place assigned the producer of this

ニョロモ⑩
おたまポケモン（NO.060）
タイプ1／みず
たかさ　　0.6m
おもさ　12.4kg

ニョロゾ⑩
おたまポケモン（NO.061）
タイプ1／みず
たかさ　　1.0m
おもさ　20.0kg

ニョロボン⑩
おたまポケモン（NO.062）
タイプ1／みず・2／かくとう
たかさ　　1.3m
おもさ　54.0kg

海のポケモン

ニョロゾの体内透視模型（オーキド博士所蔵）。

Figure 45. Changing play logics: from transformation (as in morphing super-heroes) to evolution. The *pokémon* Poliwog evolves into Poliwhirl, which evolves into Poliwrath. (Courtesy of Pokémon Company.)

brand of global fantasy making. It means that American kids can love *Poké-mon* and know, even fetishize, its origins (as in the U.S. fad for the Japanese-made trading cards), but associate Japan in all this less with a national power or cultural lifestyle ("the American dream") than with a consumer brand that can be collected and customized as one's own.

The basis of enjoyment and meaning here is not a simple one of identifi-cation: of identifying with and fantasizing about becoming a hero on the screen or trading card. Whereas this has been one of the primary structures of pleasure operating in film and, to a lesser degree, television—two of the leading visual technologies of mass culture in the twentieth century and

Figure 46. Interactivity: American kids playing competitive card tournaments with *Pokémon* trading cards. (From *Beckett Pokémon Collector* 2, no. 5, issue 9 [May 2000].)

those in which the U.S. entertainment industry has excelled—Japanese mass fantasies today are more heavily fostered by interactive technology, such as video games intermediated with comic books, *anime,* and trading cards (figure 46). Here, fantasy takes place at the interface: less through the distillation of preformed images or coherent narratives than through interactions between the player and screen/page/card deck that are transacted, assembled, and mixed in various ways. This coheres with, but also goes beyond, what Vivian Sobchack (2000) has called the "electronic presence," the perceptions and subjectivities produced by what she considers to be the third historical stage in capitalism: multinational capitalism. As outlined by Fredric Jameson (1984), each of these three stages is accompanied by a revolution in representational technologies and its own cultural logic: photography and realism for market capitalism (the first stage starting around 1840), and cinema and modernism for monopoly capitalism (the second stage starting in the 1890s). Multinational capitalism, starting roughly in the 1940s, was spurred by electronic technology, which, by the 1970s, was entering the age of flexible accumulation and informational capitalism (with a cultural logic Manuel Castells [1996] has called virtuality) marked by the rise of microelectronics, telecommunications, and computers. In this era of digital simulation rather than mechanical reproduction, the chip has replaced the copy. As Sobchack (2000:150) puts it, an electronic presence asserts neither an objective possession of the world and the self (as does a photographic presence) nor a centered and subjective spatiotemporal engagement (as does cinema) but rather a meta-world (whose constructedness is self-referential) where the primary value is the bit or the instant that can be selected, combined, and instantly replayed or remixed.

Such a logic of assemblage and disassemblage is what I have been tracing throughout this book: a cyborgian aesthetic that, given impetus by the national disruptures and reconstruction following the war, has marked Japanese mass fantasies since the 1950s starting with nuclear beasts (Gojira) and atomic superheroes (Tetsuwan Atomu). Characters with bodies and powers that are endlessly remapped, recharged, and replaced have been a commonplace throughout the postwar period as in the three properties discussed in previous chapters—*Power Rangers, Sailor Moon,* and *tamagotchi.* And, over time, what could be called a principle of identity as mutable, modular, and mixed has extended from heroes on the screen or page to the interface between player and screen advanced in the more game-based fantasies of recent years. This is where *Pokémon's* version of virtuality is of a different kind or order from that constructed by Disney. Whereas Disneyfication is more cinematic and centered by core characters, coherent narratives, and cultural values (identified as/with U.S. power), *Pokémon*ification depends on a more mobile, varied, and game-based technology and encodes a world order of networks, evolution, and endless proliferation ("opening up"). Set within and as an undulating circuitry of endlessly attaching, detaching, and recombining parts, powers, attacks, secrets, rarities, data, attributes, and natures, *Pokémon* invites a play uncannily well suited (and more aptly than Disney) to the dictates of informational capitalism.

As this has been characterized by scholars such as Castells (1996), Hardt and Negri (2000), and Morris-Suzuki (1988), productivity here relies on technologies of knowledge, and the basic unit of economic organization is not the subject (be it individual or collective) but the network (made up of a variety of subjects and organizations such as multinational corporations that must continually adapt to the market and environment). In what is a diffusion of relationships, identities, and interests, a semblance of glue is provided by "virtual cultures." Premised not on a shared set of values or stable core of institutions, these come instead from cyberspace, for example, where computers rearrange reality into digital icons, texts, and scenes. Made up of a mélange of values, projects, and cultures, virtual cultures are multifaceted and ephemeral: patchworks of experiences and interests that constantly change along with the speed of information and turnover in commodity marketing these days (Castells 1996:141–50). Reflected here is a new degree of creative destruction, something inherent in capitalism generally (where, to stimulate more profits, goods must be consumed to (re)create demand, which, in turn, triggers more production). This is even more intense today because, as information is not consumed but rather constantly expanded and amassed, the center of economic activity shifts from the production of goods to the production of innovation. In this "softening of the economy," stress is placed more on product design and diversification than on such "hard" inputs as raw materials and direct manufacturing labor.

The kiss of death for a product line today is standardization—precisely what drove the huge success and appeal of McDonaldization, with its Fordist model of mass food culture (that, suffering decline in the current era of niche marketing and customization, is spurring more flexibility and choice in McDonald's across the world). By linking profit to (perpetual) innovation, new impetus is given to creativity, discovery, and knowledge production. While these qualities are theoretically good, however, there is also a paradox in that profit not only inspires but also distorts the forms assumed by new knowledge and creativity (Morris-Suzuki 1988:84). Virtual reality falls in this camp, according to Ken Hillis, who, defining it as the technical reproduction of the process by which humans perceive the world/reality, notes that one of the prime engines driving the development of virtual technologies today is the relentless demand for ever more efficient ways to circulate capital within a global economy. Such efficiency comes from reformulating capital as "infinitely flexible data" that move "at the speed of light across a variety of geographic scales." Both capital and the spaces where it operates come to acquire a mutable identity—something that is simultaneously capital/data/virtual reality and is also malleable to perpetual innovation. But while it is necessary for achieving competitive advantage under advanced capitalism, such a mutable entity/identity is far less beneficial to the human psyche, in Hillis's opinion. People count on some semblance of continuity, stability, and relationality, and rootedness of some kind is what anchors sanity (Hillis 1999:xxx).

Intimate Virtuality

Pokémon is a playscape of images, places, and friends that also converts to a field of infinitely flexible data. *Poké*-world could be said to display a mutable identity (or interface, as I have argued), but it also offers anchors and roots—mechanisms often said, as we saw in the last chapter, to reduce rather than heighten the alienating, atomizing effects of life under conditions of informational capitalism. In a labyrinth of networks erected in the pursuit of profit ("getting"), there is also a "glue" that ties disparate elements together—a virtual culture where digital icons link to humans in relationships at once intimate and instrumental. It is in this sense of mutability that the *Pokémon* game world operates not only as capital, the infinite flexibility by which everything decomposes and recomposes into endless variations, but also as intimate virtuality—my own term for virtualization in this mobile, interactive, and addictive human-machine interface. Significantly, the creator of the *Pokémon* game felt it was their very *dētaka*, or "datafication," that gave pocket monsters this dual function. Convertibility from image to data enables them to inhabit *Poké*-balls and, as a portable medium, be traded, accumulated, or communicated by (and between) humans. But this *dētaka* also animates the pocket monsters, Tajiri believed, by making them more, rather than less, lifelike (by putting *pokémon* in a dynamic rather than static form, where they not only change and evolve but also do so according to a player's input). Like bugs, this is a version of "life" at once familiar and intriguing to kids, but in a digitalized/informational mode also conducive to the marketplace of global capital/ism.

This model of virtualization—elastic fantasy in contrast to the more closed and contained version promoted by Disney/ification—is poignantly rendered in the third of the *Pokémon* movies, *Pokémon 3 the Movie: Spell of the Unknown* (in English). In this story about attachments and home, a young girl is trapped in the huge mansion she once shared with her parents (who have disappeared while researching a new species of *pokémon*, the Unknown). Clinging to the dream of ("natural") family and (stable) household, Molly deludes herself into believing that a visiting Unknown (Entei) is actually her dad: a powerful spell that prevents her from leaving the mansion even when a wall of deadly crystal encroaches from the outside.[30] The traveling band of would-be *pokémon* masters (Ash, Misty, Brock, Team Rocket) eventually save Molly by getting her to see what is "real"—Entei is not her dad, the mansion has become a death trap, and the world outside offers a host of possible new kinship/friendships (ties with other kids and a range of *pokémon*, referred to here as "like family"). In the end, Molly survives by projecting a different desire—the will to escape rather than remain tied to the mansion and all it represents—onto Entei.[31] With this, the spell is broken; Entei disappears, the crystal erodes, and Molly matures into a girl who can now subsist outside her home. As the credits roll, we see her playing happily outside next to Himeguma, her new *pokémon*. Self-absorbed, the girl does not even notice the reappearance of her parents, who wait in the distance on the mansion's veranda until their daughter finally looks up.

In *Spell of the Unknown*, a girl is caught in the fortress of her imagination: the parents she has lost and desires to literally—albeit virtually—replace.[32] In this tale about misplaced attachments, Molly runs into danger by fetishizing the realness of family and a dreamworld that impersonates the real thing. Clinging to what entraps her—a home petrifying into crystal—Molly survives only by letting go of this dream: bonds rigidly affixed to a set and unchanging notion of place/family/domesticity/identity. The message, at once ideological and commercial, is for kids—like Molly—to turn outward in their desires and to reach for other worlds, different intimacies, alternative families. And, as embodied by "good" versus "bad" *pokémon* (ones that open kids up to the outside rather than enclose them within insular fantasies), the message is about Pokémonization as well: how its brand of virtuality is both pliable and useful in these changing times, providing kids not only with entertainment but also a resource for anchoring their lives with new relations, meanings, and (pre)occupations (of a mobile, techno-intimate sort). With a stock of different pocket monsters (and a vast, and constantly changing, array of media goods with which to access these creatures), children today have an endless supply of different and replaceable play buddies. And like Pikachu, at once Ash's favorite *pokémon* but also a species/category that all players can access, collect, and grow (as in building, altering, even evolving its identity), pocket monsters are a flexible medium for intimacy of a virtual variety.

Recall here Yokoi Akihiro's inspiration for the *tamagotchi*. Seeing an ad of a boy packing his pet turtle into a suitcase to take along on a trip, Yokoi was moved to create a traveling "pet"—a portable device that could evoke, both digitally and emotionally, the bond between human and pet. As he believed, people are drawn to cats, dogs, and turtles only initially because of these animals' cuteness. Soon, however, it is more the attention pets demand that establishes a bond: what Yokoi imprinted as *mendō*—the tasks of feeding, tending to, and cleaning up that, in the electronic *tamagotchi,* come from manipulating icons on the screen. The virtual pet proved to be a big hit, as we know, giving owners the experience of intimacy (interaction with a responsive albeit demanding "pet") encased in the convenience of New Age technology (an affordable, portable, and disposable digital machine). But most relevant to the story of intimate virtuality I am tracing here with *Spell of the Unknown* is the nature of the *tamagotchi:* an entity intended to both mimic and transgress "life" as defined by a more grounded notion of biology, geography, or parenthood. In Yokoi's words, the *tamagotchi* are a "strange life-form" *(henna ikimono):* entities that start off all head and grow legs and berets as an effect of the real care they are given by attentive owners. The resultant pet is not simply a static image on the screen but the result of labor that is expended by the player herself: the interface between player and machine that animates the *tamagotchi* into a "strange life-form."

As is extended much further in *Pokémon* (and video games and role-playing/card games like *Magic: The Gathering* more generally), fantasy characters are built from a combination of image and information. In the case of *tamagotchi,* pets appear on the screen both as bodies (Kusatchi, Mimitchi, Bill) and as data—the icons that reveal need (a frowny face), care (a ducky indicating cleaned-up poop), and current state of health (a health meter). And, for Tajiri, it is "datafication" that lends *Pokémon* its life-giving properties. By manipulating data, users build up their *pokémon* in a process that not only simulates organic life as in the bug world (*pokémon* grow bigger, stronger, and into evolved forms) but also produces a language or currency with which users establish exchanges, communication, and relationships with others. As noted earlier, Tajiri viewed trade of information as the most important aspect of the *Pokémon* game for its "gorgeous implications for communication" (Hamamura 1997). It is this—the endless deconstruction, rearrangement, calculation, and proliferation of information—that goes on forever in the Pokémonization model of play and intimate virtuality that promises to open kids up, as its marketers have reiterated so often, to a world outside. And as the movie *Spell of the Unknown* would seem to suggest, what is "outside" is interactions as much with virtual entities as

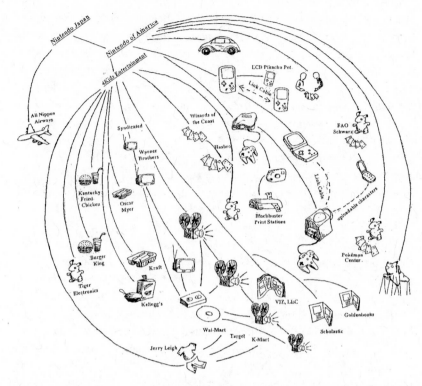

Figure 47. The spread of *Pokémon* to/in America: some of the product lines generated by *Pokémon* in its U.S. campaign. (Original artwork by Dwayne Dixon.)

with humans—Molly at the end of the film who, once freed from the mansion, plays with her new *pokémon* friend.

The model here of a strange new life-form both borrows from the familiar (family/nature/biology) and goes beyond it. This would seem to be a message of *Spell of the Unknown* as well, where the fantasy that literalizes the real—an imagined creation that preserves the girl's past/origins—threatens to wipe out life itself. It is only by breaking out of this narrow imaginary/world that Molly survives, being now—as viewers of the film will immediately understand—in a space where she will have endless opportunities to attach to endless *pokémon* as (not literal, but virtual) family and friend. As Professor Oak says about the *pokémon* in the *Poketto Monsutā Zukan,* their nature is difficult to pin down. With *pokémon* neither a race per se nor strictly monsters or pets, what they *do* share is convertibility to data and their utility to humans. So, besides the affective value they carry (as potential pals like Himeguma), they serve as capital, and in a form that can be reformulated "as infinitely flexible data that moves at the speed of light across a variety of geographic scales" (Hillis 1999:xxx). The demand for "ever more efficient ways to circulate capital with the global economy" is driving the development of not only virtual technologies today, as Hillis has noted, but also global capitalism. For Japan today, still burdened with the effects of a nagging recession as it passes into the new millennium, crafting capital in the form of cute monsters that can travel the world and transform—endlessly and polymorphously—into infinitely flexible data and products, is a boon for the economy.

As Japan circulates its fantasy monsters around the world at this millennial moment, it claims a place in the global marketplace as New Age trendsetter and play maker. This globality (figure 47) is embodied in the "Pokémon, the World" skit on the television show *Oha Sutā*, described at the beginning of the chapter. Here, *Pokémon* collapses into a monster ball that doubles as a handheld globe, projecting an image of a Japan at the center of (and in possession of) the world, empowered as it has been by *Pokémon* (and Japanese cultural and entertainment goods more generally). By contrast, the scene evoked by Molly—clinging desperately to a fantasy of home that threatens to shut off the world outside altogether—could not be more different. *Spell of the Unknown* could be read as an allegory about Japan as it navigates its place in the world at this millennial moment. A tale about loss, it is also one about new possibilities: about facing the dismantling of old attachments by adopting global capitalism/virtual intimacies—ties that compensate for, but themselves spur, the erosion of a more rooted sense of home, country, and nation. In this, a monster that can be "family-like" rather than "family" encodes a libidinal economy for millennial Japan (and global fantasy making): virtual entities that serve (as) capital and as intimacy at the same time.

Epilogue

In the film *Lost in Translation,* a Hollywood hit of 2003, Tokyo is the back-drop for a story about two Americans as lost in a foreign culture as they are in life back home. Strangers when they first meet as travelers in the same hotel, the two connect over shared insomnia and the mutual recognition of anomie in each other. Japan—a place they neither wanted to visit nor find particularly interesting—is utterly strange, yet it is a strangeness that, when the Americans venture into it together, inspires intimacy between the two. Being oddly in place while being displaced from home and culture is the story line of *Lost in Translation.* As rendered on the screen by director Sofia Coppola, the film presents scene after scene of a searingly beautiful Tokyo that, unreadable by the Americans, mystifies and amuses them. As strangers "lost in translation" is how the audience, too, is positioned to view Japan: a place signifying displacement—a not altogether uncomfortable state, as the story tells us. In this, Japan is treated less literally than metaphorically—a signifier of foreignness about which the Americans remain unremittingly clueless.

In summer 2004, ABC aired an episode of the children's television show *Abarangers* (the seasonal name of the long-running *Power Rangers*) enti-tled "Lost and Found in Translation." An obvious reference to the adult-targeted film of the previous year, the show replayed its tale about cultural difference with a significant twist. The scene opens in the United States with the Rangers working on their homework—a social science project studying two cultures. Switching on the TV, they discover a Japanese program that turns out to be the Japanese version of *Abarangers* dubbed into English. The plot line is standard for the series; confronted by a strange-looking alien, the Rangers morph into cyberwarriors, battle with stylized moves and newfan-gled weapons, and defeat the foe. Amusingly, the story also includes an

American: a caricatured vulgar, money-hungry athlete who has come to Japan in search of a good chiropractor (and is saved in a double sense by the Japanese Black Ranger who cures his back and also his drive for money). As the Americans watch the show, two are riveted. The third, however, dismisses it. Saying, "They got it all wrong," Conner discounts the enemy as a "guy in a rubber suit" and is offended by the portrayal of the American. "To make fun of our sports heroes? This represents what they think of us in Japan!" As his pals tell him it's just a show and that he should use his imagination, Conner relaxes and gets into the action. By the end of the program, all three are excited, and Conner admits, "It was kinda cool." The episode closes with a message about cultural difference voiced by the new convert: "We're not so different after all, just a slightly different interpretation." Completing his homework assignment, he announces the title to the others: "Japanese versus American Culture—Closer Than We Think."

What meaning can be derived from these two pop tales about the current Japan (play) fetish in U.S. youth culture? The two would seem to be at odds; one is about adults who get "lost" in a Japan they fail to "translate," and the other is about American Rangers who see in their Japanese counterpart a "different interpretation." Though the messages are not as divergent as they first appear (more on this later), what is most immediately striking for my subject—the globalization of children's trends from Japan—is the *Abarangers* episode. For, in the history I have laid out for *Power Rangers* in the States—its reinvention as an "American classic" and the de-Japanization of its roots—"Lost and Found in Translation" represents a radical shift. Dripping in irony, the show acknowledges the presence of a Japanese version (falling short, however, of identifying this as the original) and pokes fun at the American ethnocentrism that has so demeaned and restricted foreign fare from U.S. pop channels. (The "guy in a rubber suit" comment seems a reference to Godzilla, as does the odd voice-over by the American character whose mouth runs askew of his words, as did those of the Japanese actors in the English-dubbed Godzilla films.) Significantly, when the would-be critic Conner is told to "use his imagination" and remember that it's "just a TV show," his own cultural solipsism lifts. Seeing the Japanese show now in terms of differences that are "kinda cool," he grasps it as a valid alternative to a show whose authenticity is no longer singularly American (or Japanese). And, in this accommodation to cultural difference, *Power Rangers* would seem to have come a long way since it was first introduced in the States—and monoculturalized as American—in 1993.

This shift is self-consciously acknowledged in the title, where, in contrast to *Lost in Translation*, the show proclaims—for itself and for its audience of

Figure 48. A Godzilla Americans find cool: Nicknamed Gojira
(Godzilla), Matsui Hideki, a Japanese, plays for the New York
Yankees. (© James Porto 2000.)

American youth—that it has "found" a way not to be "lost" in the cultural
differences posed by the non-U.S. world today. Implicitly, a differentiation is
being made between the children and the adults, who are as clueless about
Japan as those in *Lost in Translation:* an attitude, as we have seen, that accompanied the *Pokémon* craze (which left adults mystified by the appeal and
even nature of pocket monsters) and that has persisted in the new millennium with the continuing fads of Japanese youth goods, from card sets and
video games to *anime* and *manga* (forty shelves are currently stocked with

manga at my local Borders bookstore, and the phenomenon, though intriguing to adults, seems as bewildering). Indeed, as *Millennial Monsters* has attempted to trace, there is a veritable boom these days in the sale, circulation, consumption, and popularization of Japanese fantasy products, both in the United States and globally. And, at least in the States, the way in which "Japan" has come to figure in and be identified with this trend has significantly changed over the last decade, as the *Abarangers* episode seems to indicate. From a show that was once entirely Americanized for U.S. broadcast, *Power Rangers* can now give at least a nod to its Japanese connection. And this move is even more visible in other waves of Japanese "cool" that are faddish in the States today.

For example, in *Duel Masters*—the newest media mix of card game, cartoon show, *manga*, and video game—the Japanese keyword of the play universe is *kaijudo,* or "the way of monsters" (*kaijūdō* properly in Japanese: *dō* for "the way," as in the way of bonsai or the way of karate, and *kaijū* for "monsters"). Players aim to become *kaijudo* masters by learning to manipulate their cards, strategies, and moves in order to battle, and defeat, the powerful monsters ruling five magical worlds. As one of the official guidebooks puts it, players must adopt a samurai-like code of discipline and resoluteness: "I make no excuses. My actions are my voice. I have no enemies" (Wizards of the Coast 2004:5). It further explains about the cartoon: "When most anime is imported to the U.S., nearly anything Japanese gets changed or dubbed over. This is untrue with *Duel Masters.* While battling, characters shout out their commands in Japanese, giving *Duel Masters* a much more distinct Eastern flavor" (5).

What do such millennial monsters—*kaijudo* as played by American kids in a game set peppered with Japanese or U.S. Power Rangers viewing their Japanese counterparts on split (American/Japanese) TV—tell us about the relationship today between Japanese toys and the global imagination, and the conditions of fantasy, capitalism, and globalism I set out to excavate in this book? One observation is that different cultural codes are juxtaposed but not jumbled together (or eradicated altogether). A "distinct Eastern flavor," the *Duel Masters* guidebook claims about its inclusion of Japanese commands. But immediately before this it has noted the card game resembles that of the U.S.-made *Magic: The Gathering* and adds that the same American company, Wizards of the Coast, has, in fact, produced it. Because the *anime* and *manga* come from Japanese creators (produced by Shōgakukan and Mitsui-Kids), *Duel Masters* is a joint production distributed—as is now commonplace for such Japanese products that are globalized in, and into, the West—differently in Japan and the rest of Asia than in the United States and "all territories outside of Asia." In terms of production, this (as well as other U.S.-Japanese fare, such as *Power Rangers* and *Pokémon*) represents a model of global power different from that associated with Americanization. The property is jointly produced, differentially distributed, and culturally mixed. Unlike McDonaldization, with its Fordist formula of one size fits all even in its glocalized iteration of today—a global commodity that is localized differently in various locales—"millennial monsters" are both "Eastern" and not, a globalized fantasy whose intermixture of the foreign and familiar is not localizable to any one place.

As a twenty-two-year-old American male puts this from a fan's perspective, what is appealing to American youth about Japanese cool today is its utter sense of difference. "It could be Mars," he says, for the strangeness of its settings, story lines, and characters. But equally important is knowing that all this comes from a real place: from a Japan that actually exists, which inspires at least some fans to learn about Japanese culture, language, or history. "Japan" signifies something important here, but the signifier is shifting: it is a marker of phantasm and difference, yet one that is anchored in a reality of sorts—a country Americans can study and visit. So fantasy and realism shift here, the one serving as the alibi for the other in what Roland Barthes describes as the construction of myth. Japan's role in the current J-pop boom among American youth is mythic: a place whose meaning shifts between the phantasmatic and real, foreign and familiar, strange and everyday. Numerous fans of Japanese *anime, manga,* card games, and toys I have talked with in the States voice their attraction in similar terms: their imaginations are piqued by the complexity and strangeness of an alternative fantasy world that they also strive to become fluent in and at home with (by learning some Japanese, downloading pirated versions of the Japanese originals, or acquiring knowledge about the cultural references). Seeing in the foreign an intriguing if bizarre otherworld is also the mind-set of the American travelers in *Lost in Translation.* But, in contrast to the adult perspective taken in the film, young American fans of J-pop want to be "found" rather than "lost" in this terrain, keeping the edginess of its difference yet acquiring the savviness—that of a global traveler/global citizen—to speak the language.

At work here is a new kind of global imagination: new, at least, in the way it differs from an older model of Americanization. As Joseph Nye has defined the latter in terms of what he calls soft power, this is the "ability to get what you want through attraction rather than coercion or payments," and it "arises from the attractiveness of a country's culture, political ideals, and policies" (2004:x). Power of this nature comes from inspiring the dreams and desires of others by projecting images about one's own culture that are globally appealing and transmitted through channels of global communication (such as television and film). As has been generally agreed, only the United States had the soft power—in the strength of its cultural industries and the appeal of a culture that has translated around the world as rich, powerful, and exciting—to dominate the global imagination throughout the twentieth century. But not only is America's soft power ebbing today (due, in part, to the global unpopularity of such U.S.-led initiatives as the Iraq War), so too is the desirability—even in the States—of a monolithic, monochromatic fantasy space. As A. O. Scott wrote about the 2004 Toronto film festival, the global currency of films made outside the United States (in India, China, South Korea, and Japan) is increasing, defying the prediction that Hollywood "would take over with its blockbuster globalism dissolving all vestiges of the local, particular and strange" (2004:86).

As Scott sees it, Hollywood is stuck in making movies that, while technologically impressive, project "counterfeit worlds" that spectacularize fantasies out of sync with the lived emotions of people in the twenty-first century. By contrast, movies set and produced elsewhere (the example he gives is *The World*, by Chinese director Jia Zhangkhe) are often on a smaller scale but more emotionally real. Through stories of ordinary people struggling to make it in cities in jagged transition (Beijing, Seoul, Calcutta, Taipei) where they are both dislocated and at home, "the anxious, melancholy feeling of being simultaneously connected and adrift" (Scott 2004:86) is projected—a state deeply recognizable to postindustrial subjects the world over. Of course, the fantasy magic making of Hollywood filmmaking embedded with attractive images of American culture remains popular both in the United States (though as of this writing, attendance at theaters has slipped for two years running) and, even more perhaps, outside it (where revenues for films like *Titanic* are much greater). But, as film critic Charles Taylor puts this, what characterizes the emotional condition of the millennial era is "being in a world where the only sense of home is to be found in a constant state of flux" (quoted in Scott 2004:86)—a state conjured up through mobility, nomadicism, travel, and the foreign. This is a descriptor, in fact, of the Hollywood movie *Lost in Translation* and also of all the waves of entertainment dealt with in this book, from the continual battles and dramas of *Power Rangers* and *Sailor Moon* to the nomadic travels of the portable *tamagotchi* and would-be "*pokémon* masters."

With this, I make three final observations. The first (already well known) concerns the diminishment, if hardly collapse, of American soft power as the hegemonic center of global culture. The second is about new models of the global imagination that, in the case of Japanese cool and its popularization around the world today, carry an attractive power but not one that is driven by or generates an attraction in others for the actual place or culture of the producing country. "Japan" does register in all this: itself a recent shift from the time when Japanese cultural products were marketed around the world by "deodorizing" their roots, a cultural influence that a number of Japanese critics have referred to as invisible colonization and that Iwabuchi has identified as cultural deodorization (2002:33). But, as described previously for American youth, it is not so much Japan itself as a compelling culture, power, or place that is signified (despite the fact that this is precisely what the Japanese government tries to capitalize on in all the rhetoric and attention currently given to Japan's new "soft power" in the globalization of J-pop). Rather, "Japan" operates more as signifier for a particular brand and blend of fantasy-ware: goods that inspire an imaginary space at once foreign and familiar and a subjectivity of continual flux and global mobility, forever moving into and out of new planes/powers/terrains/relations.

My third observation about the relationship between Japanese toys and the global imagination is that the current popularization of Japanese "cool" around the world is best understood in terms of its fantasy formation that, in turn, lends itself so productively to capitalistic marketing in the new millennium. As I argued at the start of *Millennial Monsters*, key here are the two qualities of polymorphous perversity (continual change and the stretching of desire across ever-new zones/bodies/products) and techno-animism (the forefronting of technology that is animated into spirits, creatures, and intimacies of various sorts). What emerges is a fantasy of perpetual transformation (humans who morph into Rangers, icons that "grow" into virtual pets) that, extended into the cyberfrontier, promises (New Age) companionship and connectedness albeit in a commodity form. Resonant with the fluctuation, fragmentation, and speedup facing postindustrial youth across the world, such a fantasy also becomes addictive, compelling players to keep changing and expanding their play frontiers through a capitalism of endless innovation, information, and acquisition. All this is certainly true of the four waves of products dealt with in this book.

To end, I merely add a note about the kind of fantasy enjoined here and its relationship to or signification by "Japan." If, indeed, the nature of global culture today is shifting away from one dominated and centered by the United States, it makes sense that cultures on the periphery would act as the movers and shakers in a new kind of decentered global imagination: one premised on dislocation and flux and on "losing" but also "finding" one's way in a terrain of endless change and regeneration. In the case of Japanese pop culture, what could be called its national imagination—mass fantasies reflecting the times and intended primarily for domestic rather than global sales—is filled with the same theme of uprootedness and disconnectedness.[1] The 2004 television *anime Mōsō Darinin* (Paranoia Agent) by Kon Satoshi, for example, traces the mass paranoia erupting in Tokyo over a mysterious boy on rollerblades *("shōnen batto")* who keeps attacking victims with a bat. Over the course of the thirteen episodes, most of the attention is paid not to the attacker but to the victims, who all share a nagging sense of anxiety over circumstances they seem hopelessly stuck in. A young designer of the recent fad in cute toys is cracking under the pressure to come up with a new concept; a boy who once excelled at everything is becoming unhinged by his classmates' suspicions that he is the *shōnen batto;* a woman leading a double life of demure teacher by day and wild prostitute at night is psychically unraveling. In all these cases, the victims have become mired in fantasies that are unsustainable—and the attacks come as a type of relief. So violence merges with imaginary existences and what is monstrous here is difficult to decipher.

The protagonists in *Mōsō Darinin* are characterized by yearning, loss, and the struggle for recognition. The same could be said of the less obviously edgy (and globally distributed) *Pokémon:* nomadic characters who are on the eternal quest to be "the world's greatest *pokémon* master": a path that is always somewhere but nowhere, and full of conquests but also contests that never end. There is something promising but also chilling in this capitalistic dreamworld. For, while the drive to press forward is ever present—winning more battles, keeping *tamagotchi* alive longer, getting (and getting) additional *pokémon*—one can never actually or definitively reach the goal, given that it is a frontier stretching out endlessly, into more *Rangers* toys, countless *Pokémon* Game Boy games, never-ending *Sailor Moon* play equipment. This is the formula for capitalism, of course: endless desire and continual deferment coming together in a cycle of consumptive repetition. In this, there is nothing new or particularly promising. Indeed, as noted in a 2003 report by Hakuhōdō on Japanese youth, a sense of "paralysis" about the future and interest in nothing beyond the immediacy of consumption characterizes girls (but less so boys) who have grown up in the anxious years of the post-Bubble (the report labels them the *shū kuri sedai,* or "sugar generation"). Such a paralytic sensibility is part and parcel of the capitalistic imagination embedded in the properties described in this book and exported far beyond Japan.

But there *is* something more promising and possibly new(er) as well in the imaginative strategies Japanese toys like *Pokémon* bring to the lives—both fantasy and real—of children who play with them. Continually morphing and disassembling (and reassembling) its parts is the signature of a *Sailor Moon* or *Yu-Gi-Oh!* play world: one that, as I have argued, offers kids a way of dealing with a world and identity premised on flux. This, too, though, could be said of most Marvel comics produced in the United States. More distinctive of the Japanese brand of fantasy morphability is techno-animism, which involves two components. First is the high degree of techno-interactivity in the play equipment (see chapter 8) that makes fantasy play ever more personally customizable and also prosthetic: games that are carried in one's pocket and whose (electronic/virtual) portal to the world is continuously open. Second is the profusion of polymorphous attachments: of nomadic humans finding new kinds of transhuman attachments, whether with digitalized pets, iconicized *pokémon*, or monsterish trading cards. Kids I know, both in Japan and in the United States, admit to finding in all this not only hours of great pleasure but also a fantasy world that has sustained and nourished them through what are often tough and lonely times.

Finally, of course, there is the significance and signification of Japan in the creation of a global imagination no longer dominated (or at least not so completely) by the United States. The attractive power at work here may be less for a real place than for the sense of displacement enjoined by the postindustrial condition of travel, nomadicism, and flux—generated and signified here by somewhere "not-the-United-States" but within the orbit of the globally familiar. Still, American hegemony is being challenged in the symbolic virtual medium of fantasy making. And in this I see a positive contribution to the cultural politics of global imaginings in millennial monsters and Japanese toys.

Notes

1. ENCHANTED COMMODITIES

1. Officially there were 150 *pokémon* to be caught in the original Game Boy game. In addition, though, there was one "secret" *pokémon* (Mew), increasing the real total to 151. I refer in the text here to 151 as the total, but I have included quotations that reference the number as 150. As I complete this manuscript in 2005, the number of pocket monsters has now increased to more than 300 with later Game Boy games.

2. I am not suggesting that the prominence of Japanese cultural goods in the global marketplace today is the only factor responsible for decentering the place of Euro-America in global styles, trends, and fantasy making.

3. This phenomenon, however, leaves out a sizable number of youth around the world today who lack the material or technological means to acquire toys like Game Boys and video games. Yet this does not mean that brand-name goods like *Pokémon* do not also spread far beyond the urban markets of the so-called first world (Pikachu has made it into a religious shrine in Ica, Peru, as a friend observed in June 2004, for example).

4. Writing about the trendiness of J-pop in East Asia today, Iwabuchi argues that "Japanization" is a very different model of cultural influence than "Americanization." Whereas the latter has carried strong associations with the United States and an American lifestyle (longings for which are consumed along with McDonald's, Coca-Cola, or Nike shoes), the former is tied less to Japan itself, and the passions incited are more for a particular aura of modernity and coolness than for a lifestyle conjured up as Japanese per se. In the context of the East Asian marketplace, Japan operates more as what he suggests is a hybrid(izing) or indigenizing power. Avid practitioners of glocalization (who localize their products to suit local tastes), Japanese media industries also use their resources to support and distribute local productions.

5. In the movie, Sen eats these rice balls when she first understands the enormity of her predicament—her parents will not be converted back into hu-

mans and none of them will be returned to the real world unless Sen works hard in the bathhouse and can manage to save them all. Disheartened, she is urged on by her friend, who insists she seek strength in the food and not give up. As she nibbles the rice, Sen starts to cry, and it is as much the tears as the sustenance (real and symbolic) provided by the food—and her commitment to *ganbaru*, not giving up—that is captured in the image of the rice balls, making them such a compelling and powerful symbol.

6. "Traditional" here is a construct: the rice balls are intended to represent a way of life and a cultural lifestyle that the movie portrays as both lost and (somewhat) retrievable. (I thank Susan Napier for this information about how *Sen to Chihiro no Kamikakushi* was promoted in Japan.)

7. *Pokémon: The First Movie* earned $52.1 million in revenues during the first year it ran in the States (Lippman 1999).

8. This also differed from *Princess Mononoke*, which, promoted as a children's movie in the United States, never brought in adults, who are a major contingent for Miyazaki films in Japan.

9. As in a child stimulated as much by throwing a stone as sucking a thumb, where these sensations neither build toward, nor are terminated by, a grand intensity—such as ejaculation—nor are directed to a specific, and specifically gendered, object choice. According to Freud's theory of sexuality (as laid out in *Three Essays on the Theory of Sexuality* [1910] 1963), children experience a type of sexuality that is much more plastic and malleable than adult sexuality, which, becoming anchored at the time of adolescence, is more definitively organized around a single erotogenic zone (genitals), a specific sexual aim (ejaculation for males, reproduction for females), and a particular object choice (of the opposite gender).

10. Freud's theory pertained to the sexuality of individuals, and it is not my aim to psychologize either Japanese toys or those who play with them in borrowing the concept of "polymophous perversity" here. Rather, I am speaking structurally of the organization of fantasy at work in a product like *Pokémon*, for which I find Freud's model to be a useful analytic.

11. According to Freud, sexual development is critically shaped by intrafamilial relations: the relations between the child's parents and those between the child and each parent. Presuming heterosexual, intact families, he argued that children start off closely attached to and attended by their mothers—a developmental period that coincides with polymorphous perversity. After infancy, the father assumes a greater role and presence in the child's life; he exerts social authority ("the name of the father," or what Lacan, in his retheorizing of Freud, has called the paternal signifier) and excludes the child from the (genitalic/reproductive) sexual relationship he shares with the child's mother. The familial drama has now moved from a dyadic to a triadic relationship, and navigating this shift—reorienting one's sexual energies to outside the family and de-anchoring it from the libidinal attachments to the mother—is what Freud believed was the most pivotal juncture in the path toward adulthood and adult sexuality.

12. Such a worldview predates the postwar period as well, of course, characterizing much in the way of Japanese folktales, legends, and myths (where women turn into cranes, lizards morph into children, and witches convert into dragons).

13. In the pregenital phases, prior to the navigation of the Oedipus complex, a child is far more attached to the mother than to the father, who assumes—for the time being—a more distant, peripheral role in the child's libidinal economy, according to Freud.

14. For example, characters look more Asian (fewer sprout blond hair or blue eyes), and story lines deal more with personal relationships and complex histories/worlds instead of offering high-tech special effects—Hollywood's trademark. More than anything, it is the cuteness (and the kind of cuteness) projected by Japanese characters that has garnered the huge Asian market; Mickey Mouse and Donald Duck are simply not cute, explains Dick Lee, a vice president for Sony Music's Asia division (*Newsweek*, November 8, 1999).

15. Some countries, such as South Korea, banned the importation of Japanese cultural goods such as *manga* and *anime* and lifted the ban only in 1998.

16. See Iwabuchi Kōichi's book *Recentering Globalization: Popular Culture and Japanese Transnationalism* (2002) for further discussion of the *mukokuseki* policy attached to Japanese cultural exports in the postwar era and the dynamics this has assumed in inter-Asian marketing.

17. As in Quentin Tarantino's 2003 movie *Kill Bill*, in which two U.S. actresses spend the final battle scene in Japan speaking Japanese to each other. And, on Saturday-morning television, *Xiaolin Showdown*—a Warner Brothers production released in fall 2003—much of the story takes place in China, with four lead characters: a Texan cowboy, a Chinese monk-in-training, a J-pop hipster girl, and a street-smart Brazilian.

18. By New Age, I mean contemporary technologies that accompany, and mark, the end of the twentieth century and cross over into the twenty-first, as the era of digital, informational, electronic, and surveillance machines.

19. Participants in this discourse include marketers, manufacturers, educators, commentators, and reporters—I refer to much of this later in the book.

20. Renato Rosaldo coined the phrase "imperialist nostalgia" to speak of such longing for a past that one's own imperialist/capitalist regimes have systematically eroded. Japan's toy industry is an agent of such imperialist nostalgia, I would argue, in that it actively promotes nostalgia for the past in marketing its goods (a nostalgia that parents and adults are far more susceptible to than children, obviously), all the while fully investing in capitalism and commoditization: the forces said to have promoted transparent materialism and eroded traditional communitarianism.

21. When Freud's grandson was about the age of two, he would engage in a ritual whenever his mother left the house: throwing away a spool, then retrieving it—which he accompanied with the words *fort/da* (here/there). In Freud's interpretation, the game was a type of fantasy with which the boy overcame the anxiety caused by the absence of his mother by symbolically reproducing both

her departure and her return. Important in this model of fantasy is its repetitive nature, which rehearses not only the boy's mastery over his loss, but also the loss (and presumably the anxiety this causes) itself. This analogy can be applied to a game like *Pokémon*, in which, to achieve the goal of the game (acquiring 151 *pokémon*), the same dynamic (battling new *pokémon* in order to defeat and thus capture them) is staged over and over again. But the sense of abundance and mastery so many players associate with *Pokémon* does not merely compensate for the losses and lacks incurred by growing up (serving as a fantasy in Freud's sense or what Lacan calls a "petit objet a"). Rather, following the work of Deleuze and Guattari, we could say the desire for acquisition so fetishistically replayed here is produced with its own libidinal economy and as an addictive pleasure (one always wants more and more) that feeds/is fed by the structure of capitalism (Deleuze and Guattari 1977; Holland 1999).

22. All translations from Japanese in *Millennial Monsters* are mine unless otherwise noted. I also follow Japanese name order, placing the family name first.

2. FROM ASHES TO CYBORGS

1. I wish to underscore the fact that, whereas technology became a cornerstone of the postwar state in Japan, there were older intellectual and politico-economic roots to its national embrace. From before the Tokugawa period (1603–1868) until 1945, technology and capital were geared to defense production, which, in turn, generated commercial manufacturing. As Richard Samuels argues, technology was "a matter of national security," constituting a "bundle of beliefs and practices" he calls "technonationalism" (1994:33). This was the ideology of wartime Japan, but also the national policy of the Meiji state as Japan industrialized and "modernized" with incredible rapidity starting in the second half of the 1800s. I do not mean to imply, therefore, that 1945 ushered in a totally new and newly technologized Japan, with no antecedents in the past. Japan was an advanced industrial technopower before (and for much of) the war, and its "miraculous" postwar recovery was neither an anomaly nor due to U.S. assistance alone. There were continuities between prewar and postwar Japan, and I agree with those scholars who argue against reifying the ruptures of 1945. Yet, despite major technological buildup before the war, technonationalism radically changed its scope (with radical implications) after the war. Technology was now put to the service of building national prosperity rather than defending or expanding the nation, and from a strict policy of domestic production *(koku-sanka)*, Japan began to allow the importation of foreign technology on a new scale. And to this end—and proving to yield national growth if not an equity in individual "success" or benefits, as Laura Hein has so correctly pointed out (1993)—a policy of industrial "rationalization" was adopted that encouraged technological innovation and implementation at multiple levels (Partner 1999).

2. The repetition here of the number 4 may be linked to the fact that the word for four *(shi)* in Japanese sounds like that for death.

3. As High rightly notes, the occupying forces also went overboard in this judgment, burning massive reams of wartime-made Japanese films at an airfield on the banks of the Tama River between April and May 1946. Included were not only war movies but also a number of *jidaigeki* (erroneously categorized as military films) feared to be "subject to misuse" (High 2003:505).

4. See, for example, Nakazawa Shin'ichi 1999:33–72 (in Japanese).

5. This is true of RoboCop in the Hollywood trilogy, for example: a high-tech cop machine rebuilt from the organic remains of the slain police officer, Murphy (see Allison 2001).

6. As Simon Partner has pointed out, foreign technology (mainly from the States) came in multiple forms: in product technologies but also technologies of mass production, distribution, and marketing (as in adopting American management styles). Despite the huge role this importation of foreign technology played in postwar Japan, accounting for 22.4 percent of Japanese economic growth between the years 1953 and 1971, according to one scholar (quoted in Partner 1999:108), Japan was not exactly a "blank slate" in 1945, having culled its technology during wartime, which, as Partner characterizes it, was a "period of rapid development and learning" (110).

7. This opinion was not universally shared, however. Some critics found the film crude in terms of both story and technical production, lamenting its association with a Japan trying to remake itself and its image in the eyes of the rest of the world after the war (Tsutsui 2004).

8. The 1984 film brought Gojira back as the main character and, like the original, was also entitled *Gojira*. Between and after these films, an array of other monsters made their debut, including Gigantis, Mothra, Biollante, Mechagodzilla, Gigan, and Rodan. For a good history of the entire genre in English, see Kalat 1997, Ryfle 1998, and Tsutsui 2004.

9. Tri-Star Pictures is a division of Columbia that was bought by Sony in 1989. Despite the fears raised when this move was negotiated that Japan would be taking over the minds of American kids, it is obvious that, with *Godzilla* at least, Sony did little to make the cultural coding more Japanese than American.

10. *Manga Shōnen* was founded by Katō Ken'ichi, the former editor of a prewar magazine designed for children: *Shōnen Club* (Schodt 1988a).

11. During wartime, the Japanese economy had been restructured away from textiles toward heavy industry for military use, and by 1945 it could not supply consumer goods. Marking the failure of its domestic production policy, Japan reoriented its technonationalism after the war toward growth by implementing a rationalization plan geared to the production of sophisticated (high-value-added) export goods. After attempting to upgrade its coal industry (an effort that failed), then its iron and steel industries (a success), it turned its attention to the electronics industry and also the automobile industry in the 1950s and '60s (Partner 1999; Hein 1993).

12. In the same year, West Germany had 12,400; France, 5,270; and Sweden, 2,380. The figures (also from 1986) are even more striking for density of robots

to population of workers: Japan, 100.7 (per 10,000 workers); the United States, 11.5; West Germany, 14.4; France, 14.2; and Sweden, 38.7 (Schodt 1988b:15–16).

13. The manufacturer was Tezuka Productions (from the "Tezuka Osamu Character Series").

14. These are also called the three S's *(senpūki, sentakuki, suihanki)*, with matching triumverates for the 1960s (the three C's: *kaa, kūraa, karaa terebi* [car, air conditioner, color television]) and the 1970s (the three J's: jewels, *jetto* [overseas travel], *jūtaku* [one's own house]; Kelly 1993:195).

15. The workload of *manga* artists increased about four times because of the weekly production schedule, but sales skyrocketed as well. The weekly sales of *Shōnen Magazine* were more than one million in 1966; for *Shōnen Jump* and *Shōnen Champion*, weekly sales exceeded two million in 1978; and for *Shōnen Jump*, they were over four million in 1984. Given that approximately three people read each purchased *manga*, the figures for readership are even higher (Schodt 1988a:67).

16. In the original story by Shelley, however, Frankenstein was depicted more as a sad and pathetic creature, a loner repulsive to others due to the failings of his inventor in crafting him. Of the more than forty-five movies made about Frankenstein, some are truer to Shelley's original than others, but the overall trend has been toward a greater demonization of the monster, making it into something more horrific. (I thank Kathy Rudy for her insights about this.)

17. Japanese *manga* and *anime* are well known for their large, saucer-eyed characters. This convention is attributed to Tezuka, who borrowed it, some say, from Disney (though, in Tezuka's hands, eyes became exaggerated and are used as vehicles to show a range of emotions, from excitement to sadness).

18. A new cartoon version for television of *Astro Boy* came out in Japan in 2003 and was aired by Warner Brothers on U.S. television in January 2004. After only three episodes, however, WB pulled it because of its poor ratings.

19. In 1997, *manga* accounted for 38 percent of all titles published in Japan and 22 percent of all publishing revenues. Considered very lucrative, the domestic *manga* market was earning three times that of the film industry by the 1990s, having started its rapid rise in the early 1960s (in 1965, total annual magazine sales were about 200 million, going to almost 700 million in 1975 and 900 million in 1975 [Kinsella 2000:42]).

3. MILLENNIAL JAPAN

1. Anti-Americanism also existed during this period, as Yoshimi is well aware, and it crystallized around protests against the U.S.-Japan Security Treaty signed in 1960.

2. While these principles became generalized, some of them (lifetime employment in particular) were adopted only by large companies and applied only to certain ranks and categories of workers (white-collar, full-time workers, not part-time workers or subcontractors).

3. This is literal as well as figurative, as in the masterpieces mothers design

in the *obentō* they pack for children attending nursery school: nutritionally balanced multicourse feasts, all miniaturized and artistically stylized—food shaped in the likeness of polar bears, media characters, tulips, clowns—for young tastes. As I have argued, these artworks, embedded in daily food, also carry an ideological message: that children should, like their mothers, work hard and follow the clean lines and careful detail of these lunch boxes (Allison 2000:81–104).

4. Rebecca Mead has written an interesting article on the trends and consumerism of youth fashion in Tokyo (2002). To showcase the article, the cover of the magazine(see figure 4) is a cartoon of a Japanese woman dressed in a *Pokémon*-motifed kimono holding a handful of cell phones: a commentary on how fashion bleeds into technology into character fetishism in millennial Japan.

5. This epoch was given various labels by politicians, pundits, and "new academics," such as "the age of culture" *(bunka no jidai)*, "information society" *(jōhōka shakai)*, and "posthistoric Japan" *(rekishi no shūen)* (Yoda 2000:646).

6. Originally published in the monthly journal *Bungei*, *Nantonaku Kurisutaru* (Somehow, Crystal) sold more than eight hundred thousand copies and, despite being critically panned, earned the prestigious Akutagawa Prize for new writers. Tracking a two-week period in the life of a college student and the fling she has before her boyfriend returns, the book showcases the consumerist lifestyle of its characters in terms of the brand-name boutiques, restaurants, shoe stores, florists, and cafés they shop at and the items they purchase—cataloged here in voluminous notes. As pointed out by Norma Field (1989) in her critical analysis of the novel, its popularity stemmed almost entirely from the brand-name information the book not only disseminated but also crafted into an aesthetics of "atmosphere" ("crystal") to define Japanese postmodernity in the 1980s.

7. For an excellent overview of such commentaries on millennial Japan and what, she proposes, is a convergence between neoliberals and neoconservatives, see Yoda 2000.

8. This attitude among young people was pointed out to me by my twenty-two-year-old research assistant, recently graduated from Sophia University and employed at a part-time job. In her mind this was the general mind-set and malaise of Japanese youth: something that I was often told by child experts and scholars when investigating *Pokémon*.

9. At the start of the film, the screen informs audiences that the nation has collapsed, there is 15 percent unemployment, and eight hundred thousand kids have boycotted school. When the scene then opens onto a schoolyard, it is soon apparent that youth are not only the perpetuators but also the victims of violence. By orders of the state (under the Millennial Educational Reform Act), one class of ninth graders is chosen each year to perform a survivalist game on a deserted island, where each must kill or be killed until only one youth remains alive. Under the guidance of their teacher, played by Kitano ("Beat") Takeshi, the youth start to rebel against the state, and plenty of killing and violence is enacted in the process. The movie was a huge hit among young people; a *manga* series came out the same year, and scores of tie-in products (card games, video

games) were generated. There was also considerable commentary in the press about the seeming valorization of youth crime as portrayed in *Battle Royale* (see Arai 2001).

10. I am defining *monster* here as an entity that defies the borders of normalcy. That is, given the parameters of "normal" at a particular period of time and as understood by the law, conventions, or cultural categories of a particular society, acts or beings that transgress these boundaries are considered to be, in some sense of the word, monstrous.

11. One of the proponents of this thesis is Kawakami Ryōichi, the author of *Gakkō Hōkai* (see Arai 2001 for discussion).

12. This finding is disputed, however, by the work of Nakajima, Himeno, and Yoshii, who, based on surveys they conducted with young *keitai* users in the late 1990s, have argued that Japanese youth tend to use their cell phones to maintain communication with no more than ten close friends, a pattern they refer to as "full-time intimate community" (quoted in Matsuda 2005:30). For Japanese scholarship on *keitai* usage in English, see Ito, Okabe, and Matsuda 2005.

13. *Jizo* is a bodhisattva, an incarnation of the Buddha that has renounced Enlightenment in order to guide lesser beings through the stages and realms of creation. In Japan, *jizo* statues appear in Buddhist temples, typically in the form of a bald Buddhist monk with simple features.

4. MIGHTY MORPHIN POWER RANGERS

1. As noted in the previous chapter, the period of high-speed growth peaked with the oil crisis in 1973, and growth subsequently slowed, yet impressive economic gains were made nonetheless.

2. Female orgasm is much less clearly or visually known than male orgasm, and ejaculation is harder to pin down in a graphic representation than is the erect male penis or semen. For these reasons, as well as the fact that there have been more inhibitions and social prohibitions against female sexuality in the West, Freud, as well as others, has argued that there is a fascination in regard to "what women want." Williams calls this a "secret" here, tracing how this has been dealt with and variously "solved" in literature, film, and pornography.

3. *Henshin* comes originally from the Buddhist transmutation of deities into human shape in order to better teach Buddhism to mortals.

4. Both Kōdansha and Shōgakukan put out what are called "television picture books" *(terebi ehon)* that sell for 350 or 400 yen. There are also a number of monthly children's magazines, with segmented audiences (toddler, first to third grade, and fourth to sixth grade, and separate magazines for boys and girls), that include pictures, graphs, stories, quizzes, exercises, make-your-own toys to assemble, and plenty of ads for toys that are based, mainly or exclusively, on television shows.

5. I was told this by a number of toy executives both in Japan (from Tomy and Bandai) and in the United States (Hasbro).

6. I have written about this extensively, as mentioned earlier, in *Permitted and Prohibited Desires: Mothers, Comics, and Censorship in Japan*, 81–104.

7. Nagai Gō, who, starting out with *Mazinger Z*, went on to create numerous robot series, most as animated cartoons on TV, lamented the pressure he felt from the sponsors of these shows to create characters that would sell toys. "Toy companies said they needed more characters in each story so they could sell more toys, so I complied by creating a series *Getta Robotto*, where one hero robot disassembled into three smaller ones" (cited in Schodt 1988b:84).

8. Loesch has said, "As a child I loved the old *Godzilla* movies. I couldn't get enough of them. It didn't matter if I could see the wires and the seams in the costumes and the lips moving when the words didn't—they were so fanciful and imaginative" (*Los Angeles Times*, November 25, 1993).

9. This is an argument made for karaoke by Hosokawa Shūhei (which I present in chapter 6 on *tamagotchi*). Hosokawa has also written an excellent article on the Walkman (1984).

10. These figures, however, have also been both disputed and kept something of a secret. Saban has cited costs as high as $600,000 per show for these original programs. But cheapness was definitely a major factor fueling interest for Saban and probably aided Margaret Loesch's willingness to sign the program on for Fox.

11. From the Web site www.characterproducts.com, posted on July 21, 2003.

12. I concluded this after talking with fans and also reading reviews in fanzines and on the Net. I did less systematic interviewing with fans of *Rangers* than with fans of the other waves of children's entertainment examined in this book (*Sailor Moon, tamagotchi*, and *Pokémon*).

13. Jameson calls this "historicism"—looking to the past for styles that are adopted without history or without a purpose. Citing Henri Lefebvre, he also speaks about the random cannibalization of all styles from the past that are adopted in an increasing primacy placed on the "neo" (1991:18).

14. I have written about this elsewhere in reference to violent cyborgs: movies like *RoboCop* and morphing superheroes like *Sailor Moon* (Allison 2001).

15. Interview at Bandai America headquarters, summer 1995.

5. FIERCE FLESH

1. Not all girl heroes start off as humans and morph into other stages. Some, particularly in *manga* and *anime*, are cyborgs, robots, or aliens, either built as *mecha* to begin with or born into a nonhuman species. Still, transformation (*henshin*) remains a central trope in media stories featuring girl heroes, and the display of bodies is a universal.

2. There are slight gender differences. Girls may wear earrings or have slightly different lines on their uniforms, in colors that tend to be yellow and pink.

3. This was a deviation from the normal pattern, in which usually the

manga comes first and is remade as a television cartoon only later, after its popularity has been established. In the case of *Pokémon,* this pattern was altered again. After the *Pokémon* Game Boy game appeared in February 1996 and showed promise of becoming a fad, a *manga* version was launched in the summer at the start of what became a cascading mixed-media production (including trading cards, a cartoon, a movie, books, and other merchandise).

4. The story is complicated and weaves in and out—as is characteristic of multivolume *manga* and long-running *anime*—of different time periods, geographic spaces, sets of relationships, and changing subplots. In terms of time alone, the scene continually shifts from the future to the past, so Usagi's relationships—with fellow Scouts, Prince Endymion/Darien/Tuxedo, and her daughter, Chibi-chan—change as well. Throughout all these shifts, however, she remains physically much the same: a fourteen-year-old schoolgirl whose alter ego is Sailor Moon.

5. There were boy viewers and fans of the show (some of whom I met) in Japan, but *Sailor Moon* was mainly categorized, including by its sponsor, Bandai, as a girl-targeted show. When I asked Bandai executives about this in Tokyo in 1995, they said the toy merchandise was "fashion dolls" and of interest only to girls.

6. Judith Butler, an important feminist scholar of gender, also argues that change to gender categories (and power in general) can come only from within ideological frameworks: from reworkings, remappings, and rearticulations that "play" with the borders rather than directly contest them from the outside (1990, 1993).

7. As in the setting red sun (symbolizing the national flag of Japan) at the end of the *Ōrenjā* episode synopsized at the beginning of chapter 4.

8. Women have been expected to be every bit the self-sacrificing, hardworking employees that men have been in postwar Japan, but their main responsibility has been the unpaid laborer position of mother. Maintaining the home and, most important, overseeing the upbringing (in their role as "education mothers," *kyōiku mama*) of children, women who do enter the workforce can often afford the time to do so only at part-time jobs for which benefits and wages are low. Also, Japanese men have been notoriously slow at assuming domestic responsibilities. This stems in part from the expectation that workers should make the job their number one responsibility, staying late at night, working overtime, and going out to drink with coworkers. (My first two books are both on this subject; the first is on the nightlife drinking that corporate men engage in as part of their jobs and fantasy lives [Allison 1994], and the second is on the role mothers play in the real and imaginary lives of postwar Japanese [Allison 2000].)

9. See discussion in chapter 3. Scholars who have written on cuteness and the *shōjo* fetish(ization) include Treat 1993, 1995; Kinsella 2002; Ueno 1998; and Miyadai 1999.

10. I use *symptom* here in the Freudian sense of something that sprouts up as a sign of internal disease but also as a mechanism the body/psyche uses to combat the same disease.

11. I am referring here to concepts and developments in 1980s and '90s Japan, laid out in chapter 3.

12. *Interpellate* is the word used by Louis Althusser to denote how ideology "hails" us with certain identities, such as gender, race, class, and nationality (1971).

13. Fiore's desires are mainly for friendship, but there is definitely a homo-erotic tinge here, particularly since he seems so jealous of Darien's girlfriend, Usagi/Sailor Moon.

14. As Hori Takahiro has pointed out, the story here does not add up. If Ricca's mother is thirty-three, she could not have a daughter old enough to be working as a stewardess. Also, Ricca is sometimes referred to as the firstborn child in the family (Hori 1996:80–81).

15. Although 40 percent of Japanese women currently work, their wages are only 65 percent those of their male counterparts (one of the largest gaps in the industrial world), and their percentages in specific professions are low as well: only 7.3 percent hold office in the Diet, and of civil service workers, 20 percent are women, but only 1.4 percent hold managerial positions (French 2003:A3).

16. Takara tried exporting her (to the United States, for example, under the name Lisa) but was never successful.

17. "Sailor Moon" is the title that has been given to the cartoon, comic, movies, and adventure figures, though this term includes the constellation of characters involved: the five Sailor Scouts (later, ten), plus Chibi-chan (called Rini in English), Tuxedo Mask, and the evil Queen Beryl.

18. The game did sensationally well, becoming the highest-selling game among girls to date.

19. As I finish this book in 2005, however, the situation has significantly changed. Miyazaki Hayao's *anime* are now well known and much loved by crit-ics and fans in the United States (*Spirited Away* won an Oscar in 2002 for best animated movie, and *Howl's Moving Castle*, released in 2005, inspired *New York Times* film critic A. O. Scott to call Miyazaki "the world's greatest living animated-filmmaker" (2005: sec. 2, p. 1). On Saturday-morning television as well, the networks are now filled with Japanese cartoons and programming that are identifiably from an Asian country (with Japanese script, temples, and rice balls all left in the image). I discuss this issue at greater length in the epilogue.

20. Survey conducted among girls age eight to fourteen; the last two replies are from a thirty-one-year-old woman and a thirty-six-year-old man. My re-search on *Sailor Moon* concentrated more on fans than on producers and mar-keters (to whom I gave more emphasis with *Pokémon*, for example). This sec-tion thus includes more fan responses than do other parts of the book, as well as a more concentrated examination of fan interest.

21. This age has been getting progressively younger; the peak age for play-ing with Barbie dolls is now about age five, and by eight, girls are turning away from dolls altogether.

22. Most of my research comes from 1998–99 in the United States, when I conducted intensive interviews with five teenage girls, led discussions in two

undergraduate classes I was teaching at Duke, taught a class on Japanese *anime* at a middle school in Durham, North Carolina (where one of our main subjects was *Sailor Moon*), and carried out a survey on the Internet (and closely examined the replies of three hundred respondents of both genders who varied in age, nationality, and geographic location).

23. This is a complaint often heard from fans *(otaku)* of Japanese *anime*, particularly when the shows have been dubbed and edited. Protesting such adjustment to American standards, tastes, and sometimes censorship (violence, nudity, and sexuality are all much more censored by U.S. TV than is the case in Japan), fans often seek out the original Japanese product, which they circulate on their own for the purity and authenticity of the story and images.

6. TAMAGOTCHI

1. *Tamagotchi*, in Japanese, stands for both the singular (toy/pet) and the plural. I follow this usage here.

2. Bandai was suffering from a decrease in global sales brought about by waning interest in *Power Rangers* and the failure of *Sailor Moon* in the United States.

3. By December 1996, total sales were 400,000 items, which rose to 10 million by July 1997 and 13 million by October 1997 (Yokoi 1997). Spring 1998 was a boom season; 20 million were sold in Japan and almost an equal number abroad. A Game Boy version also came out (selling about 3 million, mainly to boys) as well as a PC version, in both Windows 95 and Macintosh (selling about 250,000 copies). By later the same year, however, the *tamagotchi* fad died (and far quicker than Bandai had predicted). Stocked merchandise in several countries had to be disposed of, leading to a loss of 6 billion yen for Bandai (Nagao 1999:227–28, 235).

4. Yokoi Akihiro was an independent toy inventor who sold his idea for the *tamagotchi* to Bandai on November 23, 1996. He completed the final game system for the product, but other Bandai employees worked on different aspects. Shirotsubaka Yōko, often identified as *tamagotchi*'s creator, did all the basic designs of the characters, for example, and Mizugaki Junko, who designed the package, did investigative research on toy and fashion trends among teenage girls that contributed to final designs and marketing (Yokoi 1997).

5. This is the brilliance of the Walkman, which, otherwise, was technologically a less (rather than more) sophisticated tape recorder than what Sony was already producing. For this reason, many of Morita's top executives and engineers were opposed to its development (Hosokawa 1984).

6. The likeness was intended to look amateurish, with an image that anyone could copy (Yokoi 1997).

7. Whereas the original *tamagotchi* is simply a pet that keeps growing bigger, the "boy" version entails raising *tamagotchi* that will fight competitively against another *tamagotchi*.

8. This is a big difference from *Power Rangers*, for example, in which the Japanese actors and their Japanese names were entirely Americanized for U.S. transmission.

9. These small books are carried by women both during their pregnancies (when visiting their obstetrician) and after birth (when taking their infants to the pediatrician) and are used to record all the major growth signs of the fetus/baby.

10. In Japan, electronic game systems like Game Boys and video games (for television and computer) are played far more by boys than by girls. But in the field of handheld electronic games such as Tetris, girls (starting in middle school) are bigger owners as well as players. For this reason, when designing the *tamagotchi*, Bandai sent out one of its staff to observe teenage girls. Confirming patterns of consumption and trendsetting discussed in the last chapter, Mizugaki Junko read the teen girls' magazine *PuchiSebun*, visited the trendy haunts of Shibuya (Tower Records) and Ginza (Sony Plaza), and, noticing the fad of girls carrying Mini Tetris games on key chains, came up with the idea that *tamagotchi* too should come on a key chain (Yokoi 1997:89).

11. Associating Western symbols with fantasy is a common explanation for the heavy predominance of Western (and mainly Caucasian) bodies in *manga* and *anime* as well, as discussed in chapter 2.

12. According to Nagao Takeshi, Bandai targeted the *tamagotchi* to youth twelve years and older because "they know the importance of life and can assume the responsibility of owning pets" (1999:234).

13. I did individual interviews with five teenage girls in Boulder, Colorado, in the summer of 1997 and a group interview with ten children (from age eight to ten, boys and girls) the following spring in Durham, North Carolina.

14. The pause button was, in fact, installed later because so many teachers and parents complained about how intrusive and disruptive the toy was.

15. MUD is the acronym for "Multi-User Dungeons"—a class of virtual worlds that includes Trek Muse and LambdaMOO.

16. This is something I heard repeatedly in Japan about the overmanaged child in the era of "the enterprise society." This was often articulated in terms of children "lacking a space of their own": a logic given for *hikikomori* (social shut-ins) as well as for the appeal of mobile entertainment fads like *tamagotchi* and *Pokémon* (played on electronic game sets that travel in one's pocket). See chapter 3 for discussion of *hikikomori*.

17. Yokoi has also said that taking care of a pet involves chores, such as cleaning up a pet's droppings, that may be unpleasant, but that the player who fails to fulfill these duties is "terrible." Acquiring the skills, responsibility, and sensitivity for such work is one of the aims of *tamagotchi*, but he also has given this labor a playful quality by rendering it "cute." If poop—and cleaning it up—is displayed in a cute way, players might like it, Yokoi figured. This "cutification" process is an issue raised again with *Pokémon* (1997:78–79).

18. In the Freudian sense, a fetish covers over a sight/site troubling to the boy—his mother's genitals, which, as he now realizes, lack a penis. Replacing this lack in reality with a stand-in (fur, jewelry, high heels), the fetish is premised on ambiguity: it is both an absence and a presence at the same time (Freud 1961).

19. Sherry Turkle has noted that this very ambiguity allows people to "work through" personal and interpersonal issues by "playing" with a medium in which they can try on and assume different roles or identities. Studying fans of the role-playing game *Dungeons and Dragons*, for example, she notes how commonly they experience this play as constructive and not simply as a "place of escape"—the view given virtual reality by much academic writing. Rather than a mere escape, a game like *Dungeons and Dragons* stands "betwixt and between, both in and not in real life." In the words of one experienced player: "You are the character and you are not the character both at the same time"—an ambiguity making virtual reality a useful tool for addressing issues of both intimacy and identity (Turkle 1994:161).

20. Yokoi uses the word *communication (tsūshin)* to describe the relationship formed both between a player and her *tamagotchi* ("the act of owning a pet means the communication of life between the pet and its owner") and between humans for whom *tamagotchi*—as something to discuss, bond over, and share information about—becomes a means of and for establishing friendships (Yokoi 1997:140). "Communication" is central in the discourse surrounding *Pokémon* as well, as we shall see.

21. The *tamagotchi* has been revived, however, with two new versions. The Tamagotchi Connexion ("Connection" for the Euro-American market) was released in 2004 and, fitted with an infra-port on the top, enables two *tamagotchi* to talk with each other, become friends, exchange gifts, and—if one is female and the other male—to procreate. After the product quickly sold out, Bandai came out with a Connexion (Connection) Version 2 in 2005 that, in addition to the interactive functions of the 2004 model, allows kids to earn "Gotchi" points to shop for special items, toys, and food.

22. Furby was a megahit, grossing more than $100 million in 1999. It also, like *tamagotchi*, was publicly banned in certain places (hospitals and airlines for Furby, schools for *tamagotchi*) because, in the interests of simulating a live pet, no on/off switch was installed, making its sounds and responses virtually nonstop.

23. NEW *hāti* is one of those Japanese names that combines and transforms English words in interesting ways. *Hāti* probably stands for "hearty," as in "heartfelt."

24. See chapter 4.

7. POKÉMON

1. Following is the basic gist of how to play the original Game Boy game. When starting the *Pokémon* game, the player is faced with three choices: what to name one's character (the human-looking figure who will serve as the player's proxy in the game), what to name one's (human) rival in the game, and which *pokémon* to start with. Of the three, the last is the most important because this is the player's first weapon in achieving the game's goal: capturing all 150 (actually 151) wild monsters (that, once caught, become tamed or "pocketed" by their owners). A player must first find Professor Oak—the world's

foremost expert on *Pokémon*ology—who offers three choices for starter *pokémon:* Bulbasaur (grass type), Charmander (fire type), or Squirtle (water type). Each has different strengths and potentials (Bulbasaur increases its power levels more quickly, for example), and once the choice is made, the game commences. Manipulating the controls/icons of the Game Boy, players navigate the multiplaned and multisited world of *Pokémon*—towns, forests, mountains, amusement zones filled with houses, grass, ponds, minerals, *pokémon* centers, *Pokémarts* that house both the object of the game's quest (wild *pokémon*) and also the means (the tools, weapons, and secrets) of acquiring them.

The art of capturing *pokémon* is complex and becomes increasingly so as the game proceeds. The most basic strategy is engaging a wild monster in a competitive match (called *taisen* in Japanese): trying to outmaneuver the *pokémon* and, by therefore weakening it, then overcoming it with—one of the most common ploys—a *Poké*-ball (there are also other items, weapons, attacks, and secrets that can be used as devices in battling *pokémon*). Only monsters can fight other monsters; thus, once a *pokémon* is acquired, it becomes part of the player's arsenal of weapons. (Players must use strategy in deciding which *pokémon* to fight against which: this involves a complicated calculus rooted, originally, in which typology or species each *pokémon* is—water, grass, flame, rock, bug, ice—and determining their strengths and weaknesses; water trumps fire, for example.) *Pokémon* change upon accumulating victories; they get stronger, gain more attacks, and, in some cases, evolve into more advanced developmental states. Players must learn how to manipulate these changes to strengthen their *pokémon* (and, by thereby acquiring more and more, approach the goal of the game of catching all 151 *pokémon* and becoming a *"pokémon* master").

Prima's Official Strategy Guide sums up the *Pokémon* game this way: "Its appeal lies in the fact that there's always something new to do or accomplish. It's never boring and there are always new challenges awaiting you on the horizon. You can fight against established trainers for badges that will boost your abilities in some way or explore caves for treasure or rare, legendary Pokémon. Even those 'Random Battles' prove helpful when you're scouring the countryside for new Wild Pokémon or trying to get a favorite monster to its next evolution point. And the portable size of the Game Boy means you can take it with you anywhere!" (quoted in Hollinger 1998:ii).

2. The games have been sold by Nintendo in 141 countries, the cartoon has been broadcast in 51 countries, the movies have played in 33 countries, and the cards have been translated into nine languages.

3. The *Pokémon* craze peaked in 1997–98 in Japan and 1998–99 in the United States but remained vibrant—fed by new waves of Game Boy game editions, movies, cartoons, and other tie-in merchandise—until 2001–02 in both countries. In 2003, it was somewhat rejuvenated again by the newest Game Boy game editions as well as a fifth movie. In this chapter, I refer to the *Pokémon* craze mainly in the past tense. When speaking more generically about *Pokémon*, however, I use the present tense.

4. This is true of *Pokémon* in its cartoon iteration, where Pikachu is Satoshi's main monster. In the game version, however, Pikachu is only one of 151 *poké-mon*, and a player's attention is far more decentralized away from any particular *pokémon*. I address the issue of Pikachu at greater length later in the chapter.

5. Of course, the names do sound Japanese, though none is an actual place in Japan.

6. This figure was given me by Kubo Masakazu, executive producer in the character business planning section of Shōgakukan Inc., the publishers of *Korokoro Komikku*.

7. Many of these guidebooks are jointly published, in fact, by Nin-tendo/Creatures Inc./GAME FREAK Inc. There are also a host of unofficial guides to *Pokémon* cards, games, and products.

8. The title page of the book itself is illustrated with a *Poké*-dex (handheld computer for inputting *pokémon* data) and is followed by six sections: the "en-cyclopedia" of pocket monsters (accounts of the *pokémon* typologies/imaged by a *Poké*-ball); pocket monsters' "fields and dungeons" (maps and grids of *Poké-mon* world/folding map); pocket monsters' "data file" (charts of monster statis-tics/Satoshi standing in front of a computer); "communication with pocket monsters" (strategies for matches and trades/Satoshi on his bicycle); pocket monsters' "journal" (lectures by Professor Oak and a *pokémon* expert/futuris-tic headgear computer); and pocket monsters' "staff roll" (interviews with the creative staff of *Pokémon*/another futuristic headgear with lens).

9. This comes in the section "Pokémon journal" with two "public lectures," one by Professor Oak, in which he addresses the issue of what, precisely, pocket monsters *are*. When he dismisses the notion that they are a race, this is on the grounds that, for one, *pokémon* evolve and thereby change their basic nature. The word for "monster" he uses here (as in "They aren't merely monsters") is *kaijū* (1997:130).

10. For the two pages on extinct *pokémon*, for example, there are five entries like that for *Aum Naito*, no. 139: "It lived in the ancient sea and is a living being friendly with shellfish and cuttlefish. It swims with 10 legs and eats plankton and small fish. A whirlfish *pokémon*, Aum Naito is classified, first, as a rock type and, second, as a water type. It is 0.4 m in height and 7.5 kg in weight" (1997:49).

11. In his classic ethnography *Argonauts of the Western Pacific* (1961), Ma-linowski described a two-tiered system of exchange on the Argonaut Islands: one in which precious items are exchanged not for keep but for marking social relations, and the other, far more utilitarian, in which items are bartered for their value and benefit to the user.

12. When Japan modernized, adherence to Western notions of rationality and science spread throughout the country, as mentioned previously. Though "irrational" beliefs (as in otherwordly creatures) were scrutinized and censored in the process, they also survived, albeit in altered forms. As Freud has argued about dreams, the unconscious gives expression to emotions and desires that are socially proscribed, and thus repressed, in conscious everyday life. What is con-

sciously repressed never fully expires, and its effects live on, often "returning" in profound ways. In *Pokémon* there is such a "return of the repressed" of otherworldly creatures.

13. A sign of how this phenomenon of "criminal youth" has continued to haunt both the reality and the imagination of public culture in Japan is a movie made about this very incident that was released in summer 2005. Titled *Jūnana sai no Fūkei* (The Landscape of a Seventeen-Year-Old) and made by director Wakamatsu Kōji, the story focuses entirely on the road trip (fictionalized here as a solitary bike trek) the boy embarks upon after killing his mother. There is little dialogue, only the barest of flashbacks to the killing itself, and no explanation or even exploration of the motives compelling the boy's violence.

8. "GOTTA CATCH 'EM ALL"

1. The show's name combines *oha* (from the Japanese word for "good morning," *ohayō*) and *sutā* (the anglicized word for "star," because the three main anchors for the show are considered pop celebrities).

2. As pointed out by Iwabuchi (2002), the United States also dominates global distribution channels; this is a long-standing pattern, as seen with the movie *Gojira*, which became popular overseas (as the U.S. remake, *Godzilla*) only thanks to its U.S. distributor.

3. In August 2003, *Pokémon* was reported to have earned $15 billion in worldwide retail sales since 1998, the year it debuted in the States (*Business Wire* 2003). The Japan External Trade Organization (JETRO) announced the same month that animation-related sales in the U.S. market were rising and outearning by a factor of three the revenues for another leading Japanese export to the United States, iron and steel products. The latter earned $1.38 billion in 2002, in contrast to $3.94 billion for animation-related goods, which was down from $5.82 billion in *Pokémon*'s peak year, 2000 (Kyodo News Service, August 7, 2003).

4. *Shall We Dance?* was remade with an American cast, starring Richard Gere.

5. My emphasis in this section is on how the *Pokémon* property was handled by those producers and marketers responsible for negotiating the transactions. Thus, rather than doing a more so-called cultural studies analysis by concentrating on the textual logic of *Pokémon* itself, I concentrate here on the role played by the cultural industries in the two countries negotiating the flow of *Pokémon* from Japan to the United States. Given that much of what I learned came from interviews, I cite them in the text (and do so more in this section than in other chapters in the book), but mainly give them reference in these notes. Also, rather than burden the text with endless citations, I reference each interview only once in these notes.

6. Interview in Tokyo, December 1999.

7. Interview with Perry Drosos at Hasbro headquarters in Cincinnati, March 2000.

8. There had been successes before this time, of course, including transform-ers and Go-bots (both toys) in the 1980s and the Power Rangers, which, based on the popular television show, generated waves of kids' action figures, toys, and tie-in merchandising. Still, the perception in the U.S. toy industry when I talked with people in 2000 was that Japanese goods were just then making their way into the mainstream of American play culture (and that one of the reasons for these earlier successes was that Americanization had muted or erased their Jap-anese origins).

9. Interview with ShoPro executives at ShoPro headquarters in Tokyo, Jan-uary 2000.

10. Interview with Nancy Kirkpatrick at Warner Brothers in Burbank, Cali-fornia, March 2000.

11. Interview at Warner Brothers, March 2000.

12. The movies as well as the cartoons and comic books give a story line to the game, which otherwise is far less linear. Yet all the different sites are meant to interweave with one another, particularly in terms of the information that the stories dispense that is intended to assist players in maneuvering the game. It is this aspect of the movies/cartoons/game that American adults seemed the most clueless about to me, viewing the pocket monsters as simply and inexpli-cably alien beings (rather than complex entities that deconstruct into a geome-try of separate parts, strengths, attacks, evolutions—the parts of which assume meaning and value when battling other pocket monsters).

13. Interview conducted at NOA headquarters in Seattle, March 2000.

14. Japanese films have rarely broken into U.S. movie culture. Doing so with *Pokémon* was considered key for expanding the reach of the phenomenon.

15. Interview at 4Kids Entertainment in New York City, March 2000.

16. 4Kids Entertainment was designated one of America's "100 fastest growing companies" by *Fortune* magazine in September 2001.

17. All applications needed the approval of Ishihara, and both ShoPro and 4Kids Entertainment were involved in copyrighting *Pokémon* goods.

18. My interviews were mainly with executives, designers, and marketers at 4Kids Entertainment, Nintendo of America, Warner Brothers, Hasbro, and Wiz-ards of the Coast.

19. Personal interviews with Nancy Kirkpatrick and Massey Rafoni at Warner Brothers, March 2000.

20. The concept of a "metagame" originated with Richard Garfield, also at Wizards of the Coast.

21. The cards and Game Boys were banned from school in Japan as well.

22. In the case of *Pokémon* cards, most depict *pokémon*, but some picture at-tacks, energy, and trainers. The statistics listed include attack names, attack strengths, weaknesses, resistances, retreat costs, and hit points. In each corner there is also a marker designating the degree of rarity in a spectrum of four: common, uncommon, rare, or ultrarare (holofoil; these are also marked with a black star). See, for example, *Pokémon Unofficial Card Collector's Guide* (Searle and Slizewski 1999).

23. Of course, the cards do refer to the *Pokémon* operation in its multiple iterations, which include not only the movie, cartoon, Game Boy game, and books, but also the card game, which apparently half of all card owners play. So the cards have not only exchange value, but also use value for those who utilize them to play games.

24. This internship program is sponsored by the Advertising Educational Foundation (AEF).

25. Interview with Steve Dammer, July 1999.

26. Where, as persuasively argued by Yoshimi Shunya (2000) and Yoshimoto Mitsuhiro (1994), Tokyo Disneyland (TDL) operates as a sign not of Japanese indebtedness or inferiority to American culture but, rather, of Japan's postwar success and prosperity. To have the means to not merely visit Disneyland in the United States but to actually re-create it (as a nation) in Japan is a signifier, as Yoshimoto argues, of Japanese nationalism. And, as Yoshimi adds, TDL was erected during the Bubble economy (1983): a time when consumerism became both the form and the content of culture. Even though TDL is still symbolically "American" (all employes are required to speak English, and the entire theme park has been constructed to be almost identical to the original in the United States), Japanese take in these symbols through consumption. In this way, Japanese are "consuming America" (as Yoshimi entitles his essay), and Disney also becomes the model of and for Japanese consumer culture (what he calls the Disneyification of contemporary Japanese society). My own view is that, in the 1990s and the era of *Pokémon*ification, this model of consumerism/virtualization has shifted further in the ways I elaborate in this chapter.

27. Interview with Massey Rafoni, March 2000.

28. I thank Massey Rafoni for pointing out this distinction between evolution and transformation.

29. I would argue that this is also a trend in toy culture and kids' entertainment more generally. In the arena of action figures, for example, increased emphasis is placed these days on collection rather than mere play. Some children (and many adults) I know buy Star Wars or X-Men figures and keep them in their original boxes for the market value they are assured to have in the future. Retaining the figures for collection rather than play shifts their value (to one more of exchange than use value—or, to reword this, the structure of play is shifting from tactile interaction to accretion and collection). An adult who was a longtime fan of action figures as a kid (everything from GI Joes to Charlie's Angels) told me that he often intermixed body/figure parts, cross-pollinating and queering the identities they came packaged with (this is a point Erica Rand [1995] has also made about Barbies). But when figures remain in their boxes, accruing value as (future) collector items, such a performative impulse would seem severely hampered. I thank Dwayne Dixon for this story and insight.

30. Aptly named, the "Unknown" are an unknown species of *pokémon* that, as Professor Oak discovers over the course of the movie, create new realities by materializing the dreams and thoughts of their masters. Preserving the mansion as her familial home and seeing her father in Entei are both figments of Molly's

imagination that the dangerous powers (the "spell") of the Unknown help realize.

31. By reformatting Entei, she turns him from a replacement dad into an extension of herself: a force that can charge through the wall of crystal by trying hard and believing in herself.

32. In the service of constructing new realities to meet Molly's desires, Entei not only re-creates himself as her dad but also finds a substitute for Molly's lost mother. This is Dalia, Ash's mother, who, worried about her son when she hears about the encroaching crystal in the region where he is touring, journeys there and is promptly abducted by Entei and placed inside the doomed mansion as Molly's imaginary mom.

EPILOGUE

1. Many, if not most, *manga* and *anime* artists still craft their stories with primarily Japanese versus global audiences in mind. This was also true of the original *Pokémon* game that Tajiri designed for Japanese boys.

References

Abe Jōji. 2000. "Shōnen hanzai o kataru" (Speaking on criminal youth). *Focus*, 102–3.

Allinson, Gary D. 1997. *Japan's Postwar History*. Ithaca, NY: Cornell University Press.

Allison, Anne. 1994. *Nightwork: Sexuality, Pleasure, and Corporate Masculinity*. Chicago: University of Chicago Press.

———. 2000. *Permitted and Prohibited Desires: Mothers, Comics, and Censorship in Japan*. Berkeley and Los Angeles: University of California Press.

———. 2001. "Cyborg Violence: Bursting Bodies and Borders with Queer Machines." *Cultural Anthropology* 12:237–65.

"Amerika shiyō ni henshin yo." 1995. *Asahi Shinbun*, July 14, 1.

Anderson, Benedict. 1983. *Imagined Communities: Reflections on the Origins and Spread of Nationalism*. London: Verso.

Aoyama Rika and Bandai Kyarakutā Kenkyūjō. 2001. *87% no Nihonjin ga kyarakutā o tsukina riyū* (Why 87% of Japanese like characters). Tokyo: Gakken.

Appadurai, Arjun. 1996. *Modernity at Large: The Cultural Dimensions of Globalization*. Minneapolis: University of Minnesota Press.

Arai, Andrea G. 2001. "The 'Wild Child' of 1990s Japan." *South Atlantic Quarterly* 99:841–64.

Asahi Shinbun. 2000. "Niigata kankin jiken to otaku" (A Niigata imprisonment incident and otaku). April 17, 12.

Asupekuto. 1996. *Poketto monstā zukan* (Illustrated Pocket Monster book). Tokyo: Asupekuto.

Bandai Co. Ltd. 1997. *Tamagotchi: The Official Care Guide and Record Book*. Kansas City, KS: Andrews and McMeel.

Bandai Kabushikigaisha. 1997. *Tamagotchi boshitechō*. Tokyo: Bandai Kabushikigaisha.

———. 1998. *Corporate Guide: We Are Bandai*. Tokyo: Bandai Kabushikigaisha.

Barthes, Roland. 1957. *Mythologies*. Trans. Annette Lavers. New York: Noonday Press.

Bellafante, Ginia. 1993. "Mighty Raters: A Band of Campy Ninja-esque Teens Take the Lead in Kids' TV." *Time*, December 6, 88.

Benedict, Ruth. 1946. *The Chrysanthemum and the Sword: Patterns of Japanese Culture*. Boston: Houghton Mifflin.

Benjamin, Walter. 1999. *The Arcades Project*. Trans. Howard Eiland and Kevin McLaughlin. Prepared from the German and edited by Rolf Tiedemann. Cambridge, MA: Belknap Press of Harvard University Press.

Berfield, Susan. 1997. "Tamagotchi Madness." *Asiaweek*, July 25, 32–36.

Besser, Terry L. 1996. *Team Toyota: Transplanting the Toyota Culture to the Camry Plant in Kentucky*. Albany: State University of New York Press.

Betz, Doris. 1997. *Tamagotchi: The Official Care Guide and Record Book*. Riverside, NJ: Andrews and McMeel.

Biederman, Danny. 1994. "Those Mighty Saban Rangers Just Keep on Morphin." *Children's Business* 9, no. 10, 113.

Bok, Sissela. 1998. *Mayhem: Violence as Public Entertainment*. Reading, MA: Addison-Wesley.

Buckley, Sandra. 1993. "Altered States: The Body Politics of 'Being-Woman.' " In Andrew Gordon, ed., *Postwar Japan as History*, 347–72. Berkeley and Los Angeles: University of California Press.

Buck-Morss, Susan. 1997. *The Dialectics of Seeing: Walter Benjamin and the Arcades Project*. Cambridge, MA: MIT Press.

Burēn. 2000. "Kyarakutā no komyunikēshōn pawā" (Character communication and power). 40, no. 3 (March): 9–19.

Business Wire. 2003. "*Pokémon* Goes Full Tilt Celebrating Fifth Year in North America." August 29.

Butler, Judith. 1990. *Gender Trouble: Feminism and the Subversion of Identity*. New York: Routledge.

———. 1993. *Bodies That Matter: On the Discursive Limits of "Sex."* New York: Routledge.

Castells, Manuel. 1996. *The Rise of the Network Society*. Padstow, Cornwall, UK: Blackwell.

CBS Evening News with Dan Rather. 1999. Story on *Pokémon*, October 7.

Chambers, Iain. 1990. "A Miniature History of the Walkman." In Iain Chambers, *Border Dialogues: Journeys in Postmodernity*, 1–4. London: Routledge.

Chin, Elizabeth M. 2001. *Purchasing Power: Black Kids and American Consumer Culture*. Minneapolis: University of Minnesota Press.

Cironella, Jim. 1996. "Twenty Years of Super Sentai." *Ultra Fan* 1, no. 1 (January): 10–13.

Clark, Andy. 2003. *Natural-Born Cyborgs: Minds, Technologies, and the Future of Human Intelligence*. Oxford: Oxford University Press.

Clyde, Anne. 1998. "Electronic Pets." *Emergency Librarian*, May/June, 34–36.

Cody, Jennifer. 1994. "Power Rangers Take on the Whole World." *Wall Street Journal*, March 23, B1.

Comaroff, John, and Jean Comaroff, eds. 2001. *Millennial Capitalism and the Culture of Neoliberalism*. Durham, NC: Duke University Press.

Cox, Meki. 1999. "Those 'Pocket Monsters' Spawn a Mini Crime Wave." *Los Angeles Times*, December 1, A54.

Davis, Erik. 1994. "Half Japanese: Power Rangers Corrupt? Absolutely!" *Village Voice*, June 21, 70–75.

Davis, Paul. 1995. "Bandai's Rangers Prove Good Toys Transcend Culture." *Providence Sunday Journal*, March 19, F1–2.

Deleuze, Gilles, and Felix Guattari. 1987. *Anti-Oedipus: Capitalism and Schizophrenia*. Trans. R. Hurley, M. Seem, and H. Lane. Minneapolis: University of Minnesota Press.

Dentsū Kyarakutā Bijinesu Kenkyūkai. 1999. *Kyarakutā bijinesu* (Character business). Tokyo: Dentsū.

Dime. 1997. "Mobairu jidai no kontentsu kakumei" (The contents revolution of the mobile age). November 6, 110–13.

Dirlik, Arif. 1997. *The Postcolonial Aura: Third World Criticism in the Age of Global Capitalism*. Boulder, CO: Westview Press.

Durkheim, Émile. [1917] 1961. *The Elementary Forms of the Religious Life*. Trans. Joseph Ward Swain. New York: Collier Books.

Efron, Sonni. 2000. "Jobs Are Taking a Deadly Toll on the Japanese." *Daily Yomiuri*, April 24, 9–10.

Field, Norma. 1989. "*Somehow*: The Postmodern as Atmosphere." In Masao Miyoshi and H. D. Harootunian, eds., *Postmodernism and Japan*. Durham, NC: Duke University Press.

Figal, Gerald. 1999. *Civilization and Monsters: Spirits of Modernity in Meiji Japan*. Durham, NC: Duke University Press.

Foster, Michael Dylan. 2003. "Morphologies of Mystery: Yokai and Discourses of the Supernatural in Japan, 1666–1999." Ph.D. diss., Stanford University.

Foucault, Michel. 1980. *The History of Sexuality*. Vol. 1, *An Introduction*. Trans. R. Hurley. New York: Random House.

Freeman, Mike. 1993. "Haim Saban: The 'Power' Is His: 'Mighty Morphin Power Rangers' and Animated 'X-Men' Supplier." *Broadcasting & Cable*, December 20, 26.

French, Howard W. 2003. "Japan's Neglected Resource: Female Workers." *New York Times*, July 25, A3.

Freud, Sigmund. [1910] 1963. *Three Essays on the Theory of Sexuality*. Trans. James Strachey. New York: Basic Books.

———. [1927] 1961. "Fetishism." In *Standard Edition of the Complete Psychological Works of Sigmund Freud*, vol. 19, pp. 147–57. Trans. James Strachey. London: Hogarth Press.

Fujii, James A. 1999. "Intimate Alienation: Japanese Urban Rail and the Commodification of Urban Subjects." *Differences* 11, no. 2, 106–33.

Fujimi Yukio. 1998. "Doraemon wa dare ka?" (Who is Doraemon?). *Hato*, January, 18–20.

Fujimoto Yukari. 1997. "Onna no ko hoshii mono ga nan de mo tsumatta Sērā

Mūn no shinwa to kōzō" (The myth and structure of Sailor Moon, the embodiment of everything girls want). *Bessatsu Takarajima* 330 (special issue of *Takarajima*), 9, no. 2.

Furby. www.virtualpet.com/vp/farm/furby/furby.htm. 1998. "Furby" (accessed November 29).

Gabilondo, Joseba. 1995. "Postcolonial Cyborgs: Subjectivity in the Age of Cybernetic Reproduction." In Chris H. Gray, ed., *The Cyborg Handbook*, 423–32. New York: Routledge.

Garuba, Harry. 2003. "Explorations in Animist Materialism: Notes on Reading/Writing African Literature, Culture, and Society." *Public Culture* 15:261–86.

Gojira 2000 Mireniamu (Godzilla 2000 Millennium). 1999. Tokyo: Tōhō Kabushiki Shuppan.

Goldman, L. R. 1998. *Child's Play: Myth, Mimesis and Make-Believe.* Oxford: Berg.

Hakuhōdō Seikatsu Sōgō Kenkyūjō. 1997. *Seikatsu shinbun: kodomo no seikatsu—shōshika jidai no amenbo kizzu* (Newspaper of daily life: Children's lives—the "water spider kids" in the era of decreasing youth). Hakuhōdō.

———. 2003. *Seikatsu shinbun: kodomo no seikatsu—shū-kuri sedai* (Newspaper of daily life: Children's lives—the sweet generation). Hakuhōdō.

Halbfinger, David M. 1999. "Suit Claims Pokemon Is Lottery, Not Just a Fad." *New York Times,* September 24, 5.

Hamano Yusuki. 1999. "Pokemon haken no imi" (The meaning of Pokémon domination). *Mainichi Shinbun,* November 29, 4.

Haraway, Donna Jenne. 1991. *Simians, Cyborgs, and Women: The Reinvention of Nature.* New York: Routledge.

Hardt, Michael. 1995. "The Withering of Civil Society." *Social Text,* no. 4, 27–44.

Hardt, Michael, and Antonio Negri. 2000. *Empire.* Cambridge, MA: Harvard University Press.

Harvey, David. 1989. *The Condition of Postmodernity: An Enquiry into the Origins of Cultural Change.* Cambridge, MA: Basil Blackwell.

Hashino Katsumi and Miyashita Makoto. 2001. *Kyarakutā bijinesu shirarezaru senryaku* (Strategies for expanding the character business). Tokyo: Seishun Shuppansha.

Hatakeyama Kenji and Kubo Masakazu. 2000. *Pokemon sūtori* (Pokémon story). Tokyo: Nikkei BP.

Healy, Melissa. 1999. "Pokemon Frenzy Disrupting U.S. Schools." *Daily Yomiuri,* October 21, 27.

Heffley, Lynne. 1993. "Low-Tech Equals High Ratings; Fox's Offbeat *Mighty Morphin Power Rangers* Flexes Its Kidvid Muscle." *Los Angeles Times,* November 25, 1993, 1.

Hein, Laura E. 1993. "Growth versus Success: Japan's Economic Policy in Historical Perspective." In Andrew Gordon, ed., *Postwar Japan as History,* 99–122. Berkeley and Los Angeles: University of California Press.

High, Peter B. 2003. *The Imperial Screen: Japanese Film Culture in the Fifteen Years' War, 1931–1945.* Madison: University of Wisconsin Press.

Hillis, Ken. 1999. *Digital Sensations: Space, Identity, and Embodiment in Virtual Reality.* Minneapolis: University of Minnesota Press.

Holland, Eugene W. 1999. *Deleuze and Guattari's Anti-Oedipus: Introduction to Schizoanalysis.* London: Routledge.

Hollinger, Elizabeth. 1998. *Pokémon: Prima's Official Strategy Guide.* Roseville, CA: Prima Games.

Hori Takahiro. 1996. *Nihon no omocha anime wa kore de ii no ka?* (Are Japan's toys and anime good like this?). Tokyo: Chirekisha.

Hosokawa Shūhei. 1984. "The Walkman Effect." *Popular Music* 4:165–80.

"IGN for Men Interview: Craig McCracken." 1999. August 20. wysiwyg://29http://formen.ign.com/news/9736.html.

Ikeda Kenshō and Takahashi Nobuyuki. 2001. *Urutoraman tai Kamen Raidā* (Ultraman versus Kamen Raider). Tokyo: Bungei Shunju.

Ishidō, Toshirō. 2000. "Konna 'jūnana sai' ni daregashita" (Who made "seventeen-year-olds" like this?)? *Shinchō* 45 (June): 44–47.

Ito, Mizuko, Daisuke Okabe, and Misa Matsuda. 2005. *Personal, Portable, Pedestrian: Mobile Phones in Japanese Life.* Cambridge, MA: MIT Press.

Itoi, Kay. 2002. "Busy Little Buyers." *Newsweek International,* July 22, 19.

Ivy, Marilyn. 1993. "Formations of Mass Culture." In Andrew Gordon, ed., *Postwar Japan as History,* 239–58. Berkeley and Los Angeles: University of California Press.

———. 1995. *Discourse of the Vanishing: Modernity, Phantasm, Japan.* Chicago: University of Chicago Press.

Iwabuchi Kōichi. 2002. *Recentering Globalization: Popular Culture and Japanese Transnationalism.* Durham, NC: Duke University Press.

Jameson, Fredric. 1984. "Postmodernism, or the Cultural Logic of Late Capitalism." *New Left Review* 146:53–92.

Kaijū VOW Purojekuto. 1994. *Kaijū VOW.* Tokyo: Takarajimasha.

Kalat, David. 1997. *A Critical History and Filmography of Toho's Godzilla Series.* Jefferson, NC: McFarland.

Keizai Shinbun. 1999. "Haruna chan itai de hakken" (The discovery of Haruna's body). November 11, 30.

Kelley, Heather. 1998. "An Interview with Heather Kelley (Girl Games)." In Justine Cassell and Henry Jenkins, eds., *From Barbie to Mortal Kombat: Gender and Computer Games,* 152–71. Cambridge, MA: MIT Press.

Kelly, William W. 1993. "Finding a Place in Metropolitan Japan: Ideologies, Institutions, and Everyday Life." In Andrew Gordon, ed., *Postwar Japan as History,* 189–238. Berkeley and Los Angeles: University of California Press.

Kinsella, Sharon. 2000. *Adult Manga: Culture and Power in Contemporary Japanese Society.* Honolulu: University of Hawai'i Press.

———. 2002. "What's Behind the Fetishism of Japanese School Uniforms?" *Fashion Theory* 6, no. 1, 1–24.

Kitahara Teruhisa. 2000. "Mēdo in okyupaido Jyapan" (Made in occupied

Japan). In Tsukuda Mitsuo, ed., *Gangu no rekishi to tenbō* (The history and prospect of toys), 62–65. Tokyo: Nihon gangu shiryōkan.

Kobayashi Reiji. 1998. *Omocha gyōkai. dai hitto no himitsu* (The toy industry: Secrets of the big hits). Tokyo: Ēru Shuppansha.

Kobayashi Toyosama. 1991. *Gojira no ronri* (The logic of Godzilla). Tokyo: Chūkei Shuppan.

Kogawa Tetsuo. 1984. *Nyū media no gyakusetsu* (The paradox of new media). Tokyo: Shōbunsha.

Koh, Barbara. 1999. "Cute Power!" *Newsweek*, November 9, 56–61.

Kondo, Dorinne K. 1997. *About Face: Performing Race in Fashion and Theater.* New York: Routledge.

Kondō, Kōtarō. 1999. "Bei no Pokemon genshō" (The American Pokémon phenomenon). *Asahi Shinbun*, November 29, 4.

Kubo Masakazu. 1999. "Sekai o haikai suru wasei monustā Pikachu" (Pikachu, a Japanese monster that is wandering the world). *Bungei Shunjū*, special issue, no. 21, 340–49.

———. 2000. "Pokemon wa naze Beikoku de seikō shita ka?" (Why Pokémon succeeded in the U.S.). *Ronza*, February, 78–86.

Kuroki Yasuo. 1995. "Nihon no monotsukuri wa sekai ni eikyō o ataete iru ka?" (Does the Japanese way of producing things have an influence on the world?). In Akurosu Henshūshitsu, ed., *Sekai shōhin no tsukurikata* (The making of world products), 10–16. Tokyo: Parco.

"Kyarakutā ōkoku no michi." 1998. *Nikei Torendī*, December, 90–91.

Kyodo News Service. 2003. "Japanese Animations Rake in $4.4 Billion in Sales in U.S. Market." August 7.

Latour, Bruno. 1993. *We Have Never Been Modern.* Trans. Catherine Porter. Cambridge, MA: Harvard University Press.

Lawson, Carol. 1997. "Love It, Feed It, Mourn It." *New York Times,* May 22, A18.

Lee, Susan. 1997. "Virtual Love." *Forbes,* July 28, 264.

Levin, Diane E., and Nancy Carlsson-Paige. 1995. "The *Mighty Morphin Power Rangers:* Teachers Voice Concern." *Young Children,* September: 67–72.

Lippman, John. 1999. "Haim Saban Morphs into a Major Player in Kids' Entertainment." *Wall Street Journal,* October 1, A13.

Lyotard, Jean-François. 1984. *The Postmodern Condition: A Report on Knowledge.* Trans. Geoff Bennington and Brian Massumi. Minneapolis: University of Minnesota Press.

Malinowski, Bronislaw. 1961. *Argonauts of the Western Pacific: An Account of Native Enterprise and Advantage in the Archipelagoes of Melanesian New Guinea.* New York: Dutton.

Marx, Karl. [1867] 1977. *Capital.* Vol. 1. New York: Vintage Books.

Massey, Dorinne. 1994. *Space, Place, and Gender.* Minneapolis: University of Minnesota Press.

Masubuchi, Sōichi. 1995. *Shōjo ningyōron kindan no hyakunen ōkuku* (The debate about girls' dolls: The forbidden millennial kingdom). Tokyo: Kōdansha.

Matsuda, Misa. 2005. "Mobile Communication and Selective Sociality." In Mizuko Ito, Daisuke Okabe, and Misa Matsuda, eds., *Personal, Portable, Pedestrian: Mobile Phones in Japanese Life*, 123–42. Cambridge, MA: MIT Press.

Mauss, Marcel. 1967. *The Gift: Forms and Functions in Archaic Society*. Trans. Ian Cunnison. New York: Norton.

McCormick, Patricia S. 1995. "And a Parents' Guide to the Politics of Angel Grove." *New York Times*, February 12, 231.

McCracken, Craig. 1999. "IGN for Men Interview: Craig McCracken." August 20. wysiwvg://29http://formen.ign.com/news/9736.html: 1–6.

McCreery, John. 2000. *Japanese Consumer Behavior: From Worker Bees to Wary Shoppers*. Richmond, Surrey, England: Curzon Press.

McGray, Douglas. 2002. "Japan's Gross National Product of Coolness." *Foreign Policy*, May/June, 44–54.

McKinley, Jesse. 2002. "Anime Fans Gather, Loudly and Proudly Obsessed." *New York Times*, September 3, E1, 3.

Mead, Rebecca. 2002. "Shopping Rebellion: What the Kids Want." *New Yorker*, March 18, 104–11.

Meyer, Michael, and Dody Tsiantar, with Michael Schneideb. 1994. "Ninja Turtles Eat Our Dust." *Newsweek*, August 7, 34.

Minomiya, Kazuko. 1994. "Bishōjo hīro wa doko iku ka?" (Where are beautiful girl heroes going?). In Kōei Cult Club, ed., *Bishōjo Hīrō Senki* (War journals of beautiful young girl heroes), 128–35. Tokyo: Kōei.

Mitsui, Toru, and Hosokawa Shūhei. 1998. *Karaoke around the World: Global Technology, Local Singing*. New York: Routledge.

Miura Takeshi and Miyadai Shinji. 1999. "Korokoro bunka" (Korokoro culture). In Miyadai Shinji and Matsuzawa Kureichi, eds., *Poppu Karuchā* (Pop culture), 162–67. Tokyo: Mainichi Shinbunsha.

Mori, Masahiro. 1981. *The Buddha in the Robot*. Trans. Charles Terry. Tokyo: Kosei Publisher.

Morris-Suzuki, Tessa. 1988. *Beyond Computopia: Information, Automation and Democracy in Japan*. London: Kegan Paul International.

Murakami, Haruki. 2001. *Underground*. Trans. Alfred Birnbaum and Philip Gabriel. New York: Vintage Books.

Murakami Ryū. 2000. *Kyōseichū*. Tokyo: Kōdansha.

Nagao Takeshi. 1998. *Pokemon wa kodomo no teki ka mikata ka?* (Is Pokémon the enemy or ally of children?). Tokyo: Koseidō Shuppan.

———. 1999. *Terebi gēmu fūunroku: Inbēdā kara dorīmu kyasutā made* (Record of game trends: From *Invader* to *Dreamcaster*). Tokyo: Bungei Shunjū.

Nakazawa Shin'ichi. 1997. *Poketto no naka no yasei* (Wildness inside a pocket). Tokyo: Iwanami Shoten.

———. 1999. *Onna wa sonzai shinai* (The nonexistent woman). Tokyo: Serika Shobō.

Nihon Keizai Shinbun. 1999. "Nihon anime kaigai ni eikyōryoku" (The influence of Japanese animation overseas). *Nihon Keizai Shinbun*, December 1, 3.

Nikkei Dezain. 1998. "Mienai kazoku" (The invisible family). 24–44.

Nikkei Entertainment. 1998. "Shin hitto no shingenchi Pokekuro sedai" (The Pokémon generation from the epicenter of the new hit). January, 48–50.

Nintendo. 1999. "Nintendo jisedaiki happyōkai" (Announcement about Nintendo's next-generation machines). May 12.

Nye, Joseph S., Jr. 2004. *Soft Power: The Means to Success*. New York: Public Affairs.

Ōhira Ken. 1998. *Yutakasa no seishinbyō* (The pathology of abundance). Tokyo: Iwanami Shinsho.

Ōshita Eiji. 1995. *Nihon hīrō wa sekai o seisu* (Japanese heroes are invading the world). Tokyo: Kadokawa Shoten.

Partner, Simon. 1999. *Assembled in Japan: Electrical Goods and the Making of the Japanese Consumer*. Berkeley and Los Angeles: University of California Press.

Pogue, David. 2001. "Who Let the Robot Out?" *New York Times*, January 25, D1, D7.

Pollack, Andrew. 1996. "Barbie's Journey in Japan." *New York Times*, December 22, 1.

———. 1997. "Hoping a Virtual Chicken Can Lay a Golden Egg." *New York Times*, May 5, C37.

Pratt, Mary Louise. 1992. *Imperial Eyes: Travel Writing and Transculturation*. London: Routledge.

Price, John. 1995. "Lean Production at Suzuki and Toyota: A Historical Perspective." In Steve Babson, ed., *Lean Work: Empowerment and Exploitation in the Global Auto Industry*, 81–107. Detroit: Wayne State University Press.

Rand, Erica. 1995. *Barbie's Queer Accessories*. Durham, NC: Duke University Press.

Reid, T. R. 1995. "Move Over, Morphins, Sailor Moon Is Coming." *Washington Post*, July 22, 16.

Reynolds, Richard. 1994. *Super Heroes: A Modern Mythology*. Jackson: University Press of Mississippi.

Rony, Fatimah Tobing. 1996. *The Third Eye: Race, Cinema, and Ethnographic Spectacle*. Durham, NC: Duke University Press.

Ryfle, Steve. 1998. *Japan's Favorite Mon-Star: The Unauthorized Biography of "The Big G."* Toronto: ECW Press.

Saitō Minako. 1998. *Kōittenron* (The One Red Flower Theory). Tokyo: Birejji Sentā Shuppankyoku.

Saitō Ryōsuke. 1989. *Omocha hakubutsushi* (The encyclopedia of toys). Tokyo: Sōjinsha.

Samuels, Richard. 1994. *"Rich Nation, Strong Army": National Security and the Technological Transformation of Japan*. Ithaca, NY: Cornell University Press.

Schodt, Frederik L. 1988a. *Manga! Manga! The World of Japanese Comics*. Tokyo: Kōdansha International.

―――. 1988b. *Inside the Robot Kingdom: Japan, Mechatronics, and the Coming Robotopia*. Tokyo: Kōdansha International.

Scott, A. O. 2004. "What Is a Foreign Movie Now?" *New York Times Magazine*, November 14, 79–86.

―――. 2005. "Where the Wild Things Are." *New York Times*, June 12, sec. 2, pp. 1, 15.

Searle, Mike, and Tom Slizewski. 1999. *Pokémon: Unofficial Card Collector's Guide*. Lincolnwood, IL: Publications International.

Shaviro, Steven. 2003. *Connected: Or What It Means to Live in the Network Society*. Minneapolis: University of Minnesota Press.

Shiokura Yutaka. 1999. *Hikikomoru wakatachi* (Shut-in youth). Tokyo: Kabushikigaisha Birejji Sentā Shuppan Kyoku.

Shūkan Posuto. 2000. "Sūpā yūtōsei shōnen no 'taiken satsujin' " (Super honor student: Boy's sex-experience of murder). Vol. 5, no. 19, 30–32.

Sobchack, Vivian. 2000. "The Scene of the Screen: Envisioning Cinematic and Electronic 'Presence.' " In John Thornton Caldwell, ed., *Electronic Media and Technoculture*, 137–55. New Brunswick, NJ: Rutgers University Press.

Stevenson, Seth. 2002. "I'd Like to Buy the World a Shelf-Stable Children's Lactic Drink." *New York Times Magazine*, March 10, 38–43.

Stone, Sandy. 1995. "Split Subjects, Not Atoms; or, How I Fell in Love with My Prosthesis." In Chris H. Gray, ed., *The Cyborg Handbook*, 393–406. New York: Routledge.

Stossel, John. 1994. " 'They Saw It on TV'—Power Rangers Induce Kid Violence." *20/20* (ABC), broadcast December 16.

Strange, Susan. 1986. *Casino Capitalism*. Oxford: Blackwell.

Strom, Stephanie. 1999. "Japanese Family Values: I Choose You, Pikachu!" *New York Times*, November 7, 4.

Sutton-Smith, Brian. 1997. *The Ambiguity of Play*. Cambridge, MA: Harvard University Press.

Takahashi Toshio. 2001. "Gojira de 'genzai shakai' o kangaeru" (Thinking about "present-day society" from the perspective of Godzilla). www.waseda.ac.jp/koho/journal/j11–2.html (accessed July 13).

Takanarita, Tōru. 1999. "Pokémon kādo wa shakai genshō" (Pokémon cards are a social phenomenon). *Asahi Shimbun*, October 29, 4.

Takeda Tetsuo. 1998. "Ko to shūdan no aida o yurageru infura o" (Shaking the space between the individual and the group). *Nikkei Dezain*, February, 38–44.

Takeuchi, Hiroshi, and Yamamoto Shingo, eds. 2001. *Tsubaraya Eiji no eizō sekai: kanzen zōhoban* (The world of Tsubaraya Eiji's films: the complete works). Tokyo: Jitsugyō no Nihonsha.

Tanaka Tomoyuki. 1993. "Gojira no eikō" (The prosperity of Godzilla). In Tomoyuki, Takano, Kabuki, Aikawa, Kawaki, and Tanaka, eds., *Gojira eiga 40nenshi: Gojira deizu* (Godzilla days: The forty-year history of Godzilla movies), 22–25. Tokyo: Shueisha.

Tezuka Purodakushōn (Tezuka Production). 1998. *Tezuka Osamu kyarakutā Zukan: dai ikken* (The illustrated picture book of Tezuka Osamu's characters). Vol. 1. Tokyo: Tezuka Purodakushōn.

Toyama Masanari. 2000a. "Sengo fukkō to burikikan no omocha" (The postwar revival of tin toys). In Takayama Hideo, ed., *20seiki omocha hakubutsukan* (The twentieth-century toy encyclopedia), 60–61. Tokyo: Dobun shoin.

———. 2000b. "Kinzoku gangu no hokkan oyobi senzen ryōseiki" (The origins and prosperous times of metal toys). In Tsukuda Mitsuo, ed., *"Gangu no rekishi to tenbō"—dai ikken gangu zōsho* ("The history and prospect of toys"—The first volume of the toy library). Tokyo: Nihon Gangu Shiryōkan.

Toy Journal. 2000. "Petto robotto tokushū" (Special edition of pet robots). April, 50–52.

Treat, John Whittier. 1993. "Yoshimoto Banana Writes Home: Shōjo Culture and the Nostalgic Subject." *Journal of Japanese Studies* 19:353–86.

———. 1995. "Yoshimoto Banana's *Kitchen,* or the Cultural Logic of Japanese Consumerism." In Lise Skov and Brian Moeran, eds., *Women, Media and Consumption in Japan,* 274–98. Richmond, Surrey, England: Curzon Press.

Tsurumi, Shunsuke. 1987. *A Cultural History of Postwar Japan: 1945–1980.* London: KPI.

Tsutsui, William. 2004. *Godzilla on My Mind: Fifty Years of the King of Monsters.* New York: Palgrave.

Turkle, Sherry. 1994. "Constructions and Reconstructions of Self in Virtual Reality: Playing in the MUDs." *Mind, Culture and Activity* 1:159–66.

———. 1998. "Cyborg Babies and Cy-Dough-Plasm: Ideas about Self and Life in the Culture of Simulation." In Robbie Davis-Floyd and Joseph Dummi, eds., *Cyborg Babies: From Techno-Sex to Techno-Tots,* 317–29. New York: Routledge.

Ueno Chizuko. 1998. *Hatsujō sōchi* (The erotic apparatus). Tokyo: Chikuma Shobō.

Wada, Hideki. 2000. "Why Can't Our Children Communicate?" *Echo,* October, 35–38.

Walker, Rob. 2004. "Comics Trip: What Are American Kids Looking For in the Cultural Mix and Match of Japanese Manga?" *New York Times Magazine,* May 30, 24.

Watanabe, Naomi. 1999. "Kodomotachi ga Pokemon ni motomeru mono" (The things children want from Pokémon). *Kodomo Purasu,* no. 2, 59–75.

Watanabe Susumu. 1987. "Flexible Automation and Labour Productivity in the Japanese Automobile Industry." In Watanabe Susumu, ed., *Microelectronics, Automation and Employment in the Automobile Industry,* 41–78. Chicester, UK: Wiley.

Weber, Max. [1930] 1987. *The Protestant Ethic and the Spirit of Capitalism.* London: Unwin Hyman.

Williams, Frances. 2003. "Robots Hit Record High Order Level Industrial Survey." *Financial Times of London,* October 21, international economy section, 13.

Williams, Linda. 1989. *Hard Core: Power, Pleasure, and the "Frenzy of the Visible."* Berkeley and Los Angeles: University of California Press.

Williams, Raymond. 1975. *Television: Technology and Cultural Form.* New York: Schocken Books.

Wizards of the Coast/Shōgakukan/Mitsui-Kids. 2004. *Duel Masters and the Ultimate Anime Games.* Summer, USA: Wizards of the Coast/Shōgakukan/Mitsui-Kids.

WuDunn, Sheryl. 1997. "Hatchling of Pet Lover Is the Rage of Toylands." *New York Times,* September 7, sec. 1, p. 17.

Yamato, Michikazu. 1998. "Kūzen no shakai genshō 'Pokémon' chō hitto no nazo" (The riddle of the super hit and unprecedented social phenomenon, *Pokémon*). *Gendai,* January, 242–49.

Yang, Jeff, Dina Can, Terry Hong, and the staff of *A. Magazine.* 1997. *Eastern Standard Time: A Guide to Asian Influence on American Culture: From Astro Boy to Zen Buddhism.* Boston and New York: Mariner/Houghton Mifflin.

Yoda, Tomiko. 2000. "A Roadmap to Millennial Japan." *Southern Atlantic Quarterly* 4:629–68.

Yokoi Akihiro. 1997. *Tamagotchi tanjōki* (Annals of *Tamagotchi*'s birth). Tokyo: Bandai.

Yomiuri Shinbun. 2000. "Deisukasu: 'jūnana sai no bakuhatsu' naze aitsugu?" (Discussion: why do outbursts by seventeen-year-olds keep happening?). May 13, 17.

Yoshimi, Shun'ya. 2000. "Consuming America: From Symbol to System." In Chua Beng-Hart, ed., *Consumption in Asia: Lifestyles and Identities,* 202–24. New York and London: Routledge.

Yoshimoto Mitsuhiro. 1994. "Images of Empire: Tokyo Disneyland and Japanese Cultural Imperialism." In Eric Smoodin, ed., *Disney Discourse: Producing the Magic Kingdom,* 181–99. New York: Routledge.

Index

Italicized page numbers refer to figures.

Watanabe, Ken, 123
Watanabe, Naomi, 218–19
Watanabe Yoshinori, 117
wearability, 17, 89
Weber, Max, 13, 28, 86, 217
What's Her Face? (doll), 149
Wildness in the Pocket. See Poketto no naka no yasei (Nakazawa)
Williams, Linda, 103, 288n2
Williams, Raymond, 89, 151
Winnicott, D. W., 183, 206
Wizards of the Coast, 33, 242, 253, 274, 298n20
women warriors. *See* female warriors
work, 29–30
worker bees, 69, 71
work ethic, 59, 69, 71, 74–75, 286–87n3
The World (movie), 276
World Bank, 15
World Economic Forum, 145
World War II, 35–37, 45, 98, 116

Xena, the Warrior Princess (TV show), 119
Xiaolin Showdown (TV show), 283n17

Yamada Mitsuko, 79–80
Yamashina Makoto, 120
Yanagita Kunio, 27, 212–13
Yohji Yamamoto, 149
yōkai (spirits), 21, 27, 222. *See also* spirits
Yokoi Akihiro, 164, 166–67, 182–84, 267–68, 292n4, 293n17, 294n20
Yokoyama, Mitsuteru, 61, 104
Yomiuri Shinbun, 81, 255
Yoshii Hiroaki, 288n12
Yoshimi, Shun'ya, 67, 147, 286n1, 299n26
Yoshimoto, Banana, 139
Yoshimoto Mitsuhiro, 238, 299n26
youth crime *(shōnen hanzai)*, 76–81, 92, 216, 287–88nn9–11; and Pokémon, 232–33, 297n13; and recluses and nomads, 82–86
Yu-Gi-Oh!, 1–2, 5, 6, 24, 26, 33, 218, 257–58
Yutakasa no Seishinbyō (Ōhira), 88

Zen Buddhism, 21
Zenigame *(pokémon)*, 209
zukan (databases), 208, 213

Text: 10/13 Aldus
Display: Franklin Gothic
Compositor: Binghamton Valley Composition, LLC